ADAM SMITH.

Adam Smith

THE LEWIS WALPOLE SERIES IN EIGHTEENTH-CENTURY
CULTURE AND HISTORY

The Lewis Walpole Series, published by Yale University Press with the aid
of the Annie Burr Lewis Fund, is dedicated to the culture and history of the
long eighteenth century (from the Glorious Revolution to the accession of
Queen Victoria). It welcomes work in a variety of fields, including literature
and history, the visual arts, political philosophy, music, legal history and the
history of science. In addition to original scholarly work, the series publishes
new editions and translations of writing from the period, as well as reprints
of major books that are currently unavailable. Though the majority of books
in the series will probably concentrate on Great Britain and the Continent,
the range of our geographical interests is as wide as Horace Walpole's.

NICHOLAS PHILLIPSON

Adam Smith

An Enlightened Life

Yale

UNIVERSITY PRESS

New Haven & London

Published with assistance from the Annie Burr Lewis Fund.

Published in the United States in 2010 by Yale University Press and in the United Kingdom by Penguin Books.

Yale University Press books may be purchased in quantity for educational, business, or promotional use. For information, please e-mail sales.press@yale.edu (U.S. office) or sales@yaleup.co.uk (U.K. office).

Set in 10.5/14 pt Linotype Sabon.
Typeset by TexTech International.
Printed in the United States of America.

Library of Congress Control Number: 2010925524
ISBN 978-0-300-16927-0 (hardcover : alk. paper)

A catalogue record for this book is available from the British Library.

This paper meets the requirements of ANSI/NISO Z39.48-1992 (Permanence of Paper).

10 9 8 7 6 5 4 3 2

In Memory of
Duncan Forbes
1922–1994

Fellow of Clare College and Reader in History
University of Cambridge

The Author of the Wealth of Nations

Contents

List of Illustrations

Plates

1. The Burgh School, Kirkcaldy. (Fife Council Libraries & Museums: Kirkcaldy Museum & Art Gallery)

2–3. *Eutropii historiae breviarum ab urbe condita usque ad Valentinianum & Valentem Augustum ... In usum scholarum. Editio sexta correctior* (Edinburgh, 1725). (Fife Council Libraries & Museums: Kirkcaldy Museum & Art Gallery)

4. *The Colledge of Glasgow* (early eighteenth century), by or after John Slezer, *Theatrum Scotiae* (1693). (Hunterian Art Gallery, University of Glasgow)

5. Balliol College, Oxford, from D. Loggan, *Oxonia Illustrata* (1765). (Private collection/Giraudon/The Bridgeman Art Library)

6. Robert Simson, engraving by Alexander Baillie (1768) after de Nune. (University of Glasgow; licensor www.scran.ac.uk)

7. Francis Hutcheson, from F. Blackburn, *Memoirs of Thomas Hollis Esq.* (London, 1780). (Glasgow University Library)

8. Archibald, Earl of Islay and 3rd Duke of Argyll, engraving T. Chambars after A. Ramsay. (Collection, the author)

9. David Hume, frontispiece from his *History of England from the Invasion of Julius Caesar to the Revolution in 1688* (Edinburgh, 1770). (Getty Images)

10. *A General View of the City and Castle of Edinburgh, the Capital of Scotland* (anon., 1765). (Courtesy Edinburgh City Libraries and Information Services – Edinburgh Room)

Illustrations in the Text

Acknowledgements

This book has had an elephantine period of gestation and has incurred more debts on the way than I can hope to repay here. It was the late Duncan Forbes who introduced me to Smith, the Scottish Enlightenment and intellectual history in a legendary Cambridge special subject which few who were lucky enough to have taken will ever forget. My own students and postgraduates may recognize various themes of this book which were tried out in my own special subjects at Edinburgh and will I hope remember discussions which were always enjoyable, sometimes memorable, and have helped to shape my thinking more than they may have realized. It was from them that I came to learn that for many intelligent students, Smith's first book, the *Theory of Moral Sentiments*, was more of a living text than the *Wealth of Nations*, and it was they who helped me to understand why Smith preferred the first book to the second.

In planning this book I wanted to write about Smith's life and works in a way which would throw light on the development of an extraordinary mind and an extraordinarily approachable philosophy at a remarkable moment in the history of Scotland and of the Enlightenment. I was particularly lucky that the book began to take shape when Susan Manning, Thomas Ahnert and I were directing a research seminar, funded by the Leverhulme Trust, on the Science of Man in Scotland. Our discussions and those of our research group were invaluable in keeping my thinking on the move at an important moment in its development. At the same time, my thinking about Smith, the Scottish Enlightenment and much else besides was being refreshed, as it has been for more than twenty years, by John Pocock and Istvan Hont. My debts to them are not easily repaid.

ACKNOWLEDGEMENTS

Various sections of this book have been discussed at conferences, colloquia and seminars in Edinburgh, Glasgow and St Andrews, at Oxford, Cambridge, London and Sussex, at Budapest, Fiesole and Munich and at Chapel Hill and Columbia, and I am grateful to all of those who took part for their criticism and encouragement.

Emma Rothschild, Tony LaVopa, Richard Bourke and David Raynor read the text in draft and were more generous with their time, trouble and encouragement than I had any right to expect.

I am particularly grateful to Jane Freel at the Kirkcaldy Museum and Art Gallery, Ann Dulau at the Hunterian Art Gallery, Robert MacLean at the Glasgow University Library and to the staffs of the Research Collections at Edinburgh University Library, the Royal Commission for Ancient and Historical Monuments of Scotland and the Bridgeman Art Library for their help with illustrations and to Ann Watters for her help in mapping Smith's Kirkcaldy.

It has been the greatest pleasure working with the staff of that most civilized and professional of publishers, the Penguin Press, Phillip Birch, Richard Duguid, Charlotte Ridings, Penelope Vogler and Sarah Hunt Cooke in particular. And finally my thanks to my agent Bruce Hunter and, above all, to Stuart Proffitt, who commissioned this book, who stuck with it throughout its long period of gestation, who edited it with sympathy and acuity and who has remained a tower of strength and friendship. Without him this book might not have happened.

Nicholas Phillipson
Edinburgh, May 2010

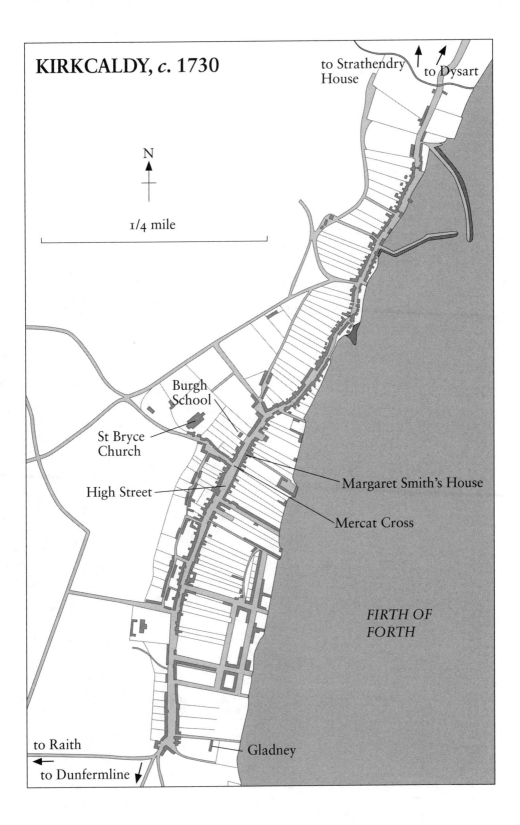

KIRKCALDY, *c.* 1730

N

1/4 mile

to Strathendry House

to Dysart

Burgh School

St Bryce Church

High Street

Margaret Smith's House

Mercat Cross

FIRTH OF FORTH

to Raith

to Dunfermline

Gladney

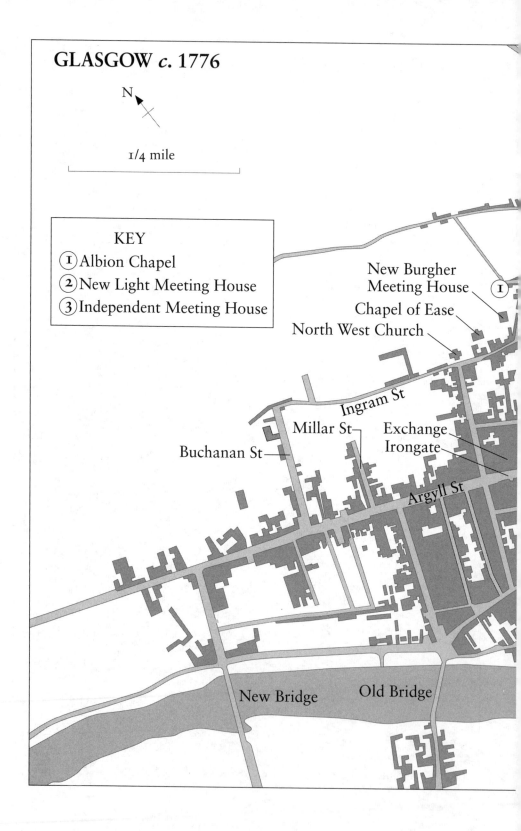

GLASGOW *c.* 1776

N

1/4 mile

KEY
①Albion Chapel
②New Light Meeting House
③Independent Meeting House

New Burgher
Meeting House
Chapel of Ease
North West Church

①

Ingram St

Millar St
Buchanan St
Exchange
Irongate

Argyll St

New Bridge
Old Bridge

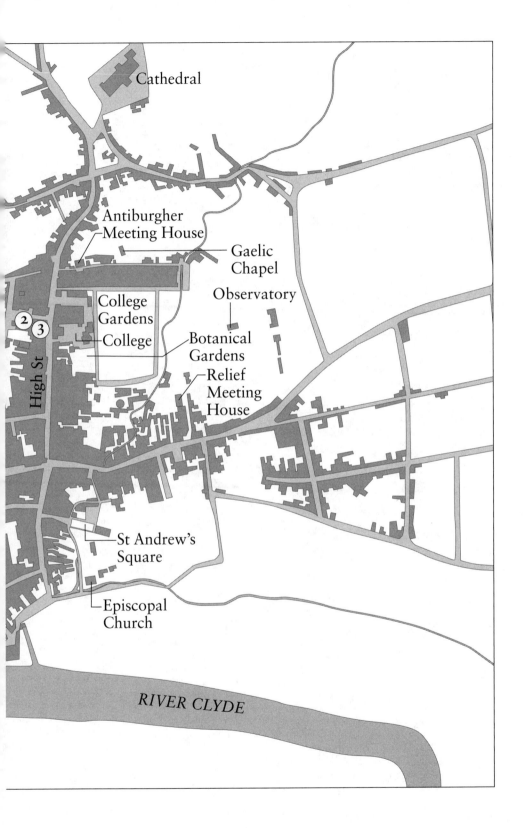

Cathedral

Antiburgher
Meeting House

Gaelic
Chapel

Observatory

College
Gardens

College

Botanical
Gardens

Relief
Meeting
House

②③

High St

St Andrew's
Square

Episcopal
Church

RIVER CLYDE

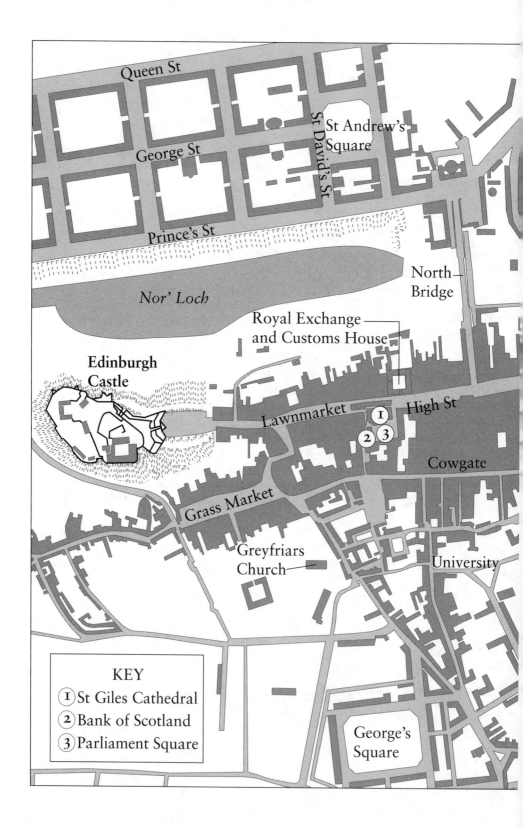

Queen St

George St

St David's St

St Andrew's Square

Prince's St

North Bridge

Nor' Loch

Royal Exchange and Customs House

Edinburgh Castle

Lawnmarket

High St

Cowgate

Grass Market

Greyfriars Church

University

KEY
1 St Giles Cathedral
2 Bank of Scotland
3 Parliament Square

George's Square

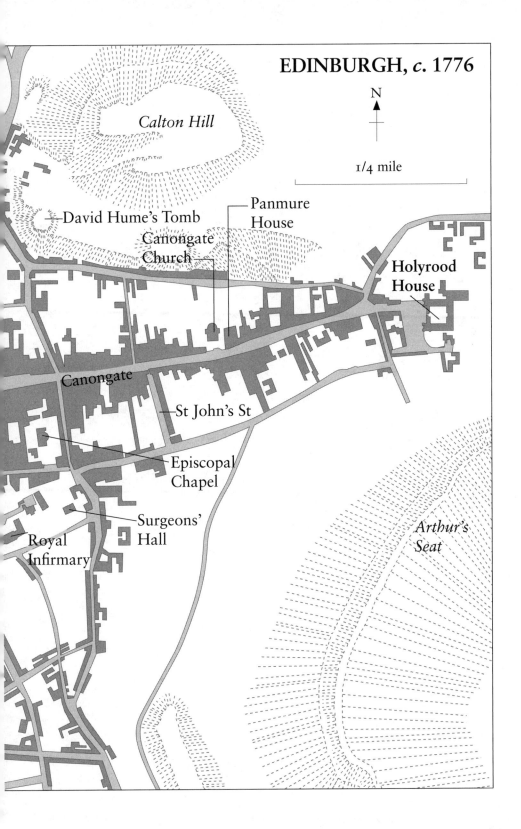

EDINBURGH, *c.* 1776

N

1/4 mile

Calton Hill

David Hume's Tomb

Panmure
House

Canongate
Church

Holyrood
House

Canongate

St John's St

Episcopal
Chapel

*Arthur's
Seat*

Surgeons'
Hall

Royal
Infirmary

Prologue

'The character of a man is never very striking nor makes any deep impression: It is a dull and lifeless thing, taken merely by itself. It then only appears in perfection when it is called out into action.'

Adam Smith, *Lectures on Rhetoric and Belles Lettres*, 17 January 1763

Adam Smith's *Inquiry into the Nature and Causes of the Wealth of Nations* was published on 9 March 1776. Although David Hume thought that 'it requires too much thought' to reach a wide audience, it immediately acquired a significant readership in political and intellectual circles in Edinburgh, London and Paris.[1] Even Smith's most intelligent critic, the former Governor of Massachusetts, Thomas Pownall, admitted that Smith had succeeded where everyone else had failed in creating 'a system, that might fix some first principles in the most important of sciences, the knowledge of the human community, and its operations. That might become *principia* to the knowledge of politick operations; as Mathematicks are to Mechanicks, Astronomy, and the other Sciences.'[2] The success of the *Wealth of Nations* transformed Smith's life. It smoothed his path to a lucrative place on the Board of Customs in Scotland, a semi-sinecure which he characteristically treated seriously, attending as many meetings of the Board as possible and apologizing whenever he was unable to be present. It turned him into the most celebrated of Scotland's enlightened literati, a man to be visited by cultural tourists on pilgrimage to Edinburgh, a man whose table-talk and eccentricities were to be cherished by locals. But in the

1780s failing health made worse by hypochondria, the death of his mother, with whom he had lived for much of his life, and the erosion of the small, tight-knit circle of lifelong friends among whom this sociable but deeply private man had lived, sapped his morale and intellectual energies and underlined what was becoming increasingly obvious – that the vast intellectual project to which he had devoted his life and of which the *Wealth of Nations* was only a part, would never be completed. For like Bacon and Hobbes, like the great natural jurists of the previous century, Grotius and Pufendorf, like his two mentors Francis Hutcheson and David Hume, like d'Alembert and the *encyclopédistes* he greatly admired, Smith believed that it was now possible to develop a genuine Science of Man based on the observation of human nature and human history; a science which would not only explain the principles of social and political organization to be found in different types of society, but would explain the principles of government and legislation that ought to be followed by enlightened rulers who wanted to extend the liberty and happiness of their subjects and the wealth and power of their dominions.

This great project had shaped the whole of Smith's intellectual career. He had first learned about it from Hutcheson and Hume in the 1730s and 40s as a student at Glasgow University and at Balliol College, Oxford. He had laid the foundations of his own system in the lectures and papers he delivered in Edinburgh in 1748–51 and developed as Professor of Logic and Metaphysics (and later of Moral Philosophy) at Glasgow between 1751 and 1764. These writings ranged astonishingly widely, dealing with the principles of language, rhetoric, morals, jurisprudence, government, the fine arts and astronomy, subjects which, his friend and biographer Dugald Stewart noted, he invariably tackled by tracing their origins in human nature. Smith had published the first part of the superstructure of his science of man in 1759 in the *Theory of Moral Sentiments*, a theory which explained how men and women seek to satisfy their moral needs and learn to live at ease with themselves and the world around them, a theory of sociability as well as a theory of ethics, providing what was in effect an account of the moral economy of a recognizably modern civil society. The *Wealth of Nations* formed the second part of that superstructure. It offered an account of the political economy of the different types of civil society known to history, and a sharply focused analysis of the problems which modern governments faced in extending the wealth, liberty and happiness of their subjects at a time when the international order was being transformed by the expansion of empire and the growth of commerce. But the two final parts of this project, 'a sort of Philosophical History of all the different branches of Literature, of Philosophy, Poetry and Eloquence' and 'a sort of theory and History of Law and Government' were never completed. 'The materials of both are in a great measure collected, and some Part of both is put in tollerable good order', Smith wrote in 1785. 'But the indolence of old age, tho' I struggle violently against it, I feel coming fast upon me, and whether I shall ever be able to finish either is extremely uncertain.'[3] He was then sixty-two and felt he had become an old man.

For Smith's health was failing. Before setting out on his last trip to London in the spring of 1787 he asked his two future executors to visit him. These were old friends, the chemist Joseph Black and the geologist James Hutton, two great scientists who, like him, had glimpses of grander, unfulfilled scientific designs. Smith told them they were to destroy all of his lecture notes, 'doing with the rest of his manuscripts what they pleased'. Two years later, and a few weeks before his death, he reminded them of what they were to do. Hutton told Dugald Stewart that

> They entreated him to make his mind easy, as he might depend upon their fulfilling his desire. He was then satisfied. But some days afterwards, finding his anxiety not entirely removed, he begged one of them to destroy the volumes immediately. This accordingly was done; and his mind was so much relieved, that he was able to receive his friends in the evening with his usual complacency.[4]

All that was left were seven unpublished essays on philosophical subjects that Smith seems to have tinkered with for most of his professional life. These were published posthumously by his executors and largely forgotten. As Stewart commented, 'he seems to have wished that no materials should remain for his biographers, but what were furnished by the lasting monuments of his genius, and the exemplary worth of his private life'.[5] He died on 17 July 1790, having done as much as was humanly possible to preserve his intellectual privacy.

3

Stewart blamed this archival bonfire on Smith's fastidious distaste for unhoned arguments which would inevitably be misunderstood, would retard 'the progress of truth' and would tarnish his posthumous reputation.[6] Smith certainly had an aesthete's taste for intellectual elegance; having finished the *Wealth of Nations* (and polished it in three subsequent editions), he turned again to the *Theory of Moral Sentiments* to develop and refine the ethical implications of his theory of sociability. On top of this there was a lifelong love of intellectual systems and the *esprit systématique* he associated with true philosophical thinking and which he had learned to admire as a student at Glasgow studying mathematics, natural science and the Stoics. It was a quality he associated with the French and found lacking in the English. As he put it in one of his two contributions to the *Edinburgh Review* of 1755–6:

> It seems to be the peculiar talent of the French nation, to arrange every subject in that natural and simple order, which carries the attention, without any effort, along with it. The English seem to have employed themselves entirely in inventing, and to have disdained the more inglorious but not less useful labour of arranging and methodizing their discoveries, and of expressing them in the most simple and natural manner.[7]

It was in this Anglo-French spirit of combining discovery and experimentation with methodizing that Smith had set out to create his own science of man. Developing and perfecting his Glasgow lectures on jurisprudence and on the arts and sciences, absorbing them into the intellectual framework of the systems he had developed in the *Theory of Moral Sentiments* and the *Wealth of Nations*, reviewing once again the arguments of the earlier works in the light of the later, would, in Smith's perfectionist hands, have become a vast intellectual undertaking, made vaster still by the fact that he was a slow worker. It was certainly not a task for a sick and valetudinarian man.

For a biographer, the trouble with this act of archival self-concealment is that it was an attempt to cap a life that was already badly documented. Next to nothing is known about the circumstances of Smith's childhood in Kirkcaldy, his student days at Glasgow and Oxford and the evidently formative years spent launching his philosophical career in the aftermath of the battle of Culloden, which had brought a bloody end to the Jacobite rebellion of 1745. His career as an active and influential philosophy professor at Glasgow from 1751 to 1764, at a time when his university was making a bid to turn itself into the model of an enlightened seat of learning, and his subsequent career as a Commissioner of Customs are both exiguously documented. This lack of institutional data would matter less if Smith had been a better correspondent. As it is, only 193 letters written by him and 129 letters written to him have survived, and more than half of these belong to the later period of his life, following the publication of the *Wealth of Nations*. No doubt this is partly because he destroyed his letters just as he destroyed his notes, to preserve his privacy. He told David Hume's publisher in 1776 that he disapproved of the plan to publish some of his old friend's correspondence because it would encourage dealers '[to] set about rummaging the cabinets of all those who had ever received a scrap of paper from him. Many things would be published not fit to see the light to the great mortification of all those who wish well to his memory.'[8]

Not that Smith needed to worry overmuch about the posthumous publication of unwelcome correspondence. He was himself a notoriously bad correspondent who only wrote letters when there was business to be done or when he was goaded into it by his friends. Even then, although his letters are good enough, they are not the work of a Hume or a Boswell, a Voltaire or a Diderot, of a man, in other words, who loved correspondence for its own sake and regarded it as a form of conversation that mattered almost as much as the company of friends. There is a general lack of visibility in Smith's life. Unlike Hume, Smith had a strictly limited taste for city life, salon culture and even, one suspects, the company of his friends, and it was only after the publication of the *Wealth of Nations* in 1776, when he was fifty-three, that he began to generate the gossip and table-talk which continues to shape our understanding of his character. Indeed, it is not until 1787 when James Tassie made two medallions of him that we have any idea of what he looked like. It is only possible to make sense of Smith's life if one accepts that he was a private and self-sufficient man who spent long periods in Kirkcaldy and Glasgow away from the social and political worlds that generate the materials upon which biographies generally rely, content to spend his life with the only woman who mattered, his mother.

How then is Smith's biography to be written? Some say, Don't try; any attempt at biography will simply turn into a broken-backed account of his ideas and the world in which he lived. But that really won't do. Biography never has been and never will be an exact science. All any biographer can do is use the materials at his disposal to construct a credible life-story which will throw light on his subject's life and works. But because biographies only come to life when one can hear the subject speak, and because the bulk of the primary data about Smith is to be found in his published and unpublished texts, this means that his biography must be, first and foremost, an intellectual biography, one which traces the development of his mind and character through the making of those texts, one that is set in a country that was generating its own forms of Enlightenment. And it is here that the biographer is in luck, for Smith's attempts at self-concealment were to be less successful than he intended. By the time he resigned the Moral Philosophy chair at Glasgow in 1764, his lectures had begun to attract world-wide attention and it was probably inevitable that sets of student notes would begin to turn up. So far there have been two such finds, in 1895 and in 1958. The first is a set of student notes of a section of the lectures on jurisprudence he probably gave in 1763–4, the last year of his professorship, when he was forty-six. The second are sets of notes of the lectures on rhetoric and the lectures on jurisprudence he gave in 1762–3. Neither is quite complete, though both are substantial and seem to be the work of students who were anxious to get as full a version of Smith's lectures as possible. In other words, they probably represent Smith's thought at the stage at which it was ready to be developed into two of the treatises that were projected but never completed.

These lecture notes are transforming our understanding of Smith's philosophy. They help us to relate the social theory and the ethics of the *Theory of Moral Sentiments* to the political economy of the *Wealth of Nations* by putting both in the wider context of Smith's unrealized science of man. They alert us to the depth and complexity of Smith's thinking about the formation of the human personality and the progress of society. They elaborate Smith's thinking about the ways in which self and society are shaped by the distribution of property and the systems of law and government that exist to preserve them. They alert us to the fact so often overlooked by students of Smith's political economy, that the human beings who inhabit the types of society about which he writes are driven by moral, intellectual and aesthetic as well as material needs. But the notes are of considerable biographical value too for the light they shed on Smith's intellectual development. For although they record the lectures he gave at the end of his professorial career, it is clear that their roots lie deeper in his past, and almost certainly in the later 1740s, when he was in his late twenties launching his philosophical career in Edinburgh with courses on the same subjects. While no notes of these Edinburgh courses have survived, it seems reasonable to suppose that they contained Smith's first thoughts on the finished articles, and that they can be read as the work of a formidably ambitious young thinker, ready to take on the leading moral philosophers of Scotland and France, prepared to offer a friendly though radical critique of the philosophy teaching of Scotland's two leading universities and confident enough to be able to see himself as the heir of Grotius, Hobbes and Pufendorf, who had set out to develop philosophical accounts of the principles of law and government which would be of use to the rulers of modern Europe. So there is still biographical work to be done by historians who are interested in the development of Smith's mind and character.

What is more, it is work of a sort that would surely have met with Smith's approval. Although he was impatient with biographers who were over-preoccupied with what he would have regarded as the trivia of everyday life – what, one wonders, would he have made of his pupil James Boswell's *Life of Johnson*? – he knew very well that there were things to be learned about an author's character from his style and use of language. In the *Lectures on Rhetoric* he reminded his students that texts were rhetorical performances which could be studied for the light they threw on an author's methods of persuasion and on the character he wished to present to his readers; indeed part of what he liked to call his 'system' was to take the form of a sophisticated gloss on the old rhetorician's adage, *'le style, c'est l'homme même'* – 'the style is the man'. It was an invitation to his students and those who were interested in his character to attend to his rhetoric as well as his ideas, and to the circumstances in which they were first delivered.

This, then, is the story of a tough-minded, ambitious young philosopher and his encounters with the intellectual world in which he found himself. It is the story of a man born into the middling ranks of Scottish society at a remarkable moment in the history of his class and nation, a man who would be known to his contemporaries as solitary as well as sociable, and more than a touch eccentric, and a man who generated affection as well as respect. It is the story of a philosopher who with the help of vast erudition, an excellent memory and a taste for reasoning *en système* constructed texts that would help to make the complexities of the modern world intelligible and manageable. And this is why this story takes the shape of an intellectual biography.

I

A Kirkcaldy Upbringing

Adam Smith was born, or baptized, on 5 June 1723 in Kirkcaldy, then, as now, a small, decent, unprepossessing port on the Firth of Forth. Like so many members of the Scottish intelligentsia, his family belonged to the middling ranks of Scottish society. Both of his parents came from the minor gentry and had connections with the law, the army and the world of office-holding on which the routines of Scottish public life and politics depended. Smith's father, Adam Smith senior, was clearly a man of some ability and ambition. Baptized in 1679, he belonged to the Presbyterian gentry of north-east Scotland. He was educated for the law at Aberdeen and Edinburgh and grew up in the turbulent world of Scottish politics between the Glorious Revolution of 1688 and the Act of Union of 1707. It was a time when the Crown and the Scottish nobility were engaged in an internecine struggle to control the machinery of Scottish government, when the Kirk was riven with doctrinal and ecclesiological disputes, when Scottish trade was being dislocated by international war and English competition, and when the entire fabric of Scottish political life was being unsettled by a rapidly deteriorating pattern of Anglo-Scottish relations and by constant (and by no means unjustified) fears that Scotland's political independence was being compromised by the English. In 1705, at the age of twenty-six, Smith became secretary to the new Secretary of State, the Earl of Loudon, a leading member of the Presbyterian nobility. Two years later he was appointed Clerk of the Court Martial in Scotland, a highly responsible office which must have given him a close insight into security matters and into the political state of the country at a time when Jacobitism was rife and the future of the Revolution Settlement and the Protestant succession was in question. In

1714 he was appointed Controller of Customs at Kirkcaldy, the most important port in Fife and a significant source of customs revenue. By 1723 he was earning around £300 per annum, a fairly substantial income by contemporary standards, and was actively campaigning for promotion to take him back to Edinburgh and the heartland of Scottish politics. He was clearly an ambitious and up-and-coming man.

In 1710, Smith married Lilias Drummond, the daughter of Sir George Drummond of Milnab, a wealthy and prominent Edinburgh politician and one of the Scottish commissioners who had negotiated the Act of Union. They had one son, Hugh, a sickly child, who seems to have worked in the customs at Kirkcaldy until his death in 1749 or 1750. Lilias Smith died sometime between 1716 and 1718. In 1720 Smith remarried and once again married well. His second wife was Margaret Douglas, the daughter of a substantial and well-connected Fife laird who had sat in the old Scots Parliament. Again it was a short marriage. Smith died in January 1723, six months before the birth of his second son, Adam. Margaret Smith never remarried. Her husband had left her comfortably off and she was to spend most of her long life in Kirkcaldy among her family and friends, and most of that life was to be devoted to her son. He for his part was to spend long periods of his life at home in Kirkcaldy. It was there that he went to school, there he returned for many of the long vacations he enjoyed as a student and professor at Glasgow, and there that he wrote much of the *Wealth of Nations* between 1767 and 1773. And when after the publication of his masterpiece he was made a Commissioner of Customs in 1778 and had to move to Edinburgh, he took his eighty-four-year-old mother with him and set up home in Panmure House in the Canongate. His relationship with his mother could not have been closer. Dugald Stewart recalled that she treated him with 'an unlimited indulgence; but it produced no unfavourable effects on his temper or his dispositions: and he enjoyed the rare satisfaction of being able to repay her affection, by every attention that filial gratitude could dictate, during the long period of sixty years.'[1] Indeed the Earl of Buchan commented that 'the three great avenues to Smith were his mother, his works and his political opinions. The conquest of him was easy through any of these channels.'[2] When she died in 1784, Smith told his publisher William Strahan:

Tho' the death of a person in the ninetieth year of her age was no doubt an event most agreable to the course of nature; and, therefore, to be foreseen and prepared for; yet I must say to you, what I have said to other people, that the final separation from a person who certainly loved me more than any other person ever did or ever will love me; and whom I certainly loved and respected more than I shall ever either love or respect any other person, I cannot help feeling, even at this hour, as a very heavy stroke upon me.[3]

Margaret Smith's devotion had been amply repaid.

Kirkcaldy is situated 10 miles north of Edinburgh. Its first and best historian, the Reverend Thomas Fleming writing in 1791, observed that '[it] is properly but one long street, with a few lanes of small extent opening on each side of it'.[4] The town, with its long, winding, narrow street, more than two miles long, and the hugger-mugger of small closes and wynds that sprouted from it, was fairly typical of the old coastal burghs of Scotland. What was odd about Kirkcaldy was the length of the High Street, which earned it the nickname it still enjoys – the Lang Toun. This it owed to geography, for eighteenth-century Kirkcaldy was bounded to the south by the long sandy beaches of the Firth of Forth, which Fleming regarded as 'a safe and agreeable walk; and by which the traveller may generally avoid the uneasy jolting of a long and rugged pavement'; to the north it was bounded by a series of sharply rising terraces that butted onto the estates of an interesting and important group of landed families with which the Smith family was closely connected.

Kirkcaldy had a long history of settlement.[5] Its name is said to be derived from the Celtic 'Culdee' and there is evidence of Roman and early Christian settlement. By the fourteenth century it had become a town of some consequence, having acquired burgh status and the right to trade freely in Scotland and overseas. By the early sixteenth century there was a small harbour and the town was developing as a centre of regional trade, importing goods from England, Ireland and the Low Countries in exchange for locally produced coarse cloth, nails and salt, as well as raw materials such as hides, wool, herring, salmon, coal and timber. A century later its merchants had extended their reach to France and the Baltic. By 1644 it was a burgh with a population of around 4,500, a fleet of around 100 ships, a complex guild system and a town council. The old church of St Bryce, which Fleming rightly described as 'a large unshapely pile', had another wing tacked onto it to accommodate the town's growing population. The Town House had been enlarged in 1678 to house the gaol, the town guard, the meal market and the weigh house. The burgh's small but evidently prosperous elite were building themselves fairly substantial houses at the west end of the town. By 1688, the town's tax returns suggest that it had become the sixth or seventh most important burgh in Scotland and its reputation as a trading port was at its height.

But the town's economy was beginning to face difficulties, a victim of historic events that were changing the face of the British state. It had been occupied and heavily taxed by both the Royalist and Covenanting armies during the Civil War. Its trade was severely disrupted by the Dutch Wars of the Restoration, and more severely still by the wars in the reigns of William III and Anne. Worse still, the town suffered badly from the Union, which brought increased English competition, a new focus on the possibilities of trade with the Americas and the Caribbean, and the exceptionally high customs and excise duties levied on the Scots in order to bring their tax system into alignment with that of England, an exercise in which Smith's father was probably heavily involved. The effects of these historic developments on Kirkcaldy's mercantile economy were disastrous. The number of ships registered in the harbour fell from around 24 in 1673 to 3 in 1760. By 1755, the town's population was 2,296, little more than half of what it had been a century before; its position as a centre of mercantile trade had collapsed.

It would be wrong, however, to think of Smith growing up in a town whose economy was in a state of terminal decline. His schooldays in the 1730s coincided with the first real signs that Kirkcaldy's economy was beginning to develop in an entirely new direction. This was a direct result of the growth of the linen industry, which was to help transform the economy of eastern Scotland in the early years of the new Anglo-Scottish Union.[6] It was an enterprise which interested merchants trading with England and the colonies, landowners concerned with rural unemployment and low rents and patriots interested in the regeneration of the economy of post-Union Scotland. It attracted the interest of the grandly named and aristocratic The Honourable the Society for Improvement in the Knowledge of Agriculture (1723–c.45) and the patronage of the Board of Trustees for Fisheries and Manufactures, an eighteenth-century quango set up in 1727 to invest the funds the Scots had been given to compensate them for the collapse of the Darien scheme, Scotland's first and only exercise in colonization. In fact, the Board was to devote most of its time and resources to the linen industry. As the Fife freeholders told the Convention of Royal Burghs, 'No-one can claim better rights than the public for [this money] to be employed for the purpose mentioned since it belongs to Scotland.'[7]

Linen manufacturing was an essentially rural, domestic industry, relying on cotters who could be induced to learn the spinning and weaving trades, and on entrepreneurs to supply them with raw materials and a market for their goods. The lairds of Fife were to play a crucial part in developing the industry in their part of the country in the early years of the century. Some, like the Oswalds of Dunnikier, the Adams of Maybole and the St Clairs of Dysart, were Edinburgh-based families who had made their money from the professions or the army and found in Fife a promising and reasonably priced land-market in which to invest. By the 1730s, these local lairds had turned themselves into an effective entrepreneurial class. They imported flax from Holland, Riga and St Petersburg and they encouraged their tenants to take up spinning and weaving, sometimes equipping them with wheels and looms at their own expense. They launched a determined campaign to produce cloth for the highly competitive export market by encouraging the recruitment of skilled flax workers and weavers from abroad and by lobbying the Board of Trustees for more and better stamp-masters to guarantee the quality of local cloth. By the 1740s they were exporting checks and tickings and napkins to England and the colonies. The Oswalds, whose estates abutted the town, were conspicuous in this enterprise, feuing (a Scottish form of leasing) most of their lands in the nearby village of Dunnikier to tradesmen engaged in the linen, woollen and nail-making businesses. In the neighbouring burgh of Dysart, General St Clair had ensured that its 'active and diligent people' were making linen goods for the home and English markets.[8] Kirkcaldy became the focal point of this activity both as a centre of production and as a market. In 1739 the town council, doubtless under pressure from local lairds, set up an annual market for linen cloth on the first Wednesday of July to encourage the local linen trade.[9] In 1733, it was producing 177,740 yards of stamped linen per year for England and the home market; by 1743 production had nearly doubled, and by the time of Smith's death in 1790, output was running at about 900,000 yards, worth around £45,000. This acted as a stimulus to further economic activity in the town. Stocking manufacturing began in 1773, cotton manufacturing in the 1780s and shipbuilding in 1788.[10] By then the population of the town was growing fast and its housing stock was increasing rapidly. It was, in short, turning into a small but prosperous town with an expanding system of commerce, ready for the much larger transformations which would follow during the Industrial Revolution. We need to think of Smith, then, growing up in a town and a region of Scotland that was undergoing a profound revolution as a result of the Union and the political and economic changes that were transforming contemporary Europe. And we need to think of his family as part of the landed and professional elite that was intent on regenerating, or, as contemporaries liked to put it, 'improving' their estates and the local economy.

As a boy, Smith's life was securely rooted in the social, economic and political world of Kirkcaldy and south Fife. Several of his father's family worked for the customs. His half-brother Hugh worked in the customs house at Kirkcaldy. His cousin Hercules Smith, one of those named as his guardian in his father's will, was Collector of Customs at Kirkcaldy before being promoted to Inspector General of the Outports in Scotland in 1740 with the task of managing the collecting of customs revenues at all the smaller Scottish ports. Another cousin, also called Adam Smith, who had been his father's clerk, was to become Comptroller and later Collector of Customs at Kirkcaldy. His mother's family was rather more patrician. The Douglases of Strathendry had estates on the outskirts of the town, in easy reach of Margaret Smith's two sisters who had married into the Fife gentry. The family was and remained in contact with the formidable, wealthy and intelligent General St Clair, one of David Hume's friends and patrons, who controlled the burgh of Dysart and much of the politics of south Fife,

and with the Fergusons of Raith, whose pretty and improved estate
butted onto the burgh. They were close neighbours of one of the
interesting newer families, the Adams of Maybole, who had moved
into the region early in the century. William Adam had made his fortune as a fashionable architect with a lucrative practice, an activity he
coupled with the equally lucrative posts of Clerk and Storekeeper of
the King's Works in Scotland, and Mason to the Board of Ordnance
in Scotland. He built Gladden House in Kirkcaldy in 1711 and began
acquiring large estates in Kincardineshire in the 1730s. His two sons,
Robert and John, were not only to become two of Scotland's greatest
architects but were to remain Smith's lifelong friends.

But by far the most important of the local landed families, for the
burgh and for Smith himself, were the Oswalds of Dunnikier. Like
William Adam, Captain James Oswald was new to district. He bought
Dunnikier in 1703, built himself the house he needed to acquire burgess rights and to hold office in the town, and had himself elected
Provost in 1717. He was now the largest landed proprietor in the
town and its most powerful local politician. Given the family's wealth,
power and interest in economic improvement, it seems certain that
Oswald and his family played a significant part in engineering the
town's economic recovery. He was a close friend of Smith's father and
was named Adam Smith's tutor, or legal guardian in his father's will.
Oswald's son, another James Oswald, was eight years older than
Smith and became one of his closest friends. This James Oswald was
a remarkable man. Like Smith, he lost his father as a child and like
him was bought up by a formidable mother who, according to her
grandson, 'cultivated James' talents with the most assiduous care and
the best education which Scotland could then afford'.[11] He became an
improving landlord and a much-admired MP for the Fife Burghs and
the county from 1741–68. In fact, he was to develop as the sort of
modern politician Smith most admired – an intelligent, literate and
independently minded man, who steered clear of party politics and
applied himself to studying the business of government, impressing
David Hume by his understanding of naval finance. As he once put it,
'the surest way of becoming remarkable here [in the House of Com-
mons] is certainly application to business, for whoever understands it
must make a figure'.[12] Oswald kept in close contact with Scottish

intellectual life and remained another of Smith's lifelong friends. As his son wrote:

> It is well known that an uninterrupted friendship and intercourse existed betwixt them for the greater part of their lives. In his early days [the author] remembers well to have heard Dr. Smith dilate, with generous and enthusiastic pleasure, on the qualities and merits of Mr. Oswald; candidly avowing, at the same time, how much information he had derived, on many points, from the enlarged views and profound knowledge of that accomplished statesman. In their frequent discussions on the science of political economy, Mr. Oswald brought his practical knowledge and experience in aid of the Doctor's theoretical deductions, and afforded him much valuable assistance in the laborious investigations in which he was so long engaged.[13]

Indeed, Dugald Stewart thought that Oswald had played a decisive part in persuading Smith to develop his interests in political economy.[14]

In the *Wealth of Nations*, Smith was to pay close attention to the role of small towns in shaping the commerce and culture of the regions of a commercial state. A small town was 'a continual fair or market' in which ordinary men and women were able to learn the meaning of fair prices and wages and would in time begin to appreciate more general truths about the meaning of liberty and order.[15] But Smith also knew how important prudent, intelligent and independent country gentlemen were in generating economic improvement in the countryside. As a class they were least likely to be corrupted by great wealth or poverty, or by 'the wretched spirit of monopoly' which Smith regarded as the cancer that threatened the economic, political and moral health of most modern states.[16] It is hard to read Smith's thinking about the progress of society in a commercial state without thinking of Kirkcaldy, Fife and the activities of energetic and ambitious incomers like the Oswalds, the St Clairs and the Adams; and although he never explicitly drew on the experience of Fife to 'illustrate' his theory of progress, it was, nonetheless, remarkably apposite.

Smith was by all accounts a sickly child, and it may be that the slight confusion about his birth day arises from his having been baptized on the day of his birth – a common enough practice in the case of infants not expected to survive. He grew up in his mother's house, which is said to have been in Rose Street at the fashionable west end of the High Street, not far from the Adams at Gladney House, the Oswalds at Dunnikier and only seven miles or so from his maternal uncle's house at Strathendry. Indeed it was at Strathendry that Smith first comes to life biographically with a curiously suggestive contemporary story that he was snatched by a tinker woman and rescued by his uncle; if true it must surely have helped to lay the foundations of the extraordinarily close relationship which this sickly only child enjoyed with his widowed mother. Unlike his half-brother Hugh, who was sent to board at school in Perth, Adam was sent to the local burgh school in Hill Street, a short walk from his mother's house which would have taken him through the local market. To be sure it was an essentially medieval market, hedged around by guild restrictions and designed to protect local traders from unwelcome competition from outsiders. Nevertheless, Smith would have grown used to watching what he famously called the 'higgling and bargaining of the market' that was to seem to him as natural a form of social intercourse as ordinary conversation and one of the forms of social exchange on which sociability and society depended.[17]

Smith was a pupil at the burgh school from 1731 or 1732 until 1737 at a remarkable moment in its history. The school had been transformed in 1724 as the result of the appointment of a new master, David Miller. Miller was the highly successful master of the burgh school at Cupar and he had at first been reluctant to move.[18] What made him change his mind is not clear, though the formidable Lady Oswald must surely have had something to do with it; after all, she had her son James to educate and a family position in the burgh to keep up. Perhaps she put pressure on the town council to increase his salary, more probably she offered to pay Miller a tutor's fee to give her son private classes. Be that as it may, Miller threw himself into the business of reorganizing the school with considerable energy. The town council agreed to build a new schoolhouse, and to increase fees to 2s. 6d. per quarter, although Miller was told 'to consider the necessity of such as cannot pay the half crown'.[19] It also agreed to Miller's proposals for a new curriculum. The school was to provide a classical education based on translation and exposition so as to 'exercise [the pupils'] judgements, to teach them by degrees to spell rightly, to write good write [handwriting], good sense and good language'.[20] Miller was a good classicist and Ian Ross is surely right to suggest that Smith left school in 1737 well versed in the standard authors; certainly he knew enough Latin and Greek to be exempted from the first year of Glasgow University's curriculum, which was largely devoted to remedial classical education. His copies of two of the history textbooks Miller used have survived. The first, Trogus' *De Historiis Philippicis*, was a well-known introduction to the history of the ancient world, much used as a source of exemplary stories about prudent military and political leadership. The second, Eutropius' *Breviarum Historiae Romanae*, which is inscribed 'Adam Smith his book May 4th 1733' in that large, slow, neat hand which would never change, was the work of a senator who had lived in the age of the Emperor Julian. The story of the rise and progress of the Roman Empire was told as a story of war and conquest, which demonstrated the dignity of war and the disgrace of making peace without honour. It was a singularly appropriate text for boys living in a militaristic age.[21]

However, the most striking glimpse into the character of Miller's teaching is to be found in a contemporary account of his use of theatre as a vehicle of civic education. This was a relatively common humanist technique in the more avant-garde schools of central Scotland. The High School of Dalkeith staged *Julius Caesar* and a comedy of Aesop in 1734 and, even more adventurously, performed Allan Ramsay's charming Scots pastoral, *The Gentle Shepherd*. Perth Grammar School performed Joseph Addison's *Cato* at much the same time. Miller wrote and staged his own play in 1734 while Smith was still a pupil; it was called 'The Royal Command for Advice: or the regular education of boys the foundation of all other national improvements'. It seems to have been about the business of a council of twelve senators who debate petitions from a tradesman, a farmer, a country gentleman, a nobleman, two schoolmasters and, last of all, 'a gentleman who complimented and congratulated the council on their noble design and worthy performance'.[22] It was clearly a play which starred middle-ranking officials rather than kings and grandees and dealt with the routines of government rather than high politics. Interestingly the boys seem to have been expected to play the parts of petitioners as well as senators. If so, it was an admirable device for giving the sons of enterprising Whig gentlemen a feeling for ordinary public life. No wonder the press reported that the performance 'was said to have given high satisfaction to the audience'.

Miller's sophisticated, politically correct curriculum strongly suggests that his teaching had a solid ethical core; the texts used in similar avant-garde classical schools in Scotland suggest that it was probably he who introduced Smith to the classical moralists and their modern admirers. A standard classical diet of this sort would have included Epictetus' *Enchiridion* and Cicero's *De Officiis*, and quite probably Addison and Steele's *Spectator* essays.[23] Smith's signed but undated copy of a 1670 edition of the *Enchiridion* bound with the *Tabula* of Cebes is generally assumed to have been bought for use at university, but it could equally well have been acquired a year or two earlier for use at Kirkcaldy.[24] And even if Miller did not make use of the *Spectator* in class, we may be sure that it would have been read at home in the edition Smith's father had once possessed.[25] Its charming, thought-provoking moral fables and ethical and aesthetic reflections were part of the staple literary diet of the middling ranks' homes. These texts provided a Stoic or, in the case of Cicero and Addison, a quasi-Stoic view of the world, inviting young people to think about the duties they owed themselves, their fellow-citizens and the deity. They taught them how to square their private interests with those of the public. They taught them how to understand and enjoy the peace of mind and sense of self-respect that comes from knowing that one is able to live an active social life at ease with one's self and with others. Above all, they taught young people the value of philosophy to public life and of public life to philosophy. Ethically and sociologically these were matters which were to interest Smith for the rest of his life. If Miller really did introduce him to these classics, he must go down as a seminal influence on his intellectual development.

These authors provided Smith with a way of looking at the moral world and a language for discussing the problems of learning to live within it. The *Enchiridion* had long been regarded as a valuable ethical primer for intelligent and well-born schoolboys. It was one of the foundation texts of Stoic ethics. Epictetus had been a slave and had written for those who feared that they were becoming slaves to their passions and victims of circumstances over which they had no control – a situation with which many schoolboys could easily sympathize. He had taught generations of schoolboys to think of liberty as a matter of learning the arts of self-command, by which he meant learning to distinguish between those aspects of life we could and could not control. 'Not up to us are body, property, reputation, office and, in a word, whatever is not in our own action,' Epictetus observed, commenting that these were *indifferentia*, things to be endured and despised. On the other hand, passions, opinions, judgements 'and, in a word, whatever is in our own action' were things we could control, sources of moral energy which could be regulated and mastered with the help of brainpower and reason. Indeed it was only when reason had established control over the passions that we could hope to live rationally as nature and the deity intended.[26] But learning the art of self-command was far from easy. It meant cultivating a philosophical detachment from the world and its transient attachments, disappointments and resentments. It meant learning to look beyond the *indifferentia* to the evidence that the moral and natural worlds provided of order and design. Above all, it meant cultivating a love of its benevolent Creator. Only then would the budding Stoic begin to feel at one with nature and experience that state of *apathaeia* that could only be enjoyed when mind and reason had established their dominion over the body and the passions. Under these circumstances, he would be free. As Epictetus put it, 'Anytus and Meletus can kill me, but they cannot harm me.'[27] Epictetus had shown how an anxious, virtuous-minded young man could learn 'to act well that part that is assigned to you' in a play that had been written and was being directed by others. But learning to act well meant learning to become a spectator of the works of the great author of nature,

> and not only [to be] a spectator, but an interpreter of them. It is therefore shameful that man should begin and end where irrational creatures do. He ought rather to begin here, but to end where nature itself had fixed our end; and that is in contemplation and understanding and a way of life in harmony with nature. Take care then, not to die without ever being spectators of these things.[28]

In learning to become a spectator, the Stoic would earn his liberty.

This image of the moral agent faced with the problem of learning how to distance himself from the uncertainties and resentments of daily life, learning to cultivate the moral and intellectual skills he needed to live rationally, at ease with himself and the world, was to attract Smith profoundly. Such men were not only happy and capable of virtue; they were also likely to be more sociable and efficient. To be sure, he found Epictetus' system unduly severe and thought that he had placed too much faith in the ethical value of contemplation, but he put that down to the fact that Epictetus had been brought up in a semi-barbarous slave society. Smith admired and exploited the spirit of Epictetus' ethics for sociological as well as ethical purposes. He was to argue that it was on our ability to master our disappointments and resentments that our capacity for sociability ultimately depended. And he believed that being able to feel that 'how untoward soever things might be without, all was calm and peace and concord within' was the mark of the truly sociable agent.[29]

Smith must have learned from a very early age that ethical systems have to be adapted to the needs of different peoples and places. He would almost certainly have been introduced to Cicero's ethics at much the same time as Epictetus', and would have learned how Cicero had adapted the ethics of the Greek slave for the needs of the free citizens of the Roman Republic. Cicero did not share Epictetus' contempt for the world or his belief that the only path to virtue lay in contemplation. He was interested in the ethical value of learning to perform the offices of ordinary life skilfully, honestly and with an eye on the public good. Indeed, Smith was to regard the cultivation of these 'imperfect, but attainable virtues' as the core of Cicero's thinking, and the useful heart of 'the practical morality of the Stoics'.[30]

Reading the *Spectator* essays would have shown Smith how the teaching of the ancients could be adapted for use by moderns living in a free commercial society, a form of civilization completely unknown to antiquity. Addison's title – *The Spectator* – was deliberately borrowed from Epictetus and drew attention to the central ethical skill Addison wanted his readers to cultivate: the ability Robert Burns was to characterize so brilliantly as seeing ourselves as others see us. Like Cicero, Addison wrote for a free citizenry – in this case, the citizenry of a great commercial city, London. Indeed, a large part of his enduring appeal lay in the fact that his essays provided young men and women from the provinces with their first view of the mightiest city in the kingdom, a city which dazzled by virtue of its wealth, power and glamour. His essays allowed his readers to glimpse life as it was lived in the city and to share vicariously in the ethical hopes and fears of its citizens. His London was a *commercial* city in the widest sense of the term, a theatre of life, as some writers put it, in which men and women were constantly engaged in the exchange of goods, services and sentiments. But it was also a world that was fragmented by party-political divisions, by religious sectarianism, by rank, profession, trade, age and gender (it was as important to Addison as it would be to Smith that modern ethics should pay attention to the needs of women as well as men). It was a world ruled by the vagaries of opinion and fashion, a world in which people looked in vain for fixed and settled standards of taste, morality, politics and religion. As one of the *Spectator*'s ever-popular fictional heroes, Sir Roger de Coverley, put it, it was a world in which a man would find himself 'hopping instead of walking', and would never be in 'his entire and proper motion'.[31]

This world of politics, religion, business and fashion was Addison's world of *indifferentia*, a world over which ordinary citizens had little control, a world from which they would have to distance themselves if they were ever to aspire to a life of virtue and peace of mind, a world which was in need of moral reform. Like Cicero, Addison had little time for the 'severer' Stoics and thought that those who tried to cultivate the more austere Epictetan virtues would end up as ridiculous social misfits. He wanted to show that life in the modern city could foster virtue as well as corruption, if only citizens would pay attention to the way in which they performed the offices of everyday life and were willing to exchange the company of cronies for the friendship of strangers who belonged to different walks of life. In the last resort it was simply a matter of cultivating good manners and politeness, of learning to be a spectator as well as an actor in the theatre of the world. The company of strangers would teach one to moderate one's own prejudices and would give one more 'extensive' views of the world. It would encourage tolerance, taste, judgement and a respect for that sense of propriety that played such an important part in securing the decencies and pleasures of ordinary life. It was a form of sociable Stoicism that would release the sort of *apathaeia* which, the polite Addisonian citizen thought, would encourage religious and political moderation and active Christian citizenship.

These ancient and modern classics provided Smith with a simple but sophisticated way of looking at the social world. They gave him a way of viewing human beings as agents whose lives and happiness depend on their ability to cultivate the moral and intellectual skills they need to live sociably, at ease with themselves, with others and with the world. They encouraged him to think of self-command as the essential skill on which sociability, success and personal happiness depends. Addison's charming and deceptively simple moral essays had a special value. They gave Smith his first glimpse of the modern commercial city as a complex pluralistic entity, which had the power to improve as well as to corrupt human nature. They showed the importance of conversation as the social skill on which the exchange of sentiments and the creation of social and moral norms depended, and presented it as a skill that could be 'improved' and cultivated in the name of fostering good manners and 'politeness'. They provided him with the first rudiments of a language of sociability which suggested that in fostering the cause of self-improvement the modern citizen would, more or less unintentionally, be fostering the good of society at large. All of this he was to glimpse from the narrow but distinctive perspective of Kirkcaldy, a town which, in its modest way, was on the road to improvement. As a Glasgow student Smith was to see how these Stoic and quasi-Stoic ethics, these insights into society, sociability and public life, could be developed philosophically and applied to the analysis of the political systems of the ancient and modern world. Eventually he was to develop an analysis of his own on very different principles.

2

Glasgow, Glasgow University and Francis Hutcheson's Enlightenment

Smith left school in the summer of 1737 and matriculated at Glasgow University in October. He was fourteen. He spent the next nine years at university, as a Glasgow student from 1737 to 1740 and as a Snell exhibitioner at Balliol College, Oxford from 1740 to 1746. His student life at Glasgow and Oxford is almost completely undocumented, nevertheless it is clear that these were crucial years in his intellectual development. By the time he returned to Scotland in 1746, fed up with Oxford, in search of a job and ready for the sophisticated intellectual life of Edinburgh, his own philosophy would be well enough developed to justify invitations to deliver public lectures on rhetoric and on jurisprudence that were to establish his intellectual credentials and to play an important part in launching his career.

The groundwork for Smith's philosophical career could not have been laid down in two more different universities. In the 1720s and 30s Glasgow became one of the most sophisticated and interesting of the tiny Protestant universities of northern Europe. Oxford was notorious – at least in the Whig Presbyterian circles to which Smith belonged – for being an intellectually stagnant, High Church and high Tory institution. Glasgow could offer Smith a distinctive philosophy curriculum and the teaching of two of the most charismatic and intellectually creative university professors in northern Europe – Robert Simson, Professor of Mathematics, and Francis Hutcheson, Professor of Moral Philosophy. Hutcheson introduced Smith to the moral philosophy of the ancient and modern world and to the problems involved in placing the study of human behaviour on what contemporaries liked to describe as 'experimental' foundations. Simson taught him to appreciate the importance of mathematics in placing moral philosophy on scientific foundations. Neither Oxford nor Balliol could hope to extend, question or supplant the teaching Smith had received at Glasgow. But it did have the Snell exhibitions, which were reserved for former Glasgow students and allowed the exhibitioners to spend up to eleven years in private study in the hope that they would enter the ministry of the Episcopal Church in Scotland. Whether Smith ever seriously intended to take that latter path is not known, though the formal requirement that Snell exhibitioners should do so had fallen into disuse by his time. But what the Snell exhibitions could and clearly did offer was unlimited time for private study, which Smith appears to have used to distance himself from the highly structured philosophical education he had received at Glasgow. His six years at Oxford gave him a unique opportunity to broaden his education and to lay the foundations of the formidable erudition which, like his love of system, was to become a distinctive characteristic of his philosophy. What is more, it is probable that it was at Oxford that he first encountered the philosophy of David Hume. The young philosopher, then, who made his first appearance in Edinburgh in 1748 as a lecturer on rhetoric and jurisprudence, was one whose development had been shaped in the two highly distinctive worlds of Glasgow and Oxford, and, above all, by his encounters with his two great mentors, Hutcheson and Hume.

Glasgow must have seemed a striking contrast to Kirkcaldy. It was a boom town that had been transformed in the course of the previous century and was to undergo an even more spectacular transformation in the 1750s and 60s during Smith's years as a professor. Its population was growing rapidly, its overseas trade expanding to the point that it now rivalled that of Bristol and Liverpool, and its manufacturing, which had previously been restricted to commodities for local consumption, now featured flourishing sugar refineries, rum (or 'Glasgow brandy') distilleries, and linens, plaids, soap, rope, snuff and refined tobacco for export. For Daniel Defoe writing in 1724–5, this evidence of progress was epitomized in the physical appearance of a city that had been almost completely rebuilt in the wake of two disastrous fires in 1652 and 1677.

Glasgow is indeed, a very fine City: the four principal Streets are the fairest for Breadth, and the finest built that I have ever seen in one City together. The Houses are all of Stone, and generally equal and uniform in Height, as well as in Front; the lower story generally stands on vast Square Dorick Columns, not round Pillars, and Arches between give Passage into the Shops, adding to the Strength as well as Beauty of the Building; in a Word, 'tis the cleanest and beautifullest, and best built City in *Britain, London* excepted.[1]

Characteristically, Defoe was not much interested in Glasgow's history; as always what interested him was what was new, modern and favourable to the progress of trade, commerce and civility. But, like Kirkcaldy, modern Glasgow was heavily indebted to its medieval past.[2] A royal charter of around 1175 had placed city government in the hands of the archbishop and an oligarchic town council, and although the abolition of episcopacy in 1690 had freed the council from episcopal control and given it the right to elect the Provost and bailies who governed the city, that had merely ensured that henceforth city government would be controlled by the Crown and local magnates. It was to turn Glasgow into a city with a reputation for unquestioning loyalty to the 1688 Revolution, the Hanoverian succession and the Act of Union. And it made it possible for the Earl of Islay, the future 3rd Duke of Argyll and one of Sir Robert Walpole's closest political advisers, to take effective control of city government and the management of the university from 1725 to 1761. He was to play a crucial part in laying the foundations of the academic culture that shaped Smith's education and his academic career.

The city's population was expanding rapidly. In the middle of the seventeenth century its inhabitants numbered around 10,000, much the same population as that of Aberdeen or Dundee. By the end of the century it was probably around 14,000, compared with Edinburgh's 30,000. By the mid-eighteenth century it would be 31,000. By the end of Smith's life it was nearly 81,000 and still expanding.[3] Economically and politically, it resembled the other royal burghs of Scotland. Its charter gave those fortunate enough to possess burgess rights a monopoly of trade within the burgh, the right to hold markets and fairs and to hold a court to regulate its general commerce and industry. These privileges were exercised through fourteen guilds or 'incorporations', of which the merchants' incorporation was by far the most important. By the late seventeenth century Glasgow had a merchant community of between four and five hundred, about a hundred of whom were engaged in overseas trade. This tiny group of 'sea adventurers', as Christopher Smout calls them, were the driving force behind the city's remarkable economic expansion in the seventeenth and early eighteenth centuries.[4] In the sixteenth century most of Glasgow's mercantile trade had been confined to coastal trade in the west of Scotland. In the early seventeenth century, its business began to expand. Merchants began trading wine and salt with France, luxury goods and foodstuffs with Holland, and timber with Norway. Pedlars from the west of the country hawked linens and yarn down the west coast of England and even to London. In 1656 it was even reported that one merchant had made an unsuccessful attempt to start trading tobacco and sugar with Barbados. Most important of all, the plantation of Ulster led to its colonization by Presbyterians from the west of Scotland, thus making Glasgow and its university the focal point of the new province's commercial and academic life.

During the century after the Restoration of 1660 Glasgow's economy took its decisive leap forward, expanding faster than that of any other Scottish burgh. Glaswegians began trading with the Canaries, the Azores and Madeira, with the English colonies in the Caribbean and with their plantations in the Carolinas, Virginia, New Jersey, New York and Massachusetts. At the same time trade with Norway and the Baltic expanded and intensified, before being interrupted and finally annihilated by the wars of 1689–1713. This trade took the form of an exchange of primary commodities such as cattle, hides, leather, herring and coal for luxury goods such as wines, brandies and fine textiles and raw materials like sugar, flax and hemp, all commodities that were unobtainable at home. But it was the tobacco trade which became the city's flagship enterprise and the source of its enormous wealth in the middle decades of the eighteenth century. Before the Union the tobacco trade had been entirely illegal and possible only because the Glaswegians were skilful smugglers who were good at evading the trade restrictions imposed on them by the English Navigation Acts, which had placed swingeing controls on the importation of various types of colonial produce. However, even after these had been removed with regard to Scotland by the Act of Union, the tobacco

trade took some time to build up strength. By the 1710s, the Glaswegians were still only legally importing 1.4 million lbs per year, and less
than 3 million lbs in the 1720s, compared with the 8 million lbs landed
in 1741 and the 21 million lbs landed ten years later; the huge,
unquantifiable volume of illegal imports was to be the subject of endless complaint in London and Edinburgh. By 1751, when Smith
returned to Glasgow as a professor, the Glasgow tobacco lords were
importing more tobacco than London and all the English outports
combined.

The key to the Glaswegians' success in the tobacco trade lay in the
simple fact that they concentrated on small planters with whom they
could deal directly, rather than the great planters with whom the London and Bristol merchants preferred to deal. The English preferred to
act as agents, selling on American tobacco to English and continental
suppliers on commission, an often intricate and time-consuming business that generated high prices for the planter at the cost of long
periods of waiting for payment. The Glasgow merchants' preference
for buying directly from the small planters allowed them to pay lower
prices in exchange for quick payment. What was even better was that
the Glaswegians' planters often accepted payment in kind in the form
of staple goods and luxuries, as well as in cash. This method of trading was flexible and profitable. It meant that Glasgow prices were
generally lower than those of England; it gave the merchants a greater
degree of control over the planters; and it stimulated manufacturing
as well as the warehousing of tradable goods. For all that, the tobacco
trade, like all overseas trade, was an expensive and risky activity. In
spite of the enormous profits to be made from importing and re-exporting
a lucrative and fashionable narcotic to England and Europe, tobacco
merchants constantly ran the risk of overstocking the market and caus-
ing prices to slump in a trade that inevitably carried high overheads.
Ships had to be bought or hired and provisioned for long journeys;
there was always the problem of maintaining cash flow on unsold car-
goes; and customs duties could have a ruinous effect on liquidity. This
last was an open invitation to merchants to rig the market. By 1737, the
leading tobacco lords had intermarried and had turned themselves into
large, well-integrated syndicates with their own rules and protocols
and ways of dealing with the peculiarities of Scots mercantile law.

Indeed, by the 1760s more than half the tobacco imported into Glasgow was controlled by three giant syndicates headed by Alexander Speirs, John Glassford and William Cunninghame.

The development of such family syndicates established the tobacco lords not only as the dominant elite in the city's trading economy but as the dominant force in the development of the city's manufactures. Between the 1660s and 1740s families like the Bogles began sugar refining, soap manufacturing, whaling and tanning, the Montgomeries began sugar refining, soap-making and bottle-making, the Dinwiddies became involved in tanning and rope-making, and so on. It was only a matter of time before they, their friends and relations began to run the city.[5] It is striking, for example, that between 1740 and 1790 nearly every Provost of Glasgow was a tobacco lord and that the merchant oligarchy went out of its way to make sure that the city kept on the friendliest terms with the reigning ministry. In other words, the city Defoe admired in 1724, the city Smith discovered in 1737, was a remarkable place at a remarkable stage of its development. Its expansion was being engineered by the skill and enterprise of a closely knit merchant oligarchy that knew how to exploit the possibilities and limitations of the old, medieval burgh system, the hazards of the Navigation Acts and the opportunities created by the expansion of Atlantic trade in an age of war and empire. It was a monument to a spirit of enterprise that flourished in spite of, or even because of, the mass of protectionist regulations that controlled the workings of the local economy. When Smith spoke so famously of 'the mean rapacity, the monopolizing spirit of merchants and manufacturers' he could perfectly well have been talking about the spirit of the merchants he knew best, the merchants whose business practises he had watched most carefully, the tobacco lords of Glasgow.[6]

Glasgow's economic growth was so spectacular that it has virtually monopolized the attention of historians to the exclusion of its Presbyterian pietism, the other remarkable fact of its eighteenth-century history. One contemporary put the paradox well when he wrote that in the middle of the century, 'the chief objects that occupied the minds of the citizens were commerce and religion, the chief means of acquiring importance among them were wealth and piety'.[7] This pietism had deep tap-roots which have never been properly studied. Before the Reformation, when Glasgow was merely a regional trading port, the city's status in national life depended entirely on its archbishopric and its university. Thereafter, for reasons which are far from clear, the south-west of Scotland became the breeding ground for a radical Presbyterianism that held strict views about sin, grace and the salvation of the elect, and regarded secular and even ecclesiastical authority with the greatest distrust. Popular, revivalist preaching flourished there throughout the seventeenth and eighteenth centuries, deeply troubling the leaders of the Presbyterian and Episcopalian churches alike. This was where the seditious covenanting movement had flourished during the Restoration period, threatening civil government as well as the Established Church, and it continued to spawn the radical, antinomian sects that troubled the restored Presbyterian Church after 1690. Most striking of all to Scots of Smith's generation, this was where the Cambuslang Revival of 1742 began, a radical movement which seemed for a moment to threaten a reversion to the bloody sectarian guerrilla warfare of the previous century and troubled moderate Presbyterians like John Clerk of Penicuick, who, recalling the radical conventicles of covenanting days, feared that this new movement would once again encourage the people 'to goe a gading after conventicles'.[8]

Inevitably, Glasgow became the focal point for this radical piety. It played host to the Kirk's General Assembly of 1638, when it had voted for the abolition of episcopacy. During the Interregnum, the university became a notable covenanting seminary under the direction of its formidable Principal, Robert Baillie. During the Restoration the city acquired a reputation for conventicling which the town council and government were never fully able to eradicate. After 1688, its Dissenting population grew rapidly to the point that by the later eighteenth century, over 40 per cent of the population were Dissenters, most of them members of radical secessionist sects. Throughout the century the local presbytery and synod had a well-earned reputation for doctrinal orthodoxy and remained implacably hostile to any more 'moderate' attempt to develop a Presbyterianism which held less pessimistic views of human nature, civil society and the possibilities of redemption. The city's culture was deeply influenced by this pietism. As Defoe noted, Glasgow's sabbatarianism was exceptional even by Scottish standards.[9] 'People were prevented by authority from walking on the Lord's Day,' John Gibson, the city's historian, noted in 1777. 'No lamps were lighted on that evening because it was presumed that no one would be out of his own house after sun-set; the indulgences, and innocent amusements of life were either unknown or were little practised.'[10]

Glaswegian Presbyterian orthodoxy had always played an important direct or indirect part in shaping the history of the university and it continued doing so for the next century. Like the other post-Reformation universities, Glasgow's primary responsibility had been to train boys for the parishes and schoolhouses of a newly reformed church, a task whose importance John Knox, for one, had never underrated. 'Above all things,' he had warned the General Assembly in 1572, 'preserve the Church from the bondage of the Universities. Persuade them to rule themselves peaceably, and order their schools in Christ; but subject never the pulpit to their judgement, neither yet exempt them from your jurisdiction.'[11] Knox's words were meant as a warning. But they were also the words of a master strategist who well knew that universities had a key role to play in the making of a godly community, words that were never forgotten by the clergy or laity.

It had always been easy for the Kirk and Crown to interfere in university affairs; unlike many Oxbridge colleges, the tiny Scottish universities were too poor and politically vulnerable to resist political intrusion. What is more, the religious and political life of the country was so volatile in the century and a half after the Reformation that interference became a continuing fact of university life in Glasgow and elsewhere. Like the other Scottish universities, Glasgow was purged during the Reformation, in the later 1630s, after the Restoration and after the Glorious Revolution (the Aberdeen colleges were additionally purged after the Jacobite rebellion of 1715). In each case the university's Principal, and the professors and regents who undertook all the teaching and who refused to sign the appropriate oaths of loyalty and confessions of faith, were removed, their 'dictates' often being scrutinized for evidence of heterodoxy or heresy. Strict Presbyterians were particularly assiduous in this task. After the re-establishment of Presbyterianism in 1638 and in 1690, the Scottish universities were purged of Episcopalians and an attempt was made to reconstruct the philosophy curriculum, on which the entire system of university education was built. The regents of the five universities were instructed to produce a new, doctrinally wholesome philosophy textbook for compulsory use in all of the universities. The first attempt in the 1640s never got off the ground. Later the project collapsed as authors squabbled about its contents. Nevertheless, the whole episode showed that the orthodox Presbyterians fully appreciated the importance of the universities and the philosophy curriculum in building a Godly state. Nor, as we shall see, was this message lost on their enemies. For one of the oddest paradoxes in the history of the university in Glasgow, this most strictly Presbyterian of cities, was that it became the intellectual powerhouse of a highly successful attempt by moderate Presbyterian professors to develop an alternative Presbyterian academic culture, which would be more in tune with the demands of a Whig regime and the polite manners demanded by a commercial age.

This remarkable exercise in rebuilding Glasgow University's academic culture had its roots in the Glorious Revolution and the restoration of Presbyterianism in 1690. At one level the university did quite well out of the Revolution. Between 1690 and 1720, the Crown supplied two formidable and politically well-connected Principals. These two men, William Dunlop (1690–1701) and John Stirling (1701–28), were responsible for establishing chairs in Ecclesiastical History, Botany, Law and Medicine, and for extracting funds from the Crown for a better botanical garden and a new collection of scientific instruments. And although it took time and persistence, the two Principals succeeded in improving the university's precarious finances. It is perhaps a measure of their success that the number of students rose from around 150 in the 1650s to around 400 in 1702, a significant number of whom came from Presbyterian communities in England and Ireland. During Stirling's period of office, however, the university developed an increasingly uneasy relationship with the city. For one thing, Stirling's firm and imperious style of management led to bitter infighting within the faculty and between himself and the students. This reached a climax in 1717 when he rashly attempted to deprive students of their constitutional right to elect the Rector, with whom many of the Principal's powers of governing the university were shared – a measure which led to riots, expulsions, litigation and an appeal from the students to Parliament. What made matters worse was that these confusions became associated with well-founded clerical suspicions that the university was becoming a hotbed of heterodoxy. The Crown had been worried by Glasgow's radical Presbyterian culture for a long time, and had encouraged the appointment of professors who would teach a moderate Presbyterianism that stressed the need for a more consensual, less adversarial relationship between the Kirk and civil society than that favoured by the orthodox.

No one was less orthodox than John Simson. He had been educated at Edinburgh and Leiden and was appointed to the Divinity chair in 1708. By 1715 he had become notorious among the radical clergy of the west of Scotland for daring to suggest that the principles of the foundational credal document of the Kirk, the Westminster Confession of Faith, could be defended on rational grounds; as his enemies put it, he attributed 'too much to natural reason and the power of corrupt nature' and not enough to revelation and 'the effectiveness of free grace'. Between 1716 and 1726 he became the *bête noire* of the orthodox. He was continually in trouble with the local presbytery and the General Assembly for fostering heresy in the forms of Arminianism, Socinianism and Arianism, in spite of strenuous efforts by the college to resist clerical intrusion into university affairs. In 1729, after protracted litigation and pressure from the Crown, Simson was finally ordered to stop teaching divinity. Throughout Smith's student days, he was to be an elderly reminder of the hazards of teaching theology on rational principles in the heartland of orthodox Presbyterianism.

These academic wranglings gave the rising man of Scottish politics, the Earl of Islay, the opportunity to strike. His close connections with the Prime Minister, Sir Robert Walpole, ensured that his power would grow rapidly during the 1720s, to the point that he became known as 'the uncrowned king of Scotland'. He was an intelligent and cultivated man, with a genuine interest in experimental science and letters and in the future of the Scottish universities. In 1726 he arranged a Visitation to overhaul the university's constitution and curriculum. New chairs in Logic and Metaphysics, in Moral Philosophy and in Natural Philosophy were established and the teaching duties of every university professor were carefully defined to prevent jurisdictional squabbles within the new professoriate. From thenceforth until his death in 1761, Islay was to keep a watchful eye on the affairs of the university. His advice was sought on the election of most professors and was generally decisive. His support for Francis Hutcheson's appointment to the Moral Philosophy chair in 1729, and for Smith's to the Logic and Metaphysics chair in 1751, was crucial; so was his opposition to David Hume's bid for the Logic and Metaphysics chair in 1752 following Smith's move to the chair of Moral Philosophy. He was a relentless opponent of orthodox, high-flying Presbyterians, whom he thought of as 'Levites', and an equally committed supporter of the moderates. During the 1730s Islay carefully built up a party of supporters in the university, including Francis Hutcheson, Alexander Dunlop, the Professor of Greek, Alexander Rosse, the Professor of Humanity (or Latin), and Robert Simson, the Professor of Mathematics, the professors who were to be responsible for much of Smith's university education.[12]

Hutcheson's appointment to the chair of Moral Philosophy in 1729 was the most important moment in the shaping of this new academic culture. This was not simply because he was the undisputed leader of the moderate Presbyterian group in the university but because he was able to give ideological and intellectual definition to a new philosophy curriculum. His was the voice of a new sort of academic philosophy, tolerant in its attitudes to religion, consensually minded in its views about the relationship between the Church and civil society, radical Whig in its attitude to politics, and committed to a new approach to the problem of educating the laity and clergy of a modern Christian state. Indeed, it was as an exemplary professor as well as a moral philosopher of the first rank that his teaching was to appeal to Smith. Hutcheson was one of the many Ulstermen who had studied for the ministry at Glasgow University. He had been introduced to moral philosophy by his predecessor, Gersholm Carmichael, a highly intelligent, orthodox Presbyterian of some originality who had given him a sophisticated introduction to Pufendorf's natural jurisprudence, and to modern theology by John Simson, who had showed him the dangers and difficulties of trying to develop a system of Christian apologetics based on natural law rather than revelation. Hutcheson returned to Ireland in 1717, ran an influential dissenting academy in Dublin and became a leading member of an intellectual circle that revolved round Viscount Molesworth, one of the most influential Whig ideologues of the day and one of the most important advocates of university reform.

Molesworth encouraged Hutcheson to set his theological interests in a wider ideological framework, and to think about the role of university education in a free state. He was a radical Whig who was deeply preoccupied with the problem of preserving and perfecting the liberties the British had won in 1688. 'Must frequent Blood-lettings be indispensably necessary to preserve our Constitution?' he wrote. 'Is it not possible for us to render vain and untrue that Sarcasm of Foreigners, who object to us that our *English* Kings have either too little Power, or too much, and that therefore we must expect no settled or lasting Peace? Shall we for ever retain the ill Character they give us of the most mutable and inconstant Nation of the World?' In an age in which Britain was becoming 'more considerable' in the world, it was time for Britons to broaden their knowledge of the world and attend to the culture and education of their political leaders. This meant reforming the country's universities, which had become hotbeds of priestcraft and provided an education only fit for schoolmasters. Molesworth was contemptuous of most modern university teachers, their teaching and their politics:

> The weightier Matters of true Learning, whereof one has occasion every hour; such as good Principles, Morals, the improvement of Reason, the love of Justice, the value of Liberty, the duty owing to ones Countrey and the Laws, are either quite omitted, or slightly passed over: Indeed they forget not to recommend frequently to [their students] what they call the *Queen of all Vertues*, viz. *Submission* to Superiors, and an entire *blind Obedience* to Authority.[13]

By the 1730s Molesworth's disciples were well positioned in the Scottish universities: George Turnbull in Marischal College, Aberdeen, William Wishart in Edinburgh and Hutcheson in Glasgow, all sharing the ambition to 'promote the interests of liberty and vertue and to reform the taste of the young generation' in what Turnbull described as 'this narrow and bigoted country'.[14] The new curriculum, like that of David Miller's school at Kirkcaldy, was to be based on the study of the ancients who, as Molesworth put it, 'were deservedly look'd upon as Supports of the State, they had their dependence wholly upon it: and as they could have no Interest distinct from it, they laid out themselves towards the advancing and promoting the good of it, insomuch that we find the very good Fortune of their *Commonwealth* often lasted no longer than they did'.[15] This gratifying portrait of professors and philosophers as the custodians of the liberties of modern Britain was one with which Hutcheson sympathized and one which would attract Smith profoundly. Hutcheson quickly established himself as a reforming, imaginative and immensely hardworking professor. He abandoned the age-old practice of dictating lectures in Latin and turned his moral philosophy lectures into celebrated rhetorical performances that attracted students from England, Ireland and Edinburgh. Hugh Blair, the first Professor of Rhetoric and Belles-Letters at Edinburgh, was one of his pupils:

> Besides his constant lectures five days of the week on natural religion, morals, jurisprudence and government; he had another lecture three days of the week, in which he explained some of the finest writers of antiquity, both Greek and Latin, on the subject of morals, and every Sunday-evening, he gave a weekly lecture on the truth and excellency of the Christian religion, to a very crowded auditory. Fond of well-disposed youth, entering into all their concerns, encouraging and befriending them on all occasions, he gained the esteem and affections of the students in a very high degree. To his honour it will be ever acknowledged, that he raised and supported an excellent spirit, and a high taste for literature in that university; and was particularly happy in reviving the study of antient learning, especially the Greek, which had been much neglected. Such an ardour for knowledge, and such a spirit of inquiry, did he spread every where around him, that . . . the usual conversation of the students, at their social walks and visits, turned with great keenness upon subjects of learning and taste.[16]

Hutcheson's friend and colleague William Leechman commented that this 'rational enthusiasm for the interests of learning, liberty, religion, virtue and human happiness' penetrated all of Hutcheson's teaching. In teaching natural theology and moral philosophy, 'when

he led [his students] from the view of the external world to the contemplation of the internal one, the soul of man, and showed them like
instances of Divine Wisdom and benignity in the contrivance of its
moral constitution, they were filled with fresh delight and wonder,
and discerned new and encreasing proofs of the glorious perfections
of the Father of our spirits'. His lectures on politics emphasized 'the
importance of civil and religious liberty to the happiness of mankind'
and set out to awaken and shape his pupils' love of public spirit. For
'public spirit in him was not a vague and undetermined kind of order,
for something unknown or not distinctly understood; but it was an
enlightened and universal zeal for every branch of human happiness,
and the means of promoting it.'[17] In a celebrated sermon delivered on
7 April 1741, a year after Smith had left for Oxford, Leechman left a
portrait of the moderate Presbyterian minister which nicely catches
the elements of the civic personality that Glasgow's Molesworthians
set out to inculcate in lay as well as clerical students. The modern
minister, Leechman observed, must be set apart from the world by his
personal integrity, his manners and an 'unbyass'd state of mind'. He
must be able to move freely and easily in the world, retaining as much
purity of mind 'as if he were living outside the world'. He must be
wary of the blandishments of the great for, 'while we shew all due
regard to their stations and characters, it must appear at the same
time, that we have a greater regard for truth, virtue, piety, and decency:
while we avoid everything like insolence and pertness, on the one
hand, and abject cringing on the other'. In a word, Leechman concluded, using an expression which orthodox Presbyterians regarded
as an abomination, he must cultivate a 'friendship' with God.[18]

In his back-breaking programme of teaching, Hutcheson succeeded
in placing the moral philosophy curriculum at the apex of the philosophy curriculum at Glasgow, as the discipline which would teach
students preparing to enter Divinity Hall or one of the professions the
duties of the Christian citizen. It was a deeply controversial programme
in Presbyterian circles and, as Hutcheson knew all too well from his
days as a Dissenting minister in Dublin, one which was bound to provoke opposition.[19] His appointment had aroused suspicion among the
orthodox, even though there were some, like Robert Wodrow, who
were prepared to give him the benefit of the doubt on the grounds

that he was a good man who might be able to introduce a modicum of order into a notoriously unruly college.[20] Hutcheson went out of his way to discuss some of the points of his inaugural lecture with potential opponents and took the precaution of delivering it 'very fast and lou [sic] being a modest man, and it was not well understood'[21]– which was just as well, because the lecture was designed to prepare the ground for some of Hutcheson's most radical thinking. Once established, Hutcheson began to push his luck, chatting to divinity students and discussing the sermons they were working on, a matter which normally lay within the province of the Professor of Divinity. He began looking out for prospective professors who shared his tastes and opinions, scoring his greatest triumph in 1743 in securing the appointment of William Leechman to the Divinity chair. 'It will put a new face upon Theology in Scotland!' he exclaimed. 'We have at last got a right Professor of Theology, the only thoroughly right one in Scotland.'[22] He was instrumental in setting up two of his former students, Robert and Andrew Foulis, as printers to the university and charging them with the business of publishing – in exquisite and highly collectable editions – the ancient and modern authors he and his colleagues admired and taught; his own works, which went through twenty-eight editions, were the most widely published of the Foulises' list.[23] By the end of his career in 1746 he had built up a substantial core of disciples among English and Irish students, as well as among the Scots who had studied with him, and many of these were to play a crucial part in shaping moderate Presbyterianism in Britain and in America. Indeed, it was predictable that when he was attacked by a troubled former student who was unable to square his professor's teaching with the provisions of the Westminster Confession of Faith, a group of students should have rushed into print in Hutcheson's defence. For Hutcheson, like Smith after him, had an extraordinary ability to generate affection and loyalty.

Hutcheson and Islay between them had transformed the reputation of the university at Glasgow and had done much to turn it into one of the most interesting in northern Europe. And although it did not yet have the resources to provide the sort of legal and medical education that its great rival at Edinburgh could provide, its philosophy curriculum was unrivalled in Scotland. Much of this must have been known to Margaret Smith and her intelligent and cultivated Kirkcaldy friends, and it was not in the least surprising that she should have decided that Glasgow was the right place for her son. Smith for his part cannot have failed to be impressed by the physical presence of the college and by its distinctive ethos, as well as by a curriculum that was to suit him very well. The college building was one of the largest public buildings in Scotland, built in the middle decades of the previous century with the proceeds of a large benefaction from a grateful alumnus, Zachary Boyd, and a large public subscription. It now resembled one of the grander Oxford colleges, with two large courts, a common hall, a well-stocked library and lodgings for students, regents and professors. When Smith matriculated in 1737, a line of houses – or manses – for the new generation of professors had just been completed. 'The whole building is of freestone,' Defoe wrote, 'very high and very august', and, with the Cathedral, it dominated the city's skyline.[24]

At the same time the university had developed a distinctive social ethos that emphasized its cultural distance from the city as well as its commanding presence within it, and stood in striking contrast to the academic ethos of its great rival at Edinburgh. Edinburgh lacked Glasgow's splendid buildings and collegiate sense of identity. Its professors generally led second lives as ministers of city parishes, as practising doctors and lawyers, and, because the university had no lodgings, its students had to make their own domestic arrangements in the city. By Smith's time, Edinburgh's professors and students had begun to see themselves as part of a wider social, political and cultural world and were even beginning to think of this environment as one which encouraged useful learning and politeness. In Glasgow, however, the academic community tended to keep itself to itself. Not many professors had church livings and, anyway, the university lacked the large and rapidly expanding medical and legal faculties which would have encouraged the growth of a professoriate with professional interests in the city. And while many better-off students preferred to lodge in the city, they soon discovered that Glasgow's puritan culture discouraged the easy passage between town and gown that was characteristic of the capital. Alexander Carlyle thought that this meant that Glasgow students worked harder than those at Edinburgh, but added (rather snobbishly) that they lacked 'knowledge of the world and a Certain Manner and Address that can only be attained in the Capital'.[25] They also lacked the clubs and societies dedicated to the cultivation of learning, letters and politeness that shaped the interplay of academic and civic life in Edinburgh and made it possible for the capital to develop its own distinctive form of enlightenment. Though Glasgow had its merchant-intellectuals like Lord Provost Andrew Cochrane, whose Political Economy Club flourished in the 1750s and whose discussions were to provide Smith with the opportunity of listening to merchants discussing their business and their attitudes to commercial policy, it was the university and its professors who shaped the city's enlightenment. However, this enclosed collegiate culture was one that suited Smith very well. In later life his friends found it difficult to get him to visit Edinburgh, and he went out of his way to describe his Glasgow years as 'by far the most useful, and, therefore, as by far the happiest and most honourable period of my life'.[26] And it was here in this newly reformed institution that he settled down to study a philosophy curriculum of intellectual sophistication and ideological interest.

In outline, the Glasgow curriculum was traditional and resembled that of any other Scottish university. The academic year ran from 10 October to mid-June almost without a break. The first two years were devoted to Humanity – or Latin – and Greek, though students who were competent in Latin were generally excused the first year. The third year was devoted to logic and metaphysics, the traditional introduction to philosophy, the fourth to moral philosophy and the fifth to natural philosophy. By Smith's time, however, this outline had been much refined. Geometry and advanced Greek were available in the third year. Advanced geometry and advanced Humanity were available in the fourth year. In the final year, it was also possible to study further mathematics, natural jurisprudence, Latin and Greek. During the three philosophy years 'the Scholars have frequent Exercises in Declaiming and Disputing, both in the several Classes and in the Common Hall: And, about the 10th of December there is a publick Examination of all the under Graduates, which continues a Fortnight or three Weeks, three Days each Week at least.'[27]

Smith's Latin and Greek seem to have been good enough already to exempt him from the first two years of the curriculum. He entered the third year in 1737 at the age of fourteen as a member of John Loudon's logic and metaphysics class and may have attended Alexander Dunlop's special Greek course. Loudon, who was no friend of Hutcheson, was a serious, intelligent orthodox Presbyterian and one of the last orthodox professors of the old school. His intellectual world was Augustinian, shaped by a belief in the natural depravity of man and by a sense of the yawning gulf which separates the world of the flesh from that of the heavenly city to which God's grace alone could grant access. It was a profoundly different intellectual world from that which Smith was to inhabit: his great pupil was to retort that, so far from being the enemy of morality, earthly needs were the parents of morality and virtue. Loudon saw his task as one of introducing his students to the different properties of the mind and to the art of thinking, and, like most orthodox Christians, he seems to have done this by relying on the sophisticated writings of modern Augustinians like Malebranche, De Vries and the Port-Royal and by using Arnauld and Nicole's classic *Art of Thinking* as his textbook. His more avant-garde students found his teaching old-fashioned – Tobias Smollett complained that the 'art of logic has been transformed into a kind of legerdemain, by which boys can syllogize'.[28] And although Loudon introduced his students to the main metaphysical systems used in the ancient and modern world, he did so in order to protect them against theological error, on the classic assumption that, in the last resort, the real purpose of philosophy was to illustrate and reinforce the fundamental truths of Christianity and, more especially, those set out for Presbyterians to observe in the Westminster Confession of Faith.

Smith must have realized that Loudon's view of the mind and his theology were controversial. Francis Hutcheson's course on pneumatology – a discipline which dealt with proofs of the being and nature of the deity – ran concurrently with Loudon's course on logic and metaphysics and was taught on very different principles. It is true that Hutcheson dealt with this explosive subject with characteristic circumspection, minimizing his differences with Loudon as far as possible. Nevertheless, his real opinions on the subject soon became apparent in his classes on moral philosophy and natural jurisprudence, in which he contradicted everything Loudon and the orthodox

Presbyterians stood for. As William Leechman put it, '[Hutcheson] still continued extremely doubtful of the justice and force of all the metaphysical arguments, by which many have endeavoured to demonstrate the existence, unity, and perfections of the Deity.' He went on: 'Such attempts instead of conducting us to the absolute certainty proposed, leave the mind in such a state of doubt and uncertainty as leads to absolute scepticism.'[29] Hutcheson regarded the study of human nature and the natural world as the only sure foundation on which theological knowledge could be built.

Smith was taught by most of the most notable scholars in the university. Robert Dick introduced him to Newtonian physics and turned him into a serious student of natural philosophy. The great mathematician Robert Simson, the heterodox Professor of Divinity's nephew, introduced him to Euclidean geometry, a discipline Smith admired for its elegance, lucidity and 'the absolute rigour of its demonstrations'.[30] Smith's friend Archibald Maclaine told Dugald Stewart that Smith's 'favourite pursuits while at that university were mathematics and natural philosophy', and he certainly retained a lifelong respect for mathematical explanation. Stewart remembered 'to have heard my father [Matthew Stewart, Professor of Mathematics at Edinburgh] remind him of a geometrical problem of considerable difficulty, about which he was occupied at the time when their acquaintance commenced, and which had been proposed to him as an exercise by the celebrated Dr. Simpson'.[31] As we shall see, Euclidean geometry was to provide Smith with important insights into methods which could be employed for placing the study of human nature on experimental foundations. But for all Smith's interests in natural philosophy and mathematics his greatest debt was to Francis Hutcheson. It was he who introduced Smith to the moral philosophy of the ancients and moderns and gave him a distinctive way of thinking about the importance of philosophy in the modern world. His total dedication to teaching and his powerful philosophical intelligence gave his courses an intellectual excitement that led Smith to describe him as 'the never to be forgotten Dr Hutcheson'.[32] For Hutcheson was one of the most ambitious, admired and innovative philosophy teachers in the English-speaking world in the early eighteenth century.

Before his appointment to the Moral Philosophy chair, Hutcheson's philosophical reputation had rested on his insights into the principles of human nature, the nature of virtue and the meaning of sociability. Much of his Glasgow teaching was devoted to working out the political implications of his philosophy and to doing so in a way that earned him his formidable reputation in radical Whig circles in Britain and the American colonies. The wider agenda to which he worked, however, had been laid down by Samuel von Pufendorf in the previous century in one of the most ambitious of all seventeenth-century philosophical projects, that of distilling an understanding of the principles of government from the principles of natural law and the principles of human nature. It was a project to which university students had been introduced in most of the serious universities of Europe since the later seventeenth century and it was one to which Hutcheson himself had been introduced by Gersholm Carmichael. It was a project the politically aware philosopher could admire for its relevance to the business of government; on the other hand, it was also a project which Hutcheson had every reason for regarding as flawed and in need of radical reconstruction. Smith was about to be introduced to one of the most powerful and ambitious undertakings in modern philosophy in a deeply revisionist spirit.

It is easy to see why Pufendorf's ideas seemed so attractive to ambitious, politically minded thinkers. He had believed profoundly in the importance of philosophy to public life, had addressed some of the most difficult and disturbing political problems faced by the rulers of late seventeenth-century Europe, and had worked in the service of several of them. He had grown up in the shadow of the wars of religion of the later sixteenth century and the Thirty Years War of 1618–48, and had seen how civil wars and lethal sectarian conflicts had undermined the political foundations of nearly every European state; indeed his earliest memory had been of sectarian slaughter in his native Saxony.[33] He had looked into the abyss of political anarchy that had threatened to engulf the political life of post-Reformation Europe and had asked how political society could be rebuilt on principles that were shared by the subjects of any state, whatever their credal loyalties.

This was no easy matter. Like Hobbes, he thought that men were naturally dangerous, unsociable, 'impolitick animals', driven by 'thirst after things superfluous', by ambition ('the most pernicious of all Evils'), and by a 'quick Resentment of injuries, and eager Desire of Revenge'.[34] Like Hobbes, his interests in philosophy, politics and the business of government were directed to the question of explaining how this naturally ungovernable species acquired the understanding of morality and justice and the overriding need to submit to government, for these were the forms of understanding on which political life and sociable living depended. Pufendorf thought that life in the family made men aware of their natural weaknesses and taught them the need for co-operation, long before they realized the need to submit to a political sovereign. In his view, so far from being a product of Hobbesian fears, civil society was the product of a series of contracts made by cautious, prudent, patriarchal heads of households who were anxious 'to guard themselves against those Injuries; which one Man was in danger of sustaining from another'; and it was on the behaviour of these patriarchs that the future of society effectively depended.[35] His view of civil society was, therefore, austere, disenchanted and authoritarian. Most rulers were faced with the problem of governing subjects whose appetites and ambitions were constantly at odds with whatever rudimentary sense of justice they might have acquired, and he worked on the assumption that in most states the threat of faction, sedition and civil war was bound to be endemic. Absolute monarchy – supported, as Pufendorf continually pointed out, by learned counsellors like himself and a carefully educated magistracy – was the only sure way of preserving peace and ensuring that subjects behaved sociably. Mixed constitutions, like that of modern Britain, in which king and people continually quarrelled about their rights and liberties, posed a constant threat to stability. Lutheran churches, which recognized the king as their supreme head, were to be preferred to Presbyterian churches, which distrusted the sovereignty of princes. Religious dissent was distrusted and luxury and commerce were suspect in Pufendorf's scheme, because conspicuous consumption tended to encourage greed and ambition. However, with luck, prudent management and well-regulated schools and universities, a sovereign could hope 'to train up some few, by long Discipline, to a tolerable Behaviour [in the performance of the civil duties]'; the vulgar 'who are the greater Part of Mankind' could only be ruled by fear.[36] What he wanted was a citizen class which had a disenchanted view of human nature, a bleak Stoic appreciation of the necessities which bound them together in civil society, and a fear of the deity. Under these circumstances there was a reasonable chance the citizens would learn to respect political authority and the rules of justice and morality and come to think of them as right in themselves and incumbent on every virtuous and god-fearing citizen. In which case there was also a reasonable chance that citizens would have learned the foundational lesson that 'in order to be safe, it is necessary for [them] to be sociable'.[37] When Pufendorf's moral philosophy is viewed as a philosopher-statesman's response to the problem of securing the tenuous state of international peace that had been made possible by the treaty of Westphalia of 1648, its political purposes seem clear enough – to secure the minimal level of sociability needed to ensure a state's survival and no more.

However, by the early eighteenth century this bleak system of natural jurisprudence began to look dated and unconvincing. The circumstances of the European state system had changed and were changing. Fears of political implosion and a descent into a state of endemic civil war were being replaced by fears of French imperialism. The expansion of commerce and overseas empires were transforming international relations and raising difficult questions about the effects of economic expansion and luxury on the political and moral fabric of the state. There were also questions being asked about the principles on which the Pufendorfian system was based. Scots and English philosophers were convinced that their mixed constitution and the limited monarchy brought into existence by the Glorious Revolution and the Revolution Settlement was a better way of fostering sociable behaviour than absolute monarchy, and many moderate theologians were repelled by Pufendorf's Lutheran vision of a harsh and retributive deity. So far as Smith was concerned, the importance of Hutcheson's teaching was not simply that he provided a critical introduction to these important questions, but that he opened up wider and more fundamental questions about the nature of sociability itself and the principles of human nature on which it rested.

Hutcheson's critique of Pufendorf was sweeping and far-reaching and must have been exhilarating for his students. Was it enough to say that human beings behave sociably simply because they fear the sovereign or the deity? Surely true and lasting sociability must have deeper roots in the principles of human nature than the selfish, prudential and always opportunistic instincts about which Pufendorf had written. And was it really true, as Pufendorf claimed, that the authority of our parents or masters or sovereigns was based on a series of contracts? Did this not represent a perilously narrow and selective view of human nature and the civilizing process? And, worse still, was it not a view of human nature that had been distorted at every level by grim theological assumptions about the corruption of human nature? In a so-called 'scientific' age, wasn't there a need, as one of Pufendorf's sharpest editors, Jean Barbyrac, put it, for a new science of morality, which placed the study of human nature and the principles of sociability on empirical foundations? Was it not time for an account of the principles on which political society and government were based that would suit the needs of a civilization which had moved far beyond the insecurities of a Pufendorfian world and was in the process of being transformed by commerce?

Hutcheson's distaste for Pufendorf's grimly Augustinian view of human nature was profound.

> We scarce ever hear any thing from [such moralists] of the *bright Side* of Humane Nature. They never talk of any kind *Instinct*s; of natural Affections *to associate*; of *natural Affections*, of *Compassio*n, of *Love of Company*, a *Sense of Gratitude*, a *Determination* to honour and love the Authors of any good Offices toward any Part of Mankind, as well as of those toward our selves; and of a *natural Delight* Men take in being esteem'd and honour'd by others for good Actions: which yet all may be observ'd to prevail exceedingly in *humane* Life.[38]

He wanted a moral theory which would take account of the fact that we have benevolent as well as selfish passions and affections, and one that would yield up a very different understanding of the functions and duties of government to Pufendorf's. Here his starting point was the 3rd Earl of Shaftesbury's idiosyncratic and influential *Characteristicks of Men, Manners, Opinions and Times* (1711) and his attempt to demonstrate that human beings were essentially 'benevolent' agents who were at their most contented, most virtuous and most sociable when they felt able to follow the dictates of their generous affections. He shared Shaftesbury's view that the vicissitudes of modern life encouraged the young – 'grown youth' as he liked to call them – to ignore the 'language of the heart' and to indulge in selfish and cynical thinking about the world and their duties. He was interested in Shaftesbury's ethics, which were designed to show how grown youth could discover their benevolent selves by cultivating a love of beauty, virtue, friendship and humanity, and learning to value them for their own sakes rather than for any vulgar material advantage they might bring, and he believed that these were lessons that could only be learned in the company of fellow-dilettanti. Above all, Hutcheson shared Shaftesbury's belief that these exercises in self-improvement would foster a sense of sociability, public spirit and liberty. The trouble with these ethics for Hutcheson, however, was that they were deist and anti-Christian: Shaftesbury thought that organized religion fostered sectarianism and undermined man's natural capacity for sociability. Moreover, as a philosopher he was well aware that Shaftesbury's analysis of the relations between the selfish and benevolent passions was far from being conclusive. It was a weakness that had recently been demonstrated with devastating clarity by Bernard Mandeville, the author of *The Fable of the Bees*, first published in 1711 and reissued in 1723 in the highly publicized edition which Hutcheson must have read in Dublin, one of the most brilliant and witty philosophical satires of the Enlightenment. Mandeville was the philosophical irritant Hutcheson was able neither to ignore nor to accommodate, and one who would shadow Smith for the rest of his life.

The Fable of the Bees was a glorious satire on the follies of human nature that ridiculed Shaftesbury's attempt to show that the sociable affections were founded on benevolence. Mandeville was a Grub Street journalist who was prepared to pit the down-to-earth language of the coffee-house and tavern against Shaftesbury's high-falutin' prose, and the apparently earthy cynicism of the ordinary citizen against the wishful thinking of the idealistic aristocratic virtuoso. 'This Noble Writer (for it is the Lord Shaftesbury I mean in his Charcteristicks)' had simply seen what he wanted to see in human nature and had naively assumed 'that as Man is made for Society, so he ought to be born with a kind Affection to the whole, of which he is a part, and a

Propensity to seek the Welfare of it'. Such sentiments, Mandeville commented dryly, 'are a high Compliment to Human-kind, and capable by the help of a little Enthusiasm of Inspiring us with the most Noble Sentiments concerning the Dignity of our exalted Nature: What Pity it is that they are not true.'[39] For Mandeville all our passions, benevolent and selfish alike, had a single purpose: to serve and gratify our pride and what he later called 'self-liking', and it was pride and its companion, shame, that explained the ultimate paradox of human nature – that man, the most selfish and wilful of animals, was also the most sociable and docile.[40] How was this to be explained? For Mandeville it was a story about how human beings were 'broke' by their parents, nurses, teachers, friends and, above all, by 'wary Politicians' who used their arts to gull us into believing that curbing our passions was a better way of gratifying our pride and self-esteem than indulging them. It was a story about 'the witchcraft of flattery', about the never-ending comedy of lives devoted to exploiting others and discovering that we have been exploited in return, about the way in which we become caught in a web of culture and language that ensnares and socializes us all. It was dangerous as well as absurd for Shaftesbury to claim that young men could be socialized by indulging their so-called benevolent affections. It was also ethically contemptible, in that it provided 'a vast Inlet to Hypocrisy, which being once made habitual, we must not only deceive others, but likewise become altogether unknown to our selves'.[41] All the virtuously minded, good-natured person could do, Mandeville seemed to suggest (for this was not a subject he ever touched on directly), was to reflect on our endless capacity for hypocrisy and self-delusion with ironic detachment and to submit cheerfully to the beneficent if scarcely edifying constraints of culture and custom.

This was a formidably brilliant social analysis. Here was a highly developed account of the civilizing process which showed that at every point of their daily lives men and women (Mandeville was interested in the formation of the female as well as the male personality) were driven by what Mandeville described as 'wants' or 'needs'. As he was well aware, his analysis could be used to show that all of the cultural institutions on which the survival of society depended, all systems of taste, morality and politics, all philosophy and art, all progress in the arts, sciences and commerce, all language even, were driven by need, by a hunger for social approval and by the ever-contemptible delusion that our self-regarding actions were virtuous and for the public good.

> So Vice is beneficial found,
> When it's by Justice lopt and bound;
> Nay, where the People would be great,
> As necessary to the State,
> As Hunger is to make 'em eat.
> Bare Virtue can't make Nations live
> In Splendor; they, that would revive
> A Golden Age, must be as free,
> For Acorns, as for Honesty.[42]

Smith was to be acutely aware of the historicity of this approach to the study of human nature and of the evolutionary nature of human civilization which was built into it. But that is not what struck his teacher. For Hutcheson, as for so many of Mandeville's contemporary critics, what was shocking was his cynicism. It was not simply that he had shown that all human behaviour was driven by pride – that, after all, was something orthodox Christians knew from St Augustine and his modern disciples. Nor was it even Mandeville's refusal to believe in the existence of that feeble spark of reason which would allow the chosen and dedicated few to learn how to control their appetites. What mattered was Mandeville's demonstration that our belief in the existence of absolute standards of taste, virtue and, by extension, justice and liberty are simply delusions and the product of our endless capacity for self-deception and hypocrisy – delusions we generate to cover our natural depravity, and which make life both contemptible and tolerable. As Hutcheson saw very clearly, *The Fable of the Bees* posed a mortal threat to true moral philosophy by encouraging citizens to distrust their own and others' motives, thus undermining those natural feelings of friendship and sociability on which trust, order and liberty depended.

This cynicism appalled Hutcheson and he returned to it continually in his writing and, it was said, in nearly every lecture; Mandeville, he said, was the most dangerous of those philosophers who would 'rather twist Self-Love into a thousand Shapes, than allow any other Principle of Approbation than Interest'.[43] Hutcheson was determined to find new ways of demonstrating the importance of the benevolent affections to human behaviour, intent to show that benevolently inclined societies were capable of a high degree of self-regulation and were therefore not in need of the attentions of absolute monarchs. It was a project that led him to think carefully about the relationship between the selfish and benevolent passions and about the civilizing process. It also, happily, provided him with an opportunity to rebut Shaftesbury's notoriously deist natural theology. He had laid the foundations of this project in Dublin in the *Enquiries* which made his philosophical reputation and was to develop his theory's ethical and political implications in Glasgow. Philosophically, Smith was to regard it as a problematical exercise on the part of his professor, but it was one which he would never forget.

Hutcheson wanted to use the resources of modern philosophy to rebuild the ethics of the ancients and to develop a theory of sociability and virtue that would dispose of the cynical errors of the moderns once and for all. What interested him were the circumstances in which we begin to reflect on our passions and interests and begin to acquire an understanding of those ideas of morality, justice and political allegiance on which our capacity for sociable behaviour ultimately depends. This meant thinking about the process of social interaction and about the way in which we perform as actors and spectators when we find ourselves engaged in moral encounters. Hutcheson saw human beings as naturally inquisitive agents. We seem to have a natural interest in other people's motives and we find ourselves naturally approving of actions which seem to be virtuous and naturally disapproving of those which seem to be vicious. To be sure, our first impressions can be mistaken; another person's motives may turn out to be more equivocal than we originally thought. But Hutcheson was struck by how quickly and almost instinctively we adjust our moral responses to new evidence, and how readily our feelings for the person concerned will adjust. He went to great trouble to show that we judge the moral behaviour of others by reckoning on the amount of benevolence that seems to motivate an action, and he was struck by the fact that our approval and affection for the person concerned seems to increase naturally in relation to the number of people we think will benefit from his actions. It also allowed him to show that we have a more complex attitude to 'benevolent' and 'selfish' behaviour than modern moralists had thought: we will naturally approve of and respect a dutiful husband who is prudent in dealing with his family's financial affairs and we may even think him virtuous for doing so; in the same way we will surely think reckless generosity a vice, particularly if it threatens our family and friends. Such conclusions showed that 'Self-love is really as necessary to the Good of the Whole, as Benevolence; as that Attraction which causes the Cohesion of the Parts, is as necessary to the regular State of the Whole as Gravitation. Without these additional Motives, Self-love would generally oppose the Motions of Benevolence and concur with Malice or influence us to the same Actions which Malice would.'[44]

The strength of Hutcheson's analysis lay in its apparently conclusive demonstration that our moral behaviour, and the social education which shapes our moral personality, was determined by a process over which reason and calculations of interest exercised no control whatever.

> The weakness of our Reason, and the avocations arising from the Infirmity and Necessitys of our Nature, are so great, that very few Men could ever have form'd those long Deductions of Reason, which shew some Actions to be in the whole advantageous to the Agent, and their Contrarys pernicious. The Author of Nature has much better furnish'd us for a virtuous Conduct, than our Moralists seem to imagine, by almost as quick and powerful Instructions, as we have for the preservation of our Bodys.[45]

He was able to observe that in the case of a fully developed moral agent 'the natural feelings of the heart' seemed to operate in such a regular and systematic way and seemed to have so little to do with custom and education, that it was possible to conclude they were controlled by an internal mechanism which was hard-wired into the constitution of human nature itself.[46] This was what he famously and controversially called the moral sense, an apparent resource of human nature whose properties continue to be debated in our own day. It was a Newtonian principle which explained the principle of moral order in the universe in exactly the same way that the principle of

51

gravity had explained the principles of order in nature. By means of it, he claimed, 'all is capable of harmony'.⁴⁷

These were conclusions which promised to breathe new philosophical life into old Stoic maxims. But they had thrown up problems that would have an important bearing on Hutcheson's thinking about political life. He was fully aware of the subjectivity that was built into his thinking. How could we ever be sure that we had interpreted a person's motives correctly? How could we be sure that our moral sense had been right in approving actions that only seemed to be virtuous? Did this not suggest that there were no absolute standards of virtue and vice, that sociability was, as Mandeville had suggested, simply a matter of convention? And wouldn't it then be better to follow Mandeville in refraining from judging others and thinking of virtue as something that was too private to be left to moralists? For Hutcheson, however, that was to repress one of the most natural of all human instincts and the source of our understanding of the human personality. It was of the utmost importance that citizens felt free to indulge their moral curiosity and exercise their natural taste for judging the conduct of others. It would show them that while our moral tastes might differ, all citizens could agree that the best way of judging the moral behaviour of others was by the evidence their actions provided of an untarnished love of the public. In a state built on toleration and benevolence, the moral sense would reign. This was the vision which inspired Hutcheson to compose his hymn to human benevolence.

Let the Obstacles from Self-love be only remov'd, and Nature it self will incline us to Benevolence. Let the Misery of excessive Selfishness, and all its Passions, be but once explain'd, that so Self-love may cease to counteract our natural Propensity to Benevolence, and when this noble Disposition gets loose from these Bonds of Ignorance, and false Views of Interest, it shall be assisted even by Self-love, and grow strong enough to make a noble virtuous Character. Then he is to enquire, by Reflection upon human Affairs, what Course of Action does most effectually promote the universal Good, what universal Rules or Maxims are to be observ'd, and in what Circumstances the Reason of them alters, so as to admit Exceptions; that so our good Inclinations may be directed by Reason, and a just Knowledge of the Interests of Mankind.⁴⁸

Hutcheson developed this highly distinctive view of political society in Glasgow in two texts on which he seems to have been working while Smith was taking his classes. The first was published in 1742 as *A Short Introduction to Moral Philosophy*. The second was abandoned, and published posthumously by his son in 1755 as *A System of Moral Philosophy*; it was, the author thought, 'a confused Book . . . a Farrago'.[49] His view of political society was certainly distinctive and curious, an exercise in using the resources of modern philosophy to reactivate a somewhat old-fashioned form of radical Whig political thinking. He showed how citizens learned about their rights and political obligations from the moral sense, and rightly claimed that this had allowed him to develop a more naturalistic account of the principles on which political society rested than the notoriously contrived system of contracts about which Pufendorf had written. Nor was this simply a matter of reinvigorating old ideologies with a new theory. States which were saddled with authoritarian constitutions, riddled with fears of faction and plagued by cynical views of human nature would inevitably encourage citizens to take narrow, partial views of their rights and these would inevitably become the subject of controversy and faction. The free Hutchesonian polity, by contrast, would be committed to the development of a society of citizens whose behaviour was regulated by the moral sense and the love that these citizens felt towards the public and their Creator. It would be a limited monarchy which recognized that citizens had a right to resist unwelcome monarchs, that guaranteed religious toleration, and which protected small landowners and tenant farmers from acquisitive and over-mighty lords. It would be a society whose merchants traded for modest profits and were motivated by a desire to increase the industry and employment of the people at large. It would extend its citizens' capacity for virtue by encouraging the diffusion of good manners and the performance of those charitable offices on which the perfection of society depended. In so doing, it would help to provide all men with those extensive views of creation on which an understanding and love of the Creator depended. For it was the virtuous, discriminating love of the deity, rather than the fearful Pufendorfian conscience, that was the ultimate source of authority on which virtue, and the performance of all the sociable virtues, depended.

Much of Hutcheson's political thinking was inspired by the radical Whiggery of the previous century and must have sounded dated to many of his Glasgow students. His strikingly radical thinking about the rights of resistance to unwelcome kings looked back to the republicanism of Algernon Sidney and to George Buchanan's alarming views that subjects had a right to change their rulers whenever they felt like it. Like the radicals of a previous generation he spoke of the need for agrarian laws, frequent elections and rotations to curb the threat of oligarchy. He too believed that the future of liberty lay with the middling ranks and particularly with the gentry, whose minds were uncorrupted by excessive wealth or poverty and who possessed the capacity for sharing in the values of the Christian Stoic Enlightenment to which he was committed.

Smith was to be indebted to Hutcheson for inspiration as much as for philosophy. Hutcheson's moral philosophy gave him an introduction to the problem which was to be of central and continuing importance to his own. For, like Hobbes, Pufendorf and Hutcheson, Smith's interests in rhetoric, jurisprudence, ethics and political economy were continually to return to questions about sociability and the processes of social exchange on which society, the progress of civilization and an understanding of the role of government in fostering the civilizing process depended. Hutcheson's subtle, nuanced analysis of the workings of the moral sense showed Smith that the study of sociability and society must begin with the process of social interaction as it is experienced in everyday life, and should revisit those classic and fundamental questions about the origins of those ideas of justice, political obligation and morality on which the citizen's capacity for sociable living depends. His interest in the citizen's need to be reassured that his ideas of morality were right as well as convenient, as well as his interest in the duties of government in fostering the development of societies which were virtuous as well as sociable, was to raise profound questions about the relationship between our never-ending desire to satisfy our moral and intellectual needs, and the material needs that animate social existence. These too were questions which would preoccupy Smith for the rest of his life.

But Smith was never able to subscribe to Hutcheson's belief in the reality of the moral sense, which was derived from the latter's convictions about the essential benevolence of human nature and the deity, both of which Smith found unphilosophical. He was to find Hutcheson's image of the benevolent virtuous citizen too arcane to supply him with a general theory of sociability. And, perhaps above all, he was to find Hutcheson's thinking short on historical vision, harking back to the world of Pufendorf and the radical Whigs of the late seventeenth century and those debates about the benevolence and selfishness of human nature that were beginning to seem redundant. For unlike the historically minded literati of Edinburgh, Hutcheson seemed relatively unaware of the transformations which were overtaking the state system in Europe and the transformational power of commerce that Mandeville had so brilliantly satirized. It was a weakness that for all his sensitivity to the moral life of well-placed citizens had meant that Hutcheson was strikingly insensitive to the changing nature of political power and the problems of government in the modern world. They were matters which had exercised Pufendorf, and were ones to which Smith would return.

3

Private Study 1740–46: Oxford and David Hume

Smith left Glasgow in May 1740, shortly before the end of the academic year. He was, apparently, 'of a cachetic [debilitated] habit, his appearance was ungracious, and his address awkward. His frequent absence of mind gave him an air of vacancy, and even of stupidity', but he was well regarded, and according to the Professor of Greek he was 'a very fine boy as any we have'.[1] He went home to Kirkcaldy to see his mother and to prepare for what he knew would be a long stay at Oxford. He had been awarded a Snell exhibition worth £40 per annum, which would allow him to spend up to eleven years at Balliol College.[2]

Smith cannot have gone to Oxford with particularly high expectations. The reformist Whig circles in which he moved in Kirkcaldy and Glasgow had long regarded Oxford as a faction-ridden sump of Jacobite and high Anglican zealotry and as a by-word for academic incompetence. 'We see Whigs engag'd against Whigs, Tories against Tories, Masters against Doctors and Heads of Colleges, Senior Fellows against Junior Fellows, one College against another College, and many Colleges against themselves', wrote Nicholas Amhurst, one of Oxford's sharpest critics, in 1721. Worse still, this was a period in which Oxford's low reputation for teaching and scholarship – gleefully exaggerated in the Whig press – became a matter of national scandal. The idle, ignorant and venal don who 'lives and moulders away in a supine and regular course of eating, drinking, sleeping and cheating the juniors' became a national figure of fun.[3] The curriculum 'in some measure defective, since we are obliged to adhere so much to the rules laid down by our forefathers' and still heavily dependent on 'the old scholastic learning' continued to be taught, according to the Regius

Professor of History David Gregory, 'because nothing else has been substituted in its place'.[4]

Throughout the early decades of the century, the threat of a Royal Visitation had hung over Oxford, as it had hung over the Scottish universities. But Oxford had managed to preserve its distance and its inglorious academic reputation from government interference, exasperating more radical Whigs like Lord Egmont who thought that the present system 'makes the Fellows lazy, whereas when pinched in their circumstances and without prospect of College livings, they would study hard to go out in the world'.[5] With the experience of six years of Balliol behind him, Smith would agree. In the *Wealth of Nations*, he used the same Whig language to suggest that these weaknesses were symptoms of a systemic failure in a university he came to despise and whose competence contrasted strikingly with Scottish practice. The interest of the Oxford professor who lived on a university salary and not on student fees, he commented,

> is, in this case, set as directly in opposition to his duty as it is possible to set it. It is the interest of every man to live as much at his ease as he can; and if his emoluments are to be precisely the same, whether he does, or does not perform some very laborious duty, it is certainly his interest, at least as interest is vulgarly understood, either to neglect it altogether, or, if he is subject to some authority which will not suffer him to do this, to perform it in as careless and slovenly a manner as that authority will permit. If he is naturally active and a lover of labour, it is his interest to employ that activity in any way, from which he can derive some advantage, rather than in the performance of his duty, from which he can derive none ... In the university of Oxford, the greater part of the publick professors have, for these many years, given up altogether even the pretence of teaching.[6]

Oxford's historians have always complained that this party political language exaggerated the university's weaknesses and overlooked the efforts of worthy individuals trying to teach an antiquated and unrewarding curriculum. But it is hard to think that either the university or, for that matter, Balliol had much to offer Smith by way of teaching. The college's fellowship was a mixed and mediocre bunch. While one of Smith's friends liked his tutor 'as I profitted very much by his superintending my studies', another had to put up with a tutor who was notorious for extracting fees from students and not teaching at all, and a third friend, Matthew Beattie, liked his tutor well enough, but admitted that his education was largely self-directed.[7] Nor was the strongly Jacobite college a particularly congenial place for studious Presbyterian Whigs. Tied fellowships and local loyalties had linked Balliol to the Tory-Jacobite south-western counties of England. In 1688, five of its fellows had been expelled as non-jurors; in 1745, the Master of the college refused to sign the Oxford 'Association', which was supposed to demonstrate the county's loyalty to the Hanoverians. To make matters worse, Balliol did not make Snell exhibitioners feel particularly welcome. The Snell exhibition itself had long been a subject of feuding between Glasgow and Balliol. It had been established in 1677 by John Snell's bequest which had endowed twelve exhibitions to allow students of Scottish universities to study at the college for periods of up to eleven years. Snell's will, however, was riddled with ambiguities, not the least of which was the requirement that the exhibitions should be given to those who were prepared to read for Holy Orders in the Church of England and to join the Episcopalian Church in Scotland, a provision which was nullified in 1738, two years before Smith's election. Balliol was constantly criticized for leaving exhibitions unfilled and using the revenue for its own purposes. Exhibitioners constantly complained that they were badly treated. Indeed, in 1744, when they complained to the Glasgow Senate of rudeness and of being left with the worst rooms, Balliol's Master retorted that as the Scots had 'a total dislike of the College' they had better go elsewhere.[8]

What then did Smith want of Oxford? Dugald Stewart thought that he was being prepared for a career in the Church of England, an option which would have been ruled out if a contemporary's view that 'he had early become a disciple of Voltaire's in matters of religion' is to be credited.[9] Margaret Smith, who must have taken advice from her son's legal guardian, William Smith, the Duke of Argyll's secretary, as well as from the Oswalds, was probably told that the Snell exhibition would give him time to work on his own until something turned up, a tutor's post in a noble household, perhaps, or a professorship at a Scottish university. What is more, because William Smith lived at

Adderbury, Argyll's residence in Oxfordshire, he would not only be able to keep an eye on his relation but might well be able to introduce him to the Duke himself. At all events, Smith's first known letter, written to his guardian shortly after his arrival at Oxford, suggests that he had few illusions about what was in store for him.

Oxford 24 Aug. 1740

Sir

I yesterday receiv'd your letter with a bill of sixteen pounds inclos'd, for which I humbly thank you, but more for the good advice you were pleased to give me: I am indeed affraid that my expences at college must necessarily amount to a much greater sum this year than at any time hereafter; because of the extraordinary and most extravagant fees we are obligd to pay the College and University on our admittance; it will be his own fault if anyone should endanger his health at Oxford by excessive Study, our only business here being to go to prayers twice a day, and to lecture twice a week. I am, dear Sir

Your most Oblig'd Servant

Adam Smith[10]

Smith was characteristically unforthcoming about his time at Oxford. Only three laconic letters from this period have survived, in one of which he apologized to his mother – as he was to apologize so often – for being a bad correspondent. 'I am quite inexcusable for not writing to you oftener,' he wrote in July 1744. 'I think of you every day, but always defer writing till the post is just going, and then sometimes business or company, but oftener laziness, hinders me.'[11] Balliol's Battells Book suggests that he was in almost continuous residence, living modestly but reasonably comfortably on his Snell exhibition, which was topped up from 1742 by a Warner exhibition, worth £8. 5s. p.a. and by periodic help from his family. What lectures he attended, even the name of his tutor, is unknown. Nor do we know what access he had to books and libraries. As a future bibliophile he presumably bought as many books as he could afford, probably relying on Edinburgh booksellers to supply him by mail order as well as on the Oxford book trade. But libraries would have been a problem. The undergraduate library at Balliol would have been inadequate for his purposes and the College Library and the Bodleian Library were only open to Masters of Arts, though friendly dons could have borrowed books on his behalf. What seems more likely is that William Smith arranged for him to use the excellent library at Adderbury, eighteen miles from Oxford.

But Smith had not gone to Oxford to be taught. What he needed and what he got was time and space to distance himself from his Glasgow education and to develop his own interests. According to Dugald Stewart, this meant developing his abiding interest in politics, polite literature, the history of ideas and 'the improvement of society':

> The study of human nature in all its branches, more particularly of the political history of mankind, opened a boundless field to his curiosity and ambition; and while it afforded scope to all the various powers of his versatile and comprehensive genius, gratified his ruling passion, of contributing to the happiness and the improvement of society. To this study, diversified at his leisure hours by the less severe occupations of polite literature, he seems to have devoted himself almost entirely from the time of his removal to Oxford; but he still retained, and retained even in advanced years, a recollection of his early acquisitions, which not only added to the splendour of his conversation, but enabled him to exemplify some of his favourite theories concerning the natural progress of the mind in the investigation of truth, by the history of those sciences in which the connection and succession of discoveries may be traced with the greatest advantage.[12]

It must have been at Oxford that he began to acquire what was to be an almost encyclopaedic knowledge of contemporary literature on the constitutions of the polities of the ancient and modern worlds, and to develop his lifelong interest in studying these constitutions for the light they shed on the manners and customs of peoples living in different ages and at different times. More particularly, this must have been the period in which he set out to master the voluminous and complex literature on the principles of human nature which had been developed in France in the previous century. Later in life he remembered teaching himself French, presumably by using the same method David Miller had used to teach him Latin and Greek in Kirkcaldy, by translating from French into English and back again.[13] Pierre Bayle's *Dictionnaire historique et critique* (1696) was an essential resource for a serious young philosopher on account of its extraordinary sceptical review of ancient and modern philosophy. Descartes, Malebranche and Pascal, La Rochefoucauld, Racine and Marivaux would have given him access to the subtleties of that dark, complex, Augustinian view of human nature on which so much of recent French philosophy and literature was built and on which Pufendorf and Mandeville had drawn. It was a view which stressed the 'weaknesses of human nature', the frailty of reason, the delusive power of the imagination, the turbulence of the passions and the difficulty of living virtuously in a corrupt world without the consolations of religion. Like Hutcheson, Smith was to find this outlook on human nature uncongenial and even silly. In the *Theory of Moral Sentiments* he described La Rochefoucauld's libertine denial of the reality of moral distinctions as elegant, superficially plausible and wholly pernicious (a remark he later withdrew in deference to the protests of a later Duc de La Rochefoucauld whom he knew and liked).[14] He regarded Pascal's moving analysis of the nature of human wretchedness as the work of a 'whining moralist'.[15] But what mattered about this sort of analysis was the psychological subtlety that these philosophers brought to the study of human nature and their insight into the nagging complexity of psychological need.

Such writers had famously written for an intelligent, educated and generally well-born elite, and they had only occasionally looked beyond their rarefied private world to that of ordinary human beings who were engaged in the pursuit of wealth, power and *amour-propre*, or self-esteem, seemingly blissfully unaware of their wretchedness. In an essay which Mandeville and Smith must have known, Pierre Nicole marvelled at the way in which even the most contemptible of passions like greed could animate our *amour-propre*, and in a way which would unintentionally serve the public good much better than random acts of charity.

We find, for example, almost everywhere when we are travelling, men who are ready to serve those who pass and have lodgings ready to receive them. We dispose of their services as we wish; we command

61

them and they obey us and make us believe that it gives them pleasure to serve us. They never excuse themselves from rendering any service demanded of them. How could such behaviour be more admirable if it were animated by the spirit of charity itself? It is greed which makes them act, and they do so with such a good grace that one believes one does them a favour by employing their services.

Think how much charity would be required to build a whole house for another man, to furnish it completely and then hand him the key. Greed does this quite joyfully. What a degree of charity would be needed to go search for medicines in the Indies, or abase oneself to the vilest services, and the most painful? Greed does all this without complaining.[16]

As we shall see, while Smith never doubted that beneficent actions might well be influenced by the basest of passions, he was more interested in our desire to be seen as acting in a way which others approve of and which we approve of ourselves. Smith's interest in the material, moral and intellectual needs of the human species at different stages of its development and in our longing for self-respect was to be of the utmost importance in shaping his moral philosophy. There was much to be learned on this subject from contemporary French literature. Smith greatly admired Racine and thought *Phaedre* 'the finest tragedy, perhaps, that is extant in any language'.[17] As he saw it, Racine had followed Euripides' excellent practice of using prologues to explain the plot so that 'we may be free to attend to the Sentiments and Actions of each scene',[18] clearing the ground for the central dramatic purpose of showing the characters struggling to control the passions which threatened to destroy their lives and honour. But Phaedre was no Euripidean heroine, responding to claims of a code of honour that transcended that of ordinary mortals. The Phaedre who interested Smith in the *Theory of Moral Sentiments* was the woman who addresses herself to an audience of ordinary spectators and is able to make them sympathize with her incestuous love for her son and even love her, 'notwithstanding all the extravagance and guilt which attend it. That very extravagance and guilt may be said, in some measure, to recommend it to us,' Smith commented. 'Her fear, her shame, her remorse, her horror, her despair, become thereby more natural and interesting. All the secondary passions, if I may be allowed to call them so, which arise from the situation of love, become necessarily more furious and violent; and it is with these secondary passions only that we can properly be said to sympathize.'[19]

This was Smith attempting to view the extraordinarily vivid and complex psychological dilemmas that interested the French moralists in the light of a very different psychology. Here, he followed the lead of the playwright and novelist Marivaux, a writer he greatly admired and must surely have read at Oxford. Marivaux was interested in the moral dilemmas of the ordinary citizens about whom Nicole had written, for these seemed to be as urgent and complex in their way as those of Pascal and his followers. Marivaux admired Addison's *Spectator* and published his own version of it, the *Spectateur Français*, between 1721 and 1724. He was interested in the study of manners because they furnished all the materials a moralist needed to lay the foundations of '*la science du coeur*', a 'science of the heart', which could be pursued by 'one who reflected on human affairs'.[20] Like Hutcheson, he was interested in 'the unreflective aspects of knowing and feeling' and, in a way Smith was to find particularly congenial, in the value of fiction in acquiring materials for such an enterprise.[21] Above all,

> It is society, it is the whole of humanity even, which stands as the only acceptable school, the only school which is always open, where every man studies the others, and is studied by them in turn, where every man is, in his turn, pupil and master. This knowledge is to be found in the commerce which we all, without exception, have with each other.[22]

Much as he admired Addison, Marivaux's approach to the *science du coeur* was deeply French. Instead of writing for a cheerful, gregarious, Addisonian coffee-house public, he addressed the salons and the *gens de lettres* of Paris, and whereas Addison had emphasized the 'easiness' of living honestly in the world, Marivaux emphasized the difficulties. This is the subject of his enormous and intricate novel of manners, *La Vie de Marianne*, which appeared between 1730 and 1742. It tells the story of an orphan who does not know who she is or where she has come from and has nothing apart from a sense of her own nobility and a sense of honour. Her story is a tale of encounters with people who befriend and abuse her. She is plagued by the problem that troubled many of her contemporaries – how to interpret the behaviour of others and know that we are interpreting it properly. Her life is 'a web of events which have given her a certain understanding of life and of the character of men' but it is never enough to give her an understanding of herself; indeed, the gigantic novel was never finished.[23] In Marivaux, Smith found a moralist who was interested in the psychological needs of ordinary citizens and who realized that these were more complex and demanding than most Anglo-Saxon moralists had perceived. It was for this reason that he commented in the *Theory of Moral Sentiments*, 'The poets and romance writers, who best paint the refinements and delicacies of love and friendship, and of all other private and domestic affections, Racine and Voltaire; Richardson, Maurivaux and Riccoboni; are, in such cases, much better instructors than Zeno, Chrysippus, or Epictetus.'[24]

If Oxford gave Smith the time and resources to extend his knowledge of ancient and modern philosophy and to deepen his understanding of the workings of the passions, his encounter with the philosophy of David Hume was to be the decisive event in his intellectual development, providing him with a resource he could use to lay the foundations of a philosophy and a deep and enduring friendship. Hume was born in 1711 and was thus twelve years older than Smith, but their backgrounds and upbringing had something in common. Both came from the middling ranks, Hume being the younger son of a Berwickshire laird whose family had connections with the law, the army and local government. Both were brought up by strongly Presbyterian widowed mothers, indeed Hume admitted to James Boswell that he had been religious as a child.[25] Hume went to Edinburgh University in 1723 at the remarkably early age of twelve, to prepare himself for a legal career, but like so many others he found the law boring and turned instead to philosophy and letters. By the late 1720s he seems to have lost all vestiges of Christian belief and had probably laid the epistemological foundations of what he was to call his 'Science of Man'. The next decade was spent working on his own in Berwickshire, and later in France and it was there that he wrote the first volume of his *Treatise of Human Nature*, which appeared in January 1739 in the last months of Smith's Glasgow career. The second volume, 'Of Morals', appeared in November 1740, three months after Smith's move to Oxford.

The publication of the *Treatise* was the great non-event of the Scottish Enlightenment for, as Hume famously commented, 'it fell *dead-born from the press*, without reaching such distinction, as even to excite a murmur among the zealots'.[26] The first volume was certainly known to Hutcheson as the lawyer and philosopher Henry Home had sent him a copy for comment. But Hutcheson was horrified by Hume's flagrant religious scepticism, to the point that he was to use all his influence to block Hume's bid for the Moral Philosophy chair at Edinburgh in 1745, and it seems unlikely that he would have advertised the work even to a star pupil like Smith. It is more likely that Smith got to know Hume's work through the publication of the first two volumes of his *Essays Moral, Political and Literary* of 1741 and 1742, in which Hume applied the principles of his theory of human nature to topical questions about morality and politics. These attracted rather more attention than the *Treatise*, not least because they were written in a quasi-Addisonian style and were addressed to what Hume described as the 'conversable' rather than the 'learned' members of society. What is more, they were puffed by Hume's friends, who included James Oswald. 'Nothing can be more agreeable to me than either to recommend our friend Hume or his book,' he told Henry Home. 'In either of these Cases the Person who recommends does himself in my opinion an honour as he becomes a Sharer of that Merit which is in both.' He concluded, 'I am convinced Mr Humes things will make their way & Nothing shall be left on my Part to lett them be known as far as I can.'[27] It is surely inconceivable that a close friend like Oswald would not have told Smith about the publication of the *Essays*, and equally inconceivable that Smith would not have found his way from the *Essays* to the *Treatise* at much the same time. At all events, it was said shortly after Smith's death that he had been caught reading the *Treatise* in his rooms at Balliol. 'We have heard that the heads of the college thought proper to visit his chamber, and finding Hume's *Treatise on Human Nature*, then recently published, the reverend inquisitors seized that heretical book, and severely reprimanded the young philosopher.'[28]

Whatever the precise timing, it is clear that by the time Smith and Hume met in 1749-50, Smith was a committed Humean who was using Hume's theory of human nature in a highly distinctive way to lay the foundations of his own philosophy. Moreover, as far as Smith was concerned the *Treatise* could not have appeared at a better time. Mandeville, the French *dévots* and Bayle had demonstrated the complexity and power of the passions, the frailty of reason and the all-pervasive power of the imagination in shaping our conduct, and had done so in a way that cleared the ground for Hutcheson's hypothesis that our moral behaviour was driven and shaped by a moral sense of whose existence these philosophers had been entirely ignorant. What Hume had to offer Smith was an approach to the study of human nature that drew these different strands together and provided a new method of looking at how we acquire those sentiments about morality, justice, political obligation and religion which make it possible for us to survive and prosper in civil society. It was, Hume claimed, an approach that was 'entirely new' and one which would form the basis for a 'science of man', constructed on genuinely experimental principles.[29]

The backbone of Hume's philosophy was an absolutely conclusive demonstration that all claims that reason has the power to supply us with knowledge about the world, and the power to regulate our understanding and conduct, rest on essentially theological claims about the special powers of reason and are therefore 'unphilosophical'. What passes as 'knowledge' has its roots in the imagination and the passions and in the use of intellectual powers we acquire through habit, custom, education and the experience of common life. As Hume asserted somewhat iconoclastically, turning conventional wisdom on its head, 'Reason is, and ought to be the slave of the passions'.[30] This was deeply sceptical, an assault on the authority of all known forms of Christian theology and, indeed, on the authority of all systems of thought, past, present and future. For in the last resort, all philosophy, all science, even mathematics itself could be shown to be products, or even figments, of the imagination. The mind, Hume concluded triumphantly (he could seldom resist the temptation of revelling in descriptions of the delusive powers of the imagination and the exploded authority of philosophy), was 'the empire' or even 'the universe' of the imagination.

Over the course of the next half-century, the Scottish intellectual community, Christian and non-Christian alike, was to take this devastating assault on reason as being decisive and of foundational importance to an understanding of human nature and to the task of rebuilding a Christian understanding of man, society and nature. Indeed it is the pattern of response to Hume's challenge that gives the Scottish Enlightenment its distinctive philosophical character. Smith was to be no exception, except that his task would be to develop the implications of Hume's philosophy and extend its reach into territories he was to make his own. For although he was no iconoclast, and studiously resisted the temptation of making fun of religion, he never forgot the fundamental Humean principle that theology, like any other system of knowledge, was a product of the imagination and one that was capable of breeding delusions that could be peculiarly destructive of society.

It is interesting to read the work Smith developed in the early years of his career as a commentary on the way in which he came to terms with the *Treatise*. He had no difficulty in accepting Hume's proposition that what conventionally passes as knowledge is better described as a form of understanding, to be considered in terms of the ideas and sentiments we acquire in the course of common life. Two things were of particular interest. The first was the nature of those ideas and sentiments and the processes by which ordinary human beings acquire them. The second was the nature and purpose of those elaborate systems of philosophy, science, literature and the arts which human beings like to develop and are instrumental in shaping the moral, political and intellectual progress of society. The elaborate thought experiments on which Hume's attack on the authority of reason was based had shown that the ideas and sentiments which shape our understanding of the world penetrated it so deeply that 'we can form no wish, which has not a reference to society'.[31] They were experiments which showed exactly how the passions were socialized and, at the same time, prepared the ground for the principle that was fundamental to Hume's theory of society (and was to become the basis for Smith's own). For Hume, all human beings were endowed with 'the principle of sympathy or communication' and it was on this that their capacity for sociability ultimately depended.[32]

No quality of human nature is more remarkable, both in itself and in its consequences, than that propensity we have to sympathize with

others, and to receive by communication their inclinations and sentiments, however different from, or even contrary to our own. This is not
only conspicuous in children, who implicitly embrace every opinion
propos'd to them; but also in men of the greatest judgment and understanding, who find it very difficult to follow their own reason or inclination, in opposition to that of their friends and daily companions. To
this principle we ought to ascribe the great uniformity we may observe
in the humours and turn of thinking of those of the same nation; and
'tis much more probable that this resemblance arises from sympathy,
than from any influence of the soil and climate, which, tho' they continue invariably the same, are not able to preserve the character of a
nation for a century together.[33]

Hume was in fact preparing the ground for a radically different
approach to Hutcheson's claim that our moral understanding was
regulated by a moral sense. His theory showed how we acquire different sorts of sentiment, which could be collectively described – though
this was not an expression Hume used himself – as a moral *sensibility*.
But this sensibility was far from being a Hutchesonian *sense*, god-given
and hardwired into the constitution of human nature. It was composed
of a set of *acquired* sentiments that collectively shaped the understanding
and personality of the individual and enabled him or her to function
as a sociable agent with a respect for the principles of morality, justice
and politics. What is more, while Hutcheson had argued that our
understanding of the principles of justice, politics and natural religion
was derived from the moral sense, Hume was to show that all of these
sentiments were built on the sense of justice every single individual
must acquire if he or she is to live sociably. A society whose inhabitants did not possess an understanding of the necessity of justice and of
the necessity of government to underwrite it was incapable of developing an understanding of morality; in fact it was not a society at all. As
he put it in his last essay, written in the last year of his life:

Man, born in a family, is compelled to maintain society, from necessity,
from natural inclination, and from habit. The same creature, in his
farther progress, is engaged to establish political society, in order to
administer justice; without which there can be no peace among them,

nor safety, nor mutual intercourse. We are, therefore, to look upon all the vast apparatus of our government, as having ultimately no other object or purpose but the distribution of justice, or, in other words, the support of the twelve judges. Kings and parliaments, fleets and armies, officers of the court and revenue, ambassadors, ministers, and privy-counsellors, are all subordinate in their end to this part of administration. Even the clergy, as their duty leads them to inculcate morality, may justly be thought, so far as regards this world, to have no other useful object of their institution.[34]

Hume's theories of justice and politics were of the utmost importance to Smith. He had no hesitation in preferring Hume's approach to the workings of sensibility to Hutcheson's theory of the moral sense and was to show a genuinely 'experimental' interest in studying the processes by which these sentiments were acquired in the course of common life. Nor did he have any hesitation in adopting Hume's theory of government and politics in preference to Hutcheson's. Hutcheson's theory envisaged constitutions which allowed subjects to depose their sovereigns at will, and regarded laws to regulate the accumulation of property as necessary for the eradication of luxury and the promotion of virtue. Hume's, on the other hand, held that the primary duty of government was to administer the rules of justice and to preserve the lives and property of subjects; all attempts to redistribute property – for whatever reason – were subversive of government, stability and the material and moral progress of society. Such progress was only possible in stable polities in which the authority of governments was respected and life and property were secure; only then would curiosity and a taste for improvement thrive. It was a theory that was built on the belief that the progress of society depended on the efforts of individuals to better their lot, rather than on radical exercises in political engineering. And as such it provided the basis for a philosophy that would explore the principles of a culture of improvement which was deeply embedded in Smith's family values and would be integral to his understanding of human nature and the progress of society.

Although the *Treatise* provided Smith with the foundations on which to base his own philosophical thinking, there was still much

69

work to be done. In developing his sceptical theory of knowledge, Hume had acknowledged the importance of language in shaping our ideas and sentiments and explaining the workings of sympathy – words like 'conversation' and 'discourse' were constantly used to character-ize what he thought of as the process of linguistic exchange. But he had no theory of language and showed no interest in developing one. One of the first philosophical tasks Smith set himself was to develop a conjectural theory of the origins of language which showed that it was possible to develop a coherent account of the origins of our capacity for language by invoking the power of the imagination and the love of improvement. It was a theory to which he attached some importance, for it was to be the basis of his theories of rhetoric, mor-als and political economy – indeed it was central to his entire under-standing of the principle of social exchange. There was also work to be done on Hume's theory of justice and politics. Hume's brilliant and tightly knit theory had emphasized the importance of scarcity and the idea of private property in explaining the origins of our belief in the necessity of justice. His theory showed that the sense of justice to be found in a primitive society that lacked a system of private property would be very different from that which would be found in a property-based society, and he knew very well that the different systems of property known to history – pastoral, feudal and commercial – were responsible for generating very different ideas of justice and needed very different systems of government to support them. A general the-ory of justice clearly needed to take account of these differences but Hume had shown little interest in developing one. It is striking that another of Smith's early tasks was to develop such a theory on which his own account of the principles of jurisprudence, politics and polit-ical economy would be based.

All of this underlined one of the greatest differences between the two philosophers: Hume's reluctance to use his brilliant insights into the cognitive processes that make it possible for us to live sociably to develop the *science* of man he had promised in the introduction to the *Treatise*. Perhaps this had something to do with a sceptic's distrust of *systems* of knowledge. Perhaps he came to believe that Smith was temperamentally better suited to the task of system-building than himself. Perhaps the reason he is said to have given to one of his friends is the most plausible of all: 'Pardon me, did I not sett out with a complete Theory of Human Nature which was so ill received that I determined to refrain from System making.'[35] At all events, he was to spend the rest of his intellectual life using his insights into the principles of human nature as critical tools which could be used to analyse the philosophical and historical roots of the political and moral culture of his own country. It was a task he characteristically performed with the utmost brilliance and culminated in the writing of a massive history of England. It also made him a very rich man.

Smith, for his part, was to find the task of developing a science of man on Humean principles very much to his taste, and was to deliver its first fruits in the later 1740s while making his debut in Edinburgh. It was here that he developed theories of rhetoric and jurisprudence which were based on the remarkable theories of language and property which were to underpin all of his subsequent moral and political thinking. Into these he was to weave his own conjectural discussion of the assumption on which all of Hume's philosophy was based, that it was necessary to think of human beings as members of a species whose nature and history were deeply determined by indigence, infirmity and need. At the same time he was to address the problem Hume had so conspicuously avoided, the meaning and nature of those systems of science and philosophy, those products of the imagination, which history teaches have the power to refine or corrupt the human understanding. They were questions he was to address in his earliest works and of which he was to be ever mindful in his own philosophical practice. For Smith became at Oxford as he remained, the perfect Humean; and it was as a perfect Humean that he was to become Hume's closest friend.

4

Edinburgh's Early Enlightenment

Smith left Oxford in late August 1746 and returned to Scotland, his final year having been overshadowed by the Jacobite rebellion of 1745 and the slaughter at Culloden on 17 April 1746. Balliol was no place for a Scottish Presbyterian Whig and Smith once commented that he had left 'in disgust'.[1] But it was time for a move. Smith was twenty-three, in need of a patron, a job and people he could talk to, and Scotland was able to supply all three. His old friend James Oswald knew David Hume and the most formidable of Edinburgh's cultural entrepreneurs, Henry Home, the future Lord Kames and one of Hume's cousins. Henry Home was to be instrumental in launching Smith's career in 1748 by means of an invitation to deliver two series of lectures in the capital, on rhetoric and on jurisprudence. It was an intelligent act of enlightened patronage. It meant exposing a well-connected and promising young philosopher to a demanding audience by giving him the chance of lecturing on subjects that were of philosophical importance and topical interest to the Edinburgh literati, and it was an opportunity Smith grasped with both hands. The lectures established his intellectual credentials and paved the way for an academic career at Glasgow, and the audiences were large enough to make him more than £100 – a professorial salary, as Hume commented rather enviously, 'tho you had not the character of Professor'.[2] And although Smith always preferred Glasgow's collegiate culture and the peace and quiet of Kirkcaldy to the more *mouvementé* life of the capital, Edinburgh was to remain close to the centre of his field of vision for the rest of his life as a city he valued for its intellectual life and its cultural politics. What is more, it was a city that, by 1746, had reached a watershed in its history.

Throughout Smith's lifetime, Edinburgh's history was shaped by the Act of Union of 1707, which had effectively sacrificed the Scottish parliament and privy council in exchange for the Scots' right of free access to English markets at home and abroad. Edinburgh citizens had feared that the loss of these political institutions would be followed by the migration of the nobility, gentry and ambitious to the new centre of power in London. The city's society and consumer economy would be destroyed and Edinburgh would become a 'widowed metropolis', as a later writer put it.[3] It didn't happen. The Union did not compromise the position of the Kirk, the legal system, the banks, the electoral system or the system of local government, and this was enough to ensure that Edinburgh would remain the focal point of the country's distinctive form of civil society. Throughout the century, English ministers responded pragmatically to this situation, preferring to supervise Scottish government and the electoral system remotely whenever possible, leaving the effective business of Scottish government to agents or 'managers' they could trust. Indeed, the two greatest 'managers' of the century, the Earl of Islay, who would succeed his brother as 3rd Duke of Argyll in 1742 and ruled from around 1725 until 1761, and Henry Dundas who ruled from 1775 to 1801, were so powerful that they were generally known as uncrowned kings of Scotland. It was a situation that meant that throughout Smith's life, Edinburgh, like Boston and Charleston and Dublin, would remain the effective centre of the public life of one of the great nations of the British Crown.

One of the reasons this worked was that for much of the century the city supported the collective life of the higher Scottish gentry and of some of the minor nobility, a class for whom the expensive and often Scotophobic attractions of London held limited appeal. This was a class of crucial importance to Scottish public life and to the future of the Union. It supplied a significant proportion of the tiny Scottish electorate; it provided the counties with most of the county Sheriffs and Justices of the Peace, on whom the burdens of local government mostly fell; and it supplied Scotland's supreme courts, the Courts of Session and Justiciary, with most of their judges and the Scottish Bar, the Faculty of Advocates, with most of its members. The restoration of lay patronage in the Church of Scotland in 1712 meant that these landowners were able to tighten their grip on country parishes and the General Assembly, the Church's ruling body. By the 1720s they expected Edinburgh to be able to maintain a university fit for their sons and a society fit for their wives and daughters. And although only a few of them made political careers in London, they provided the public life of post-Union Scotland with its middle-management, responsible, as Smith might have put it, for maintaining the rules of justice and policing a country whose political life was being transformed by an incorporating, parliamentary union.

This was Smith's world and it was one whose subjects' outlook on public life was shaped at every level by the legacy of the Union. Presbyterians knew very well that some of the Kirk's most bitter internal divisions had roots in the legislation restoring lay patronage to the Kirk and introducing toleration a year later in 1713. Lawyers and litigants – and there were few more litigious landowners than those of Scotland – were acutely aware of the problems of preserving the integrity of Scots jurisprudence and litigating in a British state in which the House of Lords had become the country's final court of appeal. Merchants and manufacturers knew that their business involved exploiting the domestic and overseas markets opened up by the Union. And those with political business to attend to and patronage to solicit were well aware that Edinburgh and London provided different points of access to the Crown and the ministry, for no churchman, lawyer, merchant or elector would ever forget that the Union had given them access to the increasingly lucrative stock of civil, military, naval and imperial patronage that lay in the hands of the British Crown. Patronage became an essential component of the cement that allowed the Union to bed down and to flourish.

By Smith's day, these brute facts of public life were being shaped by a distinctive political language, which defined the ideological character of Edinburgh's public life and provided its elite with a resource for discussing their own and their country's future. It was a language which looked back to the remarkable debate about the Union that had been staged in Edinburgh between 1698 and 1707, and to the hopes and fears that contemporaries had held for their country's future in a post-Union age. What is interesting about the debate is that, while there had been passionate differences of opinion about the possible consequences of an incorporating union, there was a fairly general agreement about the nature of the country's problems and the responsibilities that the Scots parliament faced in addressing them. No one at the time seriously doubted that seventeenth-century Scotland had been 'a failing nation', with a defective constitution, an underdeveloped, feudal economy and a fragile system of international trade that was being damaged by international war. No one doubted that the prime cause of these problems lay in the existing regal union with England, which had obstructed the development of Scottish trade, perpetuated the economic and political power of a greedy, self-serving feudal nobility and undermined the development of Scotland's political institutions. No one seriously doubted that the key to restoring Scottish fortunes lay in a renegotiated union with England which would allow the Scots to rebuild their country's economy and political life and release the energies or 'virtue' of its governing elite. English ministers and a significant number of Scottish MPs favoured an 'incorporating', or parliamentary, union, which would abolish the Scots parliament, merge its powers with that of England and create a free trade union with England. The exchange would do away with a factious institution that had become the playground for a politically ambitious nobility and was making the country ungovernable, and would lay the foundations for a system of free trade between the two countries that would allow the country's economy to be rebuilt and the fabric of its civil society to be restored. However, most Scots would have preferred a 'federal' union, built around a reformed parliament dominated by the gentry, on the grounds that economic 'improvement' and national regeneration could only be effectively directed by a free parliament and a virtuous patriotic elite.

These disagreements reflected deep anxieties about the future of the country and its landed elite, which were to become part of the mindset of ambitious young men of Smith's generation and part of the ideological underpinning of Edinburgh's enlightenment. While most could agree that a new union was necessary for curbing or even breaking the power of the great nobility, some thought that this could only be done by a British parliament which the nobility was unable to control. Others agreed with the austere and intelligent Andrew Fletcher of Saltoun, that this was a task for a reformed Scottish parliament dominated by tough, radical country gentlemen like Fletcher himself. Either way, the Union debate had had the effect of drawing questions about the problems of modernizing a country with an essentially feudal rural economy into the centre of political debate. It was a question which was to be of the deepest interest to the Edinburgh literati in Smith's day, and to Smith himself as a university professor and as the tutor and friend of the Duke of Buccleuch, one of the greatest Scottish magnates.

The Union debate also threw complex Scottish attitudes to the English into relief. The fear of the political, economic and cultural power of the English, and memories of Oliver Cromwell's attempt to govern the country by direct rule, were endemic. Pro-Unionists believed that the English would soon realize that it was not in their interest to impose direct rule on the Scots, and some went so far as to hope for a 'friendly' union between the two countries. Their opponents thought this was naive. There was nothing in the history of Anglo-Scottish relations to suggest that the English would refrain from meddling in Scottish affairs in the future, and anyway the Act of Union offered no constitutional guarantees to prevent a largely English parliament from imposing its will on the Kirk, the legal system or any of the institutions that were supposed to be preserved by the Act of Union. As we shall see, the 1745 rebellion was to present the Edinburgh literati with uncomfortable evidence that while the country had developed an informal system of devolved government that offered the prospect of a form of public life in which they could expect to play a significant part, there was nothing they could do to check the power of the Court and parliament in London, and nothing to prevent the return of direct rule.

Perhaps the most important of the ideological ambivalences thrown up by the prospect of an incorporating union was to be found in attitudes to commerce. The primary and overriding attraction of an incorporating union lay in the prospect of free access to English markets at home and abroad; as Andrew Fletcher put it, rather caustically, and in terms that Hume and Smith would echo a generation later, 'trade is now become the golden ball, for which all nations of the world are contending, and the occasion of so great partialities, that not only every nation is endeavouring to possess the trade of the whole world, but every city to draw all to itself; and that the English are no less guilty of these partialities than any other trading nation.'[4] Pro-Unionists agreed, though preferring to emphasize the importance of trade in stimulating the economic growth on which civility and national greatness depended, rather than the 'jealousy of trade' that Fletcher regarded as the natural accompaniment of the mercantile system. For those who opposed the incorporating union did so because they believed that, unless commercial activity was regulated by a virtuous elite and a reformed parliament, Scotland would become an economic satellite of England and its wealth and independence would be dissipated by luxury. These hopes and fears continually returned to questions about the role of commerce, culture and patriotism in regenerating a fallen nation – questions, above all, about the consequences of economic and political *Improvement*.

The early years of the Union appeared to justify all the sceptics' fears about the consequances of an incorporating union for Scotland. Smith himself put the matter well in 1760, in a letter to his publisher William Strahan:

> Nothing . . . appears to me more excusable than the disaffection of Scotland [after the Union]. The Union was a measure from which infinite Good has been derived to this country. The Prospect of that good, however, must then have appeared very remote and very uncertain. The immediate effect of it was to hurt the interest of every single order of men in the country. The dignity of the nobility was undone by it. The greater part of the Gentry who had been accustomed to represent their own country in its own Parliament were cut out for ever from all hopes of representing it in a British Parliament. Even the merchants seemed to suffer at first. The trade to the Plantations was, indeed, opened to them. But that was a trade which they knew nothing about: the trade they were acquainted with, that to France, Holland and the Baltic, was laid under new embarrassments which almost totally annihilated the two first and most important branches of it. The Clergy too, who were then far from insignificant, were alarmed about the Church. No wonder if at that time all orders of men conspired in cursing a measure so hurtful to their immediate interest. The views of their Posterity are now very different; but those views could be seen by but few of our forefathers, by those few in but a confused and imperfect manner.[5]

It was not until the 1720s that the tide began to turn in the optimists' direction. The worst of the period of economic readjustment was over, the Jacobite threat seemed to have been contained and the informal system of devolved governance under the Earl of Islay had begun to take shape. Edinburgh was becoming a significant centre of government and social life, and was developing a distinctive cultural infrastructure. At one level, this infrastructure resembled that of other comparable centres of provincial government and society in the Anglo-Saxon world. It was a culture that revolved round societies of men of letters, dedicated to the improvement of literature, philosophy, natural science and the fine and useful arts; small, informal clubs inspired by Addison's *Spectator*, meeting in coffee-houses and taverns and attempting to combine polite conversation with serious drinking; and assemblies, race-meetings, concert societies and theatres – somewhat late in the day in the case of Edinburgh, on account of the resolute opposition of the Edinburgh Presbytery. It was an elite culture dedicated to improvement and to providing local elites with a distinctive political identity. In Edinburgh, however, improvement was to acquire philosophical, literary and patriotic overtones. As early as 1712, a little spectator club founded by the poet Allan Ramsay, the father of the painter, set out to show that the cultivation of polite taste and manners could serve as a means of regenerating a rich vernacular poetic legacy and of providing a post-Union generation with a useable literature. The Rankenian Club, a society of gentlemen and professors founded in 1716 and lasting until 1745, thought that their metaphysical discussions would encourage 'mutual improvement by liberal conversation and rational enquiry' and so help disseminate throughout the country 'freedom of thought, boldness of disquisition, liberality of spirit, accuracy of reasoning, correctness of taste and attention to composition'.[6] The most durable of all the societies of Edinburgh's enlightenment, the Philosophical Society, originally a society of medical professors, resolved in 1737 'to carry their disquisitions into other parts of nature, besides such as more immediately relate to the branches of medicine' in the manner of the other great academies of Europe.[7] The much grander and more aristocratic The Honourable the Society for Improvement in the Knowledge of Agriculture in Scotland, which flourished from 1723 until 1745, went to some trouble to spell out the connections between improvement and patriotism in a country with an underdeveloped agrarian economy like Scotland's:

> If the Agriculture and Manufactures were improved and carried on to the height they could bear, we might be near as easy and convenient in our circumstances as our sister kingdom of *England* seeing neither our soil nor our Climate is unfriendly, and, since we enjoy the same Priviledges of Trade with them. If we are far behind, we ought to follow the faster.[8]

Perhaps the most striking cultural development of all was the way in which the teaching of the university was realigned with the culture of the city. Outside the Netherlands, most of the tiny colleges that counted as universities in northern Europe were academic enclaves, semi-detached from the public life of the towns and cities in which they were situated; Hutcheson's Glasgow, a radical moderate Presbyterian island with magnificent buildings, cocooned within a deeply suspicious orthodox and dissenting Presbyterian merchant city, was a case in point. Edinburgh was different. Radical reforms in the early decades of the century had had the effect of forging an unusually tight relationship between town and gown. Between 1708 and the 1740s, the Crown, the town council and the legal and medical corporations had joined forces to provide the College with professors of law and medicine and a new classics and philosophy curriculum modelled on that of Leiden, in order to foster the growth of moderate Presbyterianism and to encourage gentlemen to educate their sons in the city rather than in Holland. The new professors were recruited from the Faculty of Advocates, the College of Physicians and the Surgeons' Incorporation, as well as the Kirk, and they generally had legal and medical practices and local parishes to attend to. They were, in other words, professor-practitioners who were bound by loyalties to the city, its clubs and societies as well as to the university. It was a dual life which encouraged the development of the symbiotic relationship between an academic and a polite civic culture that was to be one of the hallmarks of Edinburgh's enlightenment and of Smith's understanding of the role of philosophy in public life.

Forging this relationship between town and gown was to be the achievement of the later decades of the century. Nevertheless the possibilities were evident in the 1720s and 30s. The Rankenian Club and the Philosophical Society had significant numbers of College professors among their members, including much respected figures like John Stevenson, Professor of Logic and Metaphysics, and Colin MacLaurin, Professor of Mathematics and one of Newton's brightest pupils. MacLaurin's presence was particularly interesting. His lectures on mathematics and Newton's physics were attended by a city public as well as students and even by women, who were all 'entertained with his experiments and observations; and were surprised to find how easily and familiarly he could resolve the questions they put to him'.[9] He was the moving force in persuading the original members of the Medical Society to expand their discussions to include natural philosophy and archaeology and to open their meetings to noblemen and gentlemen as well as professors, and it was he that persuaded them to rename the society the Philosophical Society. In doing this MacLaurin appeared to the Edinburgh public as the local counterpart of Hutcheson, a philosopher who had the power to improve the minds and manners of the public. It was fitting, if sad, that he should have died in 1746 of a heart attack, attempting to organize the defence of the city from the Jacobite army.

However, a fusion of the values of town and gown was far from complete in the 1720s and 30s. Popular and fashionable teachers like MacLaurin, Stevenson and the Professor of Civil History, Charles Mackie, filled classrooms but lectured on subjects that were peripheral to the core classics and philosophy curriculum. Those who came to Edinburgh reasonably well educated complained that the teaching of the Classics was rudimentary and largely remedial. Others thought the teaching of moral philosophy pedestrian compared with what was available at Glasgow. Alexander Carlyle, an ambitious young moderate Presbyterian, voiced the widely shared view that the teaching of divinity was 'Dull, Dutch, and prolix'.[10] The ever-restless young Henry Home had found the teaching of civil law pedantic. Bright medical students like William Cullen complained that the new medical curriculum was old-fashioned and that some of the professors were simply reading out the lecture notes they had taken at Leiden. For critics like these, the new curriculum seemed better suited to the needs of country clergy, law clerks and surgeons' or apothecaries' apprentices than to aspiring polite, philosophically minded citizens.

No doubt these criticisms were untypical and unfair; after all, student numbers seem to have been growing, though by how much it is impossible to say. But they came from a significant quarter, a new generation of ambitious, intellectually minded young men who had been born in the 1720s, had attended the university in the decade before the Forty-Five and were now on the threshold of significant careers in the Church, university and professions. Their subsequent influence on the cultural and intellectual life of the city was enormous. They transformed the Philosophical Society in the 1750s and 60s. In 1754 they founded the celebrated Select Society, which was to combine discussion of moral philosophy and the fine arts with practical schemes to encourage improvements in the arts and sciences. These two societies, and the many societies founded in imitation, were to be the principal mechanisms for drawing the pursuit of philosophy, science, literature and the fine arts into the public world and linking learning with the values of politeness, improvement and patriotic endeavour. Equally important, this was the generation which supplied the university with a new generation of professors, who began to take up their appointments as their predecessors died off and chairs became vacant from the later 1750s onwards. William Cullen's appointment to the chair of Chemistry in 1755, Adam Ferguson's to the chair of Natural Philosophy in 1759 and his translation to the chair of Moral Philosophy in 1764, Hugh Blair's appointment as first Regius Professor of Rhetoric and Belles-Lettres in 1762 and, above all, William Robertson's appointment as Principal in the same year, marked the arrival of the first wave of professors who brought the culture of the city into the university and developed a curriculum designed to provide the 'philosophical' professional education needed to turn budding practitioners into citizens and gentlemen. When Robertson died in 1793, the process of fusion was as complete as it would ever be. Edinburgh had established itself in the popular mind as the Athens of Britain, and later the Athens of the North. Nor did contemporaries overlook the irony in the sobriquet which the modern heritage industry has conveniently forgotten, that it had been Athens' historic destiny to provide the Empire which conquered it with its philosophy and intellectual culture.

Like Kirkcaldy and Glasgow, Edinburgh was to become an essential civic space in Smith's world. Most of its leading citizens would be known to him, some would become close friends. Some would get to know him through his Edinburgh lectures and many more were to debate themes he had raised in the clubs and societies which developed in the 1750s and 60s. Above all, it was a city whose leaders came of age politically during the Forty-Five, at a formative time in the making of Edinburgh's enlightenment and at the precise moment at which Smith's philosophical career was to begin.

The Jacobite rebellion of 1745 was a traumatic event in history of the Union. The Scottish Highlands had long been the most turbulent and inaccessible region of the country and a natural breeding ground for resistance to government. Charles Edward Stuart's attempt to restore the Stuart monarchy began in Glenfinnan in August as his army prepared to sweep through the Highlands to the central belt and to Edinburgh. The defeat of the government army at Prestonpans in October had been followed by a march on Edinburgh and its eventual occupation. News of the impending invasion closed down the city's public life. The Bank of Scotland ceased trading and destroyed what must have been a large proportion of its banknotes[11]; the judges, government officials, Presbyterian clergy and other 'principal inhabitants' hastily left for the country. The company of Irish dragoons that was detailed to defend the city deserted, leaving its defence in the hands of a few companies of volunteers and a Town Guard of 'rather elderly men' who reminded David Hume of 'Falstaff's Tatterdemalian Company'.[12] After a token resistance the city surrendered to avoid unnecessary bloodshed. Legal, financial and cultural life ceased. When Smith returned to Scotland in August 1746, four months after the battle of Culloden and the eventual routing of the Highland army, he found a city coming to terms with a bloody catastrophe. The courts and the university reopened in October, although organized intellectual life seems to have remained in abeyance until meetings of the Philosophical Society began again in 1748 or 1749.

Order was restored, but the crisis left its scars. Culloden and the atrocities which followed were a brutal reminder that the arm of the imperial British state was long and that Scotland's informal system of devolved government rested on improvised and unstable political foundations. For a short time, the unwelcome prospect of direct rule began to seem all too plausible. Some protested by wearing tartan. More thoughtful Anglo-British patriots among the lawyers and moderate clergy began to think carefully about their role and that of their professions in a post-Culloden state. In the case of the clergy the situation was brought into focus by the celebrated Torphichen case, which concerned the rights of a local presbytery to reject a patron's nominee to the charge of a parish. The case wound its way through the General Assembly between 1748 and 1752, raising fundamental questions about patronage and about the relations between the Kirk and civil society. Lawyers for their part were confronted by the future of a clan system which had been a source of political instability since time immemorial. Smith was to make his intellectual debut before a public which had good reasons for thinking that Scottish civil society had reached a crossroads and that they themselves were destined to play a significant part in managing its future.

The issues at stake for ministers and lawyers were considerable. For the young moderate Presbyterians, the Forty-Five had marked a coming of age. Many had joined the university's company of volunteers and would have fought had the Principal, William Wishart, not implored them not to expose 'the flower of the youth of Edinburgh' to the Highland army.[13] Their thinking about the place of the Church in Scottish society was shaped by their distaste for government meddling in the affairs of the General Assembly and by the indiscipline of orthodox clergy and laity who preferred to be guided by their consciences in matters of faith and church government, rather than by civil and ecclesiastical law. What they wanted was a disciplined Church that would coexist amicably with civil society and develop a form of Presbyterianism which was fertilized with the sort of learning, letters and culture that would identify ministers as polite gentlemen. As ministers, they thought of themselves in Hutchesonian terms. They wanted a religion that was based on philosophy, natural theology and the cultivation of practical morality rather than the truths of revealed religion and the teaching of the Church Fathers. They wanted their flocks to judge others by their manners and morals, rather than by their religious beliefs. They wanted to show the world that it was possible for Presbyterian ministers to live as citizens rather than as clerical isolates, and as gentlemen who would be respected for polite learning, polite manners and impeccable morals. It was during the debates in the General Assembly over the Torphichen case that the leading moderates, like the future historian and Principal of Edinburgh University, William Robertson, began to show their political muscle. They were excellent orators and formidable political tacticians who were determined to wrest control of the General Assembly from the orthodox clergy, and they were acquiring powerful allies at Court and among the gentry. Some of their leaders seem to have attended Smith's lectures on rhetoric and found his new approach to the study of the mind a welcome alternative to that of the logicians and metaphysicians. Throughout his life, and in spite of legitimate suspicions about his religious beliefs, Smith's rhetoric and moral philosophy was to become closely associated with moderate Presbyterian ideas of polite education.

Lawyers too were thinking seriously about their calling and their place in public life. Culloden and the Duke of Cumberland's ruthless campaign to exterminate Jacobitism with the sword had revived long-standing fears that the Crown would attempt to pacify the Highlands by conquest.[14] The lawyers, led by Duncan Forbes, the Lord President of the Court of Session, responded to this threat by arguing that the causes of the rebellion had more to do with the structure of clan society than with the ambitions and treachery of a few Highland chiefs, and that the problem of pacifying the Highlands could be better addressed by encouraging civility, commerce and economic improvement than by the use of military force. No one understood this better than William Crosse, Professor of Civil Law at Glasgow and, for a short while, Smith's colleague. He had written a paper on the subject for General Bland, the Commander-in-Chief of HM Forces in Scotland, pointing out that, geographically, the Highlands were barren as well as inaccessible and 'unfit for Corn Culture, [because they afforded] nothing but a coarse kind of grass fit for pasturing the low siz'd cattle of the Country'. Its people 'are always busy'd in grazing and defending their own or attacking & carrying off the cattle belonging to their Neighbours'. Blood-ties turned private quarrels into lethal blood-feuds, which were idealized in legend and song. It was a barbarous form of civilization not unlike the 'parcel of Robbers and Banditti' of ancient Greece and Rome 'that by some strange accidents got themselves form'd into regular Governments and grew to be masters of the world'. As he put it, '[their] way of living [flowed] as naturally from the present condition of their Class, as ours does from a more regular Government . . . It is our own fault they have continu'd so long in this way.'[15] Crosse was thinking of Highland culture and the laws and institutions on which it was founded in economic terms, and was proposing that its problems should be considered in historically rather than in narrowly legal terms. It was no coincidence that some senior lawyers had begun to ask whether the present state of legal education was appropriate to present needs. Some thought that advocates, like moderate ministers, should be educated as gentlemen. As the new Lord President, Robert Dundas of Arniston, told the Faculty in 1748, 'Over and above being careful to learn thoroughly the principles of the Roman Law and the Laws of Nature and Nations, they should take pains to acquire the other Sciences and accomplishments becoming the Character of Gentlemen' and, above all, 'that rational & manly eloquence' should be the mark of their profession.[16] Henry Home agreed but had other ideas about how this should be accomplished. As we shall see, he was to find Smith's view about jurisprudence very much to his taste.

Smith had easy access to this distinctive cultural world. His family and friends were well-connected with legal and clerical circles in Edinburgh, and James Oswald, now an up-and-coming MP, had already pressed his friend's claims to a place in one of the universities on the Duke of Argyll. Writing to a fellow MP, Oswald reminded him that he had already mentioned

> one Mr Adam Smith to ye late Duke when I was att ye Abbey with you who is Cousin to [William] Smith who was about ye late Duke and is a young man who was bred att Glasgow and Oxford and has made an uncommon proficiency in literature by which he is extremely well qualified for a Professorship if any opportunity should happen. This young

man I would likewise beg of you to put his Grace in mind of. For as his Grace Possesses ye laudable ambition of protecting ye letters and Industry of His Country which are ye two most genuine Marks of Patriotism applications of this nature will I dare say be made without Offence.[17]

What was almost as important was that Oswald was a friend of Henry Home. Home was a man of boundless energy and intellectual curiosity. Like his cousin David Hume, he was committed to the project of developing a science of man based on the study of the moral, political, religious and aesthetic sentiments that fitted human beings for social life. He had read and criticized his cousin's *Treatise* in manuscript, persuading him to 'castrate' the text by removing his provocative discussions of miracles and the future state. Like Smith, he thought the *Treatise* unnecessarily sceptical and was to publish his own intelligent critique in 1751 under the title *Essays on the Principles of Morality and Natural Religion*. Like Smith he was interested in strengthening the empirical base of the science of man by making an intensive, systematic study of the social sentiments as they were revealed in everyday life and in history. His earliest philosophical experiments had been in jurisprudence, publishing decisions of the Court of Session for the sake of the principles of law they illustrated. During the Forty-Five he had retired to the country and written a series of essays on British legal and political institutions 'to divert him from brooding over the Distresses of his Country', and to develop Hume's observation that judiciaries were more fundamental to the preservation of justice than parliaments.[18] This eventually led Home to the remarkable conclusion that, in post-Union Scotland, the job of developing and refining the law ought to be assigned to the courts rather than Parliament.[19] But his first love lay in constructing a 'science of rational criticism' based on the principles of human nature, 'the true source of criticism'. It was an interest he shared with Smith and Marivaux, one of his favourite authors, and was one which resulted in the publication of his best-known work, the *Elements of Criticism*, in 1762.[20]

Home had what one of his friends called an 'almost apostolical' interest in promoting 'the cultivation and improvement of polite literature and the useful arts in Scotland'.[21] He became vice-president of the Philosophical Society in about 1752, 'about which I am turned extremely keen now that I have got in a good measure the control of it'.[22] He was a founder of the best-known of the improvement societies, the Select Society, which was founded in 1754. After his appointment to the Bench in 1752 as Lord Kames, he became a Commissioner to the Forfeited Estates and member of the Board of Trustees for Fisheries, Manufactures and Improvements in Scotland. But his greatest pride and joy were his 'élèves'. 'No sooner did a young man give indications of pregnant parts,' John Ramsay of Ochtertyre commented,

> than he got acquainted with him, and took a warm part in all his concerns. Besides chalking out a course of study and pursuits, he took care to engage him in conversation, in order to try his understanding, and discover his principles and bent. If he had a philosophical turn, and was not apt to boggle at novelty, it was an additional bond of union. He then became an inmate of the family and a companion to his lordship, who used in his walks to read lectures to his juvenile disciples.[23]

To be sure, he was capable of being difficult, arrogant and overbearing, and his élèves generally dropped him. Boswell remembered David Hume saying that 'when one says of another man he is the most arrogant man in the world, it is meant only to say that he is very arrogant. But when one says it of Lord Kames it is an absolute truth.' Boswell also remembered Smith's sharp and intriguing comment that 'Every man fails soonest in his weak part. Lord Kames's weak part is writing. Some write above their parts, some under them. Lord Kames writes much worse than one should expect from his conversation.'[24] Nevertheless, on being asked to account for the fecundity of intellectual life in contemporary Scotland, he was obliged to admit that 'We must every one of us acknowledge Kames for our master.'[25]

Smith must have got on well with Home from the outset; the arrangements for the lectures on rhetoric must have been made or endorsed by him in early 1747, a matter of months after Smith's return to Scotland. Certainly, he was well enough established by 1748 to have been asked to write a short preface to an unauthorized edition of the poems of one of Home's oldest friends, the exiled Jacobite poet William Hamilton of Bangour. Smith, always the improver, cheerfully commented that he hoped that this would encourage Hamilton to publish his own edition.[26] None of this is surprising. Smith and Home had plenty in common intellectually. Both wanted to develop a science of man based on the study of the sentiments and affections. They shared interests in taste and the light it threw on the workings of the mind and in the philosophical value of sentimental fiction, particularly Marivaux's. And both were interested in the implications of the new science of man for jurisprudence. Home found in Smith a young philosopher who was exceptionally well versed in the philosophy of Hutcheson and Hume, and ready to apply their thought critically to the study of rhetoric and jurisprudence. Neither of these subjects was taught at Edinburgh in a form which interested Home. Although John Stevenson taught rhetoric and literature in the logic and metaphysics class, and clearly taught them well, earning the praise of often critical students, his teaching belonged to the world of John Locke rather than that of Hutcheson or Hume and was thus out of step with an intellectual culture that was increasingly preoccupied with questions relating to sentiment and sociability. And for a jurist like Home, jurisprudence was a sadly neglected subject in the university. The existing professor was no jurist and the professor of public law made no attempt to move beyond the teaching of Pufendorf. And while many admired Hutcheson's philosophical insights into the origins of the sentiment of justice, it was a matter of regret to lawyers that he had no interest whatever in the study of particular systems of law or government. Smith had new thinking to offer on both subjects. His lectures on rhetoric and belles-lettres would offer a new philosophical approach to the study of taste; those on jurisprudence developed a historical approach to the study of legal systems. He was to deliver both series of lectures as a historically minded philosopher who was interested in identifying the roots of those principles of improvement that were characteristic of human behaviour and which could be used to explore the principles of civilization itself. It was an agenda perfectly suited to the purposes of the remarkable cultural movement that was developing in Edinburgh. And it suited Henry Home very well indeed.

5

Smith's Edinburgh Lectures:
a Conjectural History

Smith laid out the foundations of his science of man in the courses of lectures on rhetoric and jurisprudence he delivered in Edinburgh between 1748 and 1751 and in a series of posthumously published essays on the history of philosophy and science. The lectures on rhetoric discussed the sense of propriety which regulates our social discourse. Those on jurisprudence discussed the sense of justice on which our capacity to survive and prosper in political societies depends. Both sets of lectures were heavily indebted to Hume, but were the work of a pupil who had completely mastered the philosophy of his teacher and was able to turn it to his own account in two highly distinctive and topical critiques of the academic philosophy of his day. In doing so, Smith was to employ a method which raised important questions about the nature and meaning of philosophy itself.

Smith first delivered his lectures on rhetoric in October or November 1748, the start of the professional and social seasons. The Court of Session had resumed its sittings, the College year had begun, and country gentlemen and their families were returning from their estates. They were not the only lectures on offer in the autumn of 1748; there had been a lively market for public courses in law, medicine, the natural sciences and classical languages since the Glorious Revolution, and the *Caledonian Mercury* contains advertisements for lectures on mathematics, experimental philosophy, medicine, chemistry and geography. However, not many lecturers can have enjoyed the sort of patronage Smith received, and, according to Henry Home's élève and biographer Lord Woodhouselee, he managed to attract a 'respectable auditory, chiefly composed of students in law and theology'.[1] Where the lectures were given remains a mystery. They were probably not held on university premises, given that Smith was in direct competition with the Professor of Logic and Metaphysics, John Stevenson. It is just possible that he lectured in the Philosophical Society rooms or in the Music Society's rooms in Niddry Wynd, but there were many other meeting rooms in the centre of the city in the vicinity of the College and the Parliament House.[2] The lectures were clearly a success because the course was repeated in 1749 and 1750 and, according to Woodhouselee, attracted important members of the literati like James Oswald, Hugh Blair, John Millar, Alexander Wedderburn the future Lord Chancellor, the future Sir William Pulteney, a close friend of both Hume and Home, 'and others, who made a distinguished figure both in the department of literature and in public life'.[3] Indeed, so lively had the interest in 'philosophical criticism' become that, when Smith left for Glasgow in 1751, his course was taken over by Robert Watson, another of Home's pupils and the future biographer of Philip II and Principal of St Andrews. And when Watson left for St Andrews in 1756 his place was taken by a third, more famous pupil, Hugh Blair, who was to be appointed to a new Regius Professorship of Rhetoric and Belles-Lettres at Edinburgh University in 1762, a chair founded in recognition of the fact that the appointment would bring 'additional numbers of Schollars to the College'.[4] The creation of a new chair under royal patronage and Blair's appointment marked the high point in the fashion for the discipline Smith had done so much to promote. It is one of the most striking examples of the way in which the culture of the city was penetrating the university, and it was fitting that Blair acknowledged the help he had received from 'the manuscript treatise on rhetoric' Smith had lent him.[5] Smith had promoted a novel approach to rhetoric that established it as a subject of fundamental importance to an understanding of the principles of sociability and of the science of man, and had caught the public's attention. His lectures had also established his own intellectual credentials and had helped to prepare the ground for his appointment to a Glasgow professorship.

Smith probably lectured in what was to become his usual way, by reading a text he had dictated to a clerk and garnishing it with asides. The text of the course he gave in Edinburgh is missing but it seems

Lecture 3.ᵈ Monday Nov 22
Mr. Smith.

Of the origen and progress of language.

It seems probable that those words which
denote certain substances which
exist and which we call substan-
=tives would be amongst the first
contrived by persons who were in-
=venting a language. Two savage-
=ges who met together and took
up their dwelling in the same
place would very soon endea-
=vour to get signs to denote those objects
which most frequently occurred
and with which they were most
connected. the cave they lodged in.
the tree from whence they got their food
or the fountain from whence
they drank. would all soon be
distinguished by particular
                                    names

reasonable to suppose that the notes two students took of the course in 1762–3 give a pretty fair guide to the essentials of a system of thought that had been developed in the 1740s. As the editor of the modern edition of the lecture notes comments, it is suggestive that most of the 'illustrations' Smith uses came from the period before his move to Glasgow in 1751.[6] As we shall see, it was only in the case of the remarkable third lecture, on the origins of language, that he was to develop an important theme of his lectures for publication. The essay, 'Considerations Concerning the First Formation of Languages' (1761), and the lecture on which it was based contain some of Smith's most important thinking about the principles of human nature and the methods of modern moral science. It was thinking which surely belongs in outline at least to the earliest stages of his philosophical career.

Smith lectured as a self-confident and engaging revisionist who proposed to rescue an important subject from the pedants. He was sure that his audience would agree with him that most of the classic works on the subject were 'a very silly set of books and not at all instructive',[7] that remarks about good style to be found in the text-books were distorted by the absurd popular belief that 'the farther ones stile is removed from the common manner it is so much nearer to purity and the perfection we have in view',[8] and that modern attempts to view rhetoric as an aspect of the theory of taste were underdeveloped theoretically. He proposed to relaunch the study of rhetoric by considering the workings of a sentiment with which most of his audience would have been familiar and by using a method which could show how the different characteristics of our use of language could be related to a single inclusive principle. Smith's method was 'mathematical' and derived from the Euclidean geometry he had learned at Glasgow. It involved presenting the inclusive principle on which his analysis depended as an axiom whose truth value would seem, in the eyes of his audience, to depend on the precision with which he was able to formulate the definitions on which his analysis depended, and on the quantity and quality of the 'illustrations' which he used to sustain them. The axiom on which his rhetoric was based proposed that language is at its most persuasive and pleasing when it is used with propriety, that is to say, in a way that seems fitting to others as well as to oneself.

This was a proposition which was well designed to catch the attention of the young ministers and lawyers in Smith's audience. They would have known from reading Cicero and Addison at school that propriety was important to effective social and linguistic intercourse. If they had heard John Stevenson's university lectures on rhetoric they would also have realized that Smith was proposing to reconsider a principle that Aristotle had thought to be of fundamental importance to the cultivation of an eloquent style, a principle which Smith thought had much wider implications for an understanding of the principles of human nature than Aristotle had allowed. For Smith was proposing to show that the art of using language with propriety was a skill which would refine our manners and morals as well as our powers of communication, and would help us to develop that 'character' which played such a large part in influencing the way in which others responded to our sentiments. Properly understood, then, rhetoric was a subject that had everything to do with the study of the way in which the human personality is formed and perfected, everything to do with the study of sociability and the science of man.

This was ambitious enough. Even more so was Smith's introductory discussion of language itself, which was set up in frankly conjectural terms – 'in order to [do] this, it will be proper to premise somewhat'.[9] It was surely more plausible to think of language as a human invention that was as old as the species and of fundamental importance to its survival and happiness, than to think of it as so many earlier rhetoricians had done, as God's gift to mankind. And, as if to underline the conjectural nature of his point, he presented it in the form of a fable about the circumstances that had encouraged aboriginal men and women to use signs and sounds to articulate their 'mutual wants'.[10]

Two savages who met together and took up their dwelling in the same place would very soon endeavour to get signs to denote those objects which most frequently occurred and with which they were most concerned. The cave they lodged in, the tree from whence they got their food, or the fountain from whence they drank, would all soon be distinguished by particular names, as they would have frequent occasion to make their thoughts about these known to one another, and would by mutual consent agree on certain signs whereby this might be accomplished.

Afterwards when they met with other trees, caves, and fountains concerning which they would have occasion to converse, they would naturally give the same name to them as they had before given to other objects of the same kind. The association of ideas betwixt the caves, trees, etc. and the words they had denoted them by would naturally suggest that those things which were of the same sort might be denoted by the same words. Thus it might perhaps be that those words which originally signifyed singular objects came to be Special names to certain classes of things.[11]

This was the first stage of what Dugald Stewart was to describe as a conjectural history of the progress of language, and was designed to show that there were plausible reasons for supposing that every stage of mankind's linguistic progress had been driven by need. Thus primitive mankind had progressed linguistically from the state of 'primitive jargon', in which they had simply assigned particular names to particular objects, to one in which they had begun to use general terms to describe similar objects and parts of speech to differentiate objects of the same type (the green tree, the tree above the cave, and so on). In time, they had found themselves able to ask essentially abstract questions about the nature of *greenness* and the conception of *above*. In fact, quite unintentionally, they were constructing grammatical rules and acquiring the ability to reason about things in general. Need was making them sociable and giving them the capacity for thought. It was a conjecture that invited the speculation that the history of language was synonymous with the history of mind.[12]

Some of Smith's Edinburgh audience probably realized that he was developing a line of argument that had been started by Hutcheson's *bête noire* Bernard Mandeville, in the second volume of *The Fable of the Bees*. One or two, the great Francophile Henry Home probably among them, would have realized that he was offering a critique of Condillac's newly published and seminal *Essai sur l'origine des connoissances humaines* (1746). Smith, who would always keep a close eye on contemporary French philosophy, clearly admired Condillac's attempt to use Mandeville's fable as the starting point of a natural history of grammar but doubted whether he had been able to give a satisfactory account of that epic moment in which primitive man had acquired the capacity for abstraction. Condillac's explanation turned upon what Smith and David Hume would have regarded as the 'unphilosophical' assumption that testing circumstances would have awakened man's natural and god-given power of reason. To this Smith retorted that primitive man would have been more likely to respond to the shortcomings of his primitive jargon and his limited understanding like a child, who uses his *imagination* to invest a word he already knows with new meanings. Thus in using the word for cave to denote not just this particular structure but all cave-like structures, he would be using the word in two quite distinct ways, to denote what was particular and what was general: 'A child that is just learning to speak, calls every person who comes to the house its papa or its mama; and thus bestows upon the whole species those names which it had been taught to apply to two individuals.' In the same way we say of a great orator that he is a Cicero or a great scientist that he is a Newton.[13] In all of these cases the speaker uses the language he has at his disposal, *imaginatively* to invest words which have particular meanings for him with *general* significance. He uses a figure of speech, a species of metonymy, to extend his linguistic reach.

But such figures of speech would not satisfy the linguistic needs of the child or the aboriginal for long. When their circumstances changed and the demands of ordinary life became more complicated, they would find themselves under pressure to develop more formal and powerful grammatical resources to extend their linguistic scope and satisfy their cognitive needs. 'It is in this manner that language becomes more simple in its rudiments and principles, just in proportion as it grows more complex in its composition,' he remarked in 1762,

and the same thing has happened in it, which commonly happens with regard to mechanical engines. All machines are generally, when first invented, extremely complex in their principles, and there is often a particular principle of motion for every particular movement which it is intended they should perform. Succeeding improvers observe, that one principle may be so applied as to produce several of those movements; and thus the machine becomes gradually more and more simple, and produces its effects with fewer wheels, and fewer principles of motion. In language, in the same manner, every case of every noun, and every tense of every verb, was originally expressed by a particular distinct word, which served for this purpose and for no other. But succeeding observation discovered that one set of words was capable of supplying the place of all that infinite number, and that four or five prepositions, and half a dozen auxiliary verbs, were capable of answering the end of all the declensions, and of all the conjugations in the ancient languages.[14]

In this brilliant stroke, Smith was writing off the figurative use of speech so much admired by classical rhetoricians and their admirers as symptomatic of the linguistic immaturity of the child and the aborigine. At the same time, he was unobtrusively signalling his agreement with David Hume's profoundly sceptical observation that the *imagination*, not reason, was the faculty on which all understanding ultimately depends. Additionally, in addressing the question why human beings should ever have bothered to develop the linguistic resources they had at their disposal, he was laying the foundations of a theory of improvement which showed that the seemingly natural desire to improve the resources on which we depend in everyday life had deep tap-roots in the history of an indigent and needy species. And he had done all this by using a powerful and distinctive conjectural mode of reasoning about the nature of language and the mind that he was to develop and employ in all of his later philosophical writing.

Smith only developed the full theoretical reach of his theory in the 'Considerations'. This was prudent. Not only was it a highly sceptical theory but it was not directly relevant to the system of rhetoric he was about to unfold. What mattered was that his audience should think of language as an acquired skill, learned in the course of historical time as a response to need. His message to his listeners was clear. Instead of following the advice of the old rhetoricians, instead of cultivating the grand style and the elaborate syntax, arcane vocabulary and highly mannered use of figures of speech so beloved of them, it was more sensible for the modern citizen to cultivate a plain style sustained by the sense of propriety we all develop in the hope of improving our ability to communicate effectively with others. As he put it, 'It is the custom of the people that forms what we call propriety, and the custom of the better sort from whence the rules of purity of stile are to be drawn.'[15] It followed that the best guides to style in any age were not to be found in textbooks but in the works of the authors who were most admired by men of taste and position:

> In some of our former Lectures we have given a character of some of the best English Prose writers, and made comparisons betwixt their different manners. The Result of . . . which as well as the rules we have laid down is, that the perfection of stile consists in Expressing in the most concise, proper and precise manner the thought of the author, and that in the manner which best conveys the sentiment, passion or affection with which it affects or he pretends it does affect him, and which he designs to communicate to his reader.
>
> This you'll say is no more than common sense, and indeed it is no more. But if you'll attend to it all the Rules of Criticism and morality when traced to their foundation, turn out to be some Principles of Common Sence which every one assents to; all the business of those arts is to apply these Rules to the different subjects and shew what their conclusion is when they are so applyed. Tis for this purpose we have made these observations on the authors above mentioned. We have shewn how fare they have acted agreably to that Rule, which is equally applicable to conversation and behaviour as writing. For what is that makes a man agreable company, is it not, when his sentiments appear to be naturally expressed, when the passion or affection is properly conveyed and when their thoughts are so agreable and naturall that we find ourselves inclined to give our assent to them.[16]

Smith's main examples were drawn from the moderns rather than the ancients. He was struck by the fact that the modern public admired writers as different as Sir William Temple, Jonathan Swift and Addison, and suggested that the reason was that each in his own way respected the need for perspicuity in the use of language and had acquired a particular literary voice of his own. Indeed this ability to speak in one's own voice would always be associated with speaking candidly and persuasively. But Smith's most striking illustration was an exception which proved his rule, an admired modern author whose style seemed to embody everything Smith disliked most. This was the 3rd Earl of Shaftesbury, one of the founding fathers of modern Whiggery and politeness whose abominable style was symptomatic of the problems of his age and upbringing. The idea of beauty that permeated his style was 'abstracted from his own character' and characterized by a 'polite dignity' and 'a grand and pompous diction', which was unable to disguise the thinness of his reasoning, the weakness of his character and his distasteful lack of sociability, all of which Smith proceeded to expose with a relish that rivals that of Bernard Mandeville, one of Shaftesbury's most savage critics.

> If we attend to the Character and circumstances of this nobleman we will easily perceive what it was which lead him to this Conduct. He was connected with a father and educated under a tutor [John Locke], who [had] no very strong affection to any particular sect or tenets in Religion, who cried up freedom of thought [and] Liberty of Conscience in all matters religious or philosophicall without being attached to any particular men or opinions. If these friends of his were inclined to any one sect it was rather to the puritans than the established Church, as their tenets best suited with that Liberty of Conscience they so strenuously maintained. Shaftesbury himself, by what we can learn from his Letters, seems to have been of a very puny and weakly constitution, always either under some disorder or in dread of falling into one. Such a habit of body is very much connected, nay almost continually attended by, a cast of mind in a good measure similar. Abstract reasoning and deep searches are too fatiguing for persons of this delicate frame. Their feableness of body as well as mind hinders them from engaging in the pursuits which generally engross the common sort of men. Love and Ambition are too violent in their emotions to find ground to work upon in such frames; where the passions are not very strong. The weakness of their appetites and passions hinders them from being carried away in the ordinary manner, they find no great difficulty in conforming their conduct to the Rules they have proposed to themselves. The fine arts, matters of taste and imagination, are what they are most inclined to cultivate. They require little labour and at the same time afford an entertainment very suitable to their temper and abilities.[17]

It is hard to think of a more spectacularly effective means of rubbishing the grand style than this *ad hominem* attack on an admired philosopher for lacking the character and acumen needed to place Whiggery and politeness on sound philosophical principles.

Smith was now ready to discuss literary and oratorical genres and he did so much more informally that the ancients. 'It is rather reverence for antiquity than any regard for the beauty or usefulness of the thing itself which makes me mention the ancient divisions of rhetoric,' he commented tartly.[18] All that his students needed to remember was that 'every discourse proposes either barely to relate some fact, or to prove some proposition', and that whenever the arrangement of facts was an issue, the practice of the most admired historians and the taste of modern readers was the best, and indeed only appropriate, guide. In the last resort, however, Smith's message was provocative and clear. Authors and orators should be thought of as entrepreneurs playing the literary market. Here his exemplar was the fascinating case of Tacitus, an author who had brought about a historiographical revolution by sensing that Romans had become as interested in the mental histories of the great men who had made their history as in the events themselves.

If we consider the state of the Romans at the time Tacitus wrote and the dispositions of the people which it must necessarily occasion we will find this plan of Tacitus to be a very naturall one. The Roman Empire was in the reign of Trajan arrived to its greatest pitch of Glory. The people enjoyed greater internall Tranquillity and Security than they had done in any of the former reigns or indeed in the last 150 years of the Republick. Luxury, and Refinement of manners, the naturall consequence of the former, were then as far advanced as they could be in any state. Sentiment must bee what will chiefly interest such a people. They who live thus in a great City where they have the Liberty of disposing of their wealth in all the Luxuries and Refinement of Life; who are not called to any publick employment but what they inclined to and obtained from the favour and Indulgence of the prince; Such a people, I say, having nothing to engage them in the hurry of life would naturally turn their attention to the motions of the human mind, and those events that were accounted for by the different internall affections that influenced the persons concerned, would be what most suited their taste. The French monarchy is in much the same condition as the Romans under Trajan and we find accordingly that those writers who have studied to be the most agreable have made great use of Sentiment. This is that in

which the works of Marivaux and the younger Crebillon ... resemble
Tacitus as much as we can well imagine in works of so conterary a
nature. They are Allways at great pains to account for every event by
the temper and internall disposition of the severall actors in disquisitions that approach near to metaphysicall ones.[19]

It was this, Smith might have added, that accounted for the striking
interest in sentiment being shown by the Scottish literati of his day.

In the last section of his course, discussing different forms of composition, Smith offered his first, highly sophisticated thoughts about
the methods of modern science and on the problems of offering
accounts of the world that were convincing. He was interested in the
dialectical method 'In which the design of the writer is to Lay Down a
proposition and prove this by the different arguments which lead to
that conclusion'. Aristotle had used this method, but he had produced
so many subordinate propositions 'that they produce [in the reader] the
very effect he intended to have avoided by them Viz. Confusion'. What
he called for was a Newtonian analysis in which 'we may lay down
certain principles known or proved in the beginning, from whence we
account for the severall Phenomena, connecting all together by the
same Chain'. This Newtonian method 'is undoubtedly the most Philosophical, and in every science whether of Moralls or Naturall philosophy etc.', and it was the most 'engaging' of methods. 'It gives us a
pleasure to see the phaenomena which we reckoned the most un-
accountable all deduced from some principle (commonly a well-known
one) and all united in one chain.'[20] It was a method designed to explore
propositions that appealed to the common sense of an audience, in the
hope of showing how they could develop credible maps of the world
of knowledge. It was Smith's first exercise in presenting philosophy as a
matter of mapping the world of experience as contemporaries knew it.
How far those maps could be said to represent the geography of what
was true rather than what was plausible or probable was a matter that
a Humean like Smith chose not to explore.

In spite of occasional memory lapses, confusions and moments of
exasperation ('not a word more can I remember'), the two students
made an impressive job of recording Smith's lectures in 1762–3,

unwittingly succeeding in throwing important light on his thinking at the beginning of his career. He had surely always seen himself as the revisionist who wished to place a classic ancient subject on modern philosophical foundations, the philosopher who had used Aristotle as his starting point, Hutcheson, Hume and Condillac as his modern guides, and an analytical method developed by Hobbes, Newton and Hutcheson from the principles of Euclidean geometry to establish his own philosophical voice. His hope that students of human nature would study the specialized problems of rhetoric as aspects of the principles of sociability, and would consider language and style as aspects of principles of communication that were essential to the maintenance of society, was as fundamental to his thinking in the late 1740s as it was to remain for the rest of his life. He was to speak of the way in which we trade moral sentiments, in the *Theory of Moral Sentiments*, and trade our goods and services, in the *Wealth of Nations*, as aspects of that love of persuading others that is so deeply rooted in the necessitous condition of human nature that it almost seems 'natural' to us. Indeed, 'every one is practising oratory on others thro the whole of his life'.[21] Smith was preparing the ground for a much more wide-reaching theory of human nature, which held that all our sentiments – moral, political, intellectual and aesthetic – were acquired, developed and refined in the process of learning to communicate with others. It was for these reasons that a new theory of language was of fundamental importance in understanding the nature of the human personality.

Smith's theory of rhetoric suggests that his belief that the human personality could best be understood in developmental terms as the story of how individuals learned to live sociably, was with him from the first. His discussion of authorship and literary genre suggests that he fully realized the implications of this insight for the wider understanding of the history of human society he was to develop in his lectures on jurisprudence. His practical advice about how to cultivate the art of speaking and writing persuasively and pleasingly was designed to encourage his students to attend to the tastes of their own age and culture and to the cultivation of their moral personalities and identities. But perhaps the most idiosyncratic of all Smith's early messages was contained in his remarkable attack on Shaftesbury. The attack on his philosophy, his taste and his character was an attack on a species of Whiggery and politeness that was passé, the culture of an aristocratic order that for all its rank, power and privilege was, and would remain, an obstacle to understanding the principles of commerce and liberty. It seems right to think of Smith at the start of his career as a young philosopher who saw himself as one of the heralds of a new era in the history of civilization, a Scot who was uniquely placed to provide it with a new philosophy and a new understanding of itself.

The success of the rhetoric course prepared the ground for the course on jurisprudence, a course he must have begun to plan in 1748–9 and was to deliver in 1750–51. He could reckon on there being a market from the young philosophically minded lawyers who had enjoyed the rhetoric lectures, and he would again have been able to count on enthusiastic support from Henry Home. As we have seen, Home was dissatisfied with the teaching of jurisprudence at Glasgow and Edinburgh; Hutcheson's lectures were too metaphysical and William Cleghorn, Edinburgh's Professor of Moral Philosophy had interests which lay in the field of politics rather than jurisprudence. What was wanted was a course that was based on the principles of human nature and allowed for extended discussion of the principles on which different systems of law were based. In fact Home had given some idea of what he had in mind in a volume of essays he had written during the Forty-Five and published in 1747 as *Essays upon Several Subjects concerning British Antiquities*. They were addressed primarily to lawyers and called for new thinking about the origins of legal institutions in Britain, and the feudal system. His essay on the latter would offer 'probably Conjectures at what Time, and after what Manner the Feudal Law was introduced into Scotland', and would show that this revolutionary event in Scottish history must have taken place, not 'all at once as our Authors insinuate but by Degrees' in response to changing circumstances.[22] But what made the challenge of mounting a new system of jurisprudence more appealing was the publication in 1748 of two seminal works, Montesquieu's *Défense de l'esprit des lois* and David Hume's *Three Essays: Moral and Political*. Montesquieu's great book offered a new, historically sensitive approach to politics. Hume's slender but powerful volume provided one of the most potent critiques of Montesquieu's new system, as it did also of Locke's political philosophy and the intellectual foundations of the party-political culture of contemporary England. Smith was to take on the task of responding to the greatest of all contemporary French philosophers and of laying the foundations of a new, more scientific, more historically based form of Whiggery. It would round off his attack on the Whiggery of the older generation and establish his claim to be regarded as one of the architects of the new Scottish science of man.

For Smith *De l'esprit des lois* resembled Condillac's essay on the origins of language, in that both could be regarded as brilliant but ultimately unsatisfactory French contributions to the science of man. Montesquieu regarded his book as the culmination of a lifetime spent thinking about the principles of liberty in a world dominated by enormous monarchies and the rapid extension of commerce.[23] He called for a revolution in thinking about the principles of law. He thought that it was misleading to think of laws merely as the commands of sovereigns or as the product of historical accidents. As he said, 'Many things govern men: climate, religion, laws, the maxims of the government, examples of past things, mores, and manners; a general spirit is formed as a result.'[24] Thus it was better to think of laws as systems of rules whose *spirit*, or ethos, could be understood in terms of the interplay of the physical and moral environments in which they had developed – environments that were created by climate and geography, the economy, constitution and manners. It followed from this that legislators would do well 'to follow the spirit of the nation when doing so is not contrary to the principles of government, for we do nothing better than what we do freely and by following our natural genius. If one gives a pedantic spirit to a nation naturally full of gaiety, the state will gain nothing, either at home or abroad. Let it do frivolous things seriously and serious things gaily.'[25] Montesquieu's book was written for legislators rather than philosophers, for men on whom the problem of curbing corruption and preventing the ultimate horror of despotism depended. Above all, and in spite of his admiration of the English constitution, *De l'esprit des lois* was about France, about preventing the monarchy from sliding into despotism, and about the importance of a powerful and effective nobility to its future. Smith found it hard to think of the nobility as a bastion of liberty. But what he and other Scots admired was Montesquieu's method, his typology of the different forms of government known to history, his analysis of the conditions on which their survival depended, and his erudite and acute analysis of the spirit of Roman law and the French legal system. It was a method which called for the sort of historical thinking about laws, political institutions and reform that lawyers were arguing for in their discussions of the Highland problem, and to which Home was already committed as a jurist.

But for all its strengths this was a line of enquiry the Scots thought deeply flawed. As Home put it,

> Montesquieu has dealt with all the effects that derive from the nature of government, from the difference of climate, the strength and weakness of a people, servitude etc. However, he did not develop the effects that derive from human nature itself, from our passions and from the natural spring of our actions . . . Human nature itself has a much greater influence on the establishment of laws and manners than all the other causes which Montesquieu lists.[26]

Smith's pupil John Millar put it more tactfully in an account of Smith's teaching written for Dugald Stewart, by describing Montesquieu as the Bacon to Smith's Newton, the philosopher who had cleared the way for the truly philosophical approach to jurisprudence that Smith was to develop.[27] The Scots were quick to note the classic ambivalences and lacunae in Montesquieu's system, and the unresolved tensions in his treatment of the 'physical' and 'moral' determinants of the spirit of the laws. Montesquieu was seriously interested in contemporary thinking about the effects of climate and geography on the culture of a people, and its value in explaining, for example, the apparent 'indolence' and 'barbarity' of peoples living in equatorial climates as compared with the supposed 'industriousness' of northern Europeans. On the other hand, his discussion of 'moral' causation seemed to suggest that under certain circumstances, economic, political and cultural circumstances might be powerful enough to override the constraints of geography and climate; but what these were was far from clear. What was equally troubling was Montesquieu's definition of law itself. Laws, he had said, are 'the necessary relations arising from the nature of things. In this sense all beings have their laws: the Deity has his laws, the beasts have their laws, and man has his laws' – a view that, Hume noted, rested on a quasi-theological and, therefore, 'unphilosophical' premise.[28] He also questioned the importance Montesquieu had attached to 'physical' over 'moral' causation in determining the spirit of a system of laws, by calling attention to the variety of systems of law, customs and manners that could exist within the same geographical and climatic region; his contrast between the laws, customs and manners of Highland society and those of the Lowlands in Scotland was particularly telling.[29] What he might have pointed out (but didn't) was that Montesquieu had failed to identify the precise nature of the *spirit* which apparently determined the culture of a people. It was a lacuna in Montesquieu's thinking Smith was to address directly.

Once again, no texts, reports or notes of Smith's Edinburgh course have survived; all we know of his thinking comes from a set of student notes taken in Glasgow in 1762–3 and from another which seems to derive from a rather different course and is, rather puzzlingly, dated 1766. The question of whether these notes can be taken as a guide to his thinking in 1750–51 is controversial. Some suggest that the remarkable conjectural history of property on which Smith's analysis depends belongs to a later period in his intellectual development, or was more probably undeveloped in 1750.[30] But his thinking was certainly sufficiently developed to sustain a discussion of the theory and practice of government because he referred to this himself in an unpublished paper given in 1755. Although this paper has not survived, it was seen by Dugald Stewart, who commented that 'a pretty long enumeration is given of certain leading principles, both political and literary, to which he was anxious to establish his exclusive right.' 'Many of the most important opinions in *The Wealth of Nations* are there detailed,' Stewart reported;

> but I shall quote only the following sentences: 'Man is generally considered by statesmen and projectors as the materials of a sort of political mechanics. Projectors disturb nature in the course of her operations in human affairs; and it requires no more than to lct her alone, and give her fair play in the pursuit of her ends, that she may establish her own designs'. – And in another passage: 'Little else is requisite to carry a

state to the highest degree of opulence from the lowest barbarism, but peace, easy taxes, and a tolerable administration of justice; all the rest being brought about by the natural course of things. All governments which thwart this natural course, which force things into another channel, or which endeavour to arrest the progress of society at a particular point, are unnatural, and to support themselves are obliged to be oppressive and tyrannical. A great part of the opinions (he observes) enumerated in this paper is treated of at length in some lectures which I have still by me, and which were written in the hand of a clerk who left my service six years ago [i.e. in 1749–50] . . . They had all of them been the subjects of lectures which I read at Edinburgh the winter before I left it, and I can adduce innumerable witnesses, both from that place and from this, who will ascertain them sufficiently to be mine.'[31]

Smith's somewhat pernickety claim that he had offered some distinctive comments on government and the progress of opulence in Edinburgh in 1750–51 is striking in the present context because it refers to the final part of the course that was given in Glasgow, the arguments of which formed the natural conclusion to a highly developed system of jurisprudence. It is hard to see how this most systematically minded of philosophers could have offered these conclusions in Edinburgh without having established at least the conceptual framework he needed to sustain them. As in the case of the lectures on rhetoric, it seems more plausible to suppose that the foundations of his system were laid in Edinburgh than to suppose that they weren't.

Once again, Smith presented himself to his audience as a revisionist who proposed to rebuild an important discipline on new foundations. He began by defining the purposes of jurisprudence in Pufendorfian terms: 'Jurisprudence is the theory of the rules by which civil governments ought to be directed. It attempts to shew the foundation of the different systems of government in different countries and to shew how far they are founded in reason.' And in enumerating the purposes of government he went on to announce that as well as discussing the problems of maintaining the rules of justice and national security he would discuss 'what we call police' – what we would call the practice of government – and, in particular, its role in promoting opulence. It would have been clear to anyone who knew anything of Pufendorf or

Hutcheson that this meant that he was going to raise the question of the role of opulence in promoting justice and sociability.[32]

For Smith, the *reasonableness* of any system of justice had more to do with a 'sense of justice' than with any more abstract and theologically driven principle, thus raising fundamental questions about what that sense was and where it came from. Once again Smith's reply was encapsulated in an axiom which was to be illustrated with examples drawn from common life and history. The axiom on which his system of rhetoric was based had been a commonplace that everyone would have known. His jurisprudence was based on one that was anything but commonplace and far from self-evident, that our sense of justice is enshrined in the justified resentment we feel when someone's rights are violated. As he put it, 'Justice is violated whenever one is deprived of what he has a right to and could justly demand from others, or rather, when we do him any injury or hurt without a cause'.[33] But how were we to know when this sense of resentment was justified? Smith replied that it was justified when 'an impartial spectator would be of opinion he was injured, would join with him in his concern and go along with him when he defended his subject in his possession against any violent attack, or used force to recover what had been thus wrongfully wrested out of his hands'.[34]

As the student note-taker commented, when Smith gave these lectures at Glasgow he was able to refer his students to his discussion of the sentiment of justice in his moral philosophy lectures for clarification of the psychology on which this axiom was based. In Edinburgh, that would not have been possible. Hutcheson's former students might have noted affinities with the view that our ideas of justice were shaped by some sort of internal moral sense, though they would have soon been reminded that Smith did not believe in Hutcheson's view that this moral sense was hard-wired in the human personality. Some would have remembered from school that Epictetus and Addison had thought that holding interior conversations with imaginary impartial spectators was an excellent way of learning how to cope with the resentments of everyday life, and anyone who had heard Smith lecture on the origins of language might have realized that this impartial spectator was a product of the imagination and language, a fictional resource we call into existence in response to the pressure of moral need. In the course of the lectures it soon became clear that Smith thought of impartial spectators as the embodiment of what he called 'the common sense' of mankind, as personalized sources of ethical guidance which play an unspecified but evidently crucial role in directing our moral behaviour. And it was in this 'sense' of justice that the spirit of the laws really resided. Not surprisingly, his discussion of the impartial spectator was to be the centrepiece of the system of moral philosophy he was to develop at Glasgow.

Smith's jurisprudence was derived from a theory of rights borrowed from Hume. Hume had shown that nearly all of our understanding of rights was derived from our experience of living in property-owning societies and that it was on this that our understanding of the necessity of government, morality and improvement was based; in other words, property was the mother of the civilizing process. The sentiments of right and justice were thus acquired, were the product of necessity and would take different forms in different types of societies. Hume had shown little interest in theorizing these insights. Smith's mighty achievement was to develop Hume's insights into a general theory of jurisprudence and it is probable that he began this work in Edinburgh in 1750–51. His theory was derived from a conjectural history of property that explained the evolutionary process by which a society progresses from its savage to its pastoral, feudal and commercial stages of development. By 1762, Smith had worked up a version of this conjectural history of such economy and precision that it is worth quoting at length. As in the discussion of the origins of language, he began by considering human society at its most primitive, but in a way that underlined the way in which population pressures must have been responsible for forcing some hunting societies to institute the simplest system of private property – herding.

> If we should suppose 10 or 12 persons of different sexes settled in an uninhabited island, the first method they would fall upon for their sustenance would be to support themselves by the wild fruits and wild animals which the country afforded. Their sole business would be hunting the wild beasts or catching the fishes. The pulling of a wild fruit can hardly be called an imployment. The only thing amongst them which

deserved the appellation of a business would be the chase. This is the age of hunters. In process of time, as their numbers multiplied, they would find the chase too precarious for their support. They would be necessitated to contrive some other method whereby to support themselves. At first perhaps they would try to lay up at one time when they had been successful what would support them for a considerable time. But this could go to no great length. The most naturally contrivance they would think of, would be to tame some of those wild animalls they caught, and by affording them better food than what they could get elsewhere they would enduce them to continue about their land themselves and multiply their kind. Hence would arise the age of shepherds. They would more probably begin first by multiplying animalls than vegetables, as less skill and observation would be required. Nothing more than to know what food suited them. We find accordingly that in almost all countries the age of shepherds preceded that of agriculture. The Tartars and Arabians subsist almost entirely by their flocks and herds. The Arabs have a little agriculture, but the Tartars none at all.

Smith continued, discussing the origins of that system of fixed and latterly moveable property on which civilization as the Enlightenment knew it depended.

But when a society becomes numerous they would find a difficulty in supporting themselves by herds and flocks. Then they would naturally turn themselves to the cultivation of land and the raising of such plants and trees as produced nourishment fit for them. They would observe that those seeds which fell on the dry bare soil or on the rocks seldom came to any thing, but that those which entered the soil generally produced a plant and bore seed similar to that which was sown. These observations they would . . . gradually advance in to the age of agriculture. As society was farther improved, the severall arts, which at first would be exercised by each individual as far as was necessary for his welfare, would be seperated; some persons would cultivate one and others others, as they severally inclined. They would exchange with one an other what they produced more than was necessary for their support, and get in exchange for them the commodities they stood in need of and did not produce themselves. This exchange of commodities extends in time not only betwixt the individualls of the same society but betwixt those of different nations. Thus we send to France our cloths, iron work, and other trinkets and get in exchange their wines. To Spain and Portugal we send our superfluous corn and bring from thence the Spanish and Portuguese wines. Thus at last the age of commerce arises. When therefore a country is stored with all the flocks and herds it can support, the land cultivated so as to produce all the grain and other commodities necessary for our subsistance it can be brought to bear, or at least as much as supports the inhabitants when the superfluous products whether of nature or art are exported and other necessary ones brought in exchange, such a society has done all in its power towards its ease and convenience.[35]

This conjectural history of property was to be as fundamental and characteristic of Smith's thinking about the spirit of the laws as Montesquieu's theory of climate, and has proved to be much more durable historiographically. But it no more provided Smith with a complete account of the sense of justice than Montesquieu's theory of climate had provided him with an account of the *spirit* of any system of laws. For Smith the sense of justice was not only shaped by the effects of property, but of government and police on a people's understanding; with his theory of property in place, he was in a position to develop complementary conjectural histories of government and police. These were built on another of David Hume's crucial insights: that it was only once members of a society had acquired a sense of the necessity of property that they would understand the need to submit to some form of regular government. After all, as Smith put it, property was 'the grand fund of all dispute', creating a need for 'settled laws – or agreements concerning property' and the means of enforcing them. In the first shepherd societies that was a task for the whole people; in more developed shepherd societies, for chiefs and, eventually, hereditary rulers. But property was also a cause of inequality and resentment, leading Smith to comment, sardonically, in 1762, in words which would have delighted every Mandevillian,

Laws and government may be considered in this and indeed in every case as a combination of the rich to oppress the poor, and preserve to themselves the inequality of the goods which would otherwise be soon destroyed by the attacks of the poor, who if not hindered by the government would soon reduce the others to an equality with themselves by open violence. The government and laws hinder the poor from ever acquiring the wealth by violence which they would otherwise exert on the rich; they tell them they must either continue poor or acquire wealth in the same manner as they have done.[36]

This was to enter more deeply into controversial territory. To argue as Hume and Smith were arguing, that regular government had only become necessary with the invention of property, and to claim that the first systems of governments were the work of nomadic, pastoral tribes who had lived by war and plunder, was to cut across some of the most deep-seated and emotive assumptions on which the so-called 'vulgar Whiggery' of the day rested. It challenged the notion that the first societies of property-owners had been peaceable societies of farmers, and Lockian assumptions that the origins and authority of governments rested on contracts and the consent, tacit or otherwise, of their subjects. These were assumptions Hume had challenged in the *Three Essays* on the grounds that they were wildly implausible; Smith now orchestrated the challenge by showing that they cut across the evidence of history. He drew on Homer and Thucydides to show that the pastoral barbarians who had settled Attica had done so for reasons of defence, creating camps which would in time become cities; the less fortunate Arabs and Tartars who lived in desert lands had been condemned to an eternal state of nomadic barbarism.[37] He showed how the first systems of settled property had been created by the rulers of these newly settled peoples, who had parcelled out lands to their leading followers. Before long, Smith thought, somewhat sentimentally, the pleasures of possession and cultivation would arouse an '*amor patriae*' which would be the cause of new jealousies, new assertions of power by kings, and new causes of conflict. In time these monarchies would be displaced by the fractious aristocratic republics which were characteristic of the world of Greek antiquity.[38]

This conjectural history of the origins of civilization, derived from a melding of philosophy and a revisionist reading of ancient literature, was carefully organized to underline one of the great themes of Smith's jurisprudence, the ever-menacing power of a landed nobility.

Political philosophers from Aristotle to the influential seventeenth-century theorist James Harrington had taught that power went with property. Smith showed that the power of a landed nobility to destroy monarchies and republics at will was as old as history and had survived to the present. In a pregnant comment reported in 1762, he pointed out that it was only in a modern, commercial society based on a system of movable property that it had become possible to envisage the emergence of states whose governments were capable of checking the power of great landowners.[39] So far from being the only bastion against despotism, as Montesquieu had thought, Smith would believe for the rest of his life that aristocracy posed a continuing threat to justice, sociability and the progress of civilization.

Smith's account of the origins of civilization also provided the analytical foundations of a discussion of the systems of Roman and feudal law that had developed throughout Europe before and after the fall of the Roman Empire. Each subject had an obvious attraction for a Scottish audience with a large contingent of lawyers. Together they provided Smith with the resources he needed to explain the rise of European civilization. He revisited classic accounts of the fall of the Roman Empire, the settlement of Europe by the nomadic barbarian tribes and the origins of the feudal system that had done so much to shape the legal systems of England and Scotland. So far from being a system that had strengthened the powers of the nobility, weakened the powers of kings and laid the foundations of a system of limited monarchy safeguarded by the nobility, Smith saw the origins of the feudal system as acts of policy by a formidable line of English and Scottish kings – a line of argument originally proposed by Henry Home in his essay on the origins of the feudal system. These kings had been determined to curb the power of the nobility and 'from then the power of the king was as we evidently see greatly increased, and the government administered in an orderly manner; the times after the conquest appear clear and enlightend compared with those of the Saxon race'.[40] For good government, and the liberty which good government made possible, demanded the strict administration of justice and the kings that were best able to do so were 'martiall, conquering, military kings' like Edward I and Henry IV.[41] Far from being the guardians of a system of limited monarchy, as Montesquieu and so many of Smith's contemporaries liked to believe, the nobility had unsettled the order and good government of every country in Europe and it was Smith's view, shared by Scottish theorists since the Glorious Revolution, that their power had only started to decline with 'the introduction of arts, commerce and luxury' in the modern age. What interested Smith and so many of his Scottish contemporaries was how the nobility's resurgence could be contained in an age of commerce.

This analysis, which allowed Smith to show that the systems of public and private law that had developed throughout Europe had been designed to service the needs of a feudal civilization based on principles which were very different to those developing in a commercial age, enabled him to offer some trenchant criticism of outdated laws and customs such as those relating to primogeniture and entail, which had been introduced in the feudal age as a means of preventing the dissipation of great estates and were now obstructing the progress of a civilization which was based on very different principles. These were questions which he clearly knew were of immediate interest to modern lawyers and would shortly be debated by Edinburgh's Select Society.[42]

Smith was particularly interested in the progress of government and in the seemingly natural tendency of judges and administrators to regularize and systematize the administration of law and government and to refine a people's sense of justice. Learning the necessity of the rules of justice, learning to refrain from violence even when one's own interests were at stake, was much easier when it was possible to think of justice as a system on whose integrity the security of life and property depended. For Smith a love of system – in speech and manners, in the management of domestic, business and public affairs, in the arts and sciences – was one of mankind's primary characteristics, an aesthetic sentiment that had its roots in the imagination and our natural desire to understand and improve the world. To be sure, a sceptic like Hume might be deeply ambivalent about a mental disposition that could all too easily breed religious fanaticism and political zealotry. For Smith, however, imagination and the love of system were two of the most powerful resources that had rescued humanity from extinction and had made progress possible. In the last resort they were faculties on which security, virtue and happiness depended.

But the sense of justice was also deeply influenced by the way in which a country's laws were administered, and it was this that formed the subject of the third and in many ways most remarkable section of the course. This dealt with 'police' and was devoted almost entirely to 'bon marché or the cheapness of provisions, and having the market well supplied with all sorts of commodities. This must include not only the promoting a free communication betwixt the town and the country, the internall commerce as we may call it, but also on the plenty or opulence of the neighbouring country.'[43] In this, 'the most important branch of police', Smith was to complete his theory of human nature and lay the groundwork of the system of political economy he was to develop in his two masterpieces, the *Theory of Moral Sentiments* and the *Wealth of Nations*. He was to do so in a way that marked him out as a philosopher of improvement and a pupil of Hutcheson who was, nevertheless, developing radically different ideas about liberty and the pursuit of happiness to those of his teacher.

Like Shaftesbury and Locke, Hutcheson had belonged to an older generation of Whigs who had taken the conventional path of maintaining that it was the duty of the legislator to promote virtue and a sense of liberty, as well as to provide the good government needed to check the growing economic and political power of the nobility, a class whose 'ambition, vanity, insolence, and . . . unsociable contempt of the lower orders, as if they were not of the same species, or were not fellow-citizens with them' was a patently intolerable obstacle to justice.[44] Their rack-rented estates and their political corruption were immiserating the poor, threatening the powers of the commons and opening up the horrible prospect of a constitutional slide into hereditary aristocracy – 'among the very worst forms of government'.[45] Like most of the older radical Whigs, Hutcheson looked forward to the day in which it would be possible for a virtuously minded parliament to hold the powers of the nobility in check by means of agrarian laws, rotations of office and frequent elections. However, he also went on to suggest, controversially, that this could be helped by promoting trade, manufactures and commerce. For economic growth would promote industry and employment among the poor and would provide the merchant and manufacturer with the sort of wealth that would encourage beneficence and the easy social relations on which virtue and liberty ultimately depended. This was an attempt to counter Mandeville's notorious claim that promoting economic growth depended on exploiting our capacity for luxury and conspicuous consumption. Was it really true, Hutcheson asked, 'that luxury is necessary or useful to encourage arts and manufactures?'[46] Were not habits of industry and temperance in employers and employees and a desire to live well in a state of 'sober plenty' more favourable to virtue and liberty and the progress of industry and commerce? And would not a man who chose to live his life in this prosperous but temperate and benevolent condition 'generally [make] a greater consumption than a prodigal of equal fortune; who is often punished with a long tract of diseases and penury, for the extravagance of a few years'?[47] Under the right conditions, commerce surely had the power to create a class which would be wealthy and virtuous enough to check the powers of the nobility and to secure the liberties and prosperity of a free polity. Hutcheson's thinking was speculative in the extreme, a radical dream which might have made limited sense to those living in the prosperous but puritan mercantile world of Glasgow, but one which sounded old-fashioned and utopian in the context of the ruthlessly competitive consumer culture of Mandeville's London. Nevertheless it was a critique which Smith would develop in his own way to open up his discussion of police and use as the bedrock on which his political economy would ultimately be based.

What was striking and original in the lectures on police was Smith's insistence that political stability and a sense of justice were intimately connected with 'the proper means of introducing plenty and abundance into the country, that is, the cheapness of goods of all sorts. For these terms plenty and cheapness are in a manner synonimous, as cheapness is a necessary consequence of plenty.'[48] Smith went on to consider the meaning of opulence and plenty and what he described as 'the naturall wants of mankind', developing the conjecture about need and improvement he had proposed as the basis of his lecture on the origins of language. The outcome was a powerful response to Mandeville's account of the progress of opulence that had proved so troublesome to his old teacher. 'Man,' said Smith, 'has received from the bounty of nature reason and ingenuity, art, contrivance, and capacity of improvement far superior to that which she has bestowed on any of the other animalls, but is at the same time in a much more helpless and destitute condition with regard to the support and comfort of his life.'[49] His creativity was a function of his indigence. He learned to cook because he found raw flesh difficult to digest. He learned to make clothes and build huts because he was too frail to live like the beasts. 'The same temper and inclinations which prompted him to make these improvements push him to still greater refinements.' Disgust with a 'rude and slovenly' way of life had driven him to seek 'more elegant nicities' and to value things for aesthetic rather than functional reasons, and it was this that provided a standard of value which powered the civilizing process Mandeville had described in such sardonic terms. For 'in a certain view of things all the arts, the sciences, law and government, wisdom, and even virtue itself tend all to this one thing, the providing meat, drink, rayment, and lodging for men, which are commonly reckoned the meanest of employments and fit for the pursuit of none but the lowest and meanest of the people'.[50]

Smith's discussion of need also shows him distancing himself from Hume. Hume had shown that the origins of all our social sentiments, our senses of justice, political obligation, morality and beauty, could be explained in terms of sympathy and need. In the lectures on jurisprudence, Smith had set those insights in an anthropological, or, as contemporaries thought of it, a historical framework. At one level that had meant elaborating Hume's discussion of the multiplicity of needs by applying it to the experience of different types of civilization. At another, it had meant demonstrating the overriding importance of the means of subsistence and private property in bringing political societies into existence. But what had been built into this discussion had been Smith's profound insights into the importance of security and good government in releasing that love of improvement on which the progress of civilization depended. It was that sense of security that encouraged citizens to seek the conveniences as well as the necessities of life, and which encouraged magistrates and rulers to regularize the systems of law and government on which continued security and progress depended. It would have been perfectly possible for a metaphysician or a pedant to claim that the motivation for such behaviour was selfishness or benevolence, but Smith detected a more immediate, less speculative motive at work in the behaviour of a significant number of people – an aesthetic sensibility, which led them to seek convenience or order because it was beautiful and satisfying for its own sake as well as for any benefit it might bring oneself or others. It was a response to circumstances with beneficial if unintended consequences for the progress of civilization, behaviour which Smith in one of his more poetical moments would attribute to the workings of the Invisible Hand.

In the reported version of the lectures, Smith was to use this discussion of need and improvement as the basis for a remarkable conjectural history of the progress of opulence, which provided the foundation of much of the thinking about the duties of government that is to be found in the *Wealth of Nations*. What is more, as Dugald Stewart noticed, it is clear that he had already reached important radical conclusions about the nature of those duties in his Edinburgh lectures. We do not and probably never will know whether those conclusions were reached in the same way in 1751 as they were to be in 1763, but it seems reasonably certain that Smith realized that in these lectures on police he was entering new territory in a new way. Characteristically this took the form of showing that a relatively commonplace paradox about the effects of economic growth on society could be resolved in a way which would have the most profound consequences for understanding economic development. Locke had posed the paradox in its classic form by observing that 'a King of a large and fruitful Territory there [America] feeds, lodges, and is clad worse than a day Labourer in *England*',[51] resolving the paradox by observing that civilized societies, unlike savage societies, used land productively. For Smith, the paradox ran deeper, and the way in which he resolved it laid the foundations for the sort of conclusions he was able to claim as his own in 1755. Locke, he argued, had overlooked the enormous inequalities which were characteristic of all improved societies, and their effects on the poorest members of the population. Unlike the artisan, the poor labourer

has all the inconveniencies of the soil and the season to struggle with, is continually exposed to the inclemency of the weather and the most severe labour at the same time. Thus he who as it were supports the whole frame of society and furnishes the means of the convenience and ease of all the rest is himself possessed of a very small share and is buried in obscurity. He bears on his shoulders the whole of mankind, and unable to sustain the load is buried by the weight of it and thrust down into the lowest parts of the earth, from whence he supports all the rest. In what manner then shall we account for the great share he and the lowest of the people have of the conveniencies of life[?]

Smith's historic answer was that, 'The division of labour amongst different hands can alone account for this.'[52]

By 1762 Smith was to press his insights into the economic consequences of the division of labour further by arguing that the progress of the division of labour is controlled by the market, and it was on this proposition that the economic analysis in the *Wealth of Nations* would be based. It is impossible to know how near he was to gaining this historic insight in 1750–51. A Glasgow student reported that Smith had told him he had first met David Hume at that time, when Hume was working on his *Political Discourses* and on essays on the theory of commerce that Smith was to find particularly useful.[53] We do not know whether he knew about these essays in 1750–51, or even whether he was in a position to make use of them then. Nevertheless, his assertion in 1750–51 that 'Little else is requisite to carry a state to the highest degree of opulence from the lowest barbarism, but peace, easy taxes, and a tolerable administration of justice; all the rest being brought about by the natural course of things' suggests that he was already thinking about the effects of government actions on the progress of the division of labour, and on the process of exchange upon which it depended. It was this line of thinking that allowed him to fire the first of his famous attacks on monopolies, and other restrictions on trade, manufactures and agriculture, claiming that governments could carry out their primary duty of promoting justice and encouraging the spread of sociability most effectively by removing obstacles to the progress of the division of labour. If this is indeed what Smith accomplished in 1750–51, he was not only laying the foundations of a new sort of jurisprudence but also thinking about the effects the means of subsistence, property and government had on the process of social and economic exchange and the progress of civilization. If that is so, he was laying the foundations for the two great enterprises to which he would devote himself as Professor of Moral Philosophy at Glasgow.

The two series of public lectures on rhetoric and jurisprudence were a landmark in Smith's career, establishing him as a leading member of the younger literati of ministers and lawyers around whom the intellectual life of the capital would increasingly revolve. This was when he became friends with Hugh Blair, with the formidable historian and future Principal of Edinburgh University, William Robertson, with Edinburgh's future Professor of Moral Philosophy, Adam Ferguson, with John Home, the dramatist and future political agent to the Earl of Bute, with members of the medical community and with William Cullen, another of Home's protégés who was appointed Professor of Medicine at Glasgow in 1751 and was to become one of Smith's closest friends. His lectures left their mark on the literati's intellectual life. Blair acknowledged important debts to Smith's rhetoric lectures in developing his own highly influential course, Smith having loaned him the text of his own course and having once commented 'He is very welcome, there is enough left.'[54] Whether or not Robertson heard the lectures on jurisprudence or was loaned Smith's text, the outcome was less happy. According to the antiquarian George Chalmers, one of Smith's Glasgow students told him that Smith thought that Robertson 'had borrowed the first vol. of his hist[ory] of Cha[rles] 5 from them as Every Student Could testify'.[55] Above all, this was the period in which Smith met David Hume, the man whose work had already enormously influenced his own. Thus began a friendship which was to ripen into one of the closest and most fruitful of the Scottish Enlightenment.

Smith's lectures and the circle in which they placed him made it entirely fitting that he should have shortly found himself formally recognized as one of the leading members of the younger Edinburgh literati. In 1752 he was appointed vice-president of the relaunched Philosophical Society and, two years later, became a founder-member of the Select Society, two societies which were to provide Edinburgh's enlightenment with its institutional and ideological definition. By that time he had also become one of the most notable and innovative members of the Faculty of Glasgow University.

6

Professor of Moral Philosophy
at Glasgow, 1. 1751–9

Smith gave the last of his Edinburgh lectures in the early spring of 1751 and probably returned to Kirkcaldy to prepare himself for his new appointment as Professor of Logic and Metaphysics at Glasgow. The post had fallen vacant the previous November on the death of his old professor John Loudon and there was an immediate contest to replace him. There were two candidates: Smith, and another of Francis Hutcheson's former pupils, George Muirhead. Muirhead was a serious candidate. Hutcheson had backed him for the Edinburgh Moral Philosophy chair in 1746 and David Hume thought him a suitable replacement for Smith when Smith was appointed Professor of Moral Philosophy in 1752. Muirhead was appointed Professor of Oriental Languages at Glasgow in 1753 and Professor of Humanity a year later, and was regarded as a proper candidate for the Moral Philosophy chair when Smith resigned in 1763.[1] Like Smith, he came from Fife. But Smith's Edinburgh reputation, coupled with James Oswald's lobbying, Home's backing and the Duke of Argyll's probable support, was enough to secure Smith a unanimous election and the appointment was duly announced in the *Glasgow Courant* of 7 January 1751. Shortly after, Smith went to Glasgow to sign the Confession of Faith before the Glasgow Presbytery, to take 'the usual oath de Fideli' and to deliver an inaugural dissertation, '*De Origine Idearum*' (now lost), before returning to Edinburgh to complete his lectures, leaving the new Professor of Civil Law, Hercules Lindesay, one of his sponsors, to finish Loudon's logic and metaphysics course. The whole business was settled quickly and competently. What soured the moment was the unwelcome discovery that the election had generated the sort of professorial backbiting that was all too characteristic of this most enlightened of British universities.

It is not clear exactly what happened. To judge from the draft of a long letter written by William Cullen, shortly to be appointed Professor of Medicine and Smith's main informant on university matters, the root of the trouble lay in two letters Smith had written to the Duke of Argyll and his guardian, William Smith, the previous Duke's secretary. It sounds as though Smith had reported that he was a candidate for the professorship and that he wanted to be considered on his merits and not as the Duke's protégé. However, news of the letter had leaked out. It was now being said that Smith was indeed the Duke's man and that Thomas Craigie, the Professor of Moral Philosophy, William Leechman, the Professor of Divinity, and some others had only voted for him as a 'compliment' to the Duke. Craigie was furious and there was a Faculty row. The Principal, fearing that Argyll would get to hear of it, had asked Smith to confirm what he had written so that he could assure the Duke that his name had not been taken in vain. This time it was Smith, who clearly had a temper, who was outraged, apparently threatening to write to the Duke himself to tell him his own side of the story. Cullen's instinct had been to reply 'I beg that for the sake of your quiet and health you would not indulge in any anger or vexation till you are sure of your facts and which you cannot be with regard to our affairs till you are for some time on [our Faculty].'[2] That appears to have been an end of the matter.

Smith took up residence in Glasgow in October 1751 in time for the start of the new academic year, probably taking rooms near the College while waiting for a vacant manse in Professors' Court. Once he was settled he was joined by his mother and his cousin Janet Douglas, who were to keep house for him for the rest of his professorial life. By this time he had taken on his new teaching duties. Thomas Craigie was in poor health and had been given leave to recuperate in Lisbon. His teaching was to be divided between Smith and William Leechman, Leechman lecturing on Ethics and Smith on Natural Jurisprudence and Politics, 'which it would be most agreeable for me to take upon me to teach'. Craigie was another of Hutcheson's pupils and his moral philosophy course seems to have been broadly Hutchesonian in character. Smith went out of his way to be accommodating, telling Cullen that he wanted to discuss the curriculum with Craigie before his departure for Lisbon 'that I might receive his advice about the plan I ought to follow. I would pay great deference to it in every thing, and would follow it implicitly in this, as I shall consider myself as standing in his place and representing him.'³ But the meeting never took place. Craigie died on 27 November, releasing Smith from any obligation to give the sort of course Craigie would have wanted. More importantly, Craigie's death left Smith his natural successor. He was elected to the Moral Philosophy chair on 22 April 1752. This time there was no malicious gossip and there were no tantrums.

The Glasgow Smith had known as a student was a city whose economy was at a formative stage of its development and with a university that was being remodelled under the watchful eye of the future Duke of Argyll. He returned to a Glasgow whose economy was burgeoning and to a university whose reforms were entering a new phase. The driving force of the city's economy was still the tobacco trade, which was now expanding at an astonishing rate: 8 million lbs of tobacco had been landed legally in 1741, 13 million in 1745 and 21 million in 1751 – figures which do not begin to take into account the growth of a smuggling trade that remained a thorn in the flesh of Treasury officials in Edinburgh and London. Indeed, so extensive had the Glasgow tobacco trade become by 1751 that the city was importing and re-exporting more than London and the English outports combined, and it was becoming one of the most important entrepôts in trade between the Americas and the Caribbean, and France, north Germany, the Baltic and Russia, shipping and warehousing tobacco and sugar as well as coffee, cheese, ginger, rum, canes, cottons, tar, canvas and gunpowder bound for Europe in exchange for European goods bound for America. It was a trade which flourished because the Act of Union had brought Scottish merchants under the protection of the Navigation Acts, and because the Glaswegians were good at manipulating its provisions in order to restrict foreign competition and enhance their own profits. It was also a trade that was making Glasgow tobacco merchants very rich indeed.

From 1740–90, the trade was controlled by a group of 163 merchants, knit together by family, money and interest into a series of immensely wealthy syndicates; Alexander Speirs' business, built up from scratch, was worth £135,000 by the time he was fifty-nine; William Cunninghame was able to lend his brother-in-law more than

£150,000 over a ten-year period.[4] The effect of these syndicates on the local economy was predictable. Many invested in land in neighbouring counties and built mansions and fanciful pleasure-gardens which often had more to do with conspicuous consumption than the sort of prudent improvements Smith liked to associate with merchant-landownership. Between 1750 and 1775 new public arcades and piazzas were being erected in the city centre and twelve new streets and squares were being developed to cater for a growing population and the increasingly expensive tastes of the tobacco lords. Smith was proud of the new city centre, although it was rash to commend it to Samuel Johnson in 1773. 'Pray, sir, have you ever seen Brentford?' the surly sage replied.[5] Craft trades flourished along with a rising demand for coaches and sedan chairs, exotic and expensive foods and fashions; the careful Annie Bogle, daughter of one of the richest merchants, reckoned that half of her household's total expenditure of £931 for the period 1775-80 was spent on luxuries.[6] By 1751, the city's economy was supporting new newspapers, taverns, coffee-houses, public entertainments, raree shows and exhibitions of works of art. It was symptomatic of the general expansion of mercantile wealth in the great trading cities of Britain and France. John Gibson, another of Smith's pupils, noted the effect of these changes in 1777 in his *History of Glasgow*, commenting that

> Since the year 1750, a total change has been effected, not only in Glasgow but over the whole country around it. Hitherto an attentive industry, and a frugality bordering upon parsimony, had been the general characteristic of the inhabitants of Glasgow: the severity of the ancient manners prevailed in full vigour ... An extending commerce and increasing manufactures, joined to frugality and industry, had produced wealth; the establishment of banks had rendered it easy for people possessed of credit to obtain money, the ideas of the public were enlarged, and schemes of trade and improvement were adopted and put in practice, the undertakers of which, in former times, would have been denominated madmen; a new stile was introduced in building, in living, in dress, and in furniture, the conveniences, the elegances of life began to be studied, wheel-carriages were set up; an assembly room and a playhouse were built by subscription.[7]

In the *Wealth of Nations* Smith was to argue that the carrying trade was a symptom and not a cause of economic growth, and the least efficient way of using capital to generate employment.[8] Although it was undoubtedly true that the tobacco trade fuelled a consumer boom it was also penetrating the subsoil of the city's economy much more deeply than Smith allowed. Tobacco merchants, with their vast trading interests and their enormous capital resources, were going into businesses such as sugar refining, rope manufacture, iron works, tanneries and the leather business, bottle-making, and the manufacture of stockings and hats. The greatest of all merchants, John Glassford, for example, had interests in brewing, tanning, dyeing, vitriol works and in the great Carron Iron works, as well as in print works and ribbon-making. Men like John Dunlop, whose fathers had already made fortunes in the tobacco trade, turned from overseas trade to mining the coal reserves on their estates. Others moved into banking. As Christopher Smout remarks, it was these merchants who laid the foundation for Glasgow's reputation as an industrial and financial centre before the boom in cotton and shipbuilding started in the later decades of the century.[9] While the profits of the carrying trade may not have created industry they were certainly creating the conditions in which industrial enterprise could and would thrive.

It is tempting to think of the changes which were taking place in the university in this period as a straightforward response to the cultural needs of a remarkable mercantile community, but they weren't. As Smith knew very well, the reforms that had begun in the 1720s had been designed to propagate moderate Presbyterianism rather than mercantile enterprise, and although Hutcheson had lectured on the theory of trade as part of his politics course, it was not this but the appointment of the distinguished moderate Presbyterian divine William Leechman to the Divinity chair in 1743 that he regarded as his greatest achievement. For the future, the university's priorities would lie in fostering legal and medical education and turning these subjects into disciplines which were fit for philosophically minded gentlemen.

Glasgow's law and medical professorships had been long-time sinecures, and by coincidence both fell vacant in 1750, at the same time that the Logic and Metaphysics chair fell vacant. Hercules Lindesay was appointed Professor of Civil Law in 1750 and William Cullen was appointed Professor of Medicine in 1751. Both had studied in Edinburgh, both had taught privately in Glasgow for some years. Cullen was a protégé of Henry Home and the Duke of Argyll and it seems reasonable to suppose that Lindesay was appointed with Argyll's approval. Both were known to Smith, both supported his appointment enthusiastically and both became friends and allies. Intellectually and personally, Cullen was a man after Smith's own heart. He was interested in the part played by the sentiments in forming the human personality and had a particular interest in their effects on the health of his patients. He was interested in the history of medical systems and the influence they had exercised over medical practice in former ages. He was to develop a curriculum which was notable for what some thought of as its notoriously 'philosophical' characteristics. More generally, in the same spirit as Smith, and in the words of his biographer, 'he carried into his medical lectures the same ideas of a great system of nature, and made his pupils perceive something of that affinity by which, as Cicero observes, all the senses are connected, rendering to each other a mutual illustration and assistance'.[10] Unfortunately much less is known about Lindesay, who died suddenly in 1761 having published nothing. James Boswell, who came to study with Smith, attended his lectures and thought him 'one of the best teachers I ever saw'.[11] As an advocate with academic pretensions, the chances are that he knew Home and it would be interesting to know what he thought of Home's and Smith's historical jurisprudence. He was enough of a philosopher to be able to give Smith's lectures on logic and metaphysics in the spring of 1751. What is more, as Professor of Civil Law he lectured on a branch of jurisprudence that was attracting the attention of historically and philosophically minded jurists in Holland and Germany, most notably from Henry and Samuel Cocceii, whose work was to be of some interest to Smith in the 1750s. Were Smith and Lindesay developing complementary philosophical and historical approaches to an important branch of jurisprudence? Certainly that was the approach which was to be developed by Lindesay's successor, John Millar, Smith's most intelligent pupil. Smith's appointment was thus the last in a series designed to expand the range of the curriculum and to develop the distinctive 'philosophical' style of teaching which Hutcheson had pioneered and on which Glasgow's reputation now depended. It was also the most crucial. Hutcheson's curriculum had confirmed the position of moral philosophy as the apex of the philosophy curriculum and the gateway to Divinity Hall. Smith was now faced with the task of developing a curriculum which would prepare students to enter the lay professions as well as the ministry.

One final problem remained, to fill the Logic and Metaphysics chair Smith had just vacated. It was here that the reforming impulse met its match. Intellectually, Smith had been appointed to the Logic and Metaphysics chair on the strength of lectures which John Millar had thought offered 'a more interesting and useful' introduction to philosophy than 'the logic and metaphysics of the schools'. David Hume was suggested as a suitable replacement by Lindesay, a suggestion which hints at Lindesay's philosophical orientation and suggests familiarity with the fact that Hume had once proposed to write a fourth book of the *Treatise of Human Nature*, on criticism. It was also somewhat implausibly rumoured that Edmund Burke, the author of the forthcoming and seminal *Philosophical Inquiry into the Origin of our Ideas of the Sublime and Beautiful*, was interested.[12] Smith's reaction to Hume's candidature was prudential. He told Cullen 'I should prefer David Hume to any man for a colleague; but I am afraid the public would not be of my opinion; and the interest of the society will oblige me to have some regard to the opinion of the public.'[13] Indeed, when the rumour that Hume was to be a candidate leaked out, the Glasgow Presbytery complained to the Principal, who was even more sensitive to clerical interference in Faculty business than he was to interference by the Duke of Argyll. Apparently he 'received [the Presbytery] with a hauty air & tossing up his head asked them if they were come to Dictate to the Faculty or come as his brethren. The ministers got not answer. Every body seems to imagine he will not be the man.'[14] Nor was he. In the event the chair was filled by James Clow, one of John Loudon's pupils, who followed in his master's footsteps by continuing to teach the logic of the Port-Royal, turning the class into what Thomas Reid later described as 'the drowsy shop of logic and metaphysics'.[15] It was not until 1774 when another of Smith's pupils, George Jardine, succeeded Clow that the logic and metaphysics course was rebuilt on Smithian lines to demonstrate what Jardine described as the progress of 'intellectual culture'.[16] Between 1752 and 1763 Smith would be obliged to teach rhetoric and belles-lettres as a private course to supplement his course in moral philosophy.

These professorial appointments were part of a wider attempt by the professors and their patrons to extend the intellectual reach of the College and to redefine its place in the cultural life of the city and the nation. In 1754, in a remarkable move in which Smith must have been involved, the university printers, Robert and Andrew Foulis, were given permission to open what proved to be a moderately successful Academy of the Fine Arts, to train apprentices in painting, drawing, engraving and modelling, on the grounds that 'a seat of the Sciences and Belles Lettres is the perfect nursery for the Fine Arts. The University of Glasgow who are sensible of the intrinsic value of the Fine Arts, and the excellent uses to which they may be made subservient, both moral and political, would be a proper society to have the Academy under their inspection, and to produce a noble and useful institution.'[17] In 1755 the brothers went even further, arranging an enormous exhibition of paintings, prints, drawings and sculptures, mostly copied from the great masters, for sale to the Glasgow public. Prices ranged from £70 for a copy of the Duke of Hamilton's vast painting of 'The Convention at Somerset House' and £52. 10/- for a copy of Rubens' 'Daniel in the Lion's Den', to more modest copies of landscapes, classical scenes and portraits by Poussin, Raphael and Titian. There was even a bas-relief of Francis Hutcheson on sale for 2/6 plaster and 7/6 wax. If this was an attempt to demonstrate that the fine arts were worthy of the patronage of a university and a wealthy mercantile elite, it was even more significant that the senate should have discussed and 'carried forward' a plan in which Smith is likely to have been involved, for an Academy of Dancing, Fencing and Riding to provide gentlemen with the means of completing their social education, and doubtless to attract to the university the gentlemanly clientele on which Edinburgh was beginning to build its reputation.[18]

This attempt to extend the social and cultural reach of the university was only moderately successful. To be sure, Leechman, Cullen and Smith himself would have some success in attracting international and well-born students. But the College never managed to fight off the competition for foreign and gentlemanly students from Edinburgh. Edinburgh's law and medical faculties were larger than Glasgow's and the medical professors were able to draw on the resources of the Royal Infirmary to provide clinical teaching; it is striking that William Cullen and Joseph Black, two of the greatest professors of medicine, were lured to the lusher pastures of Edinburgh from Glasgow in 1756 and 1766 respectively. And although Smith was to resist Hume's suggestion that he apply for the chair of Public Law at Edinburgh in 1758, and although his fame as a teacher did much to confirm Glasgow's enviable reputation as 'one of the most famous and illustrious' universities in Europe, as one foreign observer put it,[19] it was to be Edinburgh and the moral philosophy curricula developed in the later decades of the century by Adam Ferguson and Dugald Stewart which were to capture the lucrative and prestigious market of noble and gentle students from Scotland and abroad. In the last resort, Glasgow University was too isolated from the polite, gentlemanly, professional world of Edinburgh to compete effectively for a prestigious clientele.

Thus Glasgow's enlightenment continued to develop along some-what different lines to Edinburgh's. Although the cultural space between town and gown in Edinburgh was being bridged by the net-work of intellectual clubs and societies that cross-fertilized the city's academic and civic culture. Glasgow had few such clubs and those it did have conveyed rather different messages about cultural relations between academia and the city to those of the capital. In Smith's day, there were only three clubs of any note, to all of which he belonged. Professor Robert Simson's well-established, convivial Friday Club was a largely professorial club whose donnish culture he clearly enjoyed. The popular Hodge-Podge Club, founded in the early 1750s, began as a literary society but soon lapsed into a drinking club. The Literary Society, which was founded in January 1752 by a group of professors that included Smith and Cullen, comes over as an attempt to provide the city with a club that was roughly analogous to Edinburgh's Philo-sophical Society, in the sense of providing a forum for the professors which would link the culture of the university to that of the city, the country and the wider world. Some of its early members like Robert Bogle, William Crawford and John Graham of Douglastown were merchants, and visits from the Edinburgh literati were rare but not unknown – Adam Ferguson and Sir John Dalrymple are both known to have attended and David Hume was to provide chapters of the first volume of his *History of England* for discussion. Indeed one of the first papers given to the society, on 23 January 1752, was Smith's 'Account of some of Mr David Hume's Essays on Commerce' from his forthcoming *Political Discourses*. However, most of the society's members were professors and it is hard to resist the conclusion that, like the Friday Club, the society remained a largely professorial gathering, another extension of collegiate life, another institution which helped to ensure that the city's enlightenment would remain as it had begun, a movement largely confined to the college and its professors.

The fourth society to which Smith belonged, Lord Provost Andrew Cochrane's so-called Political Economy Club, was rather different. Cochrane was a tobacco merchant of some substance and learning. The club was founded in the early 1740s, as a means of encouraging its members to inquire 'into the Nature and the Principles of Trade in all its Branches, and to Communicate their Knowledge and Views on that Subject to each other'.[20] It was primarily a club for merchants, and Smith and the Rev. William Wight, a future Professor of Ecclesiastical History, were the only professorial members. The club's records are lost but there can be little doubt that it interested Smith because it gave him the opportunity of listening to intelligent merchants talking about their business and about their attitudes to commercial policy. It is tempting to think that it was here that Smith learned to appreciate the force that the 'wretched spirit of monopoly' exerted over the minds of even the most literate merchants. When he wrote in the *Wealth of Nations* that, 'the interest of the dealers . . . in any particular branch of trade or manufactures, is always in some respects different from, and even opposite to, that of the publick. To widen the market and to narrow the competition, is always the interest of the dealers', it is hard not to think that he was reflecting in part on thirteen years of conversations heard in Glasgow.[21] Nor was Smith a merely passive observer of the folk-ways of the merchant community. As we have already seen, Dugald Stewart saw a paper Smith had given in 1755 to what sounds like Cochrane's club in which he had somewhat testily claimed the ownership of some of the central aspects of his thinking about free trade and the police of a commercial polity. What Stewart did not say, however, was that these were ideas which were seriously at odds with those of many merchants he knew in the 1750s.

This, then, was a university reforming itself in a way which was distancing it from the heartland of the city it inhabited, and it is not altogether surprising that by the 1760s it should have been on the receiving end of a Glaswegian version of the critical invective to which Oxford had been subjected a generation earlier, an invective which castigated the professors for offering a 'philosophical' rather than a 'practical' education. 'We are generally a Commercial People,' one pamphleteer wrote in 1762. 'Except in Matters of Commerce our ideas are pretty much circumscribed. The Thoughts of great Numbers among us move in no very wide Circle and never towards Metaphysics. We figure not to ourselves any very wide or noble Plan of Education, which might dignify high Life, but would be merely imaginary and unattainable in our Circumstances: To these our Education must be suitable.'[22] This was putting it politely. Others, like the College's most doughty critic, William Thom, sneered at the greed and self-importance of professors who, by 1765, had thought themselves too grand to worship in city churches, preferring the decent seclusion of a College chapel.[23] There were calls for the establishment of new academies devoted to the practical arts and sciences needed by a commercial people. As for the civilizing power of philosophy and politeness, so much vaunted by the professors, 'who, in the name of wonder, appears with greatest dignity in a company of merchants? Or, who is listened to with the most reverent attention? Is it not the richest man? and the man who can talk experimentally of the largest transactions?'[24]

In this way, between 1751 and the publication of the *Theory of Moral Sentiments* in 1759, Smith's academic career developed in circumstances which were far from straightforward. Although there was a somewhat easier relationship between town and gown to the one he had known as a student, it was restricted by Edinburgh standards. His interest in mercantile life, the part he seems to have played in founding and running the Literary Society, his interest in developing the educational and cultural reach of the university, all suggest a sensitivity to these problems and to the wider purposes of university education and academic life in an enlightened university. Nor is it to be forgotten that during the 1750s he became an experienced and successful academic administrator with something of a taste for management. In his first year as a professor he was put in charge of moving the library into a new problem-ridden building designed by William Adam. From 1755 he was to be effectively in charge of the library as Quaestor and responsible for its accounts – which he kept meticulously – and for purchases, which were generally made through the Foulis brothers, an arrangement which incidentally gave him excellent opportunities for building up a first-rate library of his own.[25] Smith was a serious university librarian, acquiring stocks of classical literature, contemporary history, philosophy, law and, interestingly, commerce. One of his earlier and most expensive purchases was the first seven volumes of the *Encyclopédie*, to which he had already had access in the Advocates Library in Edinburgh. It was purchased for Glasgow University between 1758 and 1760 and paid for with nearly a third of his budget. By 1754 Smith had also gained a reputation for property management. He was responsible for the protracted and intricate negotiations involved in rebuilding the Principal's house, in building a new natural philosophy classroom, for accommodating the Academy of the Fine Arts, and for housing James Watt's workshop. By the late 1750s he was in charge of the university's accounts and the university's dealings with the town council on property matters and the students' tax liability. He dealt with the Barons of Exchequer in Edinburgh and the Treasury in London on matters concerning the university's accounts and its bequests. By the late 1750s seniority and competence had established him as one of the most powerful and heavily worked members of the College. He was Quaestor from 1758 to 1760, Dean of Faculty – twice – from 1760 to 1762 and Vice-Rector from 1762 to 1764. As we shall see, by the end of his professorial career he had also been drawn into the thick of the complicated and often acrimonious political life of the College.

The heart of his academic life nevertheless lay in the time-consuming business of teaching moral philosophy. Smith's timetable was governed by long-standing university tradition. The 'public' course in moral philosophy was taught every weekday from 7.30 to 8.30 a.m. from 10 October to 10 June, with a day's break at Christmas. Smith had tried to break with the custom of beginning each lecture with prayer but had not been allowed to do so. His prayers were clearly as perfunctory as possible and were said to have rehearsed the truths of natural theology. However, according to the memorialist John Ramsay of Ochtertyre, Smith did manage to abandon Hutcheson's practice of providing Sunday discourses 'suited to that day'.[26] The hour between eleven and midday was spent discussing the morning's lecture and examining students on it. The 'private' class, in which Smith delivered his lectures on rhetoric, was taught from midday until one from about mid-November to late February. The afternoons were spent teaching students privately, either by reading them lectures or by chatting, sessions which students like James Boswell, William Richardson and the future Earl of Buchan remembered with affection; Richardson, a future Professor of Humanity at Glasgow, recalled 'many of those incidental and digressive illustrations and even discussions, not only on morality, but in criticism, which were delivered by him with animated and extemporaneous eloquence, as they were suggested in the course of question and answer'.[27] Overall, it has been reckoned that by 1759 Smith could count on a public class of around eighty or ninety students and a private class of around twenty out of a total student population of about three hundred.[28]

John Millar provided Dugald Stewart with the fullest and most perceptive account we have of his old professor's course.

> About a year after his appointment to the Professorship of Logic, Mr Smith was elected to the chair of Moral Philosophy. His course of lectures on this subject was divided into four parts. The first contained Natural Theology; in which he considered the proofs of the being and attributes of God, and those principles of the human mind upon which religion is founded. The second comprehended Ethics, strictly so called, and consisted chiefly of the doctrines which he afterwards published in his Theory of Moral Sentiments. In the third part, he treated at more length of that branch of morality which relates to *justice*, and which, being susceptible of precise and accurate rules, is for that reason capable of a full and particular explanation.
>
> Upon this subject he followed the plan that seems to be suggested by Montesquieu; endeavouring to trace the gradual progress of jurispru-

dence, both public and private, from the rudest to the most refined ages, and to point out the effects of those arts which contribute to subsistence, and to the accumulation of property, in producing correspondent improvements or alterations in law and government. This important branch of his labours he also intended to give to the public; but this intention, which is mentioned in the conclusion of the Theory of Moral Sentiments, he did not live to fulfil.

In the last part of his lectures, he examined those political regulations which are founded, not upon the principle of *justice*, but that of *expediency*, and which are calculated to increase the riches, the power, and the prosperity of a State. Under this view, he considered the political institutions relating to commerce, to finances, to ecclesiastical and military establishments. What he delivered on these subjects contained the substance of the work he afterwards published under the title of An Inquiry into the Nature and Causes of the Wealth of Nations.[29]

We know nothing about the natural theology lectures except that they drew the somewhat acid comment from John Ramsay that 'his speculations ... though not extended to a great length, were no less flattering to human pride than those of Hutcheson'; they argued that the truths of religion could be discovered 'by the light of nature without any special revelation'. 'Even then,' Ramsay continued, 'from the company he kept and other circumstances, suspicion was entertained that his principles were not sound, though he was very guarded in conversation.'[30] Smith clearly hurried through this unwelcome assignment as quickly as possible so as to be able to spend most of his time on the following three sections of a course of notable sophistication and complexity, one which made demands on Smith as well as on his students, not least because of a custom that ensured that his classes were generally composed of students of mixed ages and abilities. The fee for the class was one and a half guineas per year and those who wished to hear the course a second time had to pay a second fee. Thereafter, they were free to attend the class as often as they pleased for nothing. This meant that by the mid-1750s, when he was thinking about the problem of turning his lectures into a book, Smith was facing an audience composed of some who had never heard him before and others who not only knew his ethics but knew his jurisprudence and politics as well, and were probably on the verge of qualifying as ministers or doctors. Such advanced students were in an excellent position to think about the relevance of Smith's ethics to his theories of government and his thinking about the duties of citizens and magistrates.

Smith seems to have taken time to settle down as a university lecturer. At first he followed Hutcheson's practice of lecturing extempore, but it was not a success and he reverted to the practice he had adopted at Edinburgh of reading a text he had already dictated to a clerk, interpolating as he read, a practice which some came to think of as his own form of extemporary lecturing. Millar's account of his lecturing is vivid and precise and throws light on his style and on that distinctive method of arguing from axioms which were substantiated by means of 'illustrations', and often massive displays of erudition.

There was no situation in which the abilities of Mr Smith appeared to greater advantage than as a Professor. In delivering his lectures, he trusted almost entirely to extemporary elocution. His manner, though not graceful, was plain and unaffected; and, as he seemed to be always interested in the subject, he never failed to interest his hearers. Each discourse consisted commonly of several distinct propositions, which he successively endeavoured to prove and illustrate. These propositions, when announced in general terms, had, from their extent, not unfrequently something of the air of a paradox. In his attempts to explain them, he often appeared, at first, not to be sufficiently possessed of the subject, and spoke with some hesitation. As he advanced, however, the matter seemed to crowd upon him, his manner became warm and animated, and his expression easy and fluent. In points susceptible of controversy, you could easily discern, that he secretly conceived an opposition to his opinions, and that he was led upon this account to support them with greater energy and vehemence. By the fulness and variety of his illustrations, the subject gradually swelled in his hands, and acquired a dimension which, without a tedious repetition of the same views, was calculated to seize the attention of his audience, and to afford them pleasure as well as instruction, in following the same object, through all the diversity of shades and aspects in which it was presented, and afterwards in tracing it backwards to that original proposition or general truth from which this beautiful train of speculation had proceeded.[31]

This is a description of the professor as a performer, interested in the business of holding an audience's attention and notoriously irritated by students who paid more attention to taking notes than to their professor's rhetoric – he often told note-takers 'that he hated scribblers'.[32] It also describes the practice of a philosopher who had every reason to know that the axioms from which he worked would only persuade if his illustrations caught his audience's imagination and appealed to their sense of truth. It certainly worked for a sophisticated and observant student like James Boswell, who matriculated at Glasgow in 1759 expressly to hear Smith's lectures:

> My greatest reason for coming hither was to hear Mr. Smith's lectures (which are truly excellent.) His Sentiments are striking, profound and beauitifull, the method in which they are arranged clear accurate and orderly, his language correct perspicuous and elegantly phrased. His private character is realy amiable. He has nothing of that formal stiffness and Pedantry which is too often found in Professors. So far from that, he is a most polite well-bred man, is extreamly fond of having his Students with him and treats them with all the easiness and affability imaginable.[33]

Part of Smith's technique was to begin each lecture with a meticulously crafted précis of the previous one. He also resorted to older tricks, like one he recalled later in life: 'During one whole session a certain student with a plain but expressive countenance was of great use to me in judging of my success. He sat conspicuously in front of a pillar: I had him constantly under my eye. If he leant forward to listen all was right, and I knew that I had the ear of my class; but if he leant back in an attitude of listlessness I felt at once that all was wrong, and that I must change either the subject or the style of my address.'[34] As this recollection hints, much of Smith's success as a lecturer was due to the fact that he liked students. As Ramsay put it,

> He was at great pains to discover and cherish the seeds of genius, and therefore, when he met with acute studious young men, he invited them to his house, that from their turn of conversation he might discover the bents and extent of their faculties. He took great pleasure in directing their studies and solving their doubts, adapting his hints to their plans of life. The private admonitions of such a man were likely to make a

deeper impression on the mind of an ingenious youth than the most able and eloquent lectures.[35]

His teaching was turning him into something of a cult figure, a professor whose portrait bust could be bought by students at local bookshops, a philosopher whose thinking was, according to Millar, talked about in clubs and literary societies, a guru who would succeed in turning a younger generation of Glasgow merchants into free traders.[36] Characteristically, no copy of his bust has survived.

Smith's professorial duties inevitably took a toll on his private life. There were occasional rumours of romantic attachments, but nothing ever happened; as Ian Ross puts it, 'It is to be feared that the biographer can do little more with the topic of Smith's sex life than contribute a footnote to the history of sublimation.'[37] His visits to Edinburgh were few and far between, mostly, one would guess, en route for Kirkcaldy and Glasgow at the beginning and end of the vacation. At all events his friend Miss Hepburn probably spoke for most of his friends in regretting 'very much, that you are settled at Glasgow, and that we had the Chance of seeing you so seldom'.[38] What correspondence there is suggests that Smith's Edinburgh friends were resigned to sending him letters with local news in the knowledge that he was unlikely to reply – teasing Smith on his failures as a correspondent became a recurring theme in his later correspondence. Alexander Wedderburn, one of his Edinburgh students, put it nicely in 1754: 'Though I have not heard once from you since we parted, I make very little Doubt that I have been frequently in your Thoughts. I judge so, because amidst all the variety of Objects which have since I may rather say distracted than interested me I have always in my Best hours of reflexion, had my Thoughts turned towards you.'[39] During this period Smith's friendship with Hume ripened, though more through correspondence than personal contact, Hume's letters of the 1750s picking up the thread of recent conversations or correspondence about his work on the history of England – he was at work on the volumes on the history of the reigns of James I and Charles I at the time – about forthcoming philosophical essays, about Edinburgh gossip and, all too frequently, about the worrying state of Smith's health. 'My Dear Sir,' he wrote from Edinburgh on 26 May 1753,

I was very sorry to hear by Mr Leechman that you had been ill of late. I am afraid the Fatigues of your Class have exhausted you too much, and that you require more Leizure and Rest than you allow yourself. However, the good Season and the Vacation now approaches; and I hope you intend, both for Exercise and Relaxation, to take a Jaunt to this Place. I have many things to communicate to you. Were you not my Friend, you wou'd envy my robust Constitution. My Application has been and is continual; and yet I preserve entire Health. I am now beginning the Long Parliament; which, considering the great Number of Volumes I peruse, and my scrupulous method of composing, I regard as a very great Advance. I think you shou'd settle in this Town during the Vacation; where there is always some good Company; and you know, that I can supply you with Books, as much as you please.

I beg to hear from you at your Leizure; and am

Your affectionate Friend and humble Servant

David Hume[40]

So far as we know, the offer of hospitality and good company came to nothing. For heavy professorial duties and the pressures of overwork notwithstanding, Smith, doubtless egged on by Henry Home (elevated to the bench of the Court of Session as Lord Kames in 1752), was about to launch himself on the huge task of developing a philosophy that would be fit for consumption by the polite and learned world as well as by university students. With his moral philosophy course underway by 1754-5 he was in a position to turn to the hard grind of turning his philosophy into a book in the hope of establishing his reputation in London and Paris as well as Glasgow and Edinburgh. In order to do this, he had decided to present his moral philosophy as a means of providing a philosophical defence of Hume's claim that commerce had the power to improve and perfect the human personality. It was a claim that Hume had made in *Political Discourses* of 1752 and it had been called into question in 1756 by Jean-Jacques Rousseau. As Smith was to discover in writing the *Theory of Moral Sentiments*, Rousseau's argument was not one that was easily refuted.

7

The *Theory of Moral Sentiments* and the Civilizing Powers of Commerce

Hume's theory of human nature had provided Smith with a powerful point of departure in writing his Edinburgh lectures. There Smith had developed a theory of language to reinforce Hume's theory of knowledge, and had demonstrated the importance of the sense of taste and propriety in extending our capacity for sociability. He had developed Hume's theory of justice by showing how different systems of property, government and governance shape a people's sense of justice and determine the principles of sociability on which a political society's capacity for survival depends. In so doing he had reinforced Hume's claim to have laid the foundations of a science of man based on a study of the sentiments human beings must acquire if they are to survive and prosper in organized societies. He was now ready to develop the theory of sociability on which his own contribution to the science of man would depend. When he met Hume for the first time in 1750–51, he found him working on the *Political Discourses*, which were to be his last contribution to what was now becoming their joint project. These were Hume's hugely influential attempt to draw his theory of human nature into alignment with a theory of commerce and an account of the civilizing process. They were the work of a man whom Smith would describe as 'by far the most illustrious philosopher and historian of the present age'.[1]

By 1751 Hume's intellectual career, like Smith's, was in a state of flux. Important though the *Treatise of Human Nature* had been to Smith and other members of Henry Home's circle, it had not been a popular success. During the 1740s Hume had devoted most of his literary time to applying its principles to an understanding of the moral and political culture of contemporary Britain, an analysis which

THE
THEORY
OF
MORAL SENTIMENTS.

By ADAM SMITH,
Professor of Moral Philosophy in the
University of Glasgow.

LONDON:
Printed for A. Millar, in the Strand;
And A. Kincaid and J. Bell, in Edinburgh.
MDCCLIX.

resulted in the publication of a series of *Essays, Moral, Political and Literary* in 1741, 1742 and 1748. His purpose, central to his later work as a historian, was to persuade modern Britons that the origins of their constitution and liberties were modern rather than ancient, and to urge them to think again about the nature of their rights and duties as citizens of an 'enormous monarchy' that was being transformed by war, commerce and the growth of empire. By the late 1740s his intellectual career was moving in various directions. Two years spent as secretary to a diplomatic mission had taken him to Turin and Vienna and had given him an interest in international relations and in the often confused ideas of national interest held in the courts of modern Europe. The publication of Montesquieu's *De l'esprit des lois* in 1748 had shown that it was possible to develop a system of jurisprudence out of a careful and systematic analysis of the manners of different societies. A further period of intensive reading of the classics had encouraged Hume to present his philosophical principles in a new way. This had resulted in the publication of the *Enquiry Concerning Human Understanding* of 1748 and the *Enquiry Concerning the Principles of Morals* of 1751 – the latter, 'of all my writings, historical, philosophical or literary, incomparably the best. It came unnoticed and unobserved into the world.' He wrote about the principles of natural religion in the highly sceptical *Dialogues Concerning Natural Religion*, a book that was written in 1751 and circulated in manuscript among his friends as being too controversial to publish. In his will he was to ask Smith to arrange for its posthumous publication, a request which Smith found curiously disturbing. With the publication in 1752 of his *Political Discourses*, Hume was ready to turn his attention to the grand project that was to occupy most of his time for the next decade, writing the history of England.

The twelve essays published in the 1752 edition of the *Political Discourses* stand at the meeting-point of these various strands of Hume's career. His discussion drew on important principles originally set out in the *Treatise* and now presented as principles that could be taken for granted. He used historical examples to illustrate his arguments in a way which foreshadowed the methods he was to use in the *History of England*. Most important of all, for Smith, Hume quietly introduced important refinements to his thinking about sociability by reflecting on the necessitous condition of the human species. His science of man was now as complete as it would ever be and he was ready to hand over the problem of developing it to Smith at exactly the moment at which Smith was beginning to address the same problem in his moral philosophy lectures. It could not have been more fitting that Smith's first paper to the Glasgow Literary Society should have been his 'Account of some of Mr David Hume's Essays on Commerce'.

In the *Political Discourses*, Hume was at his most acute, elegant and allusive. These were 'discourses on commerce, money, interest, balance of trade etc wherein perhaps there will occur some principles which are curious, and which may seem too refined and subtile for such vulgar subjects'. He was being ironical. Hume was proposing a philosophical review of the language merchants, politicians and philosophers used to discuss the principles and politics of commerce. He wanted to show that economic questions were, properly speaking, questions about labour and the way in which it was deployed, and that these in turn were questions about the principles of human nature. As he put it, 'everything in this world is purchased by labour and our passions are the only causes of labour'.[2] This meant that the wealth and power of any state ought to be measured in terms of the quantity and quality of its labour force and not in terms of its gold and silver reserves. Money, Hume observed, 'is not, properly speaking, one of the subjects of commerce; but only the instrument which men have agreed upon to facilitate the exchange of one commodity for another. It is none of the wheels of trade: It is the oil which renders the motion of the wheels more smooth and easy.'[3] Thus the primary duty of the sovereign in matters of commerce was to facilitate the circulation of money in ways which would stimulate trade and manufactures and enhance the quantity and quality of the nation's workforce.

Hume's ideas about money, interest and the balance of trade were among the most important contributions to Enlightenment and post-Enlightenment economic thinking, not least because of the use Smith was to make of them in the *Wealth of Nations*. Like Smith, Hume invited his readers to think of mankind as a naturally active species whose members used their labour to secure the 'necessities' and 'conveniences' of life. In primitive societies with subsistence economies, the struggle to secure the necessities of life would prevail. In modern commercial societies, men and women were better able to devote themselves to the pursuit of life's conveniences. In both cases, however, the dynamics of human life were the same, driven by the never-ending, all-consuming desire to satisfy what we think of as our needs. Broadly speaking, this was the line taken by Bernard Mandeville, and, like Mandeville, Hume realized that needs are deeply influenced by fashion and that fashion is a mechanism for creating markets. What interested him was the part merchants played in shaping and satisfying those markets. Strictly speaking, merchants were entrepreneurs who transported the fruits of the labour market of one part of the country to another, money being the mechanism which made that possible. This was why the principles of commerce could only be understood in terms of the effects of the money supply and interest rates on the workings of the market. This was to move the discussion far beyond the limits of Mandeville's and towards controversial questions about the role of government in the management of the economy, all of which returned, as Hume intended they should, to propositions about wealth, labour and need on which all of his economic thinking was based.

But Hume was still faced with the problem of Mandeville's cynicism. Mandeville's story about the civilizing process had been about the enslavement of the human personality. Primitive man might have lived in a state of wretched insecurity and indigence but he had at least been his own master. Cunning rulers had duped him into submitting to political authority and to adopting canons of taste, manners and morals that had the sole function of breaking his self-regarding passions and turning him into a 'taught animal'. Pride and gullibility, fed by fashion and the never-ending hunger for social approval, had made him a slave to social convention, unrecognizable even to himself. The only consolation Mandeville had been able to offer was that most people were so gullible that they failed to understand what was happening to them. Hume realized that his economic thinking would fail to convince unless he was able to show that commerce and economic progress were ethically beneficent and it was to this task that he was to devote some of his most eloquent and persuasive prose. Only the strictest moralists could legitimately argue that work was unnatural and deflected human beings from the state of indolence and contemplation for which they were born. 'There is no craving or demand of the human mind more constant and insatiable than that for exercise and employment; and this desire seems the foundation of most of our passions and pursuits.'[4] To argue that men were naturally indolent was to misunderstand the pleasures of indolence. 'Indolence or repose, indeed seems not of itself to contribute much to our enjoyment; but like sleep, is requisite as an indulgence to the weakness of human nature, which cannot support an uninterrupted course of business or pleasure.'[5] Primitive peoples were idle only because their societies lacked the necessary resources to make them industrious. In Hume's view scarcity, and the invention of property, were the bedrocks on which political society and the progress of civilization depended, offering the sort of security on which industry and invention, sociability and happiness ultimately depended. Indeed Hume's rhetoric suggests that because commercial civilization could offer its citizens the prospect of living more happily than the unfortunate, morally atrophied inhabitants of primitive societies, it was actually a more natural form of civilization than theirs.

In times when industry and the arts flourish, men are kept in perpetual occupation, and enjoy, as their reward, the occupation itself, as well as those pleasures which are the fruit of their labour. The mind acquires new vigour; enlarges its powers and faculties; and by an assiduity in honest industry, both satisfies its natural appetites, and prevents the growth of unnatural ones, which commonly spring up, when nourished by ease and idleness. Banish those arts from society, you deprive men both of action and of pleasure; and leaving nothing but indolence in their place, you even destroy the relish of indolence, which never is agreeable, but when it succeeds to labour, and recruits the spirits, exhausted by too much application and fatigue.

Another advantage of industry and of refinements in the mechanical arts, is, that they commonly produce some refinements in the liberal; nor can one be carried to perfection, without being accompanied, in some degree, with the other. The same age, which produces great philosophers and politicians, renowned generals and poets, usually abounds with skilful weavers, and ship-carpenters. We cannot reasonably expect, that a piece of woollen cloth will be wrought to perfection in a nation, which is ignorant of astronomy, or where ethics are neglected . . .

The more these refined arts advance, the more sociable men become: nor is it possible, that, when enriched with science, and possessed of a fund of conversation, they should be contented to remain in solitude, or live with their fellow-citizens in that distant manner, which is peculiar to ignorant and barbarous nations. They flock into cities; love to receive and communicate knowledge; to show their wit or their breeding; their taste in conversation or living, in clothes or furniture. Curiosity allures the wise; vanity the foolish; and pleasure both. Particular clubs and societies are everywhere formed: Both sexes meet in an easy and sociable manner; and the tempers of men, as well as their behaviour, refine apace. So that, beside the improvements which they receive from knowledge and the liberal arts, it is impossible but they must feel an encrease of humanity, from the very habit of conversing together, and contributing to each other's pleasure and entertainment. Thus *industry*, *knowledge*, and *humanity*, are linked together by an indissoluble chain, and are found, from experience as well as reason, to be peculiar to the more polished, and, what are commonly denominated, the more luxurious ages.[6]

This was the voice of Edinburgh's enlightenment at its most philosophical, inviting readers to reflect on the unintended consequences of a harmless and misunderstood characteristic of human nature and to ask whether these could be so easily written off as the fruits of vice. What is noticeable, however, is that Hume studiously avoided the more troubling ethical questions Mandeville had raised. If commerce and the psychological motors that drove it transformed the human personality, were there not still qualitative questions to be asked about the effects of the civilizing process on the human personality? Was there not something to Mandeville's point that by losing our primitive brutish innocence we had made ourselves utterly dependent on the opinions of others and unrecognizable to ourselves? Philosophically, Hume was not much interested in such questions, but they resurfaced in a new and troubling form at the very moment at which Smith was faced with the problem of turning his moral philosophy lectures into a book as a result of the publication of two key works of enlightened thinking: Samuel Johnson's *Dictionary of the English Language* and Rousseau's *Discours sur l'origine et les fondements de l'inégalité parmi les hommes*, published in 1755 and 1756 respectively. Smith was to review them both in two essays written for the *Edinburgh Review* of 1755–6, a short-lived, but ambitious journal founded and edited by members of the Select Society. These essays mark his debut in print as a philosopher.[7]

Smith's admiration of Johnson's *Dictionary* was real but qualified. 'Any man who was about to compose a dictionary or rather a grammar of the English language, must acknowledge himself indebted to Mr Johnson for abridging at least one half of his labour,' Smith wrote. What was wrong was its method, which Smith thought 'not to be sufficiently grammatical. The different significations of a word are indeed collected; but they are seldom digested into general classes, or ranged under the meaning which the word principally expresses. And sufficient care has not been taken to distinguish the words apparently synonomous [*sic*].' Smith went on to explain what he meant by giving two worked examples of how 'But' and 'Humour' ought to have been treated. What is interesting is that in this first published essay, Smith was in effect advertising his own methods by applying them to the problems of lexicography. Once again, he was recommending the use of the 'didactick' method of building each proposition on a general principle or axiom which could be developed and given substance through the use of a carefully organized display of erudition. Only then, Smith commented of the methods of lexicography, would the philosopher be able to show which usages were incorrect and to be avoided.

His review of Rousseau's *Discourse on Inequality* was more ambitious. He began with a call for a more cosmopolitan and less parochial approach to reviewing from the Scottish press and for more attention to be paid to the moral philosophy of England and France, the only two countries which were producing philosophy 'with such success or reputation as to excite the attention of foreign nations'. But the contrast between the character of the English and the French mind was striking. In literature the English characteristically showed imagination, genius and invention, and in philosophy had added 'something to that stock of observations with which the world had been furnished before them'. The French, on the other hand, were notable for their 'taste, judgment, propriety and order' and for their 'peculiar talent . . . to arrange every subject in that natural simple order, which carries the attention, without any effort, along with it'. He was struck by the recent revival of French philosophy, a field which had long been paralysed by Descartes' intellectually alluring errors. Here the most promising development was the appearance, volume by volume, of Diderot's and d'Alembert's *Encyclopédie*. Here was a great work which had all the philosophical strengths which Johnson's *Dictionary* lacked. It provided 'a compleat, reasoned and even critical examination of each subject' and a map of 'the different arts and sciences, their genealogy and filiation . . . [which] is nearly the same with that of my Lord Bacon'. This was the voice of a philosopher who had his own views of the problems involved in mapping the principles of knowledge according to secure philosophical principles.

What interested him most of all was the present state of French and English philosophy. It was here that the English had made the greatest strides and here that Smith quietly aligned himself with Hume by virtually reproducing his list of the philosophers who had made the science of man possible – 'Mr. Hobbes, Mr. Lock, and Dr. Mandevil, Lord Shaftsbury, Dr. Butler, Dr. Clarke, and Mr. Hutcheson'.[8] Rousseau's appearance as a philosopher of undoubted genius, with a serious interest in the principles of sociability and in the progress of commerce was thus a matter of some interest, not least because his views were seriously and diametrically at odds with his own, with Hume's and with the Scots' generally, and it was clearly necessary to challenge them. But a review was no place for such important work. Instead, Smith used his limited space to expose the bare bones of Rousseau's argument with surgical precision, his scalpel being a comparison between Rousseau's system and that of the bugbear who had come to play such an important part in shaping Hutcheson's thought and his own philosophical education, Mandeville's *Fable of the Bees*.[9] Smith's analysis is so spare and so good that it is worth quoting at length.

Whoever reads [the *Discourse on Inequality*] with attention, will observe, that the second volume of the Fable of the Bees has given the occasion to the system of Mr. Rousseau, in whom however the

principles of the English author are softened, improved, and embel-
lished, and stript of all that tendency to corruption and licentiousness
which has disgraced them in their original author. Dr. Mandeville represents the primitive state of mankind as the most wretched and miserable that can be imagined: Mr. Rousseau, on the contrary, paints it as
the happiest and most suitable to his nature. Both of them however
suppose, that there is in man no powerful instinct which necessarily
determines him to seek society for its own sake: but according to the
one, the misery of his original state compelled him to have recourse to
this otherwise disagreeable remedy; according to the other, some unfortunate accidents having given birth to the unnatural passions of ambition and the vain desire of superiority, to which he had before been a
stranger, produced the same fatal effect. Both of them suppose the same
slow progress and gradual development of all the talents, habits, and
arts which fit men to live together in society, and they both describe this
progress pretty much in the same manner. According to both, those
laws of justice, which maintain the present inequality amongst mankind, were originally the inventions of the cunning and the powerful, in
order to maintain or to acquire an unnatural and unjust superiority over
the rest of their fellow-creatures. Mr. Rousseau however criticises upon
Dr. Mandeville: he observes, that *pity*, the only amiable principle which
the English author allows to be natural to man, is capable of producing
all those virtues, whose reality Dr. Mandeville denies. Mr. Rousseau
at the same time seems to think that this principle is in itself no virtue,
but that it is possessed by savages and by the most profligate of the
vulgar, in a greater degree of perfection than by those of the most
polished and cultivated manners; in which he perfectly agrees with the
English author.[10]

Smith was scrupulous in pinpointing the aspects of Rousseau's
thinking which mattered to his own: his claims that for better or for
worse, human beings were at their most *natural* in the savage state,
that need was the mother of the civilizing process, that the civilizing
process was a tale of the progressive enslavement of human beings to
the opinions and power of others, that the ethical history of civilization was a story of deception and self-deception which was making
human beings unrecognizable even to themselves. While Hume had

gone out of his way to insist that men were at their happiest when they were active and were best able to live an active life in a commercial society, Rousseau had replied that men were naturally indolent and had only been truly at one with themselves in the savage state when they had been free to indulge their indolence by simple living. And where did Rousseau's passionate denunciation of civilization leave Hume's insistence that the human personality had been refined and perfected by the civilizing process? What Rousseau's critique had exposed were ethical questions about sociability which would have to be addressed if commerce was to be defended from its critics. These questions would confront Smith at precisely the moment when he was preparing to turn his moral philosophy lectures into a book.

The *Theory of Moral Sentiments* was Smith's extraordinary attempt to develop a coherent and plausible account of the processes by which we learn the principles of morality from the experience of common life without descending into wanton religious scepticism, Mandevillian cynicism or Rousseaunian despair. It would mean making careful experimental studies of the experiences which shape our moral understanding and teach us our duties, of the process of social exchange, and of the ways in which we learn how to evaluate our own conduct as well as that of others; above all, it would mean attending to the effects that these processes had on the human personality. It was an enterprise which meant thinking again about the principle of sympathy on which all forms of human communication ultimately depended.

Sympathy was a concept well known to contemporary moral philosophers and popular moralists. As most schoolboy readers would have known, the ancient Stoics had thought of sympathy as a principle of attraction which made it possible for human beings to live harmoniously with one another, with the natural world and with its benevolent Creator. Modern popular moralists like Addison had used the term extensively to describe the roots of those affections on which friendship and sociability depended. Hume had used the term in a more specialized, philosophical sense to explain why we find ourselves compelled to adhere to the rules of morality and justice. Indeed the notion that human beings communicate much of what they mean through sympathy as well as language was deeply embedded in the polite conversational culture of the Anglo-Saxon and French enlightenments, and had become fundamental to the Enlightenment's understanding of itself. For Smith, however, this familiar concept carried more explanatory weight than had been realized. His great achievement was to turn it into the governing principle of a theory of sociability on which a general theory of commerce could be based. And while his analysis was to do much to provide Hume's brilliant eulogy to commerce with the philosophical underpinning it now needed, ethically, his analysis presented a darker, more equivocal, more Rousseaunian even, account of the civilizing process than might have been expected, one that would raise serious problems for the moralist. For neither Rousseau nor his cynical mentor Mandeville were easily answered.

Smith's book opens with a discussion of the idea of sympathy. He began by tacitly acknowledging that Rousseau and Mandeville had been right in their way to think of *pity*, rather than selfishness or benevolence, as the affection on which our fellow-feeling for others depends. Pity was 'the emotion which we feel for the misery of others, when we either see it, or are made to conceive it in a very lively manner'.[11] But while it was a useful enough concept for explaining that almost instinctive, unreflecting sympathy we have for the sorrows of others, it was too imprecise and generalized to explain the complexities of so many of our responses to misfortune. Smith illustrated the point with the first of the graphic illustrations for which he was becoming famous, adapted, in this case, from Cicero's discussion of Stoic ethics in *De Finibus*. Smith asks you to imagine yourself in a torture chamber watching your brother on the rack. Pity does not begin to describe the depth and confusion of your response, not least because it does not begin to take account of the sheer difficulty of understanding what your brother is going through.

> Though our brother is upon the rack, as long as we ourselves are at our ease, our senses will never inform us of what he suffers. They never did, and never can, carry us beyond our own person, and *it is by the imagination only* that we can form any conception of what are his sensations

[my italics]. Neither can that faculty help us to this any other way, than by representing to us what would be our own, if we were in his case. It is the impressions of our own senses only, not those of his, which our imaginations copy. By the imagination we place ourselves in his situation, we conceive ourselves enduring all the same torments, we enter as it were into his body, and become in some measure the same person with him, and thence form some idea of his sensations, and even feel something which, though weaker in degree, is not altogether unlike them. His agonies, when they are thus brought home to ourselves, when we have thus adopted and made them our own, begin at last to affect us, and we then tremble and shudder at the thought of what he feels. For as to be in pain or distress of any kind excites the most excessive sorrow, so to conceive or to imagine that we are in it, excites some degree of the same emotion, in proportion to the vivacity or dulness of the conception.[12]

Smith gives us here a striking and rather disturbing account of human relationships. Even those who think they know each other will soon learn that the only access they have to each other's minds is via the perilously uncertain route of the imagination. Once my curiosity has been aroused by my brother's predicament, all I can do is to try to imagine sympathetically what it would be like to be in his shoes. Only when physical reactions set in and I find myself trembling and shuddering at the horrors before me am I able to feel that my sympathetic imagination has got as far as it can for the moment. From the very outset, Smith seems anxious for us to think of ourselves in Humean terms, as agents who can never hope to 'know' each other's minds. All we can do is to use our imagination sympathetically to reach what Hume describes as an 'understanding' of each other. Strictly speaking we are strangers to one another, constantly engaged in the business of trying to know each other better. In this sense the *Theory of Moral Sentiments* would develop as a study of the moral and emotional needs of strangers, and the ways in which they seek to satisfy them. The Rousseaunian question – whether those needs can ever be satisfied in society – is one that would remain with Smith for a very long time.

Like Hutcheson, Smith thought that sympathetic engagement was the function of a seemingly natural curiosity which all human beings have in the fortunes of others. Satisfying this curiosity necessarily involved evaluating the conduct of the person concerned and tacitly or overtly rewarding that person with our approval or disapproval and expressions of affection or dislike. For Smith, this process of evaluation and approbation had everything to do with taste and our sense of *propriety*, our sense of whether an emotion was appropriate to the situation in which the person seemed to be placed. He described it like this:

> When the original passions of the person principally concerned are in perfect concord with the sympathetic emotions of the spectator, they necessarily appear to this last just and proper, and suitable to their objects; and, on the contrary, when, upon bringing the case home to himself, he finds that they do not coincide with what he feels, they necessarily appear to him unjust and improper, and unsuitable to the causes which excite them. To approve of the passions of another, therefore, as suitable to their objects, is the same thing as to observe that we entirely sympathize with them; and not to approve of them as such, is the same thing as to observe that we do not entirely sympathize with them.[13]

In other words, 'I judge of your sight by my sight, of your ear by my ear, of your reason by my reason, of your resentment by my resentment, of your love by my love. I neither have, nor can have, any other way of judging about them.'[14]

Smith was doing more here than analyse our responses to the moral conduct of others: he was developing a theory which would show that moral encounters are two-way affairs, and that my attempt to make sympathetic sense of your conduct is likely to be reciprocated by your attempt to make sympathetic sense of mine. In such a situation, Smith observed, we engage in a process of 'tuning up' or 'tuning down' our responses to each other, exercising those powers of compassion or self-command that will matter so much to his ethics in the hope of developing a relationship in which our sentiments are in 'concord' with each other. In that event I shall find myself not only approving of your sentiments, and feeling affection for you, but I shall be in a position to offer you my sympathy in the hope that you will reciprocate. In that case we shall have reached a supremely pleasurable state of 'mutual sympathy', pleasurable because 'the chief part of human

happiness arises from the consciousness of being beloved'.[15] Smith
has described what may have been a testing and protracted encounter,
for experience has taught us that while mutual sympathy is a source
of pleasure, having our offer of sympathy rejected is painful in the
extreme. It soon becomes clear that the prudent Smithian will do well
to be circumspect in his moral dealings with others and offer only
what he is pretty sure will be accepted and reciprocated. It is little
wonder that Smith once commented, 'Man is an anxious animal.'[16]
We have been shown that morality is a matter of trading sentiments
in the hope of being able to conclude a rewarding emotional deal.
Smith is describing the ways of the moral market and it is with its
principles that his analysis is primarily concerned.

Smith was now ready to stretch the meaning of sympathy far
beyond its conventional bounds. He thought that his theory would
explain our responses to joy as well as sorrow, and even to 'disgust-
ing' anti-social passions like hatred or resentment, commenting that it
was clearly easier to sympathize with joy than with sorrow and with
both rather than with hatred or resentment. This was a simple observation with momentous sociological implications, throwing light on
one of the most striking and important characteristics of any reasonably well-regulated political society – the slavish admiration for the
rich and the powerful on which social deference and political stability
depend. Hume would be absolutely right in describing this principle
as 'the Hinge of your System'.[17] Smith had no hesitation in discussing
the absurd delusions on which deference depends, in terms which
could only reinforce Rousseau's conviction that the civilizing process
corrupted the human personality:

> When we consider the condition of the great, in those delusive colours
> in which the imagination is apt to paint it, it seems to be almost the
> abstract idea of a perfect and happy state. It is the very state which, in
> all our waking dreams and idle reveries, we had sketched out to our-
> selves as the final object of all our desires. We feel, therefore, a peculiar
> sympathy with the satisfaction of those who are in it. We favour all
> their inclinations, and forward all their wishes. What a pity, we think,
> that any thing should spoil and corrupt so agreeable a situation! We
> could even wish them immortal; and it seems hard to us, that death

should at last put an end to such perfect enjoyment. It is cruel, we think, in Nature to compel them from their exalted stations to that humble, but hospitable home, which she has provided for all her children. Great King, live for ever! is the compliment, which, after the manner of eastern adulation, we should readily make them, if experience did not teach us its absurdity.[18]

But the psychological damage inflicted by these delusions did not stop there, for they had the profound and unintended consequence of fuelling the spirit of improvement and competition on which the progress of civilization depended.

It is because mankind are disposed to sympathize more entirely with our joy than with our sorrow, that we make parade of our riches, and conceal our poverty. Nothing is so mortifying as to be obliged to expose our distress to the view of the public, and to feel, that though our situation is open to the eyes of all mankind, no mortal conceives for us the half of what we suffer. Nay, it is chiefly from this regard to the sentiments of mankind, that we pursue riches and avoid poverty. For to what purpose is all the toil and bustle of this world? what is the end of avarice and ambition, of the pursuit of wealth, of power, and preheminence? Is it to supply the necessities of nature? The wages of the meanest labourer can supply them. We see that they afford him food and clothing, the comfort of a house, and of a family. If we examined his oeconomy with rigour, we should find that he spends a great part of them on conveniencies, which may be regarded as superfluities, and that, upon extraordinary occasions, he can give something even to vanity and distinction. What then is the cause of our aversion to his situation, and why should those who have been educated in the higher ranks of life, regard it as worse than death, to be reduced to live, even without labour, upon the same simple fare with him, to dwell under the same lowly roof, and to be clothed in the same humble attire? Do they imagine that their stomach is better, or their sleep sounder in a palace than in a cottage? The contrary has been so often observed, and, indeed, is so very obvious, though it had never been observed, that there is nobody ignorant of it. From whence, then, arises that emulation which runs through all the different ranks of men, and what are the advantages which we propose by that great purpose of human life which we call bettering our condition? To be observed, to be attended to, to be taken notice of with sympathy, complacency, and approbation, are all the advantages which we can propose to derive from it. It is the vanity, not the ease, or the pleasure, which interests us.[19]

The easy sympathy which joy affords us, the shame we feel at allowing our poverty to disturb the sympathetic pleasures of others, has been enough to turn gullible individuals into an ethical herd, as slavishly dependent on the opinions of others as anything Mandeville and Rousseau had described. Worst of all, it was a theory of deference which explained how men became dependent on the unscrupulous as well as on the friends of justice. It was this to which he would return in 1790 in his last thoughts on the *Theory of Moral Sentiments*.

Even now, Smith was ready with more ammunition for the Rousseaunian. Why, he asked, did the citizens of a reasonably stable society think that it was particularly meritorious to obey the rules of justice? What were the origins of the belief that 'we may often fulfil all the rules of justice by sitting still and doing nothing'?[20] The answer was all too simple. In stable societies most people regard those who violated life and property with such horror and abomination that they desist from committing flagrantly unjust acts out of fear of the social as well as the legal consequences. As he put it, 'Every man is, no doubt, by nature, first and principally recommended to his own care; and as he is fitter to take care of himself than of any other person, it is fit and right that it should be so.'[21] However, he has to learn that, 'In the race for wealth, and honours, and preferments, he may run as hard as he can, and strain every nerve and every muscle, in order to outstrip all his competitors. But if he should justle, or throw down any of them, the indulgence of the spectators is entirely at an end. It is a violation of fair play, which they cannot admit of.'[22] As we shall see, Smith was to admit in the second edition of his book that for most people vanity and shame, as well as fear, were probably enough to turn them into law-abiding citizens. But this did not explain the agonies of remorse that many feel when they have acted unjustly, or have even thought of doing so. Smith's illustration of the retribution the ethically sensitive suffer is striking for its horror and psychological acuity. It underlines the violence that the civilizing process has clearly wrought on the personality of many citizens and is one of the most complex and subtle of the 'illustrations' Boswell and others admired so much in Smith's lectures.

The violator of the more sacred laws of justice can never reflect on the sentiments which mankind must entertain with regard to him, without feeling all the agonies of shame, and horror, and consternation. When his passion is gratified, and he begins coolly to reflect on his past conduct, he can enter into none of the motives which influenced it. They appear now as detestable to him as they did always to other people. By sympathizing with the hatred and abhorrence which other men must entertain for him, he becomes in some measure the object of his own hatred and abhorrence. The situation of the person, who suffered by his injustice, now calls upon his pity. He is grieved at the thought of it; regrets the unhappy effects of his own conduct, and feels at the same time that they have rendered him the proper object of the resentment and indignation of mankind, and of what is the natural consequence of resentment, vengeance and punishment. The thought of this perpetually haunts him, and fills him with terror and amazement. He dares no longer look society in the face, but imagines himself as it were rejected, and thrown out from the affections of all mankind. He cannot hope for the consolation of sympathy in this his greatest and most dreadful distress. The remembrance of his crimes has shut out all fellow-feeling with him from the hearts of his fellow-creatures. The sentiments which they entertain with regard to him, are the very thing which he is most afraid of. Every thing seems hostile, and he would be glad to fly to some inhospitable desert, where he might never more behold the face of a human creature, nor read in the countenance of mankind the condemnation of his crimes. But solitude is still more dreadful than society. His own thoughts can present him with nothing but what is black, unfortunate, and disastrous, the melancholy forebodings of incomprehensible misery and ruin. The horror of solitude drives him back into society, and he comes again into the presence of mankind, astonished to appear before them, loaded with shame and distracted with fear, in order to supplicate some little protection from the countenance of those very judges, who he knows have already all unanimously condemned him. Such is the nature of that sentiment, which is properly called remorse; of all the sentiments which can enter the human breast the most dreadful.[23]

It was at this point that Smith was ready to turn the tables on Rousseau by showing that the moral sensibility of the ethically sensitive person had been shaped by some other agency than the opinions of others and in a way that could enhance rather than damage the moral personality. This person had learned the hard way that we cannot please all the people all the time, and was able to see himself as others saw him. He was able, in other words, to view his conduct through the eyes of an impartial spectator, an imaginary 'man within the breast', whose conversation and counsel and whose praise and blame had come to mean more to him than the judgements of friends and acquaintances. Sometimes the voice of this impartial spectator would be judgemental, and sound like the voice of conscience or even of the deity himself. Sometimes it would make it possible for us to think of his judgements as being right and even beautiful in themselves as well as being useful to society. And most gratifying of all to a person who had learned to live his life according to the direction of the impartial spectator, was the feeling that his conduct was right in his own eyes as well as in the eyes of others. As Smith was to put it in the last edition of the *Theory* in one of his most luminous phrases, 'Man naturally desires, not only to be loved, but to be lovely; or to be that thing which is the natural and proper object of love. He naturally dreads, not only to be hated, but to be hateful; or to be that thing which is the natural and proper object of hatred.'[24] In learning how to 'humble the arrogance of [our] self-love, and bring it down to something which other men can go along with', we have taken the first step on the road to a life of virtue.[25] We have learned how to judge our own conduct and how to live independently of the opinions of others. The civilizing process will indeed make us unrecognizable to our former selves, but it will make us the persons we would like to be.

Smith's theory is about the ethical power of the imagination. For what is this impartial spectator who has acquired the power of regulating the ethical behaviour of virtuously minded people, but a figment of the imagination, a fictional embodiment of a moral sensibility

1. The Burgh School, Hill Street, Kirkcaldy, built in 1725, closed in 1743 and demolished in 1964. Smith was a pupil from 1731/2 to 1737.

2–3. Eutropius' *Historiae Romanae Breviarium* was a classic school text in progressive academies in the early eighteenth century. Smith's copy has survived, but the practice signatures on the endpapers hint that he did not think much of the book.

4. Glasgow's much-admired College buildings, many of which were built in the middle decades of the seventeenth century, were only finished in the 1750s, when Smith returned to the college as Professor of Moral Philosophy. John Slezer's print of the college in 1693 from his *Theatrum Scotiae* was brought up to date around 1707 and represents the College as Smith must have known it as a student. The layout of the buildings suggests that they were modelled on those of Oxford or Cambridge and which Smith was to encounter at first hand as a student at Balliol College, Oxford, from 1740 to 1746.

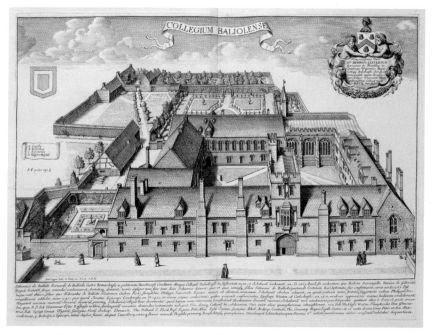

5. Balliol College, in a print from David Loggan's *Oxonia Illustrata* (1675).

6. Smith was fortunate in his teachers at Glasgow. Robert Simson (a print derived from a portrait by Peter de Nune) was Professor of Mathematics from 1711 to 1761, one of the most important mathematicians in contemporary Europe and a leading influence on Smith's thinking about philosophical method.

7. 'The Never to be forgotten Francis Hutcheson' (print derived from a portrait by Allan Ramsay) was a charismatic Professor of Moral Philosophy from 1729 to 1746 who transformed the philosophy curriculum at Glasgow and introduced Smith to the moral philosophy of the ancient and modern worlds.

8. Archibald, Earl of Islay, 3rd Duke of Argyll (1682–1761), the 'Uncrowned King of Scotland' to his contemporaries, was the College's unofficial patron (print based on a portrait by Allan Ramsay). He kept an intelligent and watchful eye on the College's affairs and took a keen interest in its modernizing agenda. His secretary, William Smith, was Adam Smith's guardian.

DAVID HUME

9. David Hume (1711–76) was one of Smith's closest friends and the most powerful influence on his philosophy. This plate, the frontispiece for the 1768 edition of Hume's *Essays and Treatises* and the 1770 edition of his *History of England*, was based on a specially commissioned drawing by an Edinburgh miniature painter, John Donaldson. Hume declared that it was 'the likest that has been done for me, as well as the best Likeness'. His publisher, Andrew Millar, took care to present Hume as historian and philosopher, and it is the complex interplay between the two forms of enquiry that characterizes Hume's and Smith's approaches to the problem of developing a Science of Man.

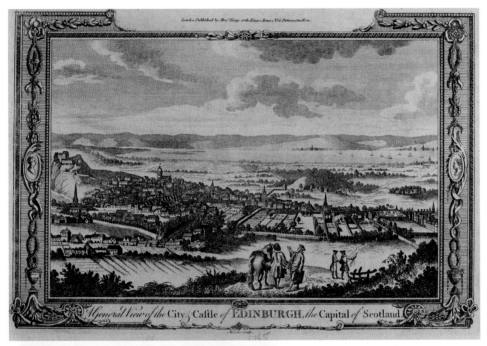

A General View of the City & Castle of EDINBURGH, the Capital of Scotland.

10. An anonymous view of Edinburgh as Smith would have known it in the late 1740s. The city is seen from the south and shows what is now called the Royal Mile from the castle, past the Cathedral to the Palace of Holyrood. In the following decade grandiose plans for developing the city as the modern and enlightened capital of an important province of the British Crown were still only dreams. They were taking shape at the end of Smith's life when he became one of the city's most prominent citizens.

11. David Martin's posthumous portrait of Henry Home, Lord Kames, presents Smith's early patron and Edinburgh's leading cultural entrepreneur in his sometimes arrogant and cantankerous old age.

SMITH AND THE FRENCH MORALISTS

Smith paid close attention to the work of contemporary French moral philosophy when developing his own systems in the 1740s and 1750s. Generally he thought of the work of the French as serious and even brilliant, but conceptually misguided.

12. The abbé E. B. Condillac (1715–78), engraving by G. Volpato, was Smith's target in developing the theory of language which underpinned his rhetoric and his understanding of the process of social exchange.

13. C.-L. de Secondat, Baron de Montesquieu (1689–1755), engraving by A. de Saint-Aubin, published his celebrated *De l'esprit des lois* in 1748. It provided a critical point of reference for the theory of justice Smith developed in his lectures at Edinburgh and Glasgow.

14. J.-J. Rousseau (1712–78), by L.-M. Halbou, gathering herbs. Smith was deeply interested in his thinking but found him to be a theorist who was 'more capable of feeling strongly than of analising accurately'.

15. *View of a Fine Art Exhibition in the Court of Old College*, based on an earlier print by David Allan of 1761, pays tribute to the College's attempt to extend the reach of its teaching to the Fine Arts. The College accommodated the Foulis Academy, and many of the paintings on display and on sale were copies of Old Masters made by its pupils.

16. Robert Paul's *View of the Middle Walk in the College Garden* (1756) is the work of one of the Foulis Academy's alumni whose prints of Glasgow provide a polite and sentimentalized image of Glasgow in its age of Enlightenment.

17. Smith was appointed tutor to the young Duke of Buccleuch in 1763. This appointment, together with the substantial pension it brought, allowed him to resign an onerous professorship that was compromising his time and his health. Smith and Buccleuch became and remained close friends for the rest of Smith's life, Smith acting as one of the Duke's closest advisers and Buccleuch helping to secure Smith a lucrative and honourable appointment as Commissioner of Customs in Scotland. This portrait by Thomas Gainsborough was probably painted to celebrate the Duke's majority in 1767. For the pupil of the greatest philosopher of sentiment in Europe, it is an appropriately sentimental portrait.

18. Hume played a minor part in securing Smith's appointment as tutor to the Duke of Buccleuch and a more significant part in arranging his stay in Toulouse and Paris. He had been appointed secretary to the British Ambassador in 1763 and was lionized by Paris society. He was preparing the ground for Smith's arrival in Paris when he was recalled with the Ambassador in 1765, only weeks before Smith and Buccleuch arrived. Louis Carrogis's portrait of Hume, painted in about 1764, shows him at this Parisian moment of his life.

19. Smith and Buccleuch's Grand Tour took the somewhat unusual step of including Geneva in 1765, a city with a sophisticated intellectual life and the home of both Rousseau and Voltaire (plate of the city taken from Baron Zurlauben's *Tableaux de la Suisse*, *c.* 1780). Rousseau was away but Smith was able to meet Voltaire, whom he greatly admired and whose portrait bust he acquired. Although their conversations were not recorded the meetings were clearly a success. Of Voltaire Smith was to exclaim, 'Sir, there is only one Voltaire,' while Voltaire said of Smith apropos the *Theory of Moral Sentiments*, 'We have nothing to compare with him, and I am embarrassed for my dear compatriots.'

20. Portrait of Voltaire from a drawing by Denon made on 6 July 1775.

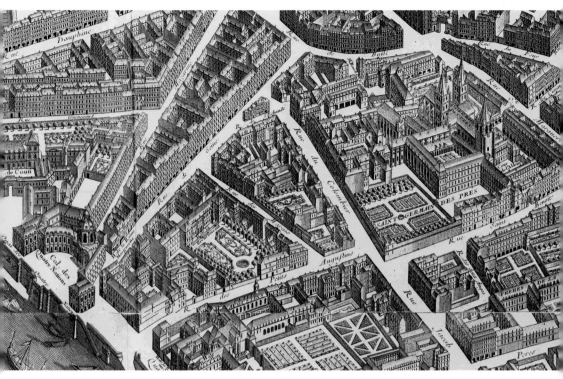

21. When Buccleuch and Smith arrived in Paris in December 1765 they stayed in the rue Colombiers, Saint-Germain, shown here in the Plan de Turgot of 1734–9.

22. François Quesnay (1694–1744) engraved by J.-G. Wille. Quesnay's circle of *économistes* formed the focal point of Smith's intellectual life in Paris when his thinking about political economy was at an important stage of its development. Smith once said that if Quesnay had lived, he would have dedicated the *Wealth of Nations* to him.

23. From 1766 onwards Smith was to be a fairly regular visitor to London, often staying in what had become the Scots' quarter of the City, Charing Cross, here portrayed by Sir John Dean Paul.

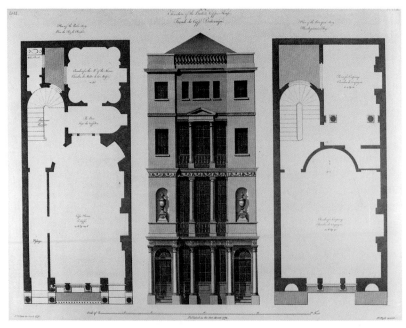

24. The centre of Scottish life was the British Coffeehouse in Cockspur Street, off Charing Cross. This was redesigned and rebuilt in the late 1770s in a notably avant-garde style by Smith's friend the Scottish architect Robert Adam, a symbol, perhaps, of the importance and pretensions of the Scots community in the age of Enlightenment. The building was demolished a century later.

25. On his appointment as Commissioner of Customs in Scotland in 1778, Smith moved with his mother and his cousin Janet Douglas from Kirkcaldy to Panmure House in Edinburgh's Canongate. Mary Elton's *View from the Walk on the Top of Calton Hill* (1820) makes it possible to identify the Canongate Church and its large churchyard (on the extreme right) where his mother probably worshipped and Smith was buried. Panmure House lies in the close immediately to the east of the church.

PHILOSOPHERS

26. Smith and his two celebrated friends the geologist James Hutton and the chemist Joseph Black set up a dining club in Edinburgh which was variously known as the Oyster Club or Adam Smith's Club, as famous in Scotland for its conversation as Samuel Johnson's Club was in London. Hutton and Black feature in James Kay's *Original Portraits* as 'Philosophers'.

27. One of Smith's first acts upon moving to Edinburgh with his mother and cousin was to commission this portrait of his mother, then in her eighties. It is said to be by Conrad Metz, a visiting artist, and has remained in her family's possession ever since. She remained a formidable social presence for the rest of her life, one of Smith's old pupils declaring that the best route to Smith's favour was via his philosophy and his mother. Margaret Smith died in 1784.

28. Smith was notoriously absent-minded. James Kay's caricature shows him wrapped in thought, carrying a nosegay to protect him from Edinburgh's notorious stench, on his way from his house in the Canongate to the Customs House opposite the Cathedral.

29. Smith died in July 1790 and was buried in the Canongate churchyard. He is commemorated by a modest but elegant memorial which stands in striking contrast to the enormous monument Hume commissioned before his death from Robert Adam. It was, Smith declared, 'the greatest piece of vanity I ever saw in my friend Hume'. Smith's own memorial is now sadly decayed. Its simple inscription reads:

HERE ARE DEPOSITED THE REMAINS OF ADAM SMITH,
AUTHOR OF THE THEORY OF MORAL SENTIMENTS
AND WEALTH OF NATIONS. HE WAS BORN, 5th JUNE 1723,
AND HE DIED, 17th JULY 1790.

we have acquired in the course of ordinary life in order to soothe our moral anxieties and help us acquire the pleasing belief that we are ethically autonomous agents? We may like to believe that the voice of the impartial spectator is the eternal voice of conscience or of the deity, but in reality his voice is that of the world to which we belong. The ethical autonomy the impartial spectator offers us is a deception that has the function of rendering us more profoundly sociable than we were when we were in a state of ethical childhood and dependency. Rousseau once famously remarked that while men were born free, everywhere they were in chains. In Smith's view the chains were those of the imagination, chains that could be loosened by a common-sense, sceptical awareness of the processes by which the moral personality was formed, but never altogether thrown off. And while Smith's account of the life of virtue lived under the direction of the impartial spectator might seem to be nothing more than a subtle deception to a Rousseaunian or a Christian, and while this fabric of deception was to trouble him at the end of his life, Smith was to argue that the satisfaction of being able to live sociably under the direction of the impartial spectator was enough for humankind, and enough to encourage the improvement of society and the progress of civilization from the self-evidently wretched condition in which it had hitherto existed.

In the *Theory of Moral Sentiments* Smith offered a powerful conjecture about the nature of the civilizing process, about the ways in which ordinary human beings engaged in the business of ordinary life set out to satisfy their moral needs, and about the way in which some citizens acquire that sense of fitness and ethical beauty which makes it possible for them to aspire to a life of virtue. He could now turn to other divisions of his science of man. In the conclusion to the *Theory of Moral Sentiments* he announced his intention to write a new book, which would 'give an account of the general principles of law and government, and of the different revolutions they have undergone in the different ages and periods of society, not only in what concerns justice, but in what concerns police, revenue, and arms, and whatever else is the object of law'.[26] This was to be the task to which he was to turn in the later years of his academic career at Glasgow. The lectures on jurisprudence were revised, reorganized and furnished with new illustrations. The lectures on police, however, presented different problems. For although they were concerned with the regulation of commerce and were thus a branch of jurisprudence, Smith was becoming increasingly interested in opulence and the general principles on which the nature and progress of opulence depended – questions which belonged to the province of something that was becoming known as political economy. Indeed, it would become clear that until these principles were addressed, it would be impossible to write effectively about the sort of legislation that was appropriate to the regulation of commerce. It was a heavy load and not one which would sit easily with ever-increasing administrative burdens.

8

Professor of Moral Philosophy
at Glasgow, 2. 1759–63

By the end of the summer vacation of 1758, the *Theory of Moral Sentiments* was virtually complete. It was published in late April 1759 in London by Andrew Millar, and shortly after in Edinburgh by Kincaid and Bell, publishers with whom Millar frequently worked. The printer was William Strahan, shortly to become a close friend of Smith and publisher of the *Wealth of Nations*. It was a well-produced, good-looking book which sold for what Millar described as 'a Cheap 6s . . . especially considering the Matter which I am sure is excellent', in a respectably sized edition of a thousand copies, two-thirds of which were destined for the London market, the rest for Edinburgh.[1] Millar and Kincaid bought Smith's copyright for an unknown but probably modest sum, on the assumption that the book would sell and that they would get their money back from subsequent editions. They were right, Millar 'exalting and bragging' that two-thirds of the London edition had sold before publication.[2] It put Smith, who had a perfectionist's love of tinkering, in the gratifying position of being able to plan a revised second edition almost as soon as the first was published. These good London sales were helped by the Scottish literary patronage machine. Hume and two fellow Select Society members, Alexander Wedderburn, the editor of the *Edinburgh Review* and the future Lord Chancellor Loughborough, and John Dalrymple, a good-natured country gentleman, man of letters and protégé of Montesquieu, arranged for copies to be sent to a carefully targeted list of London and London-Scots grandees, including the Earl of Bute, the Duke of Argyll, Lord Mansfield, the Earl of Shelburne and Charles Townshend, the stepfather to the Duke of Buccleuch. Indeed it was said that Townshend decided to offer Smith the job of tutoring his stepson on the strength of reading his book, an offer which came to nothing at the time but was renewed in 1763.

Publication of the *Theory of Moral Sentiments* proved to be an event that would allow its author to relaunch his career as a man of letters. It was an immediate literary success in London as well as in Scotland. John Home, David Hume's cousin and one of Bute's principal London advisers, told William Robertson 'that it is in the hands of all persons of the best fashion; that it meets with great approbation both on account of the matter and stile; and that it is impossible for any book on so serious a subject to be received in a more gracious manner. It comforts the English a good deal to hear that you were bred at Oxford, they claim some part of you on that account.'[3] Hume himself, then in London, turned the business of reporting a successful launch into a merciless tease.

Tho' it has been publishd only a few Weeks, I think there appear already such strong Symptoms, that I can almost to venture to fortell its Fate. It is in short this— But I have been interrupted in my Letter by a foolish impertinent Visit of one who has lately come from Scotland [whose news Hume reports at length]. But to return to your Book, and its Success in this Town, I must tell you— A Plague of Interruptions! I orderd myself to be deny'd; and yet here is one that has broke in upon me again. He is a man of Letters, and we have had a good deal of literary Conversation. You told me, that you was curious of literary Anecdotes, and therefore I shall inform you of a few, that have come to my Knowledge. [And he does, in detail.] But what is all this to my Book? say you. — My Dear Mr Smith, have Patience: Compose yourself to Tranquillity: Show yourself a Philosopher in Practice as well as Profession: Think on the Emptiness, and Rashness, and Futility of the common Judgements of Men: How little they are regulatd by Reason in any Subject, much more in philosophical Subjects, which so far exceed the Comprehension of the Vulgar. *Non si quid improba Roma, Elevet, accedas examenque improbum in illa, Perpendas trutina, nec te quaesiveris extra.* A wise man's Kingdom is his own Breast: Or, if he ever looks farther, it will only be to the Judgement of a select few, who are free from Prejudices, and capable of examining his Work. Nothing indeed can be a stronger Presumption of Falshood than the Approbation of the Multitude; and Phocion, you know, always suspected himself of some Blunder, when he was attended with the Applauses of the Poopulace.

Supposing, therefore, that you have duely prepard yourself for the worst by all these Reflections; I proceed to tell you the melancholy News, that your Book has been very unfortunate: For the Public seem disposd to applaud it extremely. It was lookd for by the foolish People with some Impatience; and the Mob of Literati are beginning already to be very loud in its Praises. Three Bishops calld yesterday at Millar's Shop in order to buy Copies, and to ask Questions about the Author: The Bishop of Peterborough said he had passd the Evening in a Company, where he heard it extolld above all Books in the World. You may conclude what Opinion true Philosophers will entertain of it, when these Retainers to Superstition praise it so highly . . .[4]

And so on! Nearer home, Smith would have been equally gratified to learn that one of his former students, the Rev. James Wodrow, was writing enthusiastically to his friend Samuel Kenrick about a book of which he had more than a glimmering of understanding.

The whole of [its philosophy] stands upon the imagining substitution of ourselves in the place of others which seems to be the foundation of his Sympathy. It is however a most ingenious book. The Language is simple & beautiful; the Painting of the Passions & situations of men admirable. There is a wonderful profusion of Examples to illustrate the different parts of the Theory which seem like so many facts and experiments in Natural Philosophy & seem to confirm & support the Author's principles in the most satisfying manner & I am perswaded these Examples will carry three fourths of the Readers along with them & make them embrace the Principles without further enquiry. To say no more his Morals seem to be pure. The Author seems to have a strong detestation of vice and Love of Virtue & perhaps a regard for Religion at least it does not appear to me that the book has any licentious tendency like the most part of David Hume's writing on those subjects tho perhaps the Principles are at the bottom the same. The Book itself I imagine will go down to Posterity as a fine Composition whatever becomes of the Theory it was intended to introduce & support.[5]

However, in the manse of Stichel, on the Borders, the Rev. George

Ridpath, another of Hume's friends, struck a more critical note. 'I can by no means join in the applauses I have heard bestowed on it.' No doubt the theory was new, but the treatment was diffuse, imprecise and marred by an 'extravagant turn to declaim and embellish' and said in four hundred pages what could have been summarized in twenty.[6] In other words, it was an over-illustrated style of philosophizing of which the minister did not approve.

Smith had interesting early reviewers: Edmund Burke in the *Annual Register* for 1759, and an author who was probably Hume himself in the *Critical Review* of May 1759.[7] Both welcomed the book as an original and accessible contribution to the theory of morals. Burke thought it offered 'a new and at the same time, a perfectly natural road of speculation' about the principles of sympathy and moral approbation, and that it had yielded up 'one of the most beautiful fabrics of moral theory, that has perhaps ever appeared'. Its 'illustrations' were those that only 'a man of uncommon observation' could have supplied.[8] In fact, Burke had already written to Smith to introduce himself and to thank him for having sent a copy of the book; it was the start of a long friendship. Burke understood what Smith was up to very well. '[T]hose easy and happy illustrations from common Life and manners in which your work abounds more than any other that I know by far', he wrote,

> are indeed the fittest to explain those natural movements of the mind with which every Science relating to our Nature ought to begin. But one sees, that nothing is less used, than what lies directly in our way. Philosophers therefore very frequently miss a thousand things that might be of infinite advantage, though the rude Swain treads daily on them with his clouted Shoon [shoes]. It seems to require that infantine simplicity which despises nothing, to make a good Philosopher, as well as to make a good Christian.

To be sure, Smith's generous use of illustrations had made his discussion 'rather a little too diffuse. This is however a fault of the generous kind, and infinitely preferable to the dry sterile manner, which those of dull imaginations are apt to fall into.'[9] For as Burke had correctly noted, it was Smith's illustrations that gave force and credibility to his speculations about the workings of sympathy.

The Humean review in the *Critical Review* provided a strikingly nuanced discussion of the theory of sympathy, 'this spring, this move-ment, this power' in shaping the passions. Once again, Smith was praised for using illustrations which appealed to 'common sense and experi-ence', for writing 'like a man of the world' rather than a pedant and – surely this is a Humean joke – for 'the strict regard which the writer every where preserves to the principles of religion: however some pre-tenders to science may endeavour to separate the philosopher from the lover of religion, it will always be found, that truth being every where uniform and consistent, it is impossible for a man to digest himself of the one character, without renouncing all just claim to the other.'[10] Hume himself had doubts about the theory of sympathy itself which were not discussed in the *Critical Review* essay. Writing to Smith on 28 July he commented, 'I am told that you are preparing a new Edition, and propose to make some Additions and Alterations, in order to obviate Objections . . . I wish you had more particularly and fully prov'd, that all kinds of Sympathy are necessarily Agreeable. This is the Hinge of your System, and yet you only mention the Matter cursorily in p. 20.' And later, 'You say expressly, *it is painful to go along with Grief and we always enter into it with Reluctance*. It will probably be requisite for you to modify or explain this Sentiment and reconcile it to your System.'[11] This was indeed the hinge of Smith's system, but the objection, as it stood, could be fairly easily answered. While it might be easier to sympathize with a person's joy than with his resentment, the emotional bond that is created by a recognition that we are in sympathy with each other is itself necessarily pleasurable. Smith was to add a footnote to this effect in the new edition, telling his friend Gilbert Elliot, 'I think I have entirely discomfitted him.'[12]

Elliot had reservations of a different sort. Like many members of the Scottish literati he was troubled by the sceptical implications of a theory that appeared to reduce the principles of ethics to social ex-perience and popular culture. Indeed, before long Smith's successor in the Moral Philosophy chair, Thomas Reid, and his old patron Henry Home (now Lord Kames), would regard the theory (and Smith's entire theory of morals) as 'a Refinement of the selfish System' of Mandeville.[13] Elliot was a rich, intelligent advocate and MP, a thought-ful Christian and a close friend of Hume, who had sent him the *Dialogues Concerning Natural Religion* in the hope that he would be able to strengthen his presentation of the argument from design, the foundation stone on which most moderate, non-enthusiastical defences of the principles of natural religion were based. Smith was to take Elliot's criticism of his moral theory equally seriously. Although Elliot's letter is missing, Smith's lengthy and belated reply of 10 October makes it clear that, like Reid and Kames, Elliot was worried by the sceptical implications of his theory. Smith replied with a fascinating elaboration of his theory of the impartial spectator, which was included in the revised edition he was preparing. It describes the situation in which we find ourselves when we try to judge our own conduct, aware of the presence of the impartial spectator and feeling like an accused person standing before the 'tribunal within the breast'.

But tho this tribunal within the breast be thus the supreme arbiter of all our actions, . . . tho it can mortify us amidst the Applauses and Support us under the Censure of the world, yet if we enquire into the origin of its institution, its jurisdiction, we shall find, is in a great measure derived from the authority of that very tribunal, whose decisions it so often and so justly reverses. When we first come into the world, being desireous to please those we live with, we are accustomed to Consider what behaviour is likely to be agreeable to every person we converse with, to our parents, to our masters, to our companions. We address ourselves to individuals, and for some time fondly pursue the impossible and absurd project of rendering ourselves universally agreable, and of gaining the good will and approbation of every body. We soon Learn, however, from experience, that this universal approbation is altogether unattainable. As soon as we come to have more important interests to manage, we find, that by pleasing one man we almost certainly disoblige another, and that by humouring an individual, we may often irritate a whole people. The fairest and most equitable conduct must frequently obstruct the interests or thwart the inclinations of particular persons, who will seldome have candour eneough to enter into the propriety of our motives, or to see that our conduct, how disagreable soever to them, is perfectly suitable to our situation. We soon learn, therefore, to sett up in our own minds a judge between ourselves and those we live with. We Conceive ourselves as acting in the presence of a person quite candid and equitable, of one who has no particular relation, either to ourselves, or to those whose interests are affected by our conduct; who is neither father, nor Brother, nor friend, either to them, or to us; but is meerly a man in general, an impartial Spectator who considers our conduct with the same indifference with which we regard that of other people.

To be sure, 'the weak, the vain, and the frivolous' will generally be content to follow public opinion in determining the way in which they choose to lead their lives. But the dutiful, virtuously minded man who wishes to escape from the Rousseaunian ethical jungle, the man who is best fitted for a useful public life, will be the man whose life is always directed by the impartial spectator. For 'it is only by consulting this judge within that we can see whatever relates to ourselves in its proper shape and dimensions, or that we can make any proper comparison between our own interests and those of other men'.[14] Elliot's intervention had elicited from Smith a remarkable portrait of the virtuous Smithian citizen and magistrate – sociable, serious, resourceful and self-reliant, and actually not at all unlike Elliot himself. It was a characterization that was to be the centrepiece of the second, and until the last year of his life, the definitive text of the *Theory of Moral Sentiments*.

There is a footnote to the story of Smith's labours in perfecting an original and provocative system of morals. In 1761 he had published an extended version of his lecture on the origins of language in a little-known and short-lived review called the *Philological Miscellany* under the title 'Considerations Concerning the First Formation of Languages'. One can see why he wanted to do so. His theory of morals and the elaborate discussion of the process of sympathetic exchange on which it was based had presupposed the theory of language on which his theory of rhetoric was based. The theory of language he had presented to his Edinburgh and Glasgow students had been designed to show that language was essentially a vehicle for communication which had a history that was probably as old as civilization. Not only was this a subject of obvious relevance to an understanding of the workings of sympathy, it was also a means of addressing Rousseau's objection that 'not even our new grammarians' (he has Condillac in mind) could convince him that all the complexities of modern grammar could be explained in naturalistic terms.[15] Smith disagreed. His expanded account of the theory of language was designed to show how this could be achieved by using a proper, Humean theory of the imagination. It completed his critique of Rousseau's theory of sociability and was reprinted in the third edition of the *Theory of Moral Sentiments* of 1763 and in every subsequent edition published in his lifetime. It is a pity that more recent editions have not followed suit. As Dugald Stewart commented, it was an essay 'on which the author himself set a high value'.[16]

By the summer of 1759 Smith had other, more immediate reasons for thinking about the practical value of his ethics. He had taken on the task of tutoring Thomas Fitzmaurice, the younger son of a wealthy, intelligent and politically ambitious Anglo-Irish peer, the 1st Earl of Shelburne. The practice of trawling universities for tutors for the sons of great men was common in early modern Europe, and in this Scotland was no exception. The normal practice was for the academic to resign his post and enter the household of his patron. The arrangement between Shelburne and Smith was unusual and, indeed in the case of Glasgow, unprecedented, in that Shelburne decided to send his son to Glasgow as a university student. He wanted him to live with Smith and for Smith to be given 'total charge and direction without any controul' of his education. For all of this, Smith was to be paid at least £100. It was an arrangement brokered by Gilbert Elliot, who was well aware that it had wider significance for the university. 'I have very little doubt, but you might even draw a good many of the youth of this part of the world [he was writing from London] to pass a winter or two at Glasgow, notwithstanding the distance and disadvantage of the dialect, provided that to your real advantages you were to add the best Masters for the exercises [i.e. riding and fencing], and also for acquiring the french language.'[17] The university, which was already developing new ways of civilizing clerical and professional education, was now being invited to civilize the education of the nobility. Smith took Shelburne's instructions at face value. The course of study he prescribed was his and his alone and although he reported his plans for his new pupil in meticulous detail, he never asked the Earl for comments or approval. For his part, Shelburne was deference itself, unfailingly appreciative of every aspect of Smith's teaching and commenting at the start of Fitzmaurice's second year, 'I wish him to stay so long as You, Sir, can endure him under your Eye, and so long as he shall continue worthy of your Attention.'[18] Smith and the head of an important political family had developed a self-consciously 'enlightened' relationship based on the mutual respect in which the philosopher and the man of rank and position held each other.

Fitzmaurice arrived in January 1759, just as the *Theory of Moral Sentiments* was going through the press, and stayed until September 1760 when he left for Oxford to study English law.[19] To start with, Smith thought him a young aristocrat who had acquired 'a somewhat flippant smartness' at Eton. His plans for his education were formidable. From January to May, he was to spend six hours a day at university classes in Latin, Greek, Philosophy and Mathematics and another two to three hours a day being taught privately by Smith. He spent the summer vacation reading ancient and modern moral philosophy with Smith – this included *De l'esprit des lois* – and in taking private mathematics classes with Smith's old professor Robert Simson; by then Fitzmaurice had acquired a taste for mathematics and mechanics. For light relief, he was taken on jaunts to Inverary, to visit the Duke of Argyll and to Edinburgh to meet the literati. The following autumn was spent on philosophy, mathematics and 'history and law', all subjects which required students to attend to the principles of the different systems of thought. As Smith put it in a letter to Shelburne explaining why he thought his son would do well to study civil law with Hercules Lindesay as a preparation for reading English law at Oxford,

> The civil Law is digested into a more regular System than the English Law has yet been, and tho' the Principles of the former are in many respects different from those of the latter, yet there are many principles common to both, and one who has studied the civil law at least knows what a System of law is, what parts it consist of, and how these ought to be arranged: so that when he afterwards comes to study the law of any other country which is not so well digested, he carries at least the Idea of a System in his head and knows to what part of it he ought to refer every thing that he reads.[20]

Fitzmaurice's domestic life was closely supervised and regarded as a sort of education in itself. He does not seem to have mixed much with other students or to have frequented the town. His days revolved around long, private conversations with Smith, which were sometimes of 'the greatest intimacy'.[21] He began to lead a blamelessly simple life, which allowed Smith to record that he 'is perfectly sober, eats no supper, or what is next to none, a roasted apple or some such trifle and drinks scarce any thing but water. There is the more merit in this part of his conduct as it is the effect of Resolution not of habit: for I find he had been accustomed to a different way of living at Eton: But your Lordships and My Lady Shelburnes good advice has, I understand, produced this change.'[22] Smith reported every detail of his financial dealings with his pupil to Shelburne. His pocket money was handed out in exchange for a receipt. He was made to 'pay all his own accounts after he has summed and examin'd them along with me. He gives me a receipt for whatever money he receives: in the receipt he marks the purpose for which it is to be applyed and preserves the account as his voucher, marking upon the back of it the day when it was payed. These shall all be transmitted to your Lordship when there is occasion.'[23] It was an attention to 'Oeconomy' of which Shelburne greatly approved. To judge from Smith's last letter to Shelburne, the eighteen months spent at Glasgow had succeeded in turning a 'very lively, and tolerably ungovernable' sixteen-year-old Etonian into a serious, independent-minded young man with a mind which was 'rather strong and firm and masculine than very graceful or very elegant'. Smith continued:

> No man can have a stronger or a more steady resolution to act what, he thinks, the right part, and if you can once satisfy him that any thing is fit to be done you may perfectly depend upon his doing it. To this excellent disposition he joins a certain hardness of character, if I may call it so, which hinders him from suiting himself, so readily as is agreeable, to the different situations and companies in which he has occasion to act. The great outlines of essential duty which are always the same, you may depend upon his never transgressing, but those little properties which are continually varying and for which no certain rule can be given he often mistakes. He has upon this account little address and cannot easily adjust himself to the different characters of those whom he desires to gain. He had learned at Eton a sort of flippant smartness which, not

having been natural to him at first, has now left him almost entirely. In a few months more it will probably fall off altogether. The real bottom of his character is very grave and very serious, and by the time he is five and twenty, whatever faults he has will be the faults of the grave and serious character, with all its faults the best of Characters.[24]

This was measuring Fitzmaurice's character in Smithian terms against the criteria he had set out in the *Theory of Moral Sentiments* for the man of duty, the budding statesman, who was capable of living his life according to the direction of the impartial spectator.

What is only implied in Smith's letters is that he and Fitzmaurice clearly become genuinely fond of each other. As Boswell and others had noticed, Smith liked students and took them seriously, and Fitz-maurice had no difficulty in treating his old tutor as a friend; his last surviving letter to Smith, written from Oxford in 1762, is a cheerful, badly written, gossipy letter which urges Smith to keep in touch and is signed off, 'With very great sincerity, yours very Affectionately, Tho-mas Fitzmaurice.'[25] A year later David Hume reported from Paris that 'Mr Fitzmaurice, your old Friend' was enthusiastically encouraging an abortive project for translating the *Theory of Moral Sentiments* into French.[26] Unfortunately, Smith's painstaking and time-consuming work preparing Fitzmaurice for public life was a *projet manqué*. After leaving Oxford, he entered Parliament as member for a succession of family seats from 1762 to 1780, dabbled disastrously in the linen industry and suffered a stroke that incapacitated him for life.[27] There is a postscript to the story of Smith's relations with the Shelburne family. Smith made his first trip to London on university business in 1761 in the company of Fitzmaurice's elder brother, the future Prime Minister and 2nd Earl of Shelburne, one of the most thoughtful politi-cians of the age. He told Dugald Stewart,

I owe to a journey I made with Mr Smith from Edinburgh to London, the difference between light and darkness through the best part of my life. The novelty of his principles, added to my youth and prejudices, made me unable to comprehend them at the time, but he urged them with so much benevolence, as well as eloquence, that they took a certain hold, which, though it did not develope itself so as to arrive at full conviction for some few years after, I can fairly say, has constituted, ever since, the happiness of my life, as well as any little consideration I may have enjoyed in it.[28]

By the early 1760s Smith's teaching was attracting attention from abroad. Théodore Tronchin, a fashionable Genevan physician who could count Voltaire and members of the French royal family among his patients, was a leading member of the Genevan literati and an early critic of Rousseau, sent his son to study at Glasgow, thus providing Smith with a useful entrée to Genevan philosophical circles when he was touring Europe with the Duke of Buccleuch in 1765. He also played an important part in the education of two Russian students, Semyon Desnitsky and Ivan Tret'yakov, protégés of Catherine the Great who were being prepared for professorial careers in the newly founded Moscow University. Both took Smith's courses in ethics and jurisprudence and studied civil law with John Millar; both became dedicated Smithians who devoted their subsequent careers to propagating and adapting his ethics and jurisprudence for Russian purposes. Desnitsky was to become a particularly formidable disciple, proposing – though never publishing – a Russian translation of the *Theory of Moral Sentiments*. According to A.H. Brown, his work on jurisprudence, and more particularly his *Proposal Concerning the Establishment of Legislative, Judicial and Executive Authority in the Russian Empire* of 1768, which was dedicated to Catherine, were the work of a jurist who understood the principles of the historical analysis on which Smith had based his jurisprudence very well, and whose thinking was to find its way into questions about monopolies and the principles of taxation which Catherine directed her ministers to address in her *Nakaz* (Instruction) of 1768.[29] Smith's theory of government and police was reaching court circles in Russia a decade before the publication of the *Wealth of Nations*.

All of this was happening at a time when Smith was becoming ever more heavily involved in College business. As Dean of Faculty in 1760–62, he was to be involved in a series of disciplinary cases involving members of the Faculty and was to find himself at the centre of a highly charged constitutional tangle concerning the powers of the Principal and the Rector. His attitude to university administration was essentially managerial in the sense of wanting to make an existing system work, and it was improvement-oriented in the sense that it was directed to developing a system of government based on principles rather than on the whims and interests of its professors.[30] Smith was as scrupulous in his attitudes to precise accounting in managing the university's library and reforming the university's accounting system as he had been in teaching Fitzmaurice the principles of 'Oeconomy'. Most suggestive was his handling of the constitutional crisis that erupted in 1762 over the respective powers of the Principal and Rector. The tangled details do not matter, but Smith's part in attempting to resolve it does. He was assiduous in attempting to mediate between the Principal and the professors and it was he and John Millar who were largely instrumental in drafting the lengthy report to the Rector's Court which proposed means of resolving it. The report, which is dated 12 August 1762, surveyed records concerning the respective powers of the Principal and Rector since the foundation of the university in 1577 in considerable detail, contrasting 'the confused and disorderly manner in which the minutes of all meetings are recorded in the previous century' with modern practice. 'The University had in this respect been no worse that almost all other Courts which have generally subsisted a century or two before they have fallen upon a proper regular and orderly method of preserving the records of their proceedings.' For this, the report commented, the present Professor of Mathematics, Robert Simson, was to be thanked. It was he, as Clerk to the university, 'who introduced order and method into the affairs of the Society in this respect as well as in many others'.[31] It was a report which showed an acute sensitivity to the way in which faulty constitutions could obstruct good government and it emphasized the crucial role that legislation and legislators play in maintaining the machinery of civil government.

It is extraordinary that in spite of working under these pressures, Smith now decided to reorganize his teaching and develop his thinking about government and police. As Dugald Stewart put it,

After the publication of the Theory of Moral Sentiments, Mr Smith remained four years at Glasgow, discharging his official duties with unabated vigour, and with increasing reputation. During that time, the

plan of his lectures underwent a considerable change. His ethical doc-
trines, of which he had now published so valuable a part, occupied a
much smaller portion of the course than formerly: and accordingly, his
attention was naturally directed to a more complete illustration of the
principles of jurisprudence and of political economy.[32]

What is more, as a set of student notes taken in 1763–4 makes clear,
he used his last year at Glasgow to reconstruct his course so as to
bring questions about the duties of government to the fore, and to
establish the central principle on which the economic thinking he was
to develop in the *Wealth of Nations* would be based.

What is known about Smith's jurisprudence in this period is to be
found in two remarkably full sets of student notes, one taken in
1762–3, the other in the following year. The contrast between them is
very striking. The earlier set of notes is as much a monument to Smith's
erudition as to his philosophy, every one of his principles fleshed out
by a lavish use of carefully formulated historical illustrations; the later
set of notes suggest that this illustrative material was drastically
pruned and used schematically to allow the basic principles of Smith's
complex system to appear with greater clarity. What is more, these
later notes show that in the final year of his academic career Smith
reorganized his course in order to emphasize the importance of government in maintaining the rules of justice and fostering the sociable
dispositions of its subjects. The earlier course he had begun with a
natural history of property ownership, because he wished to show
that the means of subsistence and the distribution of property determined the patterns of subordination and power on which the authority of governments and their peoples' sense of justice was based; he
had then gone on to discuss the principles of government and police.
In the later course, however, Smith reversed the order of the first two
sections, beginning with a discussion of the principles of government
and only then going on to discuss the changing state of property in
different forms of society, finishing with a discussion of police. What
may have happened is this.

When Smith gave the original version of his course in Edinburgh in
1750, he cannot have done much more than propose the principles on

which his theory of jurisprudence was based, that our sense of justice is derived from our sympathetic response to the resentment a person feels when the impartial spectator assures us that their person or their property has been unjustly violated. He would have then gone on to show how that sense of justice is shaped by the system of property that operates in a particular form of society, by the social system that is built upon it and, eventually, by the way in which it is governed. It was an approach to the subject that stressed the essentially historical, or as we might say, sociological roots of our understanding of justice. The Smith who had lectured in Edinburgh in 1750 could not possibly have acquired the erudition he was able to call on twelve years later to illustrate his principles. But the weight of this erudition and the lavish use of illustrations could be criticized on the grounds that they strengthened the 'sociological' dimension of the analysis at the expense of the political, a matter of some practical as well as theoretical importance to an enlightened professor concerned with preparing boys for public life. Smith saw the problem very well. As he commented at the beginning of the new version of his course,

> Property and civil government very much depend on one another. The preservation of property and the inequality of possession first formed it, and the state of property must always vary with the form of government. The civilians begin with considering government and then treat of property and other rights. Others who have written on this subject begin with the latter and then consider family and civil government. There are several advantages peculiar to each of these methods, tho' that of the civil law seems upon the whole preferable.[33]

And as if to emphasize the significance of beginning his new course with a discussion of the principles of government, Smith offered a brief critical history in which he highlighted the importance of Hobbes to a proper understanding of natural jurisprudence. For Hobbes was the supreme exponent of a theory of sociability that stressed the importance of sovereign power in making a fearful and egotistical people sociable. The reorganized course, stripped of excessive illustration, was now perfectly designed as a vehicle for helping students to concentrate on the principles and duties of governments in enforcing and improving the rules of justice and in encouraging the progress of opulence. It was a treatise on the principles of legislation in the making, the framework for the book which Smith would begin, but not complete, in the last years of his life.

Smith's jurisprudence lectures, the later version particularly, are a call for a radical rethinking of the principles of government and the sort of governance that was appropriate to a polity with a system of agriculture based on feudal principles of land tenure and a rapidly expanding system of commerce and manufactures. The Humean axioms on which his theory of government was based were introduced and developed briskly; the authority of all governments rested on opinion in the form of the natural respect we have for age, birth, talent and wealth, and was reinforced by our sense of their utility – but 'this principle is fully explained in the Theory of moral Sentiments'.[34] He reminded his students of the cardinal Humean principle that, 'Till there be property there can be no government, the very end of which is to secure wealth, and to defend the rich from the poor.'[35] He offered them a somewhat slimmed down version of his natural history of government from the age of shepherds, through the feudal era to the modern age, in order to demonstrate how different orders of men, the nobility in particular, had used government to preserve their interests and perpetuate their power. It allowed him to demonstrate that the modern system of land tenure was based on the principles of a feudal system which was fundamentally alien to what he called the 'culture of society' in an age of commerce and improvement. And he was able to argue that some of the fundamental provisions of the laws relating to inheritance, like primogeniture, testamentary succession and entail, had more to do with perpetuating the power of the nobility than with facilitating the workings of a market economy. Such questions were frequently discussed by Edinburgh's improvers and went to the heart of contemporary debate of the feudal system and the role of the nobility in Scottish society. While Montesquieu had thought that a landed nobility was the only means of defending a county like France from despotism, Smith was once again insisting that the nobility was always in danger of posing an obstacle to the development of commerce and civility. It was a reminder of the importance of providing them with an enlightened education.

Both versions of the lectures culminated in a discussion of 'police', that self-consciously used neologism he had probably first employed in Edinburgh to consider the problems involved in maintaining what he called the 'cleanliness' and internal security of a state and, above all, 'cheapness or plenty, or, which is the same thing, the most proper way of procuring wealth and abundance'.[36] This was the climax of his jurisprudence and, in a remarkable way, the climax of the curriculum he had been developing. And it is here in the last year of his academic career that it is possible to see a newer project taking shape, a project that would materialize some fourteen years later as the *Wealth of Nations*. This section of the lectures was based on a discussion of the division of labour and its significance for an understanding of the progress of 'opulence' and the principles of improvement. The subject was introduced with some care, with an account of the psychological origins of our sense of improvement. It was a discussion that his students would have realized had its roots in the lectures on rhetoric and belles-lettres and moral philosophy, and it served as a counterpoint to Hume's classic account of commerce and the civilizing process and his own critical engagement with Rousseaunian pessimism.

Nature produces for every animal every thing that is sufficient to support without having recourse to the improvement of the original production. Food, cloaths, and lodging are all the wants of any animal whatever, and most of the animal creation are sufficiently provided for by nature in all these wants to which their condition is liable. Such is the delicacey of man alone, that no object is produced to his liking. He finds that in every thing there is need of improvement. Tho' the practice of savages shews that his food needs no preparation, yet being acquainted with fire he finds that it can be rendered more wholesome and easily digested, and thereby may preserve him from many diseases which are very violent among them. But it is not only his food that requires this improvement. His puny constitution is hurt also by the intemperature of the air he breathes in, which tho' not very capable of improvement must be brought to a proper temperament for his body and an artificial atmosphere prepared for this purpose. The human skin cannot endure the inclemencies of the weather, and even in these countries where the air is warmer than the natural warmth of the constitution, and where they have no need of cloaths, it must be stained and painted to be able to endure the hardships of the sun and rain.[37]

Indeed, Smith continued, in rhetoric which not even the occasional infelicities of student note-taking can disguise, 'The whole industry of human life is employed not in procuring the supply of our three humble necessities, food, cloaths, and lodging, but in procuring the conveniences of it according to the nicety and delicacey of our taste. To improve and multiply the materials which are the principal objects of our necessities, gives occasion to all the variety of the arts.'

> Agriculture, of which the principal object is the supply of food, intro-duces not only the tilling of the ground, but also the planting of trees, the producing of flax, hemp, and inumerable other things of a similar kind. By these again are introduced different manufactures, which are so very capable of improvement. The mettals dug from the bowells of the earth furnish materials for tools, by which many of these arts are prac-tised. Commerce and navigation are also subservient to the same pur-poses by collecting the produce of these several arts. By these again other subsidiary arts are occasioned. Writing, to record the multitude of transactions, and geometry, which serves many usefull purposes. Law and government, too, seem to propose no other object but this, they secure the individual who has enlarged his property, that he may peace-ably enjoy the fruits of it. By law and government all the different arts flourish, and that inequality of fortune to which they give occasion is sufficiently preserved. By law and government domestic peace is enjoyed and security from the forreign invader. Wisdom and virtue too derive their lustre from supplying these necessities. For as the establishment of law and government is the highest effort of human prudence and wis-dom, the causes cannot have a different influence from what the effects have. Besides, it is by the wisdom and probity of those with whom we live that a propriety of conduct is pointed out to us, and the proper means of attaining it. Their valour defends us, their benevolence sup-plies us, the hungry [are] fed, the naked [are] cloathed, by the exertion of these divine qualities. Thus according to the above representation, all things are subservient to supplying our threefold necessities.[38]

Following this philosophical prelude, Smith was ready to introduce the division of labour into the discussion as the central principle on which a philosophical understanding of the progress of opulence depended. It was conventional enough for political theorists to associate the specialization that was characteristic of almost all societies – even the most primitive – with the progress or decline of civilization. It was less conventional, though by no means unknown, for theorists of trade and commerce to reflect on the effects of the division of labour on the manufacturing process; Hume's *Political Discourses* takes this for granted. Smith's remarkable achievement in the *Wealth of Nations* was to show how this experience could be used as the basis for an analysis of the workings of the economy of a nation as a whole and could set the terms in which its government ought to be discussed. Smith was to insist that freeing the market from obstructions was essential for preserving the rules of justice in a free polity. But that was for the future. In the lectures, Smith's primary purposes were to show that 'the division of labour is the immediate cause of opulence' and to explain the principles which regulated it.[39] It was not an organizational principle, which could be introduced by legislators; it was the unintended consequence of principles that were deeply embedded in human nature – the disposition to truck and barter and exchange and 'that principle to perswade which so much prevails in human nature'.[40]

> Man continually standing in need of the assistance of others, must fall upon some means to procure their help. This he does not merely by coaxing and courting; he does not expect it unless he can turn it to your advantage or make it appear to be so. Mere love is not sufficient for it, till he applies in some way to your self love. A bargain does this in the easiest manner. When you apply to a brewer or butcher for beer or for beef you do not explain to him how much you stand in need of these, but how much it would be your interest to allow you to have them for a certain price. You do not adress his humanity, but his self-love.[41]

It was language that would famously resurface in the *Wealth of Nations*.

Smith saw the division of labour as a mechanism for generating opulence whose progress could only be encouraged by removing obstructions that stood in the way of its natural development, and he ended this section of the lectures with a sometimes elaborate survey of some of the main types of obstacle which improvement-minded governments would have to contend with. These ranged from feudal laws of property, taxes, bounties, monopolies and privileges that necessarily affected prices and the workings of the market, and (strikingly, and in considerable detail) a Humean discussion of the fallacy that opulence consists of money, and a discussion of the problems involved in managing the money supply.

Smith had cast his lectures in a language of government which was juristic in origin and designed to call attention to the role of government in encouraging free trade, and by the end of his Glasgow career he was said to have had some success in turning some of the younger Glasgow merchants into free traders.[42] But Smith was still lecturing as an improver who was interested in using the division of labour as a principle that could be used to discuss the problem of improving different types of economic enterprise. At this stage, he did not have a general theory that would explain the workings of the economy as whole and draw the discussion of the interplay of agriculture, manufactures and commerce, country, town and empire, and the workings of international trade into an integrated conceptual whole. Nor did he have a general answer to the provocative question he posed at the end of his lectures – why the progress of commerce in the civilized world had been so slow. He realized that the immediate answer to his question was that in unimproved societies, men lacked the stock they needed to allow them to develop new ways of using their labour, but that begged more general questions about the workings of the economies of pre-commercial forms of society which he was, as yet, in no position to address. In 1762 such a theory was beyond his reach. Nevertheless, as A.S. Skinner and R.M. Meek have shown, in the course of his lectures on the division of labour in April 1763, he seems to have hit on the potential significance of a seemingly simple principle which Hume had taken for granted, that the division of labour is regulated by the extent of the market. As he put it in the final version of his lectures, 'From all that has been said we may observe that the division of labour must always be proportioned to the extent of commerce. If ten people only want a certain commodity, the manufacture of it will never be so divided as if a thousand wanted it.'[43] Once generalized, illustrated and applied he was to use it to analyse the workings of an entity that could properly be described as an economy, and applied to an extraordinary critical account of the entire economic development of modern Europe.

*

By 1763 Smith had developed a system of moral philosophy and a system of jurisprudence that threw new philosophical light on the idea of improvement which lay at the heart of the culture of enlightened Scotland, and in doing so he transformed European jurisprudence. He had shown that commerce and improvement were natural to human beings, a function of their natural indigence, their need for society and their love of the satisfactions improvement brings. He had orchestrated Hume's claim that commerce and the arts of exchange had a natural tendency to make men sociable and had shown that encouraging the progress of the division of labour was the best and surest way of making men sociable and society secure. And he had done all of this as his professorial career at Glasgow was reaching its climax. The university had just recognized its debt to him by awarding him a Doctorate of Laws in October 1762, in recognition of his 'universally acknowledged Reputation in letters and particularly that he has taught jurisprudence these many years in this University with great applause and advantage to the Society'.[44] On the other hand it had also taken a toll on his health. As early as 1753, Hume had warned him that 'the Fatigues of your Class have exhausted you too much, and that you require more Leizure and Rest than you allow yourself'.[45] In 1760 he was clearly in bad shape, run down through overwork and what sounds like recurrent flu. He told Lord Shelburne, only partly jokingly, that his friend and doctor William Cullen had warned him 'that if I had any hope of surviving next winter I must ride at least five hundred miles before the beginning of September'. This was expensive advice, which he took, adding mordantly: 'If, indeed, I run down as fast for these ten days to come as I have done for these ten days past, I think I shall save myself the trouble and My Mother, who is my heir, the expence of following my freinds prescription.'[46] Overwork, signs of physical wear and tear, a vast new philosophical opportunity, and the renewed offer of serious patronage from an important Scottish family convinced Smith that it was time to move on. A year later, on 8 November he resigned, to take up an appointment as tutor to the young Duke of Buccleuch.

9

Smith and the Duke of Buccleuch
in Europe 1764–6

The success of the *Theory of Moral Sentiments* had not only made Smith's philosophical reputation in Scotland and beyond; it had established his reputation as a teacher of the first rank, and was to play its part in ending his academic career. In April 1759, Hume had reported that Charles Townshend, the young Duke of Buccleuch's stepfather and guardian, 'is so taken with the Performance, that he said to Oswald he wou'd put the Duke of Buccleugh under the Authors Care, and woud endeavour to make it worth his while to accept of that Charge'. Hume wanted Townshend to follow Shelburne's example by sending Buccleuch to Glasgow, 'For I coud not hope, that he coud offer you any Terms, which woud tempt you to renounce your Professorship: But I missd him.'[1] Nothing happened, but the offer was serious and was soon to be revived.

Townshend was one of the most glamorous and ambitious politicians of his generation, a brilliant House of Commons orator of whom great things were expected. His marriage to Buccleuch's mother, the Countess of Dalkeith, in 1755 meant that he was now closely connected with a family with vast estates in Scotland and England and was in a position to use his marriage and his connection with the young Duke to bolster his own political position. Townshend and the Countess made their first visit to Scotland in the summer of 1759 and did it in style, holding large and lavish weekly receptions at Dalkeith Palace for the Scottish establishment and the Edinburgh literati. Townshend was amusing and good company, even though he was apt to put his foot in it, on one occasion gratuitously offending straitlaced opinion by making fun of the king. The Select Society elected him a member in order to hear his famous oratory, only to find that 'Like a Meteor Charles Dazzled for a Moment, But the Brilliancy soon faded away, and left no very strong Impression', as Alexander Carlyle put it.[2] It was during this visit that Smith first met him. He seems to have agreed in principle to tutor Buccleuch when he was older; he was thirteen at the time and had only just begun to settle down at Eton. And to show his willingness, Smith agreed to order a small collection of thirty-one Latin and Greek texts to prepare the boy for his future education. The collection was notable for the number of literary and historical texts Smith prescribed, in addition to appropriate texts on ethics. A menu of Homer, Virgil, Aeschylus, Euripides and Theophrastus, as well as Cicero, Marcus Aurelius and Epictetus – one copy of the latter in large print, the other a pocket edition – was a diet of literary as well as Stoic and Ciceronian texts to sensitize the Duke to questions about character and public duty in an imperfect world. Smith also took care to include in the collection the sumptuous and expensive Foulis Press edition of Homer, one of the glories of modern Scottish editing and book production.[3]

Townshend renewed his offer on 25 October 1763. His tone was friendly, serious and businesslike. This time there was no talk of the Duke becoming a student at Glasgow.

Dear Sir,

The time now drawing near when the Duke of Buccleugh intends to go abroad, I take the liberty of renewing the subject to you: that if you should still have the same disposition to travel with him I may have the satisfaction of informing Lady Dalkeith and His Grace of it, and of congratulating them upon an event which I know that they, as well as myself, have so much at heart. The Duke is now at Eton: He will remain there until Christmass. He will then spend some short time in London, that he may be presented at Court, and not pass instantaneously from school to a foreign country; but it were to be wished He should not be long in Town, exposed to the habits and companions of London, before his mind has been more formed and better guarded by education and experience.

I do not enter at this moment upon the subject of establishment, because if you have no objection to the situation, I know we cannot differ about the terms. On the contrary, you will find me more sollicitous than yourself to make the connection with Buccleugh as satisfactory and advantageous to you as I am persuaded it will be essentially beneficial to him.

The Duke of Buccleugh has lately made great progress both in his knowledge of ancient languages and in his general taste for composition. With these improvements his amusement from reading and his love of instruction have naturally increased. He has sufficient talents: a very manly temper, and an integrity of heart and reverence for truth, which in a person of his rank and fortune are the firmest foundation of weight in life and uniform greatness. If it should be agreeable to you to finish his education, and mould these excellent materials into a settled character, I make no doubt but he will return to his family and country the very man our fondest hopes have fancied him.

I go to Town next Friday, and should be obliged to you for your answer to this letter. I am, with sincere affection and esteem, dear sir, your most faithful and most obedient humble servant,

C. Townshend.

Lady Dalkeith presents her compliments to you.[4]

Townshend's terms were extremely generous – a salary of £500 to be followed by an annual pension of £300 for the rest of his life, as compared with Smith's professorial income of between £150 and £300 per year. Moreover, as Townshend had indicated and as Smith was to find to his considerable profit, the Buccleuch connection would help to pave the way to public office, a well-paid place on the Scottish Customs Board. It was not an offer to be refused. Smith accepted promptly and unequivocally, warning the university on 8 November of his intention to resign his professorship. As he told Hume, the only outstanding problem was finishing his current jurisprudence course. The matter was quickly resolved in the conventional manner by arranging for his assistant, Thomas Young, a young man from Fife about whom nothing is known, to stand in for him.

Smith's career as a university teacher ended with a pleasing incident. He was determined repay the fees he thought he owed his students for not completing the course. The students would have none of it.

But Mr Smith was not to be bent from his purpose. After warmly expressing his feelings of gratitude, and the strong sense he had of the regard
shewn to him by his young friends, he told them, this was a matter betwixt
him and his own mind, and that he could not rest satisfied unless he performed what he deemed right and proper. 'You must not refuse me this
satisfaction. Nay, by heavens, gentlemen, you shall not;' and seizing by the
coat the young man who stood next to him, he thrust the money into his
pocket, and then pushed him from him. The rest saw it was in vain to
contest the matter, and were obliged to let him take his own way.[5]

He left for London in January 1764. It was a clean break with his
academic past, underlined by his refusal to take part in the hotly con-
tested election to appoint his successor, and in spite of cries for help
from old friends like William Cullen and John Millar who feared that
his chair and much he had stood for would be undermined by the
appointment of the favourite and successful candidate, Thomas Reid,
Hume's most powerful and influential critic. Smith would not return
to Glasgow until 1784.

Smith met his new pupil for the first time in London and they travelled together to France, arriving in Paris on 13 February. It was the
start of a genuinely close friendship that was to last for the rest of
Smith's life. After Smith's death Buccleuch told Dugald Stewart, 'In
October 1766, we returned to London, after having spent near three
years together, without the slightest disagreement or coolness on my
part, with every advantage that could be expected from the society of
such a man. We continued to live in friendship till the hour of his
death; and I shall always remain with the impression of having lost a
friend whom I loved and respected, not only for his great talents, but
for every private virtue.'[6] Like Smith's previous student Thomas Fitzmaurice, Buccleuch was an Etonian, but he had none of the cockiness
and self-assurance Smith had found in his earlier aristocratic pupil.
His childhood had not been happy, having been 'almost neglected by
my mother, [and] neglected in every respect as to my learning' by the
masters of his first school. He might have added that he had grown up
in the shadow of two notably assured and self-confident siblings. It
was Townshend who had insisted on sending him to Eton and, the
Duke wrote, 'I must confess, however little I was afterwards obliged

to him, he then did me a service that amply made up for every future inattention to my affairs.'[7] Buccleuch actively distrusted his step-father's plans for turning him into a 'hereditary senator' who would be able to enter national politics under his direction. It must have been disappointing that Townshend had not taken the obvious step of ask-ing his stepson's much-liked Eton tutor to take him on the Grand Tour and he probably regarded the appointment of an academic grandee like Smith with some apprehension.[8]

Smith's appointment did not pass without comment in Edinburgh, for while no one doubted his ability as a professor there were ques-tions to be asked about his suitability as a mentor for a young noble-man who had to be groomed in the courtly skills expected of his rank. Smith's French was poor and his manners were decidedly awkward. Carlyle thought he 'still appear'd very unfit for the intercourse of the World as a Travelling Tutor', and the lawyer and antiquarian Sir David Dalrymple agreed, commenting that 'Mr Charles Townshend will make a very indifferent *compagnon de voyage* out of a very able pro-fessor of ethics. Mr Smith has extensive knowledge and in particular has much of what may be termed constitutional knowledge, but he is awkward and has so bad an ear that he will never learn to express himself intelligibly in French.'[9] Even David Hume thought it worth warning his friend the Comtesse de Boufflers that 'his sedentary recluse life may have hurt his air and appearance, as a man of the world'.[10]

But Buccleuch's character mattered much more to Townshend than his manners and, like Shelburne, he was convinced that Smith was the right man to make a statesman of his stepson, a point he underlined in June 1765.

Mr. Smith, among many other advantages, possesses that of being deeply read in the constitution & laws of your own country: he is ingenious, without being over-refin'd; he is general, without being too systematical in his notions of our government, and from him, you will grow to be a grounded politician in a short course of study. When I say a politician, I do not use the word in the common acceptance, but rather as a phrase less severe, for that reason more proper to your age, than statesman, tho' the one is the beginning of the other, and they dif-fer chiefly as *this* is the work of study, & *that* the same work finish'd by experience & a course of office. Mr Smith will make you a politician, and time will afterwards, in your example, demonstrate the truth of my opinion.[11]

Toulouse, the second city of France, was chosen as a suitable place for the intensive education Smith and Townshend had in store for the Duke for the next eighteen months. It was a choice almost certainly made with the advice of Hume, and his kinsman, the Abbé Colbert, Vicar-General of Toulouse, who undertook to introduce them to local society and probably to arrange suitable accommodation. Thereafter, Smith was to accompany his pupil to Geneva, Paris and Germany. By then, the Duke would have reached his majority and be ready to take up personal management of his estates and his career and Smith would have become a close friend and mentor who had introduced him to a much more congenial conception of the public role of a great territorial magnate than his stepfather had been able to do. Luckily for the Duke, Townshend died suddenly in 1767, and with his death, plans to turn Buccleuch into a statesman perished.

Smith could not have made his first and only visit to Europe at a more interesting moment. The Seven Years War, which had been brought to a conclusion in 1763 by the treaty of Paris, had resulted in the loss of much of France's colonial empire, had inflicted incalculable damage on the French economy, and had raised difficult questions about the management of the country's public finances and the principles of French government itself. It was only natural that a politician with a serious interest in public finance like Townshend should have urged Smith and Buccleuch to pay particular attention to recent French history and to the all-important question of how 'this insidious & vast Monarchy, so enormous in it's extent, at the completion, as it should seem, of it's ambitious plan, renowned in arms, formidable in Navy, & flourishing in Commerce, should have been found, in the last minute of decisive trial, a monster in size & Proportion, weak from that very size, and by some secret error in it's constitution, the most incapable power by land & sea that modern Times have exhibited'.[12]

Toulouse was an excellent vantage point from which a critical Scottish observer could view the progress of civilization in contemporary

France. It was the sort of city that anyone who knew Edinburgh could understand. Its social, professional and political life was dominated by lawyers and the parlement of the surrounding province, an elite and an institution which were gaining a reputation for fostering improvement and politeness in a city renowned for being 'one of the most super-stitious in Europe', as Pierre Bayle once described it.[13] The Jesuits had been expelled in 1762, the same year that had seen the appointment of the notably free-thinking and ambitious Loménie de Brienne to the archbishopric. The new archbishop was a friend of *philosophes* such as Turgot, Morellet and d'Alembert, a habitué of the leading Paris salons and the owner of a magnificent library of books on politics, trade and public finance; Smith must have looked forward to meeting him and must have hoped for access to his library. There were other signs of improvement to catch the visitor's attention. Toulouse was a university city with a well-known Faculty of Law, three royal acade-mies and ambitious plans for urban redevelopment on neo-Palladian lines. Most striking of all, it was a city that had seen the construction of the Canal des Deux Mers in the later seventeenth century, linking the Atlantic to the Mediterranean and, by the mid-eighteenth century, serving to stimulate the agricultural economy of the Midi Toulousain. Smith approved of the provisions that had been made for the upkeep of this enormous project. The engineer who had built the canal and his family had been allowed to keep the income from tolls in exchange for bearing the cost of maintaining it. While this had made them rich they now had 'a great interest to keep the work in constant repair. But had those tolls been put under the management of commissioners, who had no such interest, they might perhaps have been dissipated in ornamental and unnecessary expences, while the most essential parts of the work were allowed to go to ruin.'[14]

But for all these signs of improvement, these nods towards com-merce and politeness had only penetrated the surface of Toulousian culture by 1764. In 1762 Jean Calas, an entirely innocent Protestant merchant, had been broken on the wheel, hanged and burned for a murder he did not and could not have committed, after a trial which demonstrated the depth of local religious fanaticism and the vulner-ability of the province's courts and parlement to religious pressure. It was an atrocity that shocked Europe and was the occasion of one of

Voltaire's most memorable pamphlets. Calas' last words were remembered by Smith in the last edition of the *Theory of Moral Sentiments* as those of a man who had suffered the 'most cruel misfortune which it is possible for innocence to suffer'.[15] There must have been moments when Smith, Hume and Townshend wondered whether the city would be a suitable place for Buccleuch's education. What was equally striking, if less appalling, was Toulouse's long-standing reputation as a city without a commercial ethos or much of a will to develop one. In 1742 the Bourse des Marchands had claimed that the city 'is not a commercial town' and owed its standing and character to 'the multitude of lawyers', to the service industries, the network of guilds and corporations in which they were enmeshed, and 'the love of repose, the horror of work, the refusal to take trouble [*l'eloignement de toute peine*]' that Louis de Mandran thought characterized the local labour force.[16] What must also have caught Smith's attention at the time the tour was being planned was the crisis which was developing in relations between the French parlements and the Crown in the aftermath of the Seven Years War. The Toulouse parlement had been at the forefront of resistance to the Crown's attempt to triple the notorious tax, the Vingtième, in 1763, had seen the city occupied by royal troops, and was still engaged in a long and acrimonious quarrel with the Crown when Smith and Buccleuch arrived. Smith was to collect the voluminous pamphlet literature the quarrel provoked and send it back to Scotland: taxation and the pressure of war on public finances was and would remain of central importance to his political economy.

The visit seems to have got off to an unpromising start. The archbishop was in Paris and seems to have stayed there for the period of Smith and Buccleuch's visit. Worse still, as Smith told Hume in July 1764,

Mr Townshend assured me that the Duke de Choiseul was to recommend us to all the people of fashion here and everywhere else in France. We have heard nothing, however, of these recommendations and have had our way to make as well as we could by the help of the Abbé [Colbert] who is a Stranger here almost as much as we. The Progress, indeed, we have made is not very great. The Duke is acquainted with no french man whatever. I cannot cultivate the acquaintance of the few with whom I am acquainted, as I cannot bring them to our house and am not always at liberty to go to theirs. The Life which I led at Glasgow was a pleasurable, dissipated life in comparison of that which I lead here at Present. I have begun to write a book in order to pass away the time.[17]

Whether or not that book was the *Wealth of Nations* remains a matter of controversy and speculation. What Smith's comment does suggest, however, is that he had decided that it was time to pull together some of the thinking about jurisprudence, police and political economy he looked forward to discussing with François Quesnay and his circle of *économistes* in Paris.

As far as the Duke was concerned, all of this meant a life of hard work and, initially at any rate, relative social isolation. As Fitzmaurice had discovered at Glasgow, the cardinal principle of Smith's teaching was 'inspection and controul', and an educational regime which Smith confessed had been designed 'rather to oppress him with business for this first winter; it keeps him constantly employed and leaves no time for idleness.' In Buccleuch's case, this probably meant private reading supplemented by intensive discussion based on Smith's Glasgow moral philosophy and jurisprudence courses, and regular 'exercises' in riding and fencing with local tutors. In his second year, Smith had introduced Fitzmaurice to law and politics and he clearly followed the same practice with Buccleuch, introducing him to Montesquieu's *De l'esprit des lois* and to Hume's *History of England* for the light they shed on the constitutions of France and Britain, on the increasing militarization of modern Europe and on the extraordinary collapse of French power in the Seven Years War. As an expert on public finance, Townshend was delighted with Buccleuch's essay on the French constitution and seems to have encouraged him to pay particular attention to the tax system. What Buccleuch did not mention, and what Smith must have discussed with him, were Montesquieu's controversial views about the importance of the French aristocracy to the future of the French monarchy. It was out of discussions like these that the Duke must have begun to develop a more modest, less party-political conception of his future role as a great territorial magnate, one which was based on an appreciation of the economic and moral importance of the territorial nobility and their role as agents of improvement.

This was to be part of the bedrock on which his long and enduring friendship with Smith was to be based.

For all that, Toulouse was initially a lonely place for the Duke. With Hume's help Smith set out to lighten the load by persuading Buccleuch's brother Campbell Scott and an old Eton friend, Sir James Macdonald of Sleat, to join them in the autumn. By then things had begun to settle down. Smith and Buccleuch had begun to make their way in Toulousian political society and there were trips to Bordeaux and to Montpellier to attend debates in the local parlements. In April 1765 Townshend gave Buccleuch permission to move to Paris, provided 'the same Study & the same exercises' were continued. By then Smith was able to report 'a great change upon the Duke. He begins now to familiarize himself to French company and I flatter myself I shall spend the rest of the Time we are to live together, not only in Peace and contentment but in gayety and amusement.'[18] After a short summer tour of the south of France and the Pyrenees with Scott and Macdonald, the two set out for a two months' visit to Geneva before arriving in Paris in December 1765.

The choice of Geneva as an appropriate if somewhat unusual city for a two-month visit suggests that Smith also had a hand in the planning of the tour. The father of one of his former pupils, François-Louis Tronchin, was a leading citizen, an important member of the local literati and a royal physician to the French Court; Geneva was also, of course, the city of Rousseau and of Voltaire. Once again, the city presented Smith and Buccleuch with an interesting political situation on which to reflect. The city-state's constitution was essentially aristocratic and was currently being challenged by citizens who wished to broaden its political base; again, there was much to consider about the role of aristocracies in the management of modern states. Théodore Tronchin gave Smith and Buccleuch easy access to Genevan literary and academic society at a time when the Calvinist intelligentsia were taking a particular interest in Scottish philosophy, history and medicine.[19] Within the space of a few weeks, Smith had been introduced to leading members of Geneva's government and to professors like George Le Sage, who was interested in Joseph Black's theory of latent heat, and Charles Bonnet, both of whom were intrigued by Smith's friendship with a notorious sceptic like Hume. More importantly,

Tronchin was able to introduce Smith to the literary circle of his patient, the Duchesse d'Enville, the mother of the Duc de La Rochefoucauld, another young aristocrat who took to Smith, planned an abortive translation of the *Theory of Moral Sentiments* and remained in regular contact with him for the rest of his life. Mme d'Enville was an important contact. A highly intelligent woman, she was a close friend of Turgot and was to be valuable in preparing the ground for Smith's hugely successful introduction to French salon society and to the *économistes*. Rousseau was not in Geneva at the time and, indeed, Smith never seems to have met him. Voltaire was, however, and at one of their meetings he and Smith discussed the volatile relationships that were developing between the Court and the provincial parlements and Estates.[20] Smith, who owned a fine bust of the great man, admired Voltaire unreservedly and was reported as making the deeply Humean observation that 'the ridicule and the sarcasm which he so plentifully bestowed upon fanatics and heretics of all sects have enabled the understanding of men to bear the light of truth, and prepared them for those inquiries to which every intelligent mind ought to aspire. He has done much more for the benefit of mankind than those grave philosophers whose books are read by a few only. The writings of Voltaire are made for all and read by all.'[21] It is a reminder that the *Theory of Moral Sentiments*, the *Wealth of Nations*, and indeed Smith's entire project for a modern science of man were built on the foundations of the Enlightenment's quintessential assault on religion.

Smith and Buccleuch left Geneva in the late autumn of 1765 and arrived in Paris at Christmas for the most important stage of the Duke's educational tour. They took up residence in the Hôtel du Parc-Royal in Saint-Germain, near the British Embassy, their home for the next nine months. The ambassador, the Earl of Hertford, launched the Duke at Court and in diplomatic society, and Townshend told Buccleuch that he expected David Hume would introduce him to literary society and to 'men of the world, [who] are therefore the most useful society to you, who must be one, & ought to be the other, of these characters'.[22] No visitor could have looked forward to a more glamorous introduction to French intellectual society than the one Hume was able to offer. He had been Hertford's secretary in Paris since 1763, enjoying the cachet that a diplomatic post and a decent salary provided, as well as the reputation his *Political Discourses* and the *History of England* were making for him. What had surprised him were the unexpected joys of being lionized, an experience he reported in detail to Smith and his Scottish friends. 'Can I ever forget,' he wrote to Smith in October 1763, reflecting on the churlish reception so much of his writing had received in Edinburgh and London, 'that it is the very same Species, that wou'd scarce show me common Civilities a very few Years ago at Edinburgh, who now receive me with such Applauses at Paris?'[23] Two years later, when Smith was in Toulouse, Hume was even speculating on the possibility of settling in Paris, a proposal which alarmed Smith enough to provoke an unexpectedly sharp and prompt reply:

A man is always displaced in a forreign Country, and notwithstanding the boasted humanity and politeness of this Nation, they appear to me to be, in general, more meanly interested, and that the cordiality of their friendship is much less to be depended on than that of our own countrymen. They live in such large societies and their affections are dissipated among so great a variety of objects, that they can bestow but a very small share of them upon any individual. Do not imagine that the great Princes and Ladies who want you to live with them make this proposal from real and sincere affection to you. They mean nothing but to gratify their own vanity by having an illustrious man in their house, and you would soon feel the want of that cordial and trusty affection which you enjoyed in the family of Lord and Lady Hertford.[24]

By then, however, Hume's Parisian days were numbered. Hertford had been recalled in order to be posted to Dublin as Lord Lieutenant, Hume remaining his secretary. It was a move that would have earned Hume a handsome salary but 'it is like stepping out of Light into Darkness to exchange Paris for Dublin'.[25] Although Hertford's posting was cancelled, he returned to London with Hume, leaving Smith with the task of launching himself and his pupil on Parisian society without the direct assistance of a celebrated intellectual ambassador.

Not that Smith need have worried. Hume had taken care to advertise the visit well in advance and, anyway, Smith himself was not unknown. The *Theory of Moral Sentiments* had been well received in Paris, although it and had been published in French in a bad translation by one of the Baron d'Holbach's circle in 1764. To make matters worse it had been given a new, unhelpfully Jansenist title, *La Métaphysique de l'âme*, which encouraged French readers to discuss its theological failings as much as its generally acknowledged strengths in exploring the aetiology of the sentiments. But Smith's visit was taking place at a moment when Scottish philosophy and letters were becoming fashionable despite the vicissitudes of his own translation. The first poems of Ossian, published in 1762 and 1765, were proving to be as much of a *success de scandale* in Paris as they were in London and Edinburgh, and Lord Kames' *Elements of Criticism*, in which he had dared to criticize Voltaire's *Henriade*, had evoked the author's caustic response.

> It is a wonderful result of the progress of human culture, that at this day there come to us from Scotland rules of taste in all the arts, from epic poetry to gardening. Every day the mind of man expands, and we ought not to despair of receiving ere long treatises on poetry and rhetoric from the Orkney isles. True it is, that in this country we still prefer to see great artists than great discourses upon the arts.[26]

Smith's reception in Paris was to be almost as momentous as Hume's. Before long he had become a habitué of the leading salons, including those of the Duchesse d'Enville, Mme Geofrin, Mme de l'Espinasse, Mme de Grouchy, and Hume's old friend the Comtesse de Boufflers. Here, in a milieu in which intelligent women had discussed sentimental ethics and literature since Marivaux's day, much of the discussion of the *Theory of Moral Sentiments* took place. The Comtesse, who once idly wondered whether she should attempt a new and better translation of the book, thought that Smith's theory of sympathy seemed set fair to supplant Hume's scepticism as the fashionable opinion of female society.[27] Smith also had easy access to the world of the *philosophes* at d'Holbach's weekly dinners, at Claude-Adrien Helvétius's house and with Quesnay's circle in Paris or at Versailles (Quesnay was a royal physician). He made friends with Turgot, Morellet, Necker, d'Alembert, Marmontel and Mme Riccoboni, one of the most fashionable of contemporary novelists.[28] Never before and never again would he have a fuller and easier social life. As Rae points out, in one week in July, Smith was with Mme de L'Espinasse on the 21st, the Comtesse de Boufflers on the 25th and Baron d'Holbach on the

27th.[29] His servant's inventory of his wardrobe suggests that he began to dress rather expensively.[30] In a later essay he was to recall that he had become a keen theatre- and opera-goer, who used his time in the theatre to reflect on the arts of theatrical and vocal performance. Gossips had it that he even embarked on an inconclusive romance.[31]

What mattered most, however, were his meetings with Quesnay and his circle, 'the most intelligent men in France'.[32] For the *économistes* Smith was an unknown quantity, 'a judicious and simple man, but one who had not yet proved his worth', as Du Pont de Nemours put it[33]; a friend of Hume who had a brilliant and currently fashionable system of moral philosophy to his credit, and a system of political economy in gestation that addressed many of the *économistes* own concerns but did so in ways which were puzzlingly different to theirs. Smith's knowledge of Quesnay's work was equally incomplete. He had first got to know of him in the late 1750s through the *Encyclopédie* articles on 'Grains' and 'Fermiers', which had advocated free trade in grain and laid the foundations of Quesnay's classic claim that land was the sole source of a nation's wealth. Quesnay had developed these principles in highly abstract terms in his *Tableaux économiques*, which had been printed in 1758–9 in editions designed for a strictly limited readership and were probably unknown in Glasgow. When Smith first met the *économistes* in 1766, they were working on the wider conceptual and political implications of Quesnay's system, a development which was heralded in 1767 by the publication of the Marquis de Mirabeau's *Rural Philosophy* and continued in Quesnay's *Physiocratie* of the same year, and a series of publications by Turgot, Du Pont de Nemours and La Mercier de la Rivière which were either in preparation or production.[34] Smith was, in fact, in the extraordinary position of being able to witness at first hand the development of the only other great system of political economy of the Enlightenment to his own.

For all his shocking French, awkward manner and serious intellectual reservations about their system, Smith got on well with Quesnay and his circle, and his extended critique of them in the *Wealth of Nations* was to be notable for its friendliness as well as its severity. Quesnay, who presented Smith with a copy of his *Physiocratie*, was 'a man of the greatest modesty and simplicity' who was held in as much reverence by his disciples as 'any of the antient philosophers for the founders of their respective systems'[35]; Mirabeau was 'a very diligent and respectable author'[36]; and Turgot, he told Hume, was 'a friend every way worthy of you'.[37] For his part, Smith was to speak of the *économistes*' system 'with all its imperfections [as], perhaps the nearest approximation to the truth that has yet been published upon the subject of political oeconomy, and is upon that account well worth the consideration of every man who wishes to examine with attention the principles of that very important science'.[38] He actually told Dugald Stewart that had Quesnay lived to see the publication of the *Wealth of Nations*, it would have been dedicated to him.[39] It is language that contrasts strikingly with Hume's, who hoped that the Abbé Morellet would 'thunder them [the *économistes*], and crush them, and pound them, and reduce them to dust and ashes!' in his forthcoming *Dictionnaire du commerce*. 'They are, indeed,' Hume exclaimed, 'the set of men the most chimerical and most arrogant that now exist.'[40] It was a view with which Smith would become increasingly sympathetic at the end of his life.

Stewart thought that Smith took the *économistes*' system seriously because it helped him to clear his mind about his own, but there is surely more to it than that. His introductions to Condillac, Montesquieu and Rousseau had been encounters with systems of philosophy he took seriously but found fundamentally flawed. His introduction to Quesnay's system of economics was another such encounter. At one level they spoke the same language. They both discussed the wealth and revenue of a state in terms of its ability to satisfy the needs and desires of its inhabitants. They both thought that in one of Hume's 'enormous' European monarchies, the business of satisfying these needs and desires was a matter of using agricultural surpluses to maintain those who were not employed on the land, and they both argued that the long-term revenue and power of a state and the happiness of its people would depend on its ability to sustain a sufficiently high level of agricultural production to maintain a system of commerce and manufactures. And they both agreed that the best way of achieving this end was by removing obstacles to the free exchange of goods, services and sentiments. Indeed, the point of the highly abstract argumentation in Quesnay's *Tableaux* was to show how, in a developed economy, wealth generated by agriculture would naturally circulate through the different sectors of an economy in ways which would naturally increase the revenue of the sovereign and the wealth of his people.

The *économistes* claimed that they were developing a general theory of political economy. Smith, with his unrivalled sensitivity to the historical contexts in which thought develops, preferred to see it in a French context, as part of a long-standing preoccupation with the problem of stimulating trade and commerce and national glory in a great territorial state with an underdeveloped system of agriculture. In the *Wealth of Nations* he wrote of the *économistes'* system as an overreaction to Colbert's celebrated and abortive attempt to turn France into a great trading and manufacturing country by means of 'a system of restraint and regulation' that favoured the industry of the towns to that of the country, a scheme which Smith thought, sardonically, 'could scarce fail to be agreeable to a laborious and plodding man of business, who had been accustomed to regulate the different departments of publick offices'. The *économistes* had gone to the other extreme by proposing a scheme that 'represents agriculture as the sole source of the revenue and wealth of every country', and they consequently regarded the labour deployed in commerce and industry as useful but essentially unproductive, in the sense that it simply returned to the land the value of the labour and capital resources on which it depended.[41] Smith thought this erroneous, utopian and capable of provoking political unrest. As Mirabeau pointed out in *Rural Philosophy*, the analysis assumed the existence of the large-scale, developed agriculture characteristic of England and not the existing system of tenant farming and subsistence cultivation characteristic of France. The problem was how to set in motion the agricultural revolution on which the future prosperity and greatness of France would depend. Replacing the existing tax system by a single tax on land and the landed classes, and removing existing obstacles to internal trade and the movement of labour, would encourage the circulation of wealth through the different sectors of the economy, generate the resources on which agricultural improvement depended and increase the wealth of the sovereign. It was a recipe for the regeneration of an underdeveloped economy that could only be brought into existence by a revolutionary act of state, which Quesnay iconoclastically called an act of 'legal despotism'. So far as Smith was concerned it was a form of 'projecting' that was dangerously utopian.

Smith's critique of this system was to be notable for its sensitivity to the practicalities of installing it as well as to its economic thinking.[42] Apart from the revolutionary act of state that would be needed to create a new and obviously deeply controversial tax system, the project hinged on the assumption that the stimulus of the single tax would be enough to turn the French landowning class into a class of efficient agricultural improvers – a proposition which Smith with his long-standing lack of faith in the redeeming qualities of the Scottish nobility found hard to credit. All he was prepared to grant was that 'The class of proprietors [would contribute] to the annual produce by the expence which they *may occasionally lay out* upon the improvement of the land'[43] (my italics). Smith was struck even more forcibly by the narrow rigidity of Quesnay's system, which was like those concocted by 'speculative physicians' (like Quesnay himself), who claimed that 'the health of the human body could be preserved only by a certain precise regimen of diet and exercise, of which every, the smallest, violation necessarily occasioned some degree of disease or disorder proportioned to the degree of the violation'.[44] This critique, which must have taken shape in Paris, went to the heart of his disagreements with the French and reinforced his view that modern French thinking, for all its ingenuity, was seriously lacking in an understanding of the principles of human nature and, above all, the importance of pursuing policies that aimed at the progressive improvement of a country's institutions rather than by revolutionary acts of state.

> [Quesnay] seems not to have considered that in the political body, the natural effort which every man is continuously making to better his own condition, is a principle of preservation capable of preventing and correcting, in many respects, the bad effects of a political oeconomy, in some degree, both partial and oppressive. Such a political oeconomy, though it no doubt retards more or less, is not always capable of stopping altogether the natural progress of a nation towards wealth and prosperity, and still less of making it go backwards. If a nation could not prosper without the enjoyment of perfect liberty and perfect justice,

there is not in the world a nation which could ever have prospered. In a political body, however, the wisdom of nature has fortunately made ample provision for remedying many of the bad effects of the folly and injustice of man; in the same manner as it has done in the natural body, for remedying those of his sloth and intemperance.[45]

In the *Wealth of Nations* Smith went on to demonstrate the analytical power of the principle of improvement. The capital error of Quesnay's system was that it described the labour of artisans, manufacturers and merchants as essentially unproductive, resembling that of domestic servants in that it only 'reproduces annually the value of its own annual consumption'. But artisans, manufacturers and merchants did, after all, produce 'vendible' commodities and the labour that produced them added to the total stock of labour and capital of a country by virtue of the extra demand it created. Nor was it true that the revenue derived from agriculture was necessarily greater than the revenue generated by trade and manufactures, for the fundamental reason that the progress of the division of labour and the progress of improvement would always be slower in agriculture than in manufacturing. These were criticisms based on conclusions that were fundamental to Smith's thinking and may even have dated back to his Edinburgh lectures, that systems of political economy which were designed to favour either commerce or agriculture were equally flawed as means of maximizing the opulence of a nation. The task of political economy was to reflect on the means of giving effect to a genuinely liberal system which, so far as was possible, would remove the obstacles to free trade in both the agricultural and manufacturing sectors of the economy.

In all of this, Smith was returning to the wider questions about the relations between country and town, agriculture and commerce he had raised in Glasgow, and may well have been better able to resolve as a result of his encounters with the *économistes*. After all, by the time he left Glasgow he had developed his discussion of commerce to the point that he had been able to ask why this most beneficent of practices had developed so slowly in Europe, and had answered with an analysis of the malign and complex effects of the feudal system on the progress of agriculture and the division of labour. In the *Wealth of*

Nations he was to describe this progress as 'retrograde and unnatural', and as Istvan Hont suggests, it is likely that he learned from Mirabeau's *Rural Philosophy* (and presumably from conversation with Mirabeau himself) exactly why it was so and why exactly the *économistes*' system was so dangerous.[46] Like Smith and many others, Mirabeau viewed the progress of opulence as a natural progress from hunting to herding and agriculture, and he viewed the origins and progress of commerce as the natural consequence of the history of agriculture in its more advanced state of development. 'Thus alongside the agricultural societies there could be, and were bound to be, set up commercial societies, just as granaries are set up alongside crops.'[47] Colbert's attempt to turn France into a great trading and manufacturing nation by means of a tax system that favoured manufactures at the expense of agriculture was thus a perverse attempt to obstruct the course of nature which the *économistes* proposed to reverse by means of an act of state. By the time he came to write the *Wealth of Nations* Smith had come to see that, although this course of development could be regarded as 'natural' and 'beneficial', it did not describe the *actual* progress of commerce in modern Europe, and did not take account of the malign effects of the feudal system or of the history of war, exploration and luxury that had turned towns into little republics rather than the 'granaries' or *comptoirs* of Mirabeau's analysis, and it may well be that his discussions in Paris in 1766 led him to this conclusion. If so it would have been in Paris that Smith came to realize fully that the task of political economy was to show how states which owed their origins to such unnatural and retrograde causes should be managed.

By the summer of 1766, however, Smith's sojourn in Paris had begun to run its course. News had reached Smith and Buccleuch that the Duke's friend Macdonald of Sleat, who had joined them in Toulouse, had died in Rome, a loss which prompted Hume to write, 'Were you and I together Dear Smith we shoud shed Tears at present for the Death of poor Sir James Macdonald. We coud not possibly have sufferd a greater Loss than in that valuable young Man.'[48] Worse was to follow. In late August Buccleuch went down with a fever and what sounds like food poisoning while visiting the Court at Compiègne. In spite of his protestations, Smith was worried enough to send for Ques-

nay as the king's physician and two other doctors. He sent Townshend a meticulously detailed and precise account of the progress of
the Duke's illness, assuring him 'I never stirr from his room from eight
in the morning till ten at night, and watch for the smallest change that
happens to him. I should sit by him all night too, if the ridiculous,
impertinent jealousy of Cook [Buccleuch's servant] who thinks my
assiduity an encroachment upon his duty, had not been so much
alarmed as to give some disturbance even to his master in his present
illness.'[49] It was the same sort of assiduous care he had shown during
Thomas Fitzmaurice's illness at Glasgow.

By then Smith was ready to go home. He told the publisher Andrew
Millar that

> Tho I am very happy here, I long passionately to rejoin my old friends,
> and if I had once got fairly on your side of the water, I think I should
> never cross it again. Recommend the same sober way of thinking to
> Hume. He is light-headed, tell him, when he talks of coming to spend
> the remainder of his days here, or in France. Remember me to him most
> affectionately.[50]

It sounds as though he had got what he wanted from Paris and was
ready to write. One would guess that the Duke had had enough as
well. What settled the matter was the sudden illness and death of Buccleuch's brother Campbell Scott in Paris on 19 October. Scott had
fallen ill with a fever, vomiting and delirium. Smith reported that
Quesnay had been called in ('one of the worthiest men in France and
one of the best Physicians that is to be met with in any country'), as
had Théodore Tronchin ('my particular and intimate friend'), but to
no avail. He had gone to the Embassy to tell Buccleuch that his brother
was dying and had returned to find that he had died five minutes earlier. 'I had not the satisfaction of closing his eyes with my own hands.
I have no force to continue this letter; The Duke, tho' in very great
affliction, is otherwise in perfect health.'[51] The stay in Paris was
instantly aborted. By about mid-November Smith and Buccleuch had
returned home with Campbell Scott's body. It was the end of Smith's
first and only visit to Europe.

10

London, Kirkcaldy and the Making
of the *Wealth of Nations* 1766–76

Campbell Scott's death in October 1766 had brought Buccleuch's European tour to an abrupt end. But although Smith had told Millar a few weeks earlier that he was anxious to get home, he was to remain in London until the spring of 1767. Why he did so is not clear, although it seems likely that he was under some sort of obligation to Buccleuch and Townshend. The Duke was to enter his majority in September 1767 and it may well be that his stepfather wanted Smith's help in preparing his stepson to take over the management of his enormous estates in Scotland. At this stage Townshend still expected Buccleuch to enter politics and to follow the family practice of making one of his English houses his principal residence, running his estates from London through the elaborate system of devolved management that had evolved during the previous century. Townshend himself was a keen agricultural improver, and knowing Smith's views on the importance of agricultural improvement to a nation's wealth and its nobility's greatness it is possible that this was when discussions with Smith about the future management of the estates began.[1]

Townshend may also have had other reasons for wanting Smith to be on hand. He had been appointed Chancellor of the Exchequer in Lord Chatham's new ministry and his primary task was to bring the public finances under control in the aftermath of the Seven Years War. He had consulted Smith over taxation policy when he was still in France, and he consulted him again in the autumn of 1766 about his plans for a new sinking fund to bring the national debt under control. A paper on the subject was sent to Smith for comment, with the request to 'speak . . . upon every part of this memorial (for I cannot call it a letter) without reserve and pitty'.[2] Smith's comments are unfortunately missing. But Campbell and Skinner are probably right to suggest that the political turmoil into which this most erratic of politicians was plunged in the autumn of 1766, together with the alarming financial crisis precipitated by the affairs of the East India Company, left little time or opportunity for serious consideration of the principles of taxation.[3]

Whether or not this explains Smith's five-month stay in London, his time was clearly fully occupied. He was able to move in political circles at a time when the future of Anglo-American relations, the role of the East India Company in the government of India and public finance and taxation were under discussion, all matters of importance to the *Wealth of Nations*. Lord Shelburne, now a Secretary of State, asked him for information about the colonial policies of the Romans and was given a surprisingly perfunctory reply.[4] He was known at the Royal Society – whose President, Sir John Pringle, was a Scot – and was elected a Fellow in May 1767. He had access to the enviable resources of the recently opened British Museum. He would have undoubtedly made a point of visiting the British Coffeehouse, off Charing Cross, the regular resort of Scots in London. And it was a convenient time to see the third edition of the *Theory of Moral Sentiments*, with the addition of the 'Dissertation on the Origin of Languages', through the press. It was published that same year. Smith returned to Kirkcaldy in May 1767 preceded by four large cases of heavily insured books, and remained there until 1773. It was there that most of the *Wealth of Nations* was drafted.

Settling in Kirkcaldy came as a great relief. The burgh was far enough from Edinburgh and Glasgow to provide peace and quiet, and his mother's domestic regime provided order and security. Old school friends who had settled nearby offered the prospect of congenial and undemanding company. It was the right place to work on a demanding book. And for relaxation, he told Andreas Holt, it gave him the opportunity of studying botany '(in which however I made no great progress) as well as some other sciences to which I have never given much attention'.[5] As he told Hume in June, 'My Business here is Study in which I have been very deeply engaged for about a Month past. My Amusements are long, solitary walks by the Sea side. You may judge how I spend my time. I feel myself, however, extremely happy, comfortable and contented. I never was, perhaps, more so in all my life.'[6]

It was said that one of those long solitary walks took the form of a fifteen-mile trek to Dunfermline wrapped in thought and clad in a dressing gown, and only brought to an abrupt conclusion by the sound of the town's church bells.[7] And while Hume was able to provide Smith with news and gossip from the outside world, he constantly complained that he saw too little of him. A teasing, witty and affectionate letter proposing a trip to Edinburgh was written more in hope than in expectation of a visit.

James's Court, Edinburgh, 20 Aug. 1769

Dear Smith

I am glad to have come within sight of you, and to have a View of Kirkaldy from my Windows: But as I wish also to be within speaking terms of you, I wish we coud concert measures for that purpose. I am mortally sick at Sea, and regard with horror, and a kind of hydrophobia the great Gulph that lies between us. I am also tir'd of travelling, as much as you ought naturally to be, of staying at home: I therefore propose to you to come hither [to Edinburgh], and pass some days with me in this Solitude. I want to know what you have been doing, and propose to exact a rigorous Account of the method, in which you have employed yourself during your Retreat. I am positive you are wrong in many of your Speculations, especially where you have the Misfortune to differ from me. All these are Reasons for our meeting, and I wish you woud make me some reasonable Proposal for the Purpose. There is no Habitation on the Island of Inch-keith [halfway across the Firth of Forth]; otherwise I shoud challenge you to meet me on that Spot, and neither [of] us ever to leave the Place, till we were fully agreed on all points of Controversy. I expect General Conway here tomorrow, whom I shall attend to Roseneath, and I shall remain there a few days. On my Return, I expect to find a Letter from you, containing a bold Acceptance of this Defiance. I am Dear Smith Yours sincerely

David Hume[8]

The young Duke of Buccleuch was the only person allowed to interrupt Smith's retreat and Smith's desultory correspondence suggests that he was perfectly content for him to do so. The sudden death of Townshend on 4 September put an end to the plan to draw

Buccleuch into the 'vortex of Politics' and run his affairs from London. He chose Dalkeith House outside Edinburgh as his new centre of operations, extensively modernized it and prepared to celebrate his coming of age and his recent marriage to Elizabeth, daughter of the Duke of Montagu, before getting down to the business of taking over his estates. Smith was invited as a friend and mentor to the young couple. Buccleuch's introduction to local society does not seem to have been a conspicuous success. According to Carlyle, 'The Fare was Sumptuous, but the Company was formal and Dull. Adam Smith their only Familiar at Table, was but ill qualifi'd to promote the Jollity of a Birthday, and Their Graces were quite unexperienc'd.'[9] But Smith stayed at Dalkeith for two months, his longest absence from his Kirkcaldy retreat before 1773; it was the first of many such visits there he was to make for the rest of his life. For he became a lifelong family friend, a replacement for Townshend, someone who saw eye to eye with his former pupil on questions of estate management and had a far more palatable view of the role of great landowners in public life than his former patron.

The task of reviving the Buccleuch estates was formidable. Townshend had borrowed heavily – some said embezzled – on the credit of the estate, leaving it with serious cash-flow problems.[10] The estates were enormous; those in the so-called South Country of Ettrick, Teviotdale and Liddesdale alone consisted of 439 farms with an annual rental of £19,074. All were leased to tenants whose leases had to be reissued on the Duke's majority. The estate itself was heavily entailed, making the issue of the long leases that Smith, Buccleuch and every improver believed essential to encourage agricultural improvement, impossible. Whether or not Smith was involved in early discussions about the future of the estate in 1766, he was certainly involved in the relaunch in the autumn of 1767, and almost certainly in plans for securing the legislation needed to allow the entail to be eased, a complicated and protracted business which was only brought to a conclusion with legislation in 1770. One of his favourite Glasgow pupils, the advocate Ilay Campbell, was to be the Duke's prime legal adviser. It is inconceivable that he and Smith were not involved in discussing and drafting the remarkable advertisement that appeared in the *Edinburgh Advertiser* of 20 October, calling for applications for leases on the Duke's South Country estates. Prospective tenants were asked to state the length of the lease they wanted, to explain the sort of improvements they wished to bring about, to estimate the amount the Duke was expected to pay to finance them, and to state the rent they were prepared to offer. It was a remarkable exercise in encouraging agricultural improvement which bears all the marks of Smith's thinking, and swept aside alternative, more cautious plans proposed by other advisers. This 'General Sett' was conspicuously successful – half of the proposals coming from existing tenants, half from strangers, many from England. As Brian Bonnyman has put it, 'it was an explicit attempt to expose the land to the competition of the market',[11] and although the problems involved in implementing the plan were far from straightforward it seems likely that Smith was kept in close touch with them on his frequent visits to Dalkeith.

For Smith, Buccleuch was a model pupil with a real interest in the infrastructure and technological demands of agricultural improvement, a landlord who invested heavily in roads, bridges and canals and rewarded innovative tenants. He had been taught to think of the duties of great landowners in a commercializing economy as being the improvement of their estates rather than meddling in the business of politics, and he interpreted this as meaning playing a part in public life in Scotland rather than Westminster. He was to emerge as a popular and pre-eminent peer, well-known in Edinburgh as a 'patriot' who could have become the Duke of Argyll's successor as 'uncrowned king of Scotland' had he chosen; but that was not his style and it soon became clear that he was content to leave the government of Scotland and the management of his own political interest to the ambitious and accomplished Henry Dundas, with whom Smith soon established excellent relations. Before long Smith would be known as a close confidant of 'your duke', as John Macpherson called him, and a valuable contact when there were favours to be sought.[12] It was and remained a quiet and singularly happy relationship.

These interruptions apart, nothing was allowed to intrude on Smith's retreat in Kirkcaldy and on the hugely demanding business of writing the *Wealth of Nations*. As he told the judge and antiquarian Lord Hailes in January 1769, after apologizing for an overdue letter, "tho in my present situation I have properly speaking nothing to do,

my own schemes of Study leave me very little leisure, which go forward too like the web of penelope, so that I scarce see any Probability
of their ending'.[13] Although little correspondence from this period has
survived, it seems fairly certain that Smith's principal task was to
reflect on the principles of political economy he had developed at
Glasgow in the light of those of Quesnay and his disciples, and to
develop and refine the vast stock of historical illustrations on which
the effectiveness of his advocacy would depend. He had already established the principle that the opulence of a nation was to be measured
in terms of the flow of consumable goods and not its reserves of gold
and silver. His labour theory had established that the extent and rate
of circulation would depend on the manner in which that nation's
labour force was deployed and the extent of the division of labour,
and that the progress of the division of labour would depend on the
extent of the market. He had also developed a labour-based theory of
value and price which distinguished between the natural and market
price of commodities and provided a largely Humean theory of money
to sustain it. Moreover, he had outlined a theory of natural liberty,
which argued that a system of free markets and free exchange would
optimize a nation's wealth, and he had raised the provocative and
question-begging issue of why the progress of opulence had been so
slow in Europe. But while he had offered an account of many of the
economic, political and moral factors on which the progress of opulence depended, he had not yet worked these factors into a system
which explained precisely how they interacted.

That was the attraction of Quesnay's system. Quesnay shared
Smith's view that wealth had to be discussed in terms of a process of
consumption and production, and had shown that output could best
be maximized in an economy that allowed for the free exchange of
goods and services. But the main interest of his system had been to
explain the principles which regulated the flow of goods and services
throughout an economy and to show how that economy could sustain and reproduce itself. It was also notable for the emphasis it placed
on the role of capital in generating improvement. It was for this
reason that Smith would describe it as a system that, for all its imperfections, was worthy of serious attention.[14]

Reflecting on the implications of Quesnay's system for his own was a complex business. Developing his own account of the principle of circular flow would have to take account of his conviction that the ultimate source of a nation's wealth lay in its stock of labour, and not its land as Quesnay had argued, and that it was a mistake to argue, as Quesnay had done, that labour employed in manufactures was technically unproductive. He also thought that Quesnay's claims that the system of circular flow worked on mathematical principles were unjustified, and possibly dangerously mechanistic – questions of price and value were regulated by 'higgling and bargaining', not mathematical necessity. He regarded the act of legal despotism, which Quesnay had so notoriously claimed as necessary to set the system of natural liberty in motion, as dangerously utopian; the progress of wealth could be far better encouraged by the improvement of existing institutions than the creation of new ones. Above all, whereas Quesnay believed that economics could be turned into an exact, mathematically based science, Smith remained firmly committed to the Humean view that systems of philosophy could only appeal to the understanding, and that their credibility in the eyes of their readers would depend on the philosopher's ability to illustrate his principles with examples drawn from common life and history.

Smith clearly devoted time and erudition to illustrating the system he was developing at Kirkcaldy, and there is no better example of the way in which issues that were immediately topical were periodically used as the basis for trenchant illustration than his account of the collapse of the Ayr Bank in 1772. The Ayr Bank was founded in 1769 in response to a credit shortage at a time when the country was nearing the end of a remarkable period of economic growth affecting every major sector of the economy. In his lectures at Glasgow Smith had pointed to a major peculiarity of the Scottish banking system that had some bearing on this story of economic success: the fact that, unlike the banking system of England, the Scottish system relied almost exclusively on the circulation of paper notes and bills of exchange as the primary medium of exchange. It had prevented excessive hoarding of specie on the part of banks and had ensured that the country's stock of currency was deployed in commerce and the promotion of industry. This had worked to the advantage of the economy because banks had only issued bills to those whose creditworthiness was vouched for by two men of honour and estate, a convention which made it possible for the Scottish banks to allow repayment of loans upon easy terms. For Smith, 'this prudent and necessary reserve of the [Scottish] banks' and these easy terms 'are, so far as I know, peculiar to them, and have, perhaps, been the principal cause, both of the great trade of those companies, and of the benefit which the country has received from it'.[15] What this system could not satisfy (and what the Ayr Bank was designed to remedy) was the insatiable demand for credit from projectors and improvers anxious to cash in on a boom. The bank's founders included a substantial number of very rich land-owners who were anxious to encourage investment in agricultural improvement, Buccleuch among them. They subscribed very large capital sums indeed, and accepted liabilities to the extent of their entire fortunes. The bank expanded rapidly, its notes being said to have represented two-thirds of the entire paper currency of the country. But it overtraded, discounting bills of exchange almost on demand and accruing a dangerous amount of insecure debt.[16] By 1771 the bank's fortunes had become inextricably bound up with the fortunes of the London banks at a time when they too were becoming danger-ously overstretched. A year later it had crashed, leaving the original subscribers seriously indebted – £750,000 of landed property owned by the subscribers changed hands, much of it in Ayrshire. The Buc-cleuch estate was to remain seriously encumbered until the 1840s.

The history of Buccleuch's involvement in this ill-fated venture has not yet been written, nor is it known what Smith thought of Buc-cleuch's involvement in a venture which was intended to finance the sort of agricultural improvements that could only deliver long-term returns and had been founded under circumstances which were bound to attract 'chimerical projectors . . . who would employ the money in extravagant undertakings, which, with all the assistance that could be given them, they would probably never be able to compleat'.[17] Hume, reflecting on the 'very melancholy Situation' in London and Edin-burgh, asked, 'Do these Events any-wise affect your Theory? Or will it occasion the Revisal of any Chapters?', commenting, 'On the whole, I believe, that the Check given to our exorbitant and ill grounded Credit will prove of Advantage in the long run, as it will reduce people to more solid and less sanguine Projects, and at the same time introduce Frugality among the Merchants and Manufacturers: What say you? Here is Food for your Speculation.'[18] This was broadly Smith's view as well, although he was anxious to insist in the *Wealth of Nations* that the multiplication of banks in both kingdoms was beneficial to the banking system as a whole on the grounds that competition bred circumspection among bankers, who would learn to be wary of plots among their competitors to engineer 'malicious runs'.

Nevertheless the affair clearly made demands on his time when he felt under acute pressure to finish his book. As he told William Pulteney in September 1772, 'Tho I have had no concern myself in the Public calamities, some of the friends for whom I interest myself the most have been deeply concerned in them; and my attention has been a good deal occupied about the most proper method of extricating them.' He concluded, 'My book would have been ready for the Press by the beginning of this winter; but the interruptions occasioned partly by bad health arising from want of amusement and from thinking too much upon one thing; and partly by the avocations above mentioned will oblige me to retard its publication for a few months longer.'[19] It was to result in extending a long discussion of banking and the advantages and problems involved in using paper as a medium of exchange, with reflections on the main lesson of the Ayr Bank disaster. It was the consequence of abandoning the prudent banking practises of the chartered banks that had helped to transform the Scottish economy in the past and could continue to work for its improvement in the future. For the remarkable progress of the Scottish economy could be attributed to the system of free markets created by the Union, a spirit of improvement, and an enterprising and generally prudently managed banking system, which had developed quite naturally in response to the demands of the market. In Smith's eyes, these were also characteristics of the economic development of the American colonies, which were to furnish him with the most important of all his many illustrations in the *Wealth of Nations*. The fact that the text was to take another three years to complete was partly due to constant tinkering. But it was also due to Smith's response to the rapidly developing crisis in Anglo-American relations, a situation which could only properly be observed from London.

*

In the spring of 1773 Smith decided to end his Kirkcaldy retreat and to finish the *Wealth of Nations* in the capital. He needed company and American news. More immediately, there was the prospect of potentially rewarding future employment as tutor to the young Duke of Hamilton, to be taken up, one presumes, when the *Wealth of Nations* was finished. Before he left for London Smith made his will, appointing Hume as his executor and setting out his wishes for the disposal of his unpublished papers. All were to be destroyed with the exception of the essay on the history of astronomy which contained his thoughts about the nature of philosophical systems. 'Whether that might not be published as a fragment of an intended juvenile work, I leave entirely to your judgement; tho I begin to suspect myself that there is more refinement than solidity in some parts of it. This little work you will find in a thin folio paper book in my writing desk in my bedroom.' He concluded, 'Unless I die very suddenly I shall take care that the Papers I carry with me shall be carefully sent to you.' For in that event, Hume was to see the *Wealth of Nations* through the press.[20]

Smith arrived in London in May 1773 and took rooms in Suffolk Street, near Charing Cross and the British Coffeehouse, in the Scots quarter of Town. The Duke of Hamilton's offer was not pursued, on Buccleuch's advice, presumably because Buccleuch held out the promise of a more honourable and lucrative public appointment once the *Wealth of Nations* was published. He was to be as good as his word, using his considerable political muscle to obtain for Smith the post of Commissioner of Customs in Scotland in 1778. In retrospect, however, refusing the Hamilton offer was surely a mistake. The salary would have been accompanied by a substantial pension to add to Buccleuch's. It would have left him comfortably off and with plenty of time for philosophy. The Commissionership of Customs was certainly honourable and lucrative, but it proved to be time-consuming and wearisome and was to leave Smith constantly bewailing the lack of time for pursuing his many philosophical projects. Buccleuch undoubtedly meant well but his advice may have been a misjudgement of historic proportions.

The three years Smith spent in London with the *Wealth of Nations* nearing completion were notably sociable and provided a much-needed cathartic response to the rigours of the preceding years. He became a regular denizen of the British Coffeehouse and Alexander Wedderburn's weekly dinners. He was formally admitted to the Royal Society in May 1773, followed its proceedings with attention and went to some trouble to secure a complete set of its transactions. He attended William Hunter's public lectures on anatomy. In 1774 he became a member of The Club, the focal point of London's literary life and the much publicized theatre for Samuel Johnson's conversational talents. Although this brought him into contact with Edmund Burke and Edward Gibbon, both of whom he liked, James Boswell's chronicles suggest that his conversation was not much to Johnson's taste or that of some of the other members. Johnson did not like him, thought him 'as dull a dog as he had ever met with' and commented that he was a 'most disagreeable fellow after he had drank some wine', which, he said, 'bubbled in his mouth'.[21] Smith for his part once offered a 'very contemptuous opinion' of a man whose eccentricities offended his sense of social propriety. 'I have seen that creature, said he, bolt up in the midst of a mixed company and, without any previous notice, fall upon his knees behind a chair, repeat the Lord's Prayer, and then resume his seat at table. He has played this freak over and over perhaps five or six times in the course of an evening. It is not hypocrisy, but madness.'[22]

Nevertheless Smith seems to have been on excellent form in London. A long letter to William Cullen, now Professor of Medicine at Edinburgh, commenting on a proposal by the Royal College of Physicians that there should be new legislation to ensure that medical degrees were only awarded to those who had spent two years at university, shows him at his most cheerful and formidable, ready to deploy a full battery of philosophy, erudition and good humour to demolish a plan sponsored by one of his oldest friends. He thought that the physicians' proposal was a piece of monopolistic opportunism, which would be 'oppressive' to distinguished independent teachers of medicine like William Hunter and do nothing to guarantee that future practitioners would be men of 'sense or science'.

> The title of Doctor, such as it is, you will say, gives some credit and authority to the man upon whom it is bestowed; it extends his practice, and consequently his field for doing mischief; it is not improbable too

that it may increase his presumption, and consequently his disposition to do mischief. That a degree injudiciously conferred may sometimes have some little effect of this kind, it would surely be absurd to deny; but that this effect should be very considerable, I cannot bring myself to believe. That Doctors are sometimes fools as well as other people, is not, in the present times, one of those profound secrets which is known only to the learned. The title is not so very imposing, and it very seldom happens that a man trusts his health to another merely because that other is a doctor. The person so trusted has almost always either some knowledge or some craft which would procure him nearly the same trust, though he was not decorated with any such title. In fact the persons who apply for degrees in the irregular manner complained of, are, the greater part of them, surgeons or apothecaries, who are in the custom of advising and prescribing, that is, of practising as physicians; but who, being only surgeons and apothecaries, are not fee-ed as physicians. It is not so much to extend their practice as to increase their fees, that they are desirous of being made Doctors. Degrees conferred, even undeservedly, upon such persons can surely do very little harm to the public.

He continued: sensible physicians would be better advised 'to attend more to your characters as men, as gentlemen, and as men of letters' than to place their faith in a degree which could never 'give any tolerable security, that the person upon whom it had been conferred, was fit to practise physic. The strictest Universities confer degrees only upon students of a certain standing. Their real motive for requiring this standing is, that the student may spend more money among them, and that they may make more profit by him.' He concluded cheerfully: 'Adieu, my dear Doctor; after having delayed so long to write to you, I am afraid I shall *get my lug in my lufe*, as we say, for what I have written, But I ever am, most affectionately yours.'[23]

However, it was the American question that appears to have absorbed most of his energies – Buccleuch telling Hume that Smith was now 'very zealous in American Affairs'.[24] In the *Wealth of Nations* America was to provide him with the most striking and decisive illustration of the possibilities of the civilizing process in a part of the civilized world that had never been encumbered by feudal laws and institutions, and whose distance from Europe had ensured that the principles of natural liberty had already guided some aspects of its economic development. The book was completed against the background of worsening Anglo-American relations. The Tea Act, which American radicals saw as an attempt to strengthen British fiscal rule over the colonies, had been passed shortly before Smith's arrival in London. The Boston Tea Party, the Coercive Acts of 1774, and the Quebec Act of 1774, which raised fears in the colonies that the British were determined to govern America without elected assemblies, the subsequent outbreak of hostilities at Lexington and Concord in 1775, and the eventual outbreak of an initially popular war, were to give him a unique perspective on a crisis that suggested that Britain's future as a commercial power was at a turning point.

Smith was to end the *Wealth of Nations* with his own version of the question David Hume had raised in his *Political Discourses* of 1752, of how modern governments with overstretched systems of taxation were to manage the ruinous public debts they had incurred as a result of their incessant wars. In Hume's words of 1764, 'either the nation must destroy public credit, or public credit will destroy the nation. It is impossible that they can both subsist, after the manner they have been hitherto managed, in this, as well in some other countries.'[25] Smith was to elaborate on the problem in the *Wealth of Nations* by showing how it had been complicated and intensified by colonial wars and the continuing costs of imperial defence. The scramble for colonies had not simply been driven by a love of power, glory and wealth, but by the absurd, superstitious belief that wealth was to be measured in terms of gold reserves and fostered by a monopolistically driven system of international trade. Indeed, 'the maintenance of this monopoly has hitherto been the principal, or more properly perhaps the sole end and purpose of the dominion which Great Britain assumes over her colonies'.[26] This was to view the present state of Anglo-American relations as the function of a profound crisis in the history of commercial civilization itself, and Smith's views of its possible outcomes were carefully woven into his critique of the mercantile system and his discussion of public finance. He was to summarize them and bring them into sharp political focus in 1778 in the aftermath of General Burgoyne's disastrous defeat at Saratoga in the previous year, in a Memorial written at the request of his old friend

Alexander Wedderburn, one of the Prime Minister's closest advisers on American policy.[27]

Smith's views about the outcome of the American crisis were austere and politically uncomfortable. A successful war would almost certainly lead to conquest, to the military government of the colonies and to ruinous expense for the foreseeable future. Giving up the colonies, as favoured by the radical Dean of Gloucester, Josiah Tucker, or returning the former French and Spanish colonies to the kings of France and Spain, as Samuel Johnson had suggested, made good theoretical sense on the grounds that these measures would relieve Britain of the enormous costs of defending the colonies and would open up the possibility of negotiating 'a treaty of commerce as would effectually secure to her a free trade, more advantageous to the great body of the people, though less so to the merchants, than the monopoly which she at present enjoys'.[28] But it was an impossible dream. 'No nation ever voluntarily gave up the dominion of any province, how troublesome soever it might be to govern it.'[29] A settlement that continued the existing colonial relationship would only work if the vexed problem of how to tax the colonies was resolved. It was impossible for Britain to shoulder the entire burden of defending the colonies at her own expense indefinitely. On the other hand, the colonies could not be expected to contribute to imperial defence unless they were represented in the British parliament, or unless the power to tax was transferred from the imperial parliament to the colonial assemblies. The first option, which had had some support from Benjamin Franklin some years before and continued to attract Lord Kames, worried British MPs on the grounds that it might strengthen ministerial power in the Commons. The second relied on the improbable assumption that colonial assemblies would always be ready to vote funds to subsidize an army over which they had no control. It was perhaps with a view to lightening an unduly pessimistic conclusion that Smith was to end the *Wealth of Nations* with the only utopian vision of the future he was ever to offer. And anyway, it was time to finish. The great book was sent to Strahan late in 1775.

I I

The *Wealth of Nations* and Smith's 'Very violent attack . . . upon the whole commercial system of Great Britain'

An Inquiry into the Nature and Causes of the Wealth of Nations was finally published on 9 March 1776, in two simple but elegantly produced quarto volumes priced at £1. 16/- in boards and £2. 2/- bound, and probably in an edition of 750 copies. The author, who had insisted on being styled as Adam Smith 'without any additions either before or behind' in the third edition of the *Theory of Moral Sentiments*, was now restyled as 'Adam Smith, LL.D. and F.R.S. Formerly Professor of Moral Philosophy in the University of GLASGOW', a philosopher and man of science, rather than a man of letters. The book was a relatively expensive production directed at a serious and select readership in London and Edinburgh, and although the production costs were shared by the author and his publishers in the usual way, it sold well enough to earn Smith an initial payment of £300 at the end of the year. Its success was sufficient to prompt the publication of a Dublin edition and plans were made for what was to be a new, lightly amended second edition, which appeared in the same format in 1778. By then it had been fairly extensively reviewed and noticed in the literary and political circles for which it was intended.[1] All in all, it was a successful launch; by the end of Smith's life it would become a best-seller.[2]

Most of Smith's first readers realized that Smith's masterpiece was more than a treatise on commerce or political economy; for Scottish readers it was part of a historic exercise in placing the science of politics on philosophical foundations. 'You have formed into a regular and consistent system one of the most important parts of political science'

AN

INQUIRY

INTO THE

Nature and Caufes

OF THE

WEALTH OF NATIONS.

By ADAM SMITH, LL. D. and F. R. S.
Formerly Profeffor of Moral Philofophy in the Univerfity of GLASGOW.

IN TWO VOLUMES.

VOL. I.

LONDON:

PRINTED FOR W. STRAHAN; AND T. CADELL, IN THE STRAND.
MDCCLXXVI.

William Robertson told him,[3] John Millar adding that its author deserved to be regarded as the Newton of the science of politics. Dugald Stewart, writing in 1793 at a time when it was prudent to emphasize Smith's distaste for revolutionary solutions to current political problems, highlighted the importance of his having grasped the fundamental truth that the happiness of a people had more to do with the 'equity and expediency of the laws that are enacted' than with voting and participating in the political process.[4] A true science of politics ought to be based on a study of the municipal codes of different states at different periods of history and attend to 'the general principles which ought to run through and be the foundation of the laws of all nations'. This would '[enlighten] the policy of actual legislators' and teach them what sort of 'legislative improvements . . . the general interests of the community recommend'. 'Such speculations,' he commented,

> while they are more essentially and more extensively useful than any others, have no tendency to unhinge established institutions, or to inflame the passions of the multitude. The improvements they recommend are to be effected by means too gradual and slow in their operation, to warm the imaginations of any but of the speculative few; and in proportion as they are adopted, they consolidate the political fabric, and enlarge the basis upon which it rests.

In this respect the *Wealth of Nations* was important for '[directing] the policy of nations with respect to one most important class of its laws, those which form its system of political economy'.[5] As Stewart rightly saw, it was a treatise which offered a reformist, Whig account of the politics of improvement, not a democratic one; a treatise which was firmly rooted in distinctive jurisprudence which had been in a state of gestation for perhaps a quarter of a century.

In writing the *Wealth of Nations* Smith faced the same problem he had encountered in writing the *Theory of Moral Sentiments*: developing lectures originally designed for university students for a different sort of readership. In the case of the *Theory of Moral Sentiments* that had meant presenting his philosophy as a response to Rousseau's brilliant but misguided attack on the civilizing process. The case of the *Wealth of Nations* was more complicated. As Robertson, Millar and

Stewart had realized, his political economy was deeply embedded in a system of moral philosophy, jurisprudence and politics about which most of his readers knew nothing. The question was, how much of it did they need to know if they were to make sense of his political economy? Smith's answer was, not much. He made no formal attempt to explain the principles of the history of property and government in which his discussion of the progress of civilization was enmeshed. The long, subtle discussion of 'the natural wants and demands of mankind' and their consequences for the progress of civilization and the human mind which had prefaced the Glasgow lectures was reduced to a series of strategically placed aphorisms and aperçus about the power of self-interest and a love of improvement in determining the way in which men used their labour. Nevertheless, these were often aphorisms of some force and consequence. In observing that, 'It is not from the benevolence of the butcher, the brewer, or the baker, that we expect our dinner, but from their regard to their own interest. We address ourselves, not to their humanity, but to their self-love, and never talk to them of our own necessities but of their advantages'; in commenting that, 'The property which every man has in his own labour, as it is the original foundation of all other property, so it is the most sacred and inviolable'; and in concluding that, 'Civil government, so far as it is instituted for the security of property, is in reality instituted for the defence of the rich against the poor, or of those who have some property against those who have none at all', he was developing a rhetoric which was to become an essential part of the language of political economy itself, admired and reviled by the new discipline's disciples and detractors.[6]

Instead of introducing his system as a moral philosopher, Smith introduced it as a political economist, speaking a language that Quesnay and the *économistes* could understand; they were the only economists he took seriously. In the 'Introduction and Plan' he spoke of his subject as the 'fund' or 'stock' of annual labour which supplies a nation with the 'necessaries and conveniences of life which it annually consumes', the 'skill, dexterity and judgment' with which it was deployed in different societies and the ratio of 'useful' and unproductive labour to be found in different types of nation. This would allow him to discuss the causes of 'improvements' in the productive powers of labour and the commercial policies of modern governments, and to take on board Quesnay's view that wealth should be studied as a function of the process by which revenue circulated through the different sectors of an economy in a free market. But Smith's famous demonstration that the wealth of a nation depended on the division of labour in different sectors of the economy was at odds with Quesnay's assertions that agriculture was the 'mother of all goods' and the only form of economic activity capable of increasing the wealth of a great monarchy, and that all labour not employed in agriculture was 'unproductive'. What is more, Quesnay's model presupposed the existence of a system of 'bonne culture' such as that practised in England or in Holland, and not the system of subsistence farming characteristic of France and most of Europe. Worse still, it assumed that a system of improved agriculture could be introduced by an act of 'legal despotism', a utopian suggestion that led David Hume to exclaim that, 'They are, indeed, the set of men the most chimerical and most arrogant that now exist, since the annihilation of the Sorbonne.'[7] For Smith, Quesnay's approach to political economy was too speculative and ahistorical, and too closely geared to the experience of France and contemporary concerns with the future of the French monarchy to be the basis of a viable general theory of economic progress. His own theory would attend to the very different experience of Britain and the British Empire in America and Asia, as well as that of France and the rest of Europe. For in the last resort, Smith was proposing to treat Quesnay as he had treated Condillac, Montesquieu and Rousseau in developing his rhetoric, jurisprudence and ethics – as the author of a brilliant, provocative but flawed contribution to the science of man.

There was much in the first book of the *Wealth of Nations* that Smith's former Glasgow students would have found familiar, from the classic restatement of his great axiom, that the progress of opulence depends on the division of labour, through his account of the process of truck, barter and exchange which determines the price of labour, to the discussion of the limitations imposed on the progress of the division of labour by the market. Familiar, too, would have been his account of the origins of money, the claim that labour and not money was the true determinant of price and value, and the all-important distinction he made between the natural and market price of labour and commodities, the distinction on which his analysis of the causes of the slow progress of opulence in Europe and his attack on laws and customs which obstructed the workings of a free market depended. In the *Wealth of Nations*, however, this attack was to range wider and deeper and was able to draw on the full reserve of Smith's powers of irony and indignation, precisely because its roots lay in the general economic theory Smith had been able to develop and refine in his last year at Glasgow, in France, and in the company of Quesnay and the *économistes*. It was a theory about the creation of wealth that drew on his understanding of the principles of human nature and the progress of society but was articulated in a language which was concerned with the principles of exchange, circulation and the workings of the market.

First, important parts of his theory had to be expanded. The discussion of price and value, which had hitherto been focused on the price of labour, was now extended to a discussion of the way in which the price and value of commodities were 'adjusted', 'not by any accurate measure, but by the higgling and bargaining of the market, according to that sort of rough equality which, though not exact, is sufficient for carrying on the business of common life'.[8] Characteristically, earlier luminous suggestions that this seemingly natural disposition had its origins in the love of persuading he had discussed in his rhetoric lectures were omitted, no doubt on the grounds that they would divert the reader's attention from the all-important discussion of the real and nominal (or money) price of goods and its significance for an understanding of the workings of the market.

But this was for later consideration. In this extended discussion of economic principles, Smith's central task was to establish the three determinants of price – rent, wages and the profit of the 'undertaker' or entrepreneur – and to identify landowners, wage earners and manufacturers and merchants as 'the three great, original and constituent orders of every civilized society, from whose revenue that of every other order is ultimately derived'. It was a discussion which was designed to show that rents and wages would naturally rise and fall as the economy expanded and contracted, but that the profits earned by merchants and manufacturers would be low in rich countries, high in poorer countries, and highest of all 'in the countries which are going fastest to ruin', a factor which pointed to the crucial political conclusion that the interests of merchants and manufacturers could never be exactly the same as those of landowners or wage-earners. It was a discussion that culminated in a characteristically sardonic discussion of the capacity of each of the three constituent orders' ability to understand the true nature of their own interests and those of the public. Landowners were too rich and too indolent to be able to acquire 'that application of mind which is necessary in order to foresee and understand the consequences of any publick regulation'. Wage earners were too poor, and lacked the time, education and habits needed to judge, 'even though ... fully informed'. As for merchants and manufacturers, while they had 'more acuteness of understanding than the greater part of country gentlemen', they had no hesitation in using it to gull others into believing that their interests were the same as their own. Smith concluded acidly:

> The interest of the dealers, however, in any particular branch of trade or manufactures, is always in some respects different from, and even opposite to, that of the publick. To widen the market and to narrow the competition, is always the interest of the dealers. To widen the market may frequently be agreeable enough to the interest of the publick; but to narrow the competition must always be against it, and can serve only to enable the dealers, by raising their profits above what they naturally would be, to levy, for their own benefit, an absurd tax upon the rest of their fellow-citizens. The proposal of any new law or regulation of commerce which comes from this order, ought always to be listened to with great precaution, and ought never to be adopted till after having been long and carefully examined, not only with the most scrupulous, but with the most suspicious attention. It comes from an order of men, whose interest is never exactly the same with that of the publick, who have generally an interest to deceive and even to oppress the publick, and who accordingly have, upon many occasions, both deceived and oppressed it.[9]

The message Smith wished to convey was implicit but clear. In a country whose politics and governance was in the hands of the landed and mercantile classes, it was the job of philosophers, who understood the principles of political economy, to safeguard the public interest by educating their masters. Never before had the Ciceronian ideal of the philosopher-statesman seemed so challenging and so urgent.

In the long first book of the *Wealth of Nations*, Smith elucidated a set of principles to explain how the stock of labour on which a nation's survival and prosperity depended would be deployed in a society in which individuals were free to deploy their labour as they wished. In doing this he had used the methods of conjectural history to contrast the experience of savage societies with those which possessed systems of private property and government and enjoyed 'tolerable security', and had argued that under the same conditions the stock of labour of whole societies will be deployed in exactly the same way as that of individuals. It was an analogy which pointed towards a discussion of what instantly became Smith's most famous doctrine, that of the unintended social consequences of individual actions. It was a problem he addressed in the short second book in discussing the accumulation and circulation of stock or capital, and in so doing he was to complete the theorizing of the principle of improvement which had for so long lain at the centre of his, and the Scottish literati's, understanding of the science of man.

The importance of capital in generating economic growth had been highlighted by the *économistes*. If the progress of opulence depended on the division of labour, the love of improvement and relative security, it also depended on the existence of an adequate stock of investable capital. However, as Smith had put it in Glasgow, 'till some stock be produced there can be no division of labour, and before a division of labour take place there can be very little accumulation of stock'.[10] In modern societies, the stock of the labouring poor was so small that it could only be used for immediate consumption and the progress of opulence would therefore depend on the surplus stock of those engaged in trade, manufactures and agriculture. Smith was interested in the way in which these resources would circulate through the different sectors of a society in a relatively free market. It was a process he described in terms of a cyclical process of consumption and replenishment, a model which made it possible for Smith to remind the statesman that, 'To maintain and augment the stock which may be reserved for immediate consumption, is the sole end and purpose both of fixed and circulating capitals. It is this stock which feeds, cloaths, and lodges the people. Their riches or poverty depends on the abundant or sparing supplies which those two capitals can afford to the stock reserved for immediate consumption.'[11] This analysis allowed Smith to develop a complex discussion of the role of money and banking – Scottish banking in particular – in acting as 'the great wheel of circulation and distribution', a means of circulating the stock and capital of society in a way which would maximize the progress of the division of labour and increase the private and public revenue of a nation.[12] The analysis also showed the *économistes* that it was the labour force engaged in a never-ending process of consumption and production, and not merely agriculture, on which the real wealth of a nation depended. And this made it possible to introduce one of the most characteristic and deeply seated principles on which his political economy and his understanding of improvement rested: the character and the natural parsimony of the improver.

> But the principle which prompts to save, is the desire of bettering our condition, a desire which, though generally calm and dispassionate, comes with us from the womb, and never leaves us till we go into the grave. In the whole interval which separates those two moments, there is scarce perhaps a single instant in which any man is so perfectly and completely satisfied with his situation, as to be without any wish of alteration or improvement, of any kind. An augmentation of fortune is the means by which the greater part of men propose and wish to better their condition. It is the means the most vulgar and the most obvious . . .[13]

This natural parsimony explained the silent accumulation of the capital on which England's economic progress had always depended. As for governments, 'They are themselves always, and without any exception, the greatest spendthrifts in the society. Let them look well after their own expence, and they may safely trust private people with theirs. If their own extravagance does not ruin the state, that of their subjects never will.'[14]

Smith was now almost ready to apply theory to practice and to develop the critique of contemporary commercial policy for which the *Wealth of Nations* became instantly famous, using his theory to address the problem he had posed in the lectures, how to explain the slow progress of opulence in Europe. He was now in a position to contrast the *natural* progress of opulence in Europe, with its *actual* progress. The discussion was focused on the economic relations between the country and town. To contemporaries, who thought that towns drained the countryside of natural resources, Smith replied that their relationship was, naturally, a reciprocal one, the country being the source of the subsistence and raw materials on which the economy of towns depended, and towns being markets for the produce of the country and a source of manufactured goods and capital which could be invested in agriculture. 'Compare the cultivation of the lands in the neighbourhood of any considerable town, with that of those which lie at some distance from it, and you will easily satisfy yourself how much the country is benefited by the commerce of the town,' Smith commented, with the example of Glasgow doubtless in mind.[15] For in the last resort 'the inhabitants of the town and those of the country are mutually the servants of one another'. Theoretically, at any rate, and 'all things and all profits being equal', it was a relationship that would ensure that, 'According to the natural course of things ... the greater part of the capital of every growing society is, first, directed to agriculture, afterwards to manufactures, and last of all to foreign commerce. This order of things is so very natural, that in every society that had any territory, it has always, I believe, been in some degree observed.'[16] The trouble was that this natural order had somehow been subverted; it was 'manufactures and foreign commerce' that had given birth to much of the agricultural improvement that had taken place in the west; the commercial system was a product of 'this un-natural and retrograde order'.[17]

For Smith the root cause of the slow progress of opulence and this inversion of the natural order of things, was the feudal system. As he had shown in the lectures on jurisprudence, the feudal system had encouraged landowners to extend rather than improve their estates, reducing their tenantry to a state of dependency and even slavery – always in Smith's reckoning the least productive form of labour. What is more, it was a system that had been artificially preserved by means of primogeniture and a system of tenures and entails which were as offensive to a people's sense of natural justice as to the cause of economic efficiency. The Scots literati probably knew the outlines of

Smith's story well enough from his conversation and from Select Society debates, but French readers sympathetic to physiocracy were more likely to have seen it as a radical attack on the claim that the estates of the great nobility were the ultimate source of the real wealth of a modern polity. What sharpened Smith's analysis was his powerful discussion of the consequences of the feudal system for the relationship between town and country, on which the real wealth of a modern polity ultimately depended. The primitive state of feudal agriculture and baronial power had retarded the economic and political development of smaller towns and the regions to which they belonged, while overseas trade in luxuries, encouraged by cash-strapped rulers who were anxious to check the growth of baronial power, had allowed some coastal towns to develop as 'a sort of independent republicks' with money to invest in the neighbouring countryside. As a result, the commerce and manufactures, which ought to have been the *effect* of agricultural improvement, had become its 'cause and occasion'. It was a development which Smith thought had retarded the overall economic growth of feudal nations and had led to a disastrous misunderstanding of the role of overseas trade in promoting economic growth.

Smith was just as curious, just as indignant about the causes of this inversion of the natural order as he was in its disastrous consequences. Like Hume writing about English party ideology, he saw the problem as one which had its roots in the political culture of Europe and in the frailties of human nature. The belief that a nation's wealth and power depended on its foreign and not its domestic trade was built on the idea that 'wealth consists in money, or in gold and silver' and not in labour. It was a belief that had taken hold in all European nations. It had been theorized by scholars, manipulated by merchants and had become the intellectual engine of national policies that were threatening the peace and prosperity of the modern world, a belief as dangerous to the progress of civilization as the religious superstitions that had fuelled the wars of religion and still stalked the corridors of every European state. Smith devoted Book IV to exploding this new superstition and attacking the merchants and theorists who propagated it with the same vehemence that Voltaire and Hume had attacked priestcraft. But the basis of his assault had already been carefully set out in the difficult and, as he admitted, potentially 'tedious' discussion of value and price in Book I. Here he had carried out a meticulously executed thought experiment to explain why we find it so easy to think of the value of labour and commodities in terms of money when the ordinary experience of higgling and bargaining in everyday life provides us with a much juster understanding of value and price. Smith's explanation was one Hume would have understood. It was the result of a confusion 'which naturally arises from the double function of money, as the instrument of commerce, and as the measure of value' and feeds into common language to the point that 'this ambiguity of expression has rendered this popular notion so familiar to us, that even they, who are convinced of its absurdity, are very apt to forget their own principles, and in the course of their reasonings to take it for granted as a certain and undeniable truth'.[18]

Smith's first example of the power and destructive potential of this superstition was conventional enough, the 'sacred thirst of gold' that had fuelled the exploration and colonization of Spanish America and the genocidal atrocities that had been visited on native Americans. But this was merely a curtain-raiser for his main purpose of showing how this primitive belief had become the superstition that now lay at the centre of the political culture of a whole civilization and was fuelling policies which were distorting its economic development. The analysis is tight and sardonic, both an example of Smith's skill as a moral anatomist and a classic example of the later Enlightenment's determination to combat superstition with philosophy and history. Smith began with a review of contemporary arguments defending the policy of accumulating national stocks of gold and silver.

> Such as they were, however, those arguments convinced the people to whom they were addressed. They were addressed by merchants to parliaments, and to the councils of princes, to nobles and to country gentlemen; by those who were supposed to understand trade, to those who were conscious to themselves that they knew nothing about the matter. That foreign trade enriched the country, experience demonstrated to the nobles and country gentlemen, as well as to the merchants; but how, or in what manner, none of them well knew. The merchants knew perfectly in what manner it enriched themselves. It was their business to know it. But in what manner it enriches the country, was no part of

their business. This subject never came into their consideration, but when they had occasion to apply to their country for some change in the laws relating to foreign trade. It then became necessary to say something about the beneficial effects of foreign trade, and the manner in which those effects were obstructed by the laws as they then stood. To the judges who were to decide the business, it appeared a most satisfactory account of the matter, when they were told that foreign trade brought money into the country, but that the laws in question hindered it from bringing so much as it would otherwise do. Those arguments therefore produced the wished-for effect. The prohibition of exporting gold and silver was in France and England confined to the coin of those respective countries. The exportation of foreign coin and bullion was made free. In Holland, and in some other places, this liberty was extended even to the coin of the country. The attention of government was turned away from guarding against the exportation of gold and silver, to watch over the balance of trade as the only cause which could occasion any augmentation or diminution of those metals. From one fruitless care it was turned away to another care much more intricate, much more embarrassing, and just equally fruitless. The title of Mun's book, England's Treasure in Foreign Trade, became a fundamental maxim in the political oeconomy, not of England only, but of all other commercial countries. The inland or home trade, the most important of all, the trade in which an equal capital affords the greatest revenue, and creates the greatest employment to the people of the country, was considered as subsidiary only to foreign trade. It neither brought money into the country, it was said, nor carried any out of it. The country therefore could never become either richer or poorer by means of it, except so far as its prosperity or decay might indirectly influence the state of foreign trade.[19]

With this analysis to hand, Smith was ready to relaunch the 'very violent attack' on the entire commercial system he had begun in Edinburgh in 1750, pursued in Glasgow and was now able to bring to an intellectually and polemically devastating conclusion. In Glasgow, his critique of policies which had obstructed free trade had been piecemeal; now they could be viewed as part of this superstition that lay at the heart of an entire civilization, and was infecting the governance of

every European state. He was now able to attack restraints on foreign imports, which had been designed to seal off domestic markets from foreign competition, and attempts to create a favourable balance of trade with foreign competitors. Protected domestic markets had the effect of artificially raising prices, discouraging improvement and promoting trade policies designed to increase national wealth by 'beggaring' one's neighbours. It was all a function of 'the wretched spirit of monopoly' which had afflicted mercantile and manufacturing activity throughout history and was now reshaping the history of the world. It had fostered the growth of the great, 'exclusive' trading companies that were opening Asia and the Americas to European commerce and were taking over the governance of countries like Bengal, leaving Smith to comment sourly that, 'The government of an exclusive company of merchants, is, perhaps, the worst of all governments for any country whatever.'[20] As for what Hume had called the 'jealousy of trade', that was fostering ruinously expensive wars in Europe and overseas which threatened the very survival of every great power. 'Commerce,' said Smith,

> which ought naturally to be, among nations, as among individuals, a bond of union and friendship, has become the most fertile source of discord and animosity. The capricious ambition of kings and ministers has not, during the present and preceding century, been more fatal to the repose of Europe, than the impertinent jealousy of merchants and manufacturers. The violence and injustice of the rulers of mankind is an ancient evil, for which, I am afraid, the nature of human affairs can scarce admit of a remedy. But the mean rapacity, the monopolizing spirit of merchants and manufacturers, who neither are, nor ought to be the rulers of mankind, though it cannot perhaps be corrected, may very easily be prevented from disturbing the tranquillity of any body but themselves.[21]

So far, Smith's attack on the commercial system had been theoretical and based on his discussion of the division of labour and the natural progress of opulence in a nation unencumbered by the relics of feudalism and enjoying a system of free trade and perfect liberty. He had, of course, been meticulous in illustrating different aspects of his theory with carefully, and often painstakingly chosen historical examples. But what his theory and his attack on the commercial system had lacked was any strong example of a nation whose economic progress had actually followed the route laid out in an essentially conjectural analysis. He had naturally called attention to Scotland's remarkable economic and political progress since the creation of its free-trade union with England to illustrate his Glasgow lectures, and he made copious use of Scottish examples to illustrate various themes of the *Wealth of Nations*. But Scotland, still encumbered by the constraints of the feudal system, was not the perfect example of the sort of natural progress Smith had envisaged. His masterstroke was to introduce the experience of colonial America as the classic, and indeed the only possible, example of a society whose progress had been rapid and natural by comparison with that of Europe.

In his eyes, the root cause of the American colonies' progress was simple enough: 'plenty of good land, and liberty to manage their own affairs their own way'.[22] American land was cheap, and inheritance – in some colonies at least – was unencumbered by primogeniture, entails and high taxes. The colonists themselves appeared educated, frugal, tractable and hardworking. They were natural Smithian improvers who invested their stock in agriculture and simple manufactures and, because labour was relatively scarce, paid their labourers high wages, which encouraged them to set up on their own. Above all, they possessed a spirit of equality that encouraged a 'republican' attitude to government. For whatever claims the mother country might make in matters of sovereignty, taxation and the regulation of trade, it was too far away for these claims to be enforced. As a result the American and West Indian colonies had developed a system of regional trade that was everything Smith could have longed for in Europe. 'The most perfect freedom of trade is permitted between the British colonies of America and the West Indies, both in the enumerated and in the non-enumerated commodities. Those colonies are now becoming so populous and thriving, that each of them finds in some of the others a great and extensive market for every part of its produce. All of them taken together, they make a great internal market for the produce of one another.'[23]

Smith's analysis was schematic and introduced what became a celebrated contribution to contemporary debate about Britain's future relations with America. It was also the basis of his crucial discussion of the consequences of colonial trade for the colonies and the mother country. Smith had to show that the Navigation Acts and the various regulations that had turned trade with the colonies into a 'monopoly trade' had retarded the overall development of the British economy. His argument was fairly predictable: the monopoly trade had diverted capital from European to American trade, with the result that

> The industry of Great Britain, instead of being accommodated to a great number of small markets, has been principally suited to one great market. Her commerce, instead of running in a great number of small channels, has been taught to run principally in one great channel. But the whole system of her industry and commerce has thereby been rendered less secure; the whole state of her body politick less healthful, than it otherwise would have been. In her present condition, Great Britain resembles one of those unwholesome bodies in which some of the vital parts are overgrown, and which, upon that account, are liable to many dangerous disorders scarce incident to those in which all the parts are more properly proportioned. A small stop in that great blood-vessel, which has been artificially swelled beyond its natural dimensions, and through which an unnatural proportion of the industry and commerce of the country has been forced to circulate, is very likely to bring on the most dangerous disorders upon the whole body politick. The expectation of a rupture with the colonies, accordingly, has struck the people of Great Britain with more terror than they ever felt for a Spanish armada, or a French invasion.[24]

This vivid and suggestive pathology of current fears about the consequences of the loss of the American colonies emphasized Smith's virtuosity as an analyst of contemporary beliefs. But it is also notable for Smith's uncharacteristic failure to provide the illustrations that were needed to give substance to his conjectures about the effects of colonial trade on America and the mother country's trade with Europe. It was to provoke the early and powerfully argued retort from Thomas Pownall, a recent governor of Massachusetts, that '*you stretch your reasoning nicely.* You in words advance upon the ground of *probable reasons for believing* only, you prove by probable suppositions only; yet most people who read your book, will think you mean to set up an absolute proof, and your conclusion is drawn as though you had.'[25] It was the response of a critic who understood Smith's method better than most and was in a good position to question the way in which he had used America as the illustration on which the credibility of a vast system had come to depend.

Smith's attack on the commercial system and the wretched spirit of monopoly of its mercantile apostles was animated by more than an enlightened philosopher's outrage at the triumph of superstition. Having dismissed the claims of the nobility, merchants and manufacturers that theirs and the public interest were the same, Smith was now in a position to wind up his discussion with his new philosophical claims about the nature of the public interest. He had shown Quesnay and the *économistes* that a system of perfect liberty did not have to be created by a single revolutionary act of legal despotism. All that was needed was a sovereign who was prepared to remove 'obstructions' to the workings of the market, leaving the rest to nature. For surely a man living in a state of perfect liberty would prefer to employ his resources at home, in a place whose laws, customs and people he knew best rather than in overseas ventures. And would this not contribute more effectively to the task of stimulating local industry and circulating wealth than 'an equal capital employed in the foreign trade of consumption'? For every individual

> generally, indeed, neither intends to promote the publick interest, nor knows how much he is promoting it. By preferring the support of domestick to that of foreign industry, he intends only his own security; and by directing that industry in such a manner as its produce may be of the greatest value, he intends only his own gain, and he is in this, as in many other cases, led by an invisible hand to promote an end which was no part of his intention.[26]

Not only was this to become the most famous and most influential claim of the *Wealth of Nations*, it was the foundational political claim of the enlightened philosopher whose understanding of the public interest had deeper philosophical roots than all but a handful of his Scottish friends can have realized.

It went without saying that Smith's political prescriptions for creating a system of perfect liberty were pragmatic, and recognized the need for a gradual approach to the removal of obstructions – anything else would inevitably provoke serious and probably dangerous opposition. 'To expect, indeed, that the freedom of trade should ever be entirely restored in Great Britain, is as absurd as to expect that an Oceana or Utopia should ever be established in it. Not only the prejudices of the publick, but what is much more unconquerable, the private interests of many individuals, irresistibly oppose it.'[27] This was the pragmatism of the jurist who was always mindful of the fact that the supreme end of government was preserving the rules of justice on which sociability ultimately depended. Smith summed it up in this way:

> All systems either of preference or restraint, therefore, being thus completely taken away, the obvious and simple system of natural liberty establishes itself of its own accord. Every man, as long as he does not violate the laws of justice, is left perfectly free to pursue his own interest his own way, and to bring both his industry and capital into competition with those of any other man, or order of men. The sovereign is completely discharged from a duty, in the attempting to perform which he must always be exposed to innumerable delusions, and for the proper performance of which no human wisdom or knowledge could ever be sufficient; the duty of superintending the industry of private people, and of directing it towards the employments most suitable to the interest of the society.[28]

Smith was now ready to consider the problems modern rulers faced in matters of defence, justice, public works, education and that bane of all early modern sovereigns, religion, all of which played their part in helping to preserve and, if possible, enhance the citizen's capacity for sociability. Much of the review drew on his Glasgow lectures and his habit of analysing problems historically in order to identify practices and beliefs that had been inherited from earlier periods of history and now seemed redundant. He was particularly interested in the costs of different aspects of government and their implications for taxation, realizing that nothing did more to provoke outrage than unfair, arbitrary taxes. Promoting sociability had everything to do with maintaining an acceptable tax system.

Smith clearly relished the task of using conjectural history to explain the changing needs of society in matters of defence, justice and public works; the discussions are lavishly illustrated and generally provocative. The discussion of defence was designed to show libertarians who believed that the country's defence needs could be best secured with citizen militias that, 'It is only by means of a standing army ... that the civilization of any country can be perpetuated, or even preserved for any considerable time.'[29] In the discussion of justice he reiterated his uncomfortably luminous dictum that, 'Civil government, so far as it is instituted for the security of property, is in reality instituted for the defence of the rich against the poor, or of those who have some property against those who have none at all.'[30] It was a way of reminding citizens and magistrates that the task of maintaining a viable system of justice meant preserving inequality and fostering the sense of security on which improvement depended, something that demanded a rigorously impartial enforcement of the rules of justice in societies in which partialities were deeply ingrained. Smith's doubts about the competence of modern governments were pervasive, nowhere more so than in his discussion of the duties of sovereigns in providing roads, canals, bridges and so forth, on which the progress of commerce depended. (In later editions he would add a complementary chapter on trading companies.) These were resources whose costs should fall on users and local organizations, and not on taxpayers and the sovereign. 'The abuses which sometimes creep into the local and provincial administration of a local and provincial revenue, how enormous soever they may appear, are in reality, however, almost always very trifling, in comparison of those which commonly take place in the administration and expenditure of the revenue of a great empire. They are, besides, much more easily corrected.'[31] In the same way, Smith thought that the costs of maintaining a judiciary could always be met out of the fees of court. The real problem was the cost of defence. This was bound to be a charge on the taxpayer, would be heaviest in technologically advanced societies, and could all too easily become ruinous in an age of incessant warfare. Smith's fears of the costs of modern warfare pervade the entire discussion of governance.

Smith's treatment of these fundamental sovereign duties was largely distilled from his Glasgow lectures and earlier sections of the *Wealth of Nations.* However, in considering the sovereign's educational duties, he turned to a subject he had not discussed before, drawing on his own academic experience and on the lessons that could be learned from Scotland's recent past. How were the schools and universities, on which the education of citizens and magistrates depended, to be funded? Rich countries with wealthy churches were more likely to have had well-endowed universities like Oxford, which soon became little more than closed corporations run for the benefit of professors rather than students. In poor countries like Scotland, with poorly endowed universities, professors had to live off student fees and were thus naturally more responsive to the interests of their students. Only an experienced and committed teacher like Smith could have written: 'Such is the generosity of the greater part of young men, that, so far from being disposed to neglect or despise the instructions of their master, provided he shows some serious intention of being of use to them, they are generally inclined to pardon a great deal of incorrectness in the performance of his duty, and sometimes even to conceal from the publick a good deal of gross negligence.'[32] Smith wrote at surprising length about the history of the philosophy curriculum, a subject which particularly interested him; his notes and essays on the subject were to survive the bonfire on which the rest of his unpublished papers perished. What he had to say about the way in which the teaching of philosophy had been perverted by theology in the Christian era would have been familiar enough to most readers, but it mattered because these theologically contaminated universities would always be responsible for training up most of the teachers on whom public education depended.

While there was nothing that could be done about this, Smith was generally optimistic about the future of education in Protestant states that encouraged the sort of independency and toleration characteristic of the Quaker culture of Pennsylvania and the moderate Presbyterianism of modern Scotland. In states like Scotland ministers of religion were obliged to rely on learning, good manners and the respect of rich and poor, rather than on flattery and state patronage for preferment. A clergy of this sort would be likely to produce good teachers who understood the great enlightened dictum that, 'Science is the great antidote to the poison of enthusiasm and superstition', and that well-educated men made good citizens.[33] 'An instructed and intelligent people . . . are always more decent and orderly than an ignorant and stupid one. They feel themselves, each individually, more respectable, and more likely to obtain the respect of their lawful superiors, and they are therefore more disposed to respect those superiors.'[34] Nor would the costs of such education be excessive, universities being funded out of student fees, and the cost of a system of compulsory parochial education run on Scottish lines being negligible. It was for this reason that Smith was able to comment 'there is scarce perhaps to be found any where in Europe a more learned, decent, independent, and respectable set of men, than the greater part of the presbyterian clergy of Holland, Geneva, Switzerland, and Scotland'.[35] Indeed, the only positive role that the sovereign might possibly play in the provision of popular education was by encouraging 'the frequency and gaiety of publick diversions . . . that is by giving entire liberty to all those who for their own interest would attempt, without scandal or indecency, to amuse and divert the people by painting, poetry, musick, dancing', for this would 'easily dissipate . . . that melancholy and gloomy humour which is almost always the nurse of popular superstition and enthusiasm'.[36]

Smith's discussion of taxation and the public debt brought the *Wealth of Nations* to a close and returned for the last time to the two philosophers whose presence pervades the entire book – Quesnay and, above all, Hume. In the discussion of the problems of taxing a commercialized nation Smith paid particular attention to the fashionable view that land should form the basis of a modern tax system, and more particularly to the 'very ingenious' version of that view on which the *économistes*' fiscal system was based, a version which, as we have seen, he thought impracticable as well as being theoretically unsound.[37] His own views were largely an elaboration of Hume's: a viable tax system was one that reflected the distribution of national wealth and was easy and cheap to collect; anything else would be seen as arbitrary and oppressive. His meticulous review of the British tax system was carefully designed to show that the space for new tax opportunities was much more restricted than some politicians and theorists were apt to believe, and concluded that, in spite of all its imperfections, it was probably the most equitable in Europe: a system which could be improved but could not be transformed without a constitutional revolution so massive as to be utopian.

Smith left utopian theorizing to the final pages of his book. His more immediate purpose was to discuss public credit and the consequences of war for public finance, the most topical of all the subjects discussed in the last book of the *Wealth of Nations*. The analysis followed much the same course as Hume's had in 1752. In modern societies, it was all too easy for governments to finance warfare by mortgaging future tax revenues and piling up massive public debts which future generations would have to shoulder. It was a serious error to assume, as some had done, that these public debts were to be regarded as 'the accumulation of a great capital superadded to the other capital of the country, by means of which its trade is extended, its manufactures multiplied, and its lands cultivated and improved much beyond what they could have been by means of that other capital only'.[38] The cost of servicing 'the enormous debts which at present oppress, and will in the long-run probably ruin, all the great nations of Europe' would inevitably mean higher taxation and less economic activity.[39] In 1764 Hume had followed this grim analysis through to a catastrophic conclusion by predicting ruinous increases in the land tax, which would ruin the landed classes and give rise to a new, deadly form of despotism. 'Either the nation must destroy public credit,' Hume exclaimed, 'or public credit will destroy the nation. It is impossible that they can both subsist, after the manner they have been hitherto managed, in this, as well as in some other countries.'[40]

Hume had written with the costs of the War of the Austrian Succession and the Seven Years War in mind; Smith was thinking about the options open to government with a costly American war to finance. His analysis showed that the tax system could not be squeezed much further. Devaluation, apart from being contemptible, was only likely to produce marginal results at great cost to the economy. For Smith, the only practical solution was one based on recent Scottish experience. What, he asked, had done more to stimulate economic growth and tax takings in Scotland than the free trade with England and the colonies as established by the parliamentary Union of 1707? And would not a similar union between Great Britain, Ireland and the

American colonies bring political as well as economic benefits? For it went without saying that this new union would be 'incorporating' in the sense that Ireland and America would be represented in the imperial parliament.

> By the union with England, the middling and inferior ranks of people in Scotland gained a compleat deliverance from the power of an aristocracy which had always oppressed them. By an union with Great Britain the greater part of the people of all ranks in Ireland would gain an equally compleat deliverance from a much more oppressive aristocracy; an aristocracy not founded, like that of Scotland, in the natural and respectable distinctions of birth and fortune; but in the most odious of all distinctions, those of religious and political prejudices.

As the centre of political gravity shifted from America to London, Americans would discover that they had been delivered 'from those rancorous and virulent factions which are inseparable from small democracies, and which have so frequently divided the affections of their people, and disturbed the tranquillity of their governments, in their form so nearly democratical'. No doubt Ireland and America would be more heavily taxed than at present, but with a prudent management of tax resources, that burden 'might not be of long continuance'. And the English might well discover that this new union would do something to keep alive that childish, 'golden dream' of Empire that had been so sedulously fostered by the mercantile interest. Smith's conclusion may have lacked the touch of paranoia that characterized so much of Hume's thinking about contemporary politics in the last years of his life, but it was still deeply pessimistic.

> The rulers of Great Britain have, for more than a century past, amused the people with the imagination that they possessed a great empire on the west side of the Atlantic. This empire, however, has hitherto existed in imagination only. It has hitherto been, not an empire, but the project of an empire; not a gold mine, but the project of a gold mine; a project which has cost, which continues to cost, and which, if pursued in the same way as it has been hitherto, is likely to cost immense expence, without being likely to bring any profit; for the effects of the monopoly of the colony trade, it has been shewn, are, to the great body of the

people, mere loss instead of profit. It is surely now time that our rulers should either realize this golden dream, in which they have been indulging themselves, perhaps, as well as the people; or, that they should awake from it themselves, and endeavour to awaken the people. If the project cannot be completed, it ought to be given up. If any of the provinces of the British empire cannot be made to contribute towards the support of the whole empire, it is surely time that Great Britain should free herself from the expence of defending those provinces in time of war, and of supporting any part of their civil or military establishments in time of peace, and endeavour to accommodate her future views and designs to the real mediocrity of her circumstances.[41]

The *Wealth of Nations* is the greatest and most enduring monument to the intellectual culture of the Scottish Enlightenment. It contains a theory about the behaviour of human beings when they are seen through the lens of Scottish politeness, about agents who are deeply committed to the improvement of mind, manners and property, and are able to believe that in following what seems to be the path of nature they are acting in a way that will serve the public good. But it is also one of the supreme achievements of a remarkable intelligentsia that was engaged in the project for distilling a theory of sociability out of a popular culture of politeness, a theory whose founding fathers were Smith's two great mentors, Hutcheson and Hume. Hume had provided the philosophical resources Smith needed to develop a theory to explain how the experience of common life teaches human beings how to become social animals, capable of surviving, prospering and living virtuously in society. It was Hume who had shown him how to develop an account of the progress of civilization which paid as much attention to the material, moral and intellectual progress of humanity as to the lamentable story of the follies of so many of its rulers. Smith's contribution to this enterprise had arisen from an absorbing interest in the exchange and circulation of goods, services and sentiments, and in the creation of those cultures on which the survival of human society and the progress of civilization depends. It was an interest fostered by vast erudition, by that remarkable *esprit de système* which characterized all his work, and by a profound seriousness of purpose. For in the last resort, the *Wealth of Nations*, like the *Theory of Moral Senti-ments* and the lectures on which it drew, was a call to his contempor-aries to take moral, political and intellectual control of their lives and the lives of those for whom they were responsible. It is in such con-texts that the *Wealth of Nations* needs to be read by historians. The rest can be left to his disciples and critics.

12

Hume's Death

Predictably the first reactions to the *Wealth of Nations* came from Smith's Scottish friends, who had no hesitation in tempering praise with criticism. Hugh Blair, who recalled the occasion on which Smith had read him sections of the book in draft, told him that he had expected much, 'yet I Confess you have exceeded my expectations. One writer after another on these Subjects did nothing but puzzle me. I despaired of ever arriving at clear Ideas. You have given me full and Compleat Satisfaction and my Faith is fixed.' The attack on 'all that interested Sophistry of Merchants' and the 'good Sense and Truth in your doctrine about Universities' was particularly effective, although Smith's comments about the civilizing tendencies of Scottish Presbyterianism were far too optimistic; it 'gives too much aid to that Austere System you Speak of, which is never favourable to the great improvements of mankind', an intriguing remark from a Presbyterian minister, albeit a moderate one. But Blair's greatest regret was Smith's discussion of the American question, which was 'too much like a publication for the moment', a comment which suggests that Blair had not realized how deeply Smith's treatment of the American question was embedded in the entire analysis. He hoped that in future editions Smith would include an index and a 'Syllabus of the whole; expressed in short independent Propositions, like the Syllabus's we are in use to give of our College Lectures'.[1] Smith was to adopt the first suggestion but not the second. The *Wealth of Nations* was a book for statesmen, not students.

Other members of Smith's Scottish circle followed much the same line. Like Blair, William Robertson admitted that Smith had exceeded his expectations and thought that he might even succeed in liberalizing the vulgar Whiggery of the day.

> You have formed into a regular and consistent system one of the most intricate and important parts of political science, and if the English be capable of extending their ideas beyond the narrow and illiberal arrangements introduced by the mercantile supporters of Revolution principles, and countenanced by Locke and some of their favourite writers, I should think your Book will occasion a total change in several important articles both in police and finance.[2]

Adam Ferguson, characteristically relishing the prospect of controversy, looked forward to the outrage the book would cause in Scotland in the Church, the universities and the merchant communities, although as an ardent libertarian defender of militias he warned Smith that he himself would have things to say about Smith's criticisms of militias. 'The gentlemen and peasants of this country do not need the authority of philosophers to make them supine and negligent of every resource they might have in themselves, in the case of certain extremities, of which the pressure, God knows, may be at no great distance. But more of this at Philippi.'[3] These were marginal criticisms and it is clear that more substantial points were being reserved for future dinner-table discussion. John Millar told Hume that he had problems with Smith's 'great leading principle concerning the unbounded freedom of trade', and wondered how far it should be carried; was it really true that the interests of manufacturers and merchants were necessarily opposed to those of the public?[4] But Hume's opinions must have been the ones Smith most wanted to hear. He had reservations about Smith's style, which have not survived, although Millar thought them too severe, but these were kept to himself. But his letter of congratulation was notable for tempering generous praise with intimations of serious doubts about Smith's theory of price.

> Edinburgh, 1 Apr. 1776
>
> Euge! Belle! Dear Mr Smith: I am much pleas'd with your Performance, and the Perusal of it has taken me from a State of great Anxiety. It was a Work of so much Expectation, by yourself, by your Friends, and by the Public, that I trembled for its Appearance; but am now much

relieved. Not but that the Reading of it necessarily requires so much Attention, and the Public is disposed to give so little, that I shall still doubt for some time of its being at first very popular: But it has Depth and Solidity and Acuteness, and is so much illustrated by curious Facts, that it must at last take the public Attention. It is probably much improved by your last Abode in London. If you were here at my Fireside, I shoud dispute some of your Principles. I cannot think, that the Rent of Farms makes any part of the Price of the Produce, but that the Price is determined altogether by the Quantity and the Demand. It appears to me impossible, that the King of France can take a Seignorage of 8 per cent upon the Coinage . . . . But these and a hundred other Points are fit only to be discussed in Conversation; which, till you tell me the contrary, I shall still flatter myself with soon. I hope it will be soon: For I am in a very bad State of Health and cannot afford a long Delay.[5]

This letter opened what was to be the last chapter in a long, close and fruitful friendship. Hume had not been well for some time and was losing weight; he told Smith in February 1776 that he had lost five stones since 1773 and that if he delayed his return to Scotland much longer 'I shall probably disappear altogether'.[6] In April, Joseph Black diagnosed what sounds like a form of cancer and urged Smith to return to Scotland as soon as possible, 'that he may have the Comfort of your Company so much the sooner'.[7] Hume was resigned to the fact that he was dying, having told Black that his mother had died of the same condition, but he agreed to make the uncomfortable journey to London to consult his old friend Sir John Pringle, and to take the waters at Bath. He travelled south in May 1776, crossing Smith's journey north at Morpeth, where they discussed Hume's will and Smith's duties as his literary executor. Hume was deeply preoccupied with the future of his philosophical and historical works, and later correspondence suggests that their discussions revolved around the disposal of his unpublished papers and the publication of the new edition of his works, on which he had been working for several years. Much of the business was straightforward. Smith would see the posthumous edition through the press and would make suitable arrangements for publishing the short autobiography, *My Own Life*, Hume had just completed. He would ensure that anything not written in the last five years would remain unpublished and would be destroyed 'at your leisure'. There was one exception, however, the *Dialogues Concerning Natural Religion* Hume had written in 1750–51 for circulation among his closest friends in the belief that they were too sceptical for public consumption. Hume wanted Smith to publish them posthumously and this Smith absolutely refused to do. It was a disagreement that was to cast a shadow over their relationship in the last weeks of Hume's life.

Nothing mattered more to Hume than the publication of the *Dialogues* for they had come to occupy an essential place in the architecture of a carefully constructed literary and philosophical legacy. In *My Own Life* he had written a brief and memorably cogent Plutarchian account of his life and character, in which he consigned himself to history in exactly the same way that he had signed off the rulers of England at the end of their reigns in his *History of England*. He had written of himself as a philosopher whose *Treatise of Human Nature* had fallen 'dead born' from the press, whose subsequent career as an essayist had got off to a slow start, and whose reputation had only begun to rise with the publication of the *Political Discourses* of 1752 and the increasingly popular *History of England*. Nature had given him a sanguine and equable temper; belated literary fame had brought him a small fortune and had exposed him at every turn to the obloquy of the clergy and the party-political ideologues. The new edition of his works, on which he had spent his last years, and whose proofs he was correcting on his deathbed, was designed to eradicate unnecessary signs of iconoclasm in order to preserve the reputation for 'impartiality' he had always striven to achieve. It was to include a new political essay, 'Of the Origins of Government', which distilled his thinking about the principles of government and political obligation. By publishing the *Dialogues* he would be leaving the essence of his thinking about natural religion. With their publication his legacy would be complete.

Smith's objections to the publication of the *Dialogues* were anything but straightforward. At one level they were prudential. As he told William Strahan, Hume's publisher, after his death, publication would provoke outrage, it would affect the sales of the new edition, and it would put Smith, as the man charged with their publication, in an invidious and embarrassing personal position.[8] Indeed, as Hume proposed to leave him £200 in recognition of his work as literary executor, some would even think Smith had published the *Dialogues* for his own profit.[9] Hume would have none of it. He doubted whether they would really cause outrage, and thought that Smith's fears about the consequences of being associated with the publication of an outrageous document largely specious. He proposed a compromise. While the decision on whether or not to publish posthumously would be 'entirely to your Discretion', Hume's opinion was

> that, if upon my Death, you determine never to publish these papers, you shoud leave them, seal'd up with my Brother and Family, with some Inscription, that you reserve to Yourself the Power of reclaiming them, whenever you think proper. If I live a few Years longer, I shall publish them myself. I consider an Observation of Rochefoucault, that a Wind, though it extinguishes a Candle, blows up a fire.[10]

Smith replied that he would take 'every possible measure which may prevent anything from being lost which you wish should be preserved' and would ensure that the *Dialogues* were returned to Hume's nephew after his own death. But Hume was still troubled. A week before his death on 25 August, he ordered new copies of the *Dialogues* to be made for his nephew, his publisher and Smith: 'It will bind you to nothing, but will serve as a Security.' His last letter to 'My Dearest Friend', written two days before his death, told Smith that he had left the property of the *Dialogues* to his nephew 'in case by any accident it should not be published within three years after my decease'. The letter ends 'Adieu My dearest Friend.'[11]

Two weeks later Smith gave Strahan his own account of the affair:

> I once had persuaded him to leave it entirely to my discretion either to publish them at what time I thought proper or not to publish them at all. Had he continued of this mind the manuscript should have been most carefully preserved and upon my decease restored to his family; but it never should have been published in my lifetime. When you have read it you will, perhaps, think it not unreasonable to consult some prudent friend about what you ought to do.
>
> I propose to add to his life a very well authenticated account of his behaviour during his last Illness. I must, however, beg that his life and

those dialogues may not be published together; as I am resolved, for many reasons, to have no concern in the publication of those dialogues.[12]

Smith's behaviour in the last weeks of his closest friend's life is not easy to fathom. It certainly had nothing to do with his own views about religion, which he kept to himself but show every sign of being substantially the same as Hume's – Smith was as deeply committed to Hume's sceptical theory of human nature as Hume himself. Nor did he think the *Dialogues* were in any way unworthy of their author – he admitted to Strahan that they were indeed 'finely written'. And his admiration for Hume's manner of dying was unreserved and Humean in its contempt of traditional Christian morality. He told a mutual friend, 'Poor David Hume is dying very fast, but with great chearfulness and good humour and with more real resignation to the necessary course of things, than any Whining Christian ever dyed with pretended resignation to the will of God.'[13] But experience of orthodox polemic at Glasgow, Oxford and Edinburgh must have given Smith a horror of violent religious controversy and of the sort of arguments which were impervious to his or anyone else's philosophy. Indeed one wonders whether it was Voltaire's fearlessness in attacking *l'infame* in a way that was beyond him that had made Smith a lifelong admirer. At all events, by 1776 he was prepared to admit to Strahan that the prospect of being associated with the publication of the *Dialogues* had disturbed his peace of mind.[14]

But Smith was to make substantial amends for his timidity with his supplement to *My Own Life*. As he had told Hume, it would give 'some account, in my own name, of your behaviour in this illness, if, contrary to my own hopes, it should prove your last'.[15] The tribute took the form of a letter to William Strahan, which was published as a supplement to *My Own Life* in 1777. It is a meticulously recorded, moving account of Hume's last months and a portrait of an unashamed pagan who had faced death cheerfully and with 'the most perfect complacency and resignation'. It ends with Smith's final tribute to his closest friend, a character sketch which has probably done more than any other to shape the portrait of an iconic philosopher and man of letters:

Thus died our most excellent and never to be forgotten friend; concerning whose philosophical opinions men will, no doubt, judge variously, every

one approving or contemning them, according as they happen to coincide
or disagree with his own; but concerning whose character and conduct
there can scarce be a difference of opinion. His temper, indeed, seemed to
be more happily balanced, if I may be allowed such an expression, than
that perhaps of any other man I have ever known. Even in the lowest state
of his fortune, his great and necessary frugality never hindered him from
exercising, upon proper occasions, acts both of charity and generosity. It
was a frugality founded, not upon avarice, but upon the love of independency. The extreme gentleness of his nature never weakened either the
firmness of his mind, or the steadiness of his resolutions. His constant
pleasantry was the genuine effusion of good-nature and good-humour,
tempered with delicacy and modesty, and without even the slightest tinc-
ture of malignity, so frequently the disagreeable source of what is called
wit in other men. It never was the meaning of his raillery to mortify; and
therefore, far from offending, it seldom failed to please and delight, even
those who were the objects of it. To his friends, who were frequently the
objects of it, there was not perhaps any one of all his great and amiable
qualities, which contributed more to endear his conversation. And that
gaiety of temper, so agreeable in society, but which is so often accompanied
with frivolous and superficial qualities, was in him certainly attended
with the most severe application, the most extensive learning, the greatest
depth of thought, and a capacity in every respect the most comprehensive.
Upon the whole, I have always considered him both in his lifetime and
since his death, as approaching as nearly to the idea of a perfectly wise
and virtuous man, as perhaps the nature of human frailty will permit.[16]

But even this last tribute was tempered with caution and a determination not to arouse the fury of the zealots. It was built around a recent
conversation about one of Hume's favourite books, Lucian's *Dialogues*.
Smith reported the conversation to a mutual friend in London, on
14 August, a few days before Hume's death. Hume had remembered
Lucian's amusing account of the reasons different ghosts had given the
boatman Charon for delaying their departure to the underworld.

[He] represents one Ghost as pleading for a short delay till he should
marry a young daughter, another till he should finish a house he had
begun, a third till he had provided a portion for two or three young

Children, I began to think of what Excuse I could alledge to Charon in order to procure a short delay, and as I have now done everything that I ever intended to do, I acknowledge that for some time no tolerable one occurred to me; at last I thought I might say, Good Charon, I have been endeavouring to open the eyes of people; have a little patience only till I have the pleasure of seeing the churches shut up, and the Clergy sent about their business; but Charon would reply, O you loitering rogue; that wont happen these two hundred years; do you fancy I will give you a lease for so long a time? Get into the boat this instant.[17]

In the published letter to Strahan, the story has been tweaked and the remarks about the Church and the clergy removed. 'Have a little patience, good Charon,' Hume is now reported as saying; 'I have been endeavouring to open the eyes of the Public. If I live a few years longer, I may have the satisfaction of seeing the downfal of some of the prevailing systems of superstition.'

The final irony was to be that when the *Dialogues* were finally published anonymously by Strahan in 1779 on the authority of Hume's nephew, there was no public uproar at all, but Smith's *Letter to Strahan* itself provoked outrage from High Churchmen in England, led by George Horne, the President of Magdalen College, Vice-Chancellor of Oxford and future Bishop of Norwich. Horne had already set himself up as the scourge of 'that modern paper building of philosophical infidelity' and his *Letter to Adam Smith, LL.D. on the Life, Death and Philosophy of his Friend David Hume, Esq.* excoriated Smith for his blatant failure to present Hume as a man who ought to have sought the consolations of religion on his deathbed. 'You would persuade us', he said,

by the example of David Hume, Esq., that atheism is the only cordial for low spirits and the proper antidote against the fear of death, but surely he who can reflect with complacency on his friend thus employing his talents in this life, and thus amusing himself with Lucian, whist and Charon at his death, can smile over Babylon in ruins, esteem the earthquakes which destroyed Lisbon as agreeable occurrences, and congratulate the hardened Pharaoh on his overthrow in the Red Sea.[18]

It was a pamphlet which detonated a short and violent press controversy which must have reminded Smith of the Oxford zealotry he had encountered some thirty years earlier. According to Ramsay of Ochter-tyre, it caused some of his Edinburgh friends 'who revered his character and admired his writings' to think of him 'as an avowed sceptic', something that caused him 'very great pain'.[19] More surprising, however, was the reaction of some of Smith's friends in Johnson's Club. James Boswell, who had recently referred to his old professor as 'a professed infidel with a bag-wig', reported a dismissive attack on the *Letter to Strahan* by Edmund Burke, a friend of Smith as well as Hume. Burke thought Smith's eulogy typical of the clannishness of modern infidels.

> Talking of David Hume, Mr Burke laughed at his life and at Smith's appendix 'most virtuous,' etc. 'This,' said he, 'is said for the credit of their church, and the members of no church use more art for its credit.' He said, 'Here was a man [Hume] at a great age [sixty-five], who had been preparing all along to die without showing fear, does it, and rout is made about it. Men in general die easily ... Almost all men have a belief and hope of futurity, without any very clear certainty, which supports them at death.' BOSWELL. 'But death is terrible.' BURKE. 'Yes, to us at present. Because it is like an execution, dying in full health. But when we're gradually prepared for it, not shocking.' While he talked thus my mind was illuminated, and I looked forward to death with ease and resolution and even a flutter not unpleasing.[20]

The episode provoked Smith's wry comment: 'A single, and as, I thought a very harmless Sheet of paper, which I happened to Write concerning the death of our late friend Mr Hume, brought upon me ten times more abuse than the very violent attack I had made upon the whole commercial system of Great Britain.'[21]

Smith was to resolve the anxieties about religious controversy which had tested his oldest and most important friendship with all the fastidiousness of the aesthete. Texts should be allowed to speak for themselves, their philosophy uncontaminated by the vulgarities of public curiosity about their authors or, worse still, by their authors' capacity for self-advertisement. He was appalled by Strahan's suggestion that *My Own Life* should be prefaced by a selection of Hume's letters. 'If a collection of Mr Humes letters ... was to receive the public approbation, as yours certainly would, the Curls of the times would immediately set about rummaging the cabinets of all those who had ever received a scrap of paper from him. Many things would be published not fit to see the light to the great mortification of all those who wish well to his memory.'[22] He was equally offended by the vulgarity of Hume's plans for his own memorial, a conspicuously expensive monumental tomb designed by Robert Adam for the Calton Burying Ground in Edinburgh: 'I don't like that monument. It is the greatest piece of vanity I ever saw in my friend Hume.'[23] This distaste for self-advertisement helps to explain why Smith, almost alone among the Scottish literati, was never painted by the great portraitists of the Scottish Enlightenment, Allan Ramsay, David Martin and Henry Raeburn, and why he would be so determined to destroy nearly all of his private papers. It was part of a mindset that would be infused with the deeply idiosyncratic Stoicism with which the final edition of the *Theory of Moral Sentiments* was to be coloured.

With the controversies after Hume's death behind him, Smith was able to give his full attention to a project he had begun in May or June on his return to Kirkcaldy, the book on the imitative arts which was to be his contribution to the theory of taste and criticism. It is clear from the contents of his library that this was a subject that had interested him for some time, and it arose quite naturally from the remarkable theory of need that had prefaced the Glasgow lectures on police and had been removed from the *Wealth of Nations*. In considering the consequences of the division of labour for the progress of civilization, he had shown how the material progress of mankind created the aesthetic and intellectual needs which science and the arts set out to satisfy. Having spent some fifteen exhausting years on the material needs of mankind and the creation of wealth, he was now turning to the supremely elusive question of man's aesthetic needs and the role of the imitative arts in satisfying them.

Although the book never materialized, Smith gave two papers on the subject to the Glasgow Literary Society in 1788 and left notes for a third. These dealt with imitation in the visual arts, in music and in dancing, and were among the papers spared from the forthcoming archival bonfire. The first two lectures show Smith at the height of his powers, engaged on a subject that was central to his philosophical interests, indebted to Hume, and critical of the French and above all of Rousseau. The debts to Hume were deep and long-standing. In his *Treatise* Hume had identified the philosophy of criticism as one of the essential components of a philosophy of the understanding on which a science of man depended but had, disappointingly, devoted only two rather slender essays to the subject: 'Of Tragedy' and 'Of the Standard of Taste', both published in 1757, five years after the *Political Discourses*. Nevertheless, they would be of as much importance in opening up Smith's aesthetic thinking as Hume's essays on commerce had been for his thinking about political economy. Hume's essays were a contribution to a largely French-led debate about the pleasure we derive from the horrors of tragedy, and about the wider question of whether there could ever be a fixed standard of taste by which to judge the merits of a work of art. So far as Smith was concerned, the essay on tragedy was particularly relevant. Here Hume had suggested that the pleasure we derive from tragedy or any work of art derives from an appreciation of the author's rhetorical skills in representing the passions, and from the curious fact that 'tragedy is an imitation; and imitation is always of itself agreeable.'[24] For Smith, the view that imitation *always* pleases was an overstatement because it failed to take account of the intensity of the pleasure aroused by different forms of imitation:

> What, for example, would be the most perfect imitation of the carpet which now lies before me? Another carpet, certainly, wrought as exactly as possible after the same pattern. But, whatever might be the merit or beauty of this second carpet, it would not be supposed to derive any from the circumstance of its having been made in imitation of the first. This circumstance of its being not an original, but a copy, would even be considered as some diminution of that merit; a greater or smaller, in proportion as the object was of a nature to lay claim to a greater or smaller degree of admiration. It would not much diminish the merit of a common carpet, because in such trifling objects, which at best can lay claim to so little beauty or merit of any kind, we do not always think it worth while to affect originality: it would diminish a good deal that of a carpet of very exquisite workmanship. In objects of still greater importance, this exact, or, as it would be called, this servile imitation, would be considered as the most unpardonable blemish. To build another

St. Peter's, or St. Paul's church, of exactly the same dimensions, proportions, and ornaments with the present buildings at Rome, or London,
would be supposed to argue such a miserable barrenness of genius and
invention as would disgrace the most expensive magnificence.[25]

If imitation of this sort failed to please as much as a great classical
sculpture or a fine modern painting of a Dutch interior, what was one
to make of the enormous appeal of instrumental music, which had no
obvious claim to be regarded as imitative at all? He was interested in
Hume's view that we derive aesthetic pleasure from the skill and eloquence of the playwright or artist, but characteristically preferred to
think of that pleasure as arising from our sense of wonder at the artist's ability to represent an object or a situation in another medium.

But though a production of art seldom derives any merit from its
resemblance to another object of the same kind, it frequently derives a
great deal from its resemblance to an object of a different kind, whether
that object be a production of art or of nature. A painted cloth, the work
of some laborious Dutch artist, so curiously shaded and coloured as to
represent the pile and softness of a woollen one, might derive some
merit from its resemblance even to the sorry carpet which now lies
before me. The copy might, and probably would, in this case, be of
much greater value than the original. But if the carpet was represented
as spread, either upon a floor or upon a table, and projecting from the
back ground of the picture, with exact observation of perspective, and
of light and shade, the merit of the imitation would be still greater.[26]

This proposition was to be the axiom on which Smith's theory of
the pleasure arising from the imitative arts was to rest, the last such
axiom he was to propose in the course of his philosophical career.
However, compared with the confidently posed axioms on which
earlier systems had been based, this was presented with some caution
and hesitation, as though Smith was not yet quite sure whether its
reach was wide enough to encompass a general theory of aesthetics:
'a production of art *seldom* derives any merit from its resemblance to
another object of the same kind, it *frequently* derives a great deal from
its resemblance to an object of a different kind' (my italics).[27] Just what
the problems of extending the reach of this axiom were would become

clear in the discussion of music, and above all in Smith's extraordinary discussion of the pleasures we derive from music and particularly from that most abstract of musical forms, the concertos and
overtures which have no obvious connection with imitation at all.

To develop this dimension of his theory he returned to the natural
history of language he had first explored in Edinburgh in 1748, which
remained at the core of his science of man. There he had suggested
that our capacity for language had its origins in need, and had developed a suggestive conjecture about the natural progress of language
from the inchoate signs and sounds of the child or the aborigine to the
highly structured language systems on which the progress of civilization had depended. Smith used this conjecture to accommodate his
account of the origins and progress of music and dancing, 'perhaps,
the first and earliest pleasures of [man's] own invention'.[28] These were
pleasures which belonged to the world of leisure rather than of work,
to the long periods of inertia between hunting expeditions characteristic of savage societies and to the leisure enjoyed by the fortunate few
in a modern commercial society. In origin, all music was probably
vocal, 'as [the voice] is always the best, so it would naturally be the
first and earliest of musical instruments', and dancing was originally
the natural accompaniment of song; Smith commented that he had
been much struck by the spectacle of an African slave performing a
war dance to his own song 'with such vehemence of action and expression, that the whole company, gentlemen as well as ladies, got up
upon the chairs and tables, to be as much as possible out of the way
of his fury'.[29] The subsequent natural history of music was a story of
the way in which musical voice-sounds and rhythm developed as a
medium for expressing different passions, acquiring a new level of
imitative reach when coupled with words, poetry and narratives.
Indeed while poetry and prose could only hope to describe the succession of a person's passions, vocal music had the unique ability of being
able to imitate them:

> It is upon this account that the words of an air, especially of a passionate
> one, though they are seldom very long, yet are scarce ever sung straight
> on to the end, like those of a recitative; but are almost always broken
> into parts, which are transposed and repeated again and again, according

to the fancy or judgment of the composer. It is by means of such repetitions only, that Music can exert those peculiar powers of imitation which distinguish it, and in which it excels all the other Imitative Arts.[30]

Indeed, in modern opera, music had become a complex and distinctive vehicle of imitation through its use of words, music and performance. Smith's illustrative portrait of the fine opera singer engaged in a uniquely complex act of imitation is notably cogent and equally suggestive of Smith's interest in an art form he must have encountered in Handel's London and Rameau's Paris.

> In a good opera actor, not only the modulations and pauses of his voice, but every motion or gesture, every variation, either in the air of his head, or in the attitude of his body, correspond to the time and measure of Music: they correspond to the expression of the sentiment or passion which the Music imitates, and that expression necessarily corresponds to this time and measure. Music is as it were the soul which animates him, which informs every feature of his countenance, and even directs every movement of his eyes. Like the musical expression of a song, his action adds to the natural grace of the sentiment or action which it imitates, a new and peculiar grace of its own; the exquisite and engaging grace of those gestures and motions, of those airs and attitudes which are directed by the movement, by the time and measure of Music; this grace heightens and enlivens that expression.[31]

Thus far Smith had argued that it was its association with words that had turned vocal music into a singularly complex imitative art. Indeed Rousseau – 'an Author, more capable of feeling strongly than of analising accurately' – had been largely responsible for developing a general theory of music on this basis. But none of this explained the appeal of purely 'instrumental music', which was seldom imitative in any recognizable sense whatever. It was here that the force of Smith's original observation could be found: that the essential appeal of music lay, as the ancients had seen, in a succession of sounds and measures capable of arousing or soothing the mind, for

> time and measure are to instrumental Music what order and method are to discourse; they break it into proper parts and divisions, by which

we are enabled both to remember better what is gone before, and frequently to foresee somewhat of what is to come after ... and, according to the saying of an ancient philosopher and musician, the enjoyment
of Music arises partly from memory and partly from foresight.[32]

It led him to the striking conclusion that the appeal of non-vocal, instrumental music lay in its systemic character, whose appeal was not unlike
that of a system of philosophy. 'In the contemplation of that immense
variety of agreeable and melodious sounds, arranged and digested, both
in their coincidence and in their succession, into so complete and regular
a system, the mind in reality enjoys not only a very great sensual, but a
very high intellectual, pleasure, not unlike that which it derives from the
contemplation of a great system in any other science.'[33]

This raised the question whether music itself could be described as
an imitative art, or whether the notion of imitation was capable of
sustaining the general theory of aesthetics demanded by the terms of
Hume's science of man. It was presumably a question Smith would
have had to consider if he had been able to finish the book. The last,
aborted paper was intended to deal with dancing and tragedy. 'Yes
dancing,' wrote William Richardson, one of Smith's former students,
who heard his papers in Glasgow in 1788, 'for he conceives it to be an
Imitative art; and I believe means to prove, that the Greek tragedy was
no other than a musical Ballet.'[34] However, neither the lecture nor the
proposed book were to be finished. On 24 January 1778 Smith was
appointed to what the Solicitor General Alexander Wedderburn
described as 'a very good office', a seat on the Board of Customs in
Scotland at a salary of £600.[35] It was an appointment which meant
moving with his mother and cousin from Kirkcaldy to Edinburgh.
It was by his own account not an onerous job, but it was time con-
suming. Worse still, Hume's death was to establish him as the iconic
philosopher of the Scottish Enlightenment, a man whose company
was always in demand by his friends and whose acquaintance was
sought by the growing procession of cultural tourists who visited the
city. It was not a situation to encourage a philosopher, accustomed to
work in relative isolation, to develop what would surely have become
a general theory of aesthetics of uncommon power.

Smith's new appointment cannot have been wholly unexpected.

Hugh Blair had anticipated something of the sort when he congratulated Smith on the publication of the *Wealth of Nation*s: 'I Cannot
believe but that they will place you at some of the great Boards in
England. They are Idiots if they do not', though William Strahan was
right in thinking that Margaret Smith's declining health would make
any move to London impossible.[36] Nor was Smith averse to public
recognition of this sort. When the Duke of Buccleuch proposed him
for a vacancy on the Scottish Board in October 1777 he was quick to
announce 'I am now a candidate for a seat at that Board'. The Buc-
cleuchs, the Duchess in particular, lobbied on his behalf. Grey Cooper,
one of the Lords of Treasury, regarded the appointment agreed.[37] So
did London gossip, as reported by Edward Gibbon, a fellow-member
of Johnson's Club, on 26 November:

Dear Sir

Among the strange reports, which are every day circulated in this
wide town, I heard one to-day so very extraordinary, that I know not how
to give credit to it. I was informed that a place of Commissioner of the
Customs in Scotland had been given to a Philosopher who for his own
glory and for the benefit of mankind had enlightened the world by the
most profound and systematic treatise on the great objects of trade and
revenue which had ever been published in any age or in any Country.
But as I was told at the same time that this Philosopher was my particular friend, I found myself very forcible inclined to believe, what I
most sincerely wished and desired.[38]

When the appointment was confirmed on 24 January 1778, Smith
told Buccleuch that he wished to surrender the annuity of £300 the Duke
had been paying him. The Duke refused, saying, as Smith recalled in a
letter to a Danish correspondent, 'that though I had considered what was
fit for my own honour, I had not consider'd what was fit for his; and that
he never would suffer it to be suspected that he had procured an office
for his friend, in order to relieve himself from the burden of such an
annuity. My present situation is therefore fully as affluent as I could wish
it to be.'[39] In the winter of 1778 Smith and his household moved to
Panmure House in Edinburgh's Canongate, a wealthy and celebrated
man. It was to be his home for the last twelve years of his life.

13

Last Years in Edinburgh 1778–90

Smith had returned to Edinburgh as an affluent public intellectual with excellent political connections in London and Edinburgh, a man of some political influence who would not be slow in exercising it when he thought it was proper to do so. For his friends among an ageing literati, his return was particularly welcome. They had recently suffered what Robertson called some 'cruel loppings', not least being the death of David Hume, and Smith already knew from Hugh Blair that 'we often flattered our Selves with the prospect of your Settling amongst us in a Station that could be both Creditable and Usefull' so that Smith could help to help revitalize the city's intellectual life, a role he was happy to perform.[1]

By the late 1770s, the old city was in the middle of the vast and vastly expensive building programme that was designed to turn it into the modern provincial metropolis its literati had long dreamed of. In the *Proposals for Carrying on Certain Public Works in the City of Edinburgh* of 1752, they had envisaged a city with new public buildings and a new suburb on the far side of the North Loch to provide private housing fit for the middling ranks of a polite and commercial nation. The Royal Exchange, situated in Parliament Square and facing the cathedral, had been completed in 1760 and its upper floor had been leased back to the Crown for £360 p.a. to accommodate the Board of Customs. An enormous Register House to house the nation's public records had been begun in 1774 and was to be completed in 1788, two years before Smith's death. The wealthy College of Physicians had built themselves new rooms and a new library in the new town, and an observatory had been erected on Calton Hill. The stinking North Loch had been drained and spanned by an enormous bridge to link the old town to the lands on the far side of the loch on which the new town was being developed.² There were even grandiose plans afoot to replace the existing squalid university buildings ('Hae miseriae nostrae' as William Robertson called them) with a vast new building set in a new academic suburb to the south of the city. It would be approached by a grand avenue leading from the old town and would provide the city's intellectual life with the institutional focal point it had hitherto lacked. These were all massively expensive developments which had been made possible by the building boom following the end of the Seven Years War in 1763, and had been brought to a sudden halt by the collapse of the Ayr Bank in 1772. Smith must have noticed them with some interest. For one thing, the Duke of Buccleuch owned lands in the city which were being proposed for development, and there is some evidence that he relied on Smith to represent him at appropriate town council meetings.³ For another, Smith had known members of the Adam family since childhood, and these celebrated and energetic architects were involved in every aspect of the city's architectural development. The Royal Exchange and the Register House were the work of John Adam. Robert Adam was responsible for building a riding school near the university. He also submitted unsuccessful plans for the development of the new town to the north of the city and the grand avenue and academic suburb to the south, but he did win the contract for building the elegant and desirable Charlotte Square and the new university building, which he expected to be his masterpiece.

In choosing a place to live Smith was to be mindful of his status as well as the needs of an old and increasingly frail mother. He showed no interest in following Hume's somewhat iconoclastic path by settling in neoclassical splendour in a new town suburb somewhat remote from the centre of city life. He confessed that he would have preferred a house in George Square, the largest of the residential squares built on the south side of the city and much favoured by the city's social elite. In the end he opted for Panmure House in the Canongate, once the aristocratic suburb of the city and known for its large houses and gardens and for its newer, more fashionable dwellings; Lord Kames' house in New Street, like that of Lord Hailes, was much admired for its elegance. Panmure House was a fairly large, architecturally nondescript house built in the late seventeenth century for a Jacobite peer. Overlooking the Calton crags and Hume's distressingly vulgar tomb, it was in easy reach of the Customs House and the houses of most of his friends. Most important of all it had the inestimable advantage of being next door to the Canongate Church, a matter of no small importance to the devout and increasingly frail Mrs Smith. It was large enough to house Smith, his mother, his cousin Janet Douglas, who had kept house for him in Glasgow, and his nine-year-old cousin and heir David Douglas, whose education he had agreed to supervise. And it was well enough placed and suited to the business of keeping open house every Sunday evening to his friends and the growing number of visitors and cultural tourists who wished to meet him. 'House magnificent and place fine,' William Windham commented in 1785 when visiting with Edmund Burke. 'Felt strongly the impression of a family completely Scotch.'[4] One of the first things Smith did was to adorn it with a newly commissioned and observant portrait of the formidable Mrs Smith by a visiting painter, Conrad Metz.

The office of Commissioner of Customs may have been well-paid and honourable but it was no sinecure. By Smith's day, there were eight hundred separate acts of parliament affecting customs duties to superintend, endless adjudications to attend to and an entire revenue service to supervise.[5] The Board met four days a week throughout the year, breaking only for public holidays and, as Smith commented, it was all too likely that the remaining three days would be interrupted by Board business. The Board itself was small, composed in 1778 of a Senior Commissioner, four Commissioners, a Solicitor and Inspector General, and a Secretary. It seems to have worked amicably enough; Smith probably already knew two fellow-Commissioners, George Clerk Maxwell, a noted agricultural improver who would shortly become a regular member of the Oyster Club, and James Edgar, a dedicated classicist and, like Smith, a member of the Poker Club. He liked the Solicitor and Inspector General Alexander Osborne, who at 6'6" was said to be the tallest man in Scotland (and built to match). He even took Osborne to a raree show to see two skinny Irish giants who were only a few inches taller than him. He told Henry Mackenzie that the Irishmen scented competition and were not amused.[6] No Commissioner could have been more assiduous in attending the Board than Smith. He did not miss a single meeting from 3 February, when he took the oath of office, to 19 March 1782, when he was granted four months' leave to go to London to work on the next edition of the *Wealth of Nations*, and probably to check on his health. From July 1782 to 3 January 1787 he only missed twenty-four meetings, six of which were occasioned by his mother's death. By then, however, his health was failing and his attendance began to tail off.[7] All in all it was the attendance record of a Commissioner who took his office seriously and who understood the importance of maintaining the rules of justice for the security, prosperity and happiness of a nation.

Given his reputation as an expert on taxation, it would not have been surprising if Smith's appointment had been regarded by the Treasury as an opportunity for reviewing the workings of the Scottish Customs at the end of the American War. Lord North, and after him the Earl of Shelburne, were deeply concerned with the disastrous state of public finances. The new Lord Advocate Henry Dundas, soon to be in virtual control of Scottish government, was under pressure from the Treasury to improve the rate of return of Scottish tax revenue to London.[8] In the end, however, the confused state of Westminster politics at the end of the war ensured that nothing much was done, and although Dundas and Smith seem to have discussed Scottish customs business in London in the spring of 1782, it only resulted in Smith being asked to look into a request by the Convention of Royal Burghs to standardize the fees taken by Customs officers in different parts of Scotland and to place those taken in the firths and estuaries on the same footing as their equivalents in England. Smith did as he was asked, but he did his best to discourage the Treasury from implementing the new table of fees, on the grounds that they would result in a loss of income to the officials concerned and would encourage yet more mercantile corruption.

> Of many Officers the Income may even be so far reduced as to make it difficult for them to subsist suitably to that Rank in the Society which in reason ought to belong to them; The narrowness of their Circumstances may even force many of them into a dependency upon the Merchants which must immediately prove hurtful to the Public Revenue and in the end probably ruinous to the unhappy Persons who may have

thus endeavoured to relieve their necessities by accepting of improper Gratuities.

It led one of Shelburne's friends to report that '[Smith] is very well provided for in the customs, where he does not innovate'.[9] Innovation was a matter for ministers, not government officials.

In 1780, Smith told a Danish correspondent, Andreas Holt, 'I am occupied four days in every Week at the Custom House; during which it is impossible to sit down seriously to any other business: during the other three days too, I am liable to be frequently interrupted by the extraordinary duties of my office, as well as by my own private affairs, and the common duties of society.'[10] These, too, were in their way demanding enough. Not only was he meticulous in following local practice by keeping open house on Sunday evenings to his friends, their acquaintances and peripatetics armed with letters of introduction, he, and two old fellow-bachelor friends, Joseph Black and the geologist James Hutton, started a weekly dining club, which met initially in an unobtrusive tavern in the Cowgate. This was the Oyster Club, better known to its members as 'Adam Smith's Club', and it was to become almost as famous in Edinburgh for its conversation as Samuel Johnson's Club in London, though its style was very different.[11] If Johnson was the conversational source of energy in London, the conversation of the three Edinburgh bachelors was regarded as the Oyster Club's reason for existence. 'Their conversation was always free,' Hutton's biographer John Playfair wrote, 'often scientific but never didactic or disputatious and this club was much the resort of the strangers who visited Edinburgh from any object connected with art or science; it derived from these an extraordinary degree of variety and interest.' Hutton's conversation was characterized by 'ardour' and even enthusiasm, Black's by caution and coolness; indeed, 'While Dr Black dreaded nothing so much as error ... Dr Hutton dreaded nothing so much as ignorance ... the one was always afraid of going beyond the truth, and the other of not reaching it.'[12] As for Smith, Dugald Stewart recalled, 'In the society of his friends, he had no disposition to form those qualified conclusions that we admire in his writings; and he generally contented himself with a bold and masterly sketch of the object, from the first point of view in which his temper, or his fancy, presented it.' This was the conversational practice of a philosopher who could be surprisingly iconoclastic and loved arguing from bold premises which might or might not be susceptible of systematic illustration. As Stewart rather primly put it, 'it was the fault of his unpremeditated judgments, to be too systematical, and too much in extremes'.[13]

It was as a public figure of this sort that Smith lived his last years in Edinburgh and began to generate the mythology that has surrounded him ever since. His friends noted conversation which was as free and easy with those he liked as it had been with his Glasgow students, but smacked of pedagogy to the less sympathetic. His capacity for self-abstraction became a matter of frequent comment. John Kay, a local cartoonist, left two cartoons of Smith, one of which, made in 1787, shows him on his way to the Customs House, totally wrapped in thought, his cane over his shoulder and carrying a bunch of flowers, perhaps as protection against Edinburgh's notorious and distracting stench.[14] That great memorialist and mythmaker Walter Scott reported that

> When walking in the Street, Adam had a manner of talking and laughing to himself, which often attracted the notice and excited the surprise of the passengers. He used himself to mention the ejaculation of an old market-woman, 'Hegh, sirs' shaking her head as she uttered it; to which her companion answered, having echoed the compassionate sigh, 'and he is well put on too!' expressing their surprise that a decided lunatic, who, from his dress, appeared to be a gentleman, should be permitted to walk abroad.[15]

In these last years of his life Smith continued to live in the hope of having enough time to write, but it was not to be. An ex-student, David Callander of Craigforth, told Dugald Stewart that his Edinburgh friends were horrified to learn that 'he, in some measure gave up his books' on entering the Customs House and remonstrated with him, presumably because they had expected him to treat the post as a semi-sinecure. Callander went on to allege that Smith had even proposed exchanging his place in the Customs for a pension of lesser value which had just been awarded to an acquaintance, 'but this was not allowed'.[16] Smith himself told Andreas Holt in October 1780 that, 'The only thing I regret [in my present situation] is the interruptions to my literary pursuits, which the duties of my office necessarily occasion. Several Works which I had projected are likely to go on much more slowly than they otherwise would have done.'[17] In 1782 he told Sir Joshua Reynolds that he was 'about finishing an Essay' on the imitative arts, but as his theory was still incomplete in 1787, this was over-optimistic.[18] In 1785 he was writing to another friend, the Duc de La Rochefoucauld, about

> two other great works upon the anvil; the one is a sort of Philosophical History of all the different branches of Literature, of Philosophy, Poetry and Eloquence; the other is a sort of theory and History of Law and Government. The materials of both are in order. But the indolence of old age, tho' I struggle violently against it, I feel coming fast upon me, and whether I shall ever be able to finish either is extremely uncertain.[19]

In 1779 or 1780, an old Edinburgh friend, Henry Mackenzie, perhaps realizing that Smith's time for writing philosophy was over, suggested that he might be interested in using his limited time to contribute to the *Mirror*, Mackenzie's immensely successful journal of polite letters. It was a shrewd suggestion. The journal's ethics were strongly Smithian and two of its regular contributors, William Craig and Robert Cullen, were favourite former pupils, successful lawyers and, like Smith, men with limited time for writing. But Smith refused. 'He half promised to comply with my request; but afterwards told me he had tried a Paper without Success. "My Manner of Writing, said he, will not do for a Work of that Sort; it runs too much into Deduction and inference."'[20]

Perhaps the severest blow of all was the death of his mother on 23 May 1784. Throughout his career Smith had relied on the isolation of Kirkcaldy and the domestic world over which his mother presided to make philosophical work possible. If the move to Edinburgh had violated that state of domestically controlled isolation, her death destroyed it. Ramsay of Ochtertye described it as 'a dreadful shock to his spirits, and made him fancy himself a helpless forlorn being . . . In truth the poor man seemed to sorrow as those without hope.'[21] His tribute in a letter to Strahan apologizing for a delay in returning proofs was written for a friend who had known his mother for many years and probably understood better than most how completely Smith had depended on her. It is a letter that has already been quoted but is worth repeating here.

> I had just then come from performing the last duty to my poor old Mother; and tho' the death of a person in the ninetieth year of her age was no doubt an event most agreable to the course of nature; and, therefore, to be foreseen and prepared for; yet I must say to you, what I have said to other people, that the final separation from a person who certainly loved me more than any other person ever did or ever will love me; and whom I certainly loved and respected more than I ever shall either love or respect any other person, I cannot help feeling, even at this hour, as a very heavy stroke upon me. Even in this state of mind, however, it gives me very great concern to hear that there is any failure in your health and spirits. The good weather, I hope, will soon reestablish both in their ordinary vigour. My friends grow very thin in the world, and I do not find that my new ones are likely to supply their place.

The letter is signed 'My Dear friend, most faithfully and affectionately ever yours, Adam Smith'.[22]

Whatever hopes Smith may have had of realizing his greater philosophical designs, what really mattered was leaving his two great published works in as perfect a state as possible. His most immediate concern was a new edition of the *Wealth of Nations*. This was partly because his work at the Customs was generating useful illustrative material, partly because its message needed to be sharpened in the light of the catastrophic consequences of the American War of Independence, but mostly because Smith wished to make one final assault on the commercial system. The first edition had been published at the start of a relatively popular war which Britain was expected to win. General Burgoyne's defeat at Saratoga in 1777 and the subsequent entry of France and Spain into the conflict had escalated what many were beginning to think of as an unwinnable war fought by an incompetent and corrupt ministry. The fall of Lord North's government in 1782 was to usher in two years of political turmoil, made all the more disturbing by signs of serious political unrest in the English counties and demands from the Irish parliament for legislative independence from Westminster and free trade with Britain. It led Horace Walpole to exclaim: 'I shall not be surprised if our whole trinity is dissolved, and if Scotland should demand a dissolution of the Union. Strange if she does not profit of our distress.'[23] Politicians of all parties were now faced with questions of the utmost magnitude: the peace treaty with America and the future of Anglo-American relations; the future of Anglo-Irish relations; and, running though it all, the problem of paying for a disastrous war which was dangerously overstretching public finances. Because he was a senior Customs official, a friend of Henry Dundas, Lord North, Lord Shelburne and Edmund Burke, Smith was known, if only by repute, to politicians of different parties who debated these issues and were involved in the intricate political manoeuvres of these two fraught years. Because he was a philosopher who believed profoundly in the importance of stable and regular government for the progress of civilization, he could write in October 1783 of the ill-fated Fox–North Coalition, which included several of his friends,

> It would give me the greatest pleasure to believe that the present Administration rests on a solid Basis. It comprehends the worthiest and ablest men in the nation, the heads of the two great Aristocracies, whose disunion had weakened the . . . Government so much as at last to occasion the dismemberment of the empire. Their coalition, instead of being unpopular, was most devoutly to be wished for . . . I trust that the usual folly and impertinence of next winters opposition will more effectually reconcile the King to his new ministers, than . . . any address of theirs has yet been able to do.[24]

Smith had taken leave from the Customs House from March to July 1782 to visit London and work on the new edition, but the *mouvementé* life of the capital was clearly not conducive to work and he was forced to apologize to Thomas Caddell, who was now his publisher, in December 1782 that it was still not ready. In spite of more apologies for further delays ('I have been labouring as hard as the continual interruption which my employment necessarily occasions, will allow me'[25]) the text was not finished until November 1783, and not published until November 1784. The new edition had a curious publishing history. Smith's amendments consisted of 'Some new arguments against the corn bounty; against the Herring buss bounty; a new concluding Chapter upon the mercantile System; A short History and, I presume, a full exposition of the Absurdity and hurtfulness of almost all our chartered trading companies', and an index.[26] Smith was particularly anxious that the readers of the two earlier editions should have access to his latest thoughts and he persuaded his publisher to publish them in a 24,000-word pamphlet, the *Additions and Corrections to the first and second editions of Dr Adam Smith's Inquiry into the Nature and Causes of the Wealth of Nations*, which was to be made available to these earlier readers and then assimilated into what was to be the third edition of 1784.

The *Additions and Corrections* contains Smith's final onslaught on the commercial system and his last thoughts about Britain's future in a post-mercantilist world. The 'Conclusion of the Mercantile System' deepened his assault with an attack on statutes which fostered the insidious practice of encouraging the importation of cheap foreign raw materials, a policy particularly favoured by linen manufacturers, and the corresponding use of bounties to discourage exports and to undercut foreign competition – a practice long favoured by the woollen industry. Smith had no new theoretical point to make but his discussion is striking because it is so densely illustrated from evidence of the statutes, which he had clearly been studying intensively in the Customs House and which showed that parliament had not only actively encouraged such measures, but was in danger of becoming the creature of the mercantile lobby. He was outraged by parliament's willingness to encourage the importation of foreign linen yarn regardless of its consequences for domestic producers and the wages of the poor. Not only were arguments that this would preserve the balance of trade and increase national prosperity spurious and a cloak to naked self-interest, Smith exclaimed, but they were an affront to parliament and to liberty. As he put it in one of the last of the great juristic aphorisms that gave ethical depth to the *Wealth of Nations*, 'To hurt in any degree the interest of any one order of citizens, for no other purpose but to promote that of some other, is evidently contrary to that justice and equality of treatment which the sovereign owes to all the different orders of his subjects.'[27] It was a reminder that the liberalization of trade would have to proceed cautiously if it was not to provoke outrage.

The second new chapter, dealing with the history of trading companies, drew heavily on a 'sober and judicious writer', Adam Anderson's *Historical and Chronological deduction of the Origin of Commerce* (1764), and brilliantly displayed Smith's erudition as a historically minded jurist.[28] His theme was the constitutions of deeply oligarchic companies which served the interests of proprietors rather than the public. Indeed, in time all 'regulated companies' came to resemble 'in every respect, the corporations of trades, so common in the cities and towns of all the different countries of Europe; and are a sort of enlarged monopolies of the same kind.'[29] It was not unreasonable for new trading companies to be granted a 'temporary monopoly' and military assistance from government, in order to allow hazardous enterprises to take root, in much the same way as 'the monopoly of a new machine is granted to its inventor, and that of a new book to its author'.[30] It was not acceptable to allow these monopolies to become all but permanent in a way that ensured that the civil and military government of vast territories like India were subordinated to the interests of a single commercial organization.

The East India Company was, of course, Smith's primary target. Its affairs had been high on the political agenda since 1772 and were now reaching a climacteric. It had fared badly as a result of the bank crash of 1772 and had turned to government for financial help, which Lord North had been willing to provide as long as steps were taken to disentangle the civil and military government of the subcontinent from the affairs of the company by means of new constitutional arrangements. The point of Smith's history was to show that, whatever the constitutional reforms, the civil government of India would always fall into the hands of the company and its dependants. 'It seems impossible, by any alterations, to render those courts, in any respect, fit to govern, or even to share in the government of a great empire; because the greater part of their members must always have too little interest in the prosperity of that empire, to give any serious attention to what may promote it.'[31] Smith's remedy proposed a gradualist approach to a liberal objective. The company's monopoly should be revoked, trade liberalized and the company left to the mercy of the market. He predicted that, 'Without a monopoly . . . a joint stock company, it would appear from experience, cannot long carry on any branch of foreign trade', and concluded:

> The East India Company, upon the redemption of their funds and the expiration of their exclusive privilege, have a right, by act of parliament, to continue a corporation with a joint stock, and to trade in their corporate capacity to the East Indies in common with the rest of their fellow-subjects. But in this situation, the superior vigilance and attention of private adventurers would, in all probability, soon make them weary of the trade.[32]

Gradually and quietly the hold of the East India Company on trade and government would shrivel and die. In theory, it was a simple and unassuming exercise in political and constitutional improvement that would bring about as great a revolution in Britain's relations with the orient as the loss of the American colonies had brought about in the west, a revolution which would usher in a new liberal global order. In fact the company's rule would be succeeded by a singularly illiberal imperial regime which sought to use Smith's liberal proposals to justify its own ends.

The publication of the new edition of the *Wealth of Nations* in November 1784 was an important event in Smith's intellectual career, the moment at which a book originally designed for the political classes and the intelligentsia began to reach a broader market. The first two editions had consisted of about 1,250 quarto copies, selling at £1. 16/- in boards or £2. 2/- bound. The new edition was more affordable – 1,000 copies, in three octave volumes priced at 18s. in boards and 21s. bound. The fourth and fifth editions of 1786 and 1789 were virtually reprints of the third, consisting of 1,250 and 1,500 copies respectively, providing Smith with a revenue of £1,500–£1,800 in his lifetime, and future generations with the text which was to form the basis of subsequent editions and translations.[33]

Revising the *Theory of Moral Sentiments* was to be Smith's last literary venture. It was a larger-scale, theoretically more demanding task than that of revising the *Wealth of Nations* and it was one which

Smith must have known would be his last. Nothing was heard of the project for nearly a year after his mother's death. As he told James Menteath, an old friend from Kirkcaldy, who was thinking of moving to Edinburgh in February 1785, his world was shrinking. 'You are now, except one or two old Cousins, the oldest friend I have now remaining in the world, and it gives me the most unspeakable satisfaction to think that I have some chance of ending my days in your Society and neighbourhood. I ever am, my Dearest friend, your most affectionate and most faithful humble servant Adam Smith.'[34] Smith first announced his intention of revising the *Theory of Moral Sentiments* somewhat offhandedly in April 1785, in a letter to Thomas Caddell: 'If a new edition of the theory is wanted I have a few alterations to make of no great consequence which I shall send to you', but nothing happened.[35] In January 1787 he took a six-month leave of absence from the Customs, and visited London in May and June to see friends and to be treated for piles and an obstruction to the bowel which was painful and debilitating.[36] One of Gibbon's friends was shocked by his physical condition and wrote, 'You will find near the Adelphi poor Adam Smith. I say poor because he seems very weak and not far from the end of his career; some fundamental operation has lately been performed on him by John Hunter since when he seems to pick up a little, I nevertheless fear that the machine is nearly worn out.'[37]

However, the London visit had its consolations for the gratifying reason that government was now in the hands of men who knew and admired the *Wealth of Nations*. By 1787 William Pitt's ministry was firmly in power and attempting to negotiate a series of treaties with leading European states to liberalize trade. 'The present Rage for Commercial Treaties' had so far only resulted in one with France in 1786, and in a set of failed negotiations to create a free-trade union with Ireland, but in 1787 it also gave rise to legislation to revise and simplify the chaotically complex laws relating to customs duties, which Pitt had described as a set of 'clogs and fetters' on trade. Pitt, William Grenville, the Paymaster of the Forces and Henry Dundas had all read the *Wealth of Nations* and discussed it with Smith, and his reputation as a philosopher whose system seemed brilliantly designed to treat philosophically some of the most profound and difficult problems of contemporary government was to give rise to a possibly apocryphal story that, like the tale of Smith having been snatched by gypsies as a child, has become an essential part of the Smith legend. On arriving at Henry Dundas's house at Wimbledon, Smith is supposed to have found a company that included Pitt, Grenville, Addington and Wilberforce. When they rose to receive him he asked them to be seated, Pitt is supposed to have replied, 'No, we will stand till you are first seated, for we are all your scholars.'[38] Pitt's governance was enough to turn Smith for a moment from a Whig to a Pittite Tory. 'I think myself much honoured by the slightest mark of Mr Pitts approbation. You may be assured that the long and strict friendship in which I have lived with some of his opponents, does not hinder me from discerning courage, activity, probity, and public spirit in the great outlines of his administration.'[39] Rather later, the Earl of Buchan reported that he had reverted to his customary Whiggery.[40]

Shortly after his return to Edinburgh in July, Smith was to be gratified in a different way by being elected Rector of Glasgow University, in November 1787. As he wrote to the Principal, Archibald Davidson:

> No preferment could have given me so much real satisfaction. No man can owe greater obligations to a Society than I do to the University of Glasgow. They educated me, they sent me to Oxford, soon after my return to Scotland they elected me one of their own members, and afterwards preferred me to another office, to which the abilities and Virtues of the never to be forgotten Dr Hutcheson had given a superior degree of illustration. The period of thirteen years which I spent as a member of that society I remember as by far the most useful, and, therefore, as by far the happiest and most honourable period of my life; and now, after three and twenty years absence, to be remembered in so very agreable manner by my old friends and Protectors gives me a heartfelt joy which I cannot easily express to you.[41]

This was the occasion on which he proposed to deliver three papers on the imitative arts to the Literary Society, the last of which he was unable to complete. Once again his failing health and the demands of the Customs House were proving troublesome. It was under these circumstances that he was at last to turn to the business of revising the *Theory of Moral Sentiments* in March 1788.

Smith told Thomas Caddell that he had taken four months' leave from the Customs House 'and I am at present giving the most intense application'. By now his plans for revision had become much more elaborate and more extensive; the new edition was to be a third longer than previous ones.

> The chief and the most important additions will be to the third part, that concerning *the sense of Duty* and to the last part concerning *the History of moral Philosophy*. As I consider my tenure of this life as extremely precarious, and am very uncertain whether I shall live to finish several other works which I have projected and in which I have made some progress, the best thing, I think, I can do is to leave those I have already published in the best and most perfect state behind me. I am a slow a very slow workman, who do and undo everything I write at least half a dozen of times before I can be tolerably pleased with it; and tho' I have now, I think, brought my work within compass, yet it will be the month of June before I shall be able to send it to you.[42]

A year later the work was still not done, although promised for mid-summer – 'I am very much ashamed of this delay; but the subject has grown upon me.'[43] In the event, Caddell was not to receive the text until November 1789. It was sent for printing in January 1790 and appears to have been published some weeks later. By then Smith was still receiving visitors like the poet Samuel Rogers, and still entertaining at home and in the Oyster Club in spite of the fact that his health was finally giving way. The Earl of Buchan, a former pupil, saw him in February 1790 and told him he looked forward to seeing him again in a year's time. 'He squeezed my hand, and said, "My dear [friend], I may be alive then, and perhaps half-a-dozen of Februaries; but you will never see your old friend any more. I find that the machine is breaking down; so that I shall be little better than a mummy."'[44] He supervised the destruction of his papers in early July and died on 17 July 1790, shortly after one of his Sunday suppers. He was buried in the Canongate Churchyard.

One of Smith's reasons for revising the *Theory of Moral Sentiments* was to reply to criticism that had dogged his moral philosophy since its publication in 1759, that his ethics had effectively reduced morality to public opinion. At one level, it was not an altogether unreasonable charge. His subtle and nuanced discussion of the origin of our moral sentiments had shown that we owe our understanding of the principles of morality to sympathy, the imagination and the experience of common life. The core of his moral theory had dealt with the situation that arises when we feel that our own moral sentiments are at odds with those of others. Under these circumstances, Smith had claimed, our response was to turn in on ourselves, so that we could invoke the counsel of an internalized impartial spectator whose approbation could sometimes seem to mean more to us than that of real people in the real world. A Christian might have argued that this was because the voice of the internal spectator was that of conscience or the deity, but Smith had made it perfectly clear that it was the voice of an entirely fictitious being, an imaginary person who we invoke in difficult ethical situations to help us clarify our sense of ethical propriety and allow us to act in a way we ourselves could approve of. It meant that, strictly speaking, the impartial spectator speaks of rules of morality which have roots in our own ethical lives and that of our nation and civilization, and cannot properly be regarded as the eternal, never-changing voice of a deity. It was this that had led critics like Thomas Reid, Smith's successor at Glasgow, to write off his ethical theory as 'only a Refinement of the selfish System', in the sense that however much we might delude ourselves into believing that the impartial spectator spoke the language of disinterested virtue, it was in fact no more than the voice of self-love.[45]

Such criticism was easily made but for Smith it missed the point. Whatever metaphysicians might say about the selfish or benevolent roots of our sense of morality, what mattered in common life was that we judge people we believe to be following an internally directed sense of morality quite differently from the way in which we judge those who seem to be responding to the opinions of those around them. We think of the former as people who are acting on principle and the others as people who are simply acting in a way which will avoid the disapproval of others. What is more, we feel quite differently about ourselves when we follow an internal voice rather than that of the crowd. We have deliberately abstracted ourselves from the opinion of the world in an attempt to act as morally responsible individuals, even though we know that our actions may disturb our relations with those around us. Smith had presented this response to ethical difficulty as one that any reader would recognize as being like his own; it could therefore be described as a 'natural' characteristic of human nature. What is more, it was a characteristic that was fundamental to understanding the process of socialization and the workings of the moral economy of a political society.

Smith's revisions were designed to refine and deepen this analysis in a way which would underline its 'natural' characteristics and would demonstrate that the civilizing process was one that could turn human beings into virtuous as well as sociable agents. The new section – 'Of the Character of Virtue' – looked back to the remarkable discussion of the wants and necessities of mankind that had prefaced Smith's early discussions of political economy and had been so conspicuously omitted from the opening pages of the *Wealth of Nations*. There he had shown that man's industriousness, ingenuity and love of improvement were a response to indigence and necessity. It was out of necessity that primitive man had learned how to cook, clothe and house himself, how to improve the raw materials provided by the natural world and the patterns of co-operation on which his survival and ability to live 'conveniently' depended. It was to supply the basic wants of feeding, clothing and housing that property, law, government and the arts and sciences had been invented. Smith began his revisions to the *Theory of Moral Sentiments* by extending the reach of this natural history to ethics. We learn the meaning of prudence and the duties we owe to ourselves from the experience of living co-operatively with others. This experience teaches us to think of the prudent man as one who values security and caution, who respects the rules of justice, who is generally competent, sincere, decent and discriminating in his choice of friends and has learned to be guided by the impartial spectator. We regard prudence of this sort 'as a most respectable and even in some degree, as an amiable and agreeable quality, yet it never is considered as one, either of the most endearing, or of the most ennobling of the virtues'.[46] No doubt it was an 'inferior' species of prudence in the sense that it was only motivated by the need for self-preservation, but it was on the existence of a prudent citizenry that the preservation and improvement of society depended.

What was more, it was the basis for our admiration of the higher forms of prudence we admire in the greatest generals and patriots.

> Prudence is, in all these cases, combined with many greater and more splendid virtues, with valour, with extensive and strong benevolence, with a sacred regard to the rules of justice, and all these supported by a proper degree of self-command. This superior prudence, when carried to the highest degree of perfection, necessarily supposes the art, the talent, and the habit or disposition of acting with the most perfect propriety in every possible circumstance and situation. It necessarily supposes the utmost perfection of all the intellectual and of all the moral virtues. It is the best head joined to the best heart. It is the most perfect wisdom combined with the most perfect virtue. It constitutes very nearly the character of the Academical or Peripatetic sage, as the inferior prudence does that of the Epicurean.[47]

Whatever Christian moralists might claim to the contrary, Smith was arguing that in common life we should always think of prudence as an essential component of virtue.

But what of beneficence and the duties we owe to others? It was easy to show how our sympathies and sense of duty move outward from ourselves to our families, friends and country and shape the way in which we respond to the beneficent instincts of others, particularly when we feel that family duty is coming into conflict with the duties we feel we owe our friends or country, and Smith took it for granted that the beneficence we show to our families and to the friends who have been of service to us would always be motivated by a degree of self-love. The much more difficult ethical question for the modern citizen was in deciding how much he owed his country. An uncritical love of country could all too easily lead him to view 'with the most malignant jealousy and envy, the prosperity and aggrandisement of any other neighbouring nation' and was a form of false patriotism that he and Hume had always regarded as a potentially fatal threat to the security, prosperity and public finances of Britain and France.

> France and England may each of them have some reason to dread the increase of the naval and military power of the other; but for either of them to envy the internal happiness and prosperity of the other,

the cultivation of its lands, the advancement of its manufactures, the increase of its commerce, the security and number of its ports and harbours, its proficiency in all the liberal arts and sciences, is surely beneath the dignity of two such great nations. These are all real improvements of the world we live in. Mankind are benefited, human nature is ennobled by them. In such improvements each nation ought, not only to endeavour itself to excel, but from the love of mankind, to promote, instead of obstructing the excellence of its neighbours. These are all proper objects of national emulation, not of national prejudice or envy.[48]

What complicated this age-old problem of the citizen's duties to his country was the way in which the claims of patriotism had been caught up with those of political parties (and he might have added churches) and other associations. What worried Smith, as it had worried Hume, was that political life, like religious life in previous centuries, was becoming increasingly factious and ideologically charged. Like Hume he was troubled by the ease with which public spirit could become infected with a 'certain spirit of system' which spawned ideologies and utopias and 'always animates it, and often inflames it even to the madness of fanaticism'. It was this deeply Humean fear that led him to insist that

> The man whose public spirit is prompted altogether by humanity and benevolence, will respect the established powers and privileges even of individuals, and still more those of the great orders and societies, into which the state is divided ... He will accommodate, as well as he can, his public arrangements to the confirmed habits and prejudices of the people; and will remedy as well as he can, the inconveniencies which may flow from the want of those regulations which the people are averse to submit to. When he cannot establish the right, he will not disdain to ameliorate the wrong; but like Solon, when he cannot establish the best system of laws, he will endeavour to establish the best that the people can bear.[49]

These last political reflections, more discursive than Smith generally allowed, were his prelude to the discussion of the ethical quality which he thought would always be regarded as essential to a virtuous character whatever the metaphysicians and theologians might say – the capacity for self-command. His analysis had shown how hard it was even for the best-intentioned person not to be misled by his passions, 'sometimes to drive him and sometimes to seduce him to violate all the rules which he himself, in all his sober and cool hours, approves of'.[50] In earlier editions of the *Theory of Moral Sentiments* Smith had assumed that we think of the virtuous person as one who acts in accordance with the directions of the impartial spectator; but now this definition seemed too abstract, particularly when it was set in the context of the often conflicting demands made on the modern citizen's loyalties in troubled times. He now made the simpler point that we admire the virtuous man for the consistency of his ethical conduct, and for the capacity for self-command that one needs to live a life directed by the impartial spectator. Nor were this sense of consistency and self-command easily acquired. It would always be difficult to square the duties we owed to ourselves with those we owed to family, friends, country and association in troubled times. It would be just as hard to prevent our ethical behaviour from becoming over-rigid, over-indulgent or over-sceptical. At the end, Smith was returning to his intellectual roots to show that in the modern world we recognize virtue as a quality which is built on prudence, beneficence and a Humean understanding of the principles of human nature. It was the finishing touch to Smith's intellectual legacy, his ethical message to the citizens and magistrates of a commercial and what he hoped would become an enlightened civilization. It was, perhaps, for this reason that he told that intelligent young MP Samuel Romilly, he always considered the *Theory of Moral Sentiments* 'a much superior work to his [*Wealth of Nations*]'.[51]

Smith's death attracted little attention. Romilly was 'surprised and, I own, a little indignant to observe how little impression [Smith's] death has made [in London]. Scarce any notice has been taken of it, while for above a year together after the death of Dr Johnson [in 1784] nothing was to be heard but panegyrics of him, – lives, letters, and anecdotes.'[52] The Edinburgh press all but ignored the event, while in London the press did little more than circulate a short, anonymous, anecdotal memoir that first appeared in the *St. James' Chronicle* of

31 July 1790. This somewhat snide article by someone who clearly knew Smith, noted his oddities, his ungainliness, his respect for the French Encyclopaedists, his admiration of Hume 'as by far the greatest Philosopher that the world had ever produced' and his '[jealousy] of the property of his lectures'. The *Theory of Moral Sentiments* was written off as 'ingenious but fanciful' and the *Wealth of Nations* as a system of political economy which was 'not essentially different from that of [the Milanese philosopher] Count Verri, [the English political writer] Josiah Tucker and Hume'. It was based on data derived from the *Encyclopédie*, although 'fortified with stronger proofs than any of his predecessors'. The author concluded that '[Smith] deserves the chief praise and blame, of propagating a system, which tends to confound national wealth with national prosperity.' It was left to Dugald Stewart to present the canonical portrait of Smith in his *Account of the Life and Writings of Adam Smith, LL.D.*, on which he began work immediately after Smith's death, presented to the Royal Society of Edinburgh in the winter of 1793, published in an abridged form in the Society's *Transactions* in 1794 and in full in 1795. It was subsequently republished as an introduction to many editions of the *Wealth of Nations*. It is this portrait that continues to shape our understanding of Smith's character.

Stewart knew Smith well and fully appreciated the elusiveness of his character, commenting that 'it would require a very skilful pencil to present [this] to the public eye'.[53] Stewart's Smith was a kind, gentle, endearing eccentric who was 'certainly not fitted for the general commerce of the world, or for the business of active life'. He was a genius who was constantly absorbed in speculation, 'habitually inattentive to familiar objects, and to common occurrences', and even when in company 'was apt to be engrossed with his studies; and appeared, at times, by the motion of his lips, as well as by his looks and gestures, to be in the fervour of composition.' Strangers – and some members of Johnson's Club – were taken aback by his inability to take part in ordinary conversation and by his tendency 'to convey his own ideas in the form of a lecture', and Stewart's portrait suggests that he was only truly at ease in the company of close friends. What does not come over in Stewart's portrait is the contrast his portrait of the private man provides with the portrait of the public intellectual which has taken shape in this book. His professorial voice was commanding. He lectured as a man who knew that he was placing the study of human behaviour on new foundations and was well aware that in doing so, he was taking on the philosophical world at large. The axioms from which the different parts of his philosophy were derived were set out with daring and illustrated with the formidable erudition for which he rightly became famous. Nor does Stewart's portrait of the unworldly philosopher obviously square with Smith's evident abilities as a much respected and powerful academic administrator, with the value which Buccleuch attached to his advice in running his estates, with the respect with which his advice on public finance was treated by cabinet ministers, or with his career as a conscientious Customs Commissioner. Although the inconsequentialities of ordinary social life and conversation seemed to bore him, perhaps he was too gentle, too good-natured and too little of a committed recluse to be able to do without company, and certainly without the company of his friends. He made friends easily and kept those he had for life. It was of these that Stewart wrote, 'The serenity and gaiety he enjoyed, under the pressure of his growing infirmities, and the warm interest he felt to the last, in every thing connected with the welfare of his friends, will be long remembered by a small circle, with whom, as long as his strength permitted, he regularly spent an evening in the week; and to whom the recollection of his worth still forms a pleasing, though melancholy bond of union.'

Perhaps the most enduring characteristic of his life and philosophy is its modesty. For all its scope, ambition and daring, his philosophy is the work of a modest man who set out to reflect on a simple, apparently unremarkable characteristic of human nature – our desire, when all things are equal, to improve our own lot, that of our families and that of the civil society to which we belong, It was a disposition the day labourer shared with the aristocrat, the young person making his or her way in the world with the sage and elder statesman. It was a disposition which taught the prudent citizen to value small and progressive adjustments to life and to the management of public affairs over millenarian attempts to create new heavens and a new earth. It was a disposition which came naturally to members of an indigent species, and evidence of its quiet and unassuming power was to be seen in the remarkable material, moral and intellectual progress of mankind and the advance of civilization. And to Smith, born into and educated in a world of improving landowners in Fife, and in the improvement-minded civil society of post-Union Scotland, it was the disposition of a family, class and country whose fortunes were being transformed by the seemingly natural consequences of an enlightened Union.

Epilogue

When Smith made his first will in 1773 and made Hume his executor, he asked him to destroy all of his unpublished papers after his death with the possible exception of that 'juvenile' essay on the history of astronomy of which he was rather fond. The decision whether or not to publish it posthumously was left to Hume's discretion. By 1790 his thoughts about the future of his unpublished papers had changed. In the advertisement to the last edition of the *Theory of Moral Sentiments* he admitted that he now had 'very little expectation of ever being able to execute' the book on jurisprudence he had planned in 1759, 'when I entertained no doubt of being able to execute every thing which [the first edition] announced'.[1] His lecture notes had been destroyed, but a small number of unpublished and often fragmentary essays were spared and their future left to the discretion of his executors, Joseph Black and James Hutton. These, they said, 'appeared to be parts of a plan he had once formed, for giving a connected history of the liberal sciences and elegant arts. It is long since he found it necessary to abandon that plan as far too extensive; and these parts of it lay beside him neglected until his death.' It was a reminder that the *Theory of Moral Sentiments* and the *Wealth of Nations* had been part of a grander plan for a Science of Man that had proved to be beyond his physical resources.

Smith seems to have realized that his project for developing a Science of Man as he and Hume had known it had run its course. They had set out to show that processes by which the human personality, and the customs, habits and institutions which made political life and the progress of civilization possible, could be explained in terms of the imaginative and sympathetic response of an indigent species to the never-ending pressures of need. Hume had made the enterprise possible by providing Smith with the sceptical account of the processes which teach us how to survive and prosper in political society. It was he who had shown how deeply this needs-driven view of the making of the human mind penetrated and shaped a person's understanding of the natural and supernatural worlds, of politics, morality and religion. And it was he who had prescribed its agenda.

Hume had left it to Smith to develop this new science and it is Smith's published and unpublished, finished and unfinished texts that have provided an insight into what was being attempted, as well as what was accomplished. He had shown that it was possible to study the workings of the mind and the process of socialization by means of a study of the sentiments and the different strands of the sensibility in which the human personality was embodied. Smith had explored the processes by which we acquire the senses of propriety, justice, political obligation and beauty on which our skills in the arts of social intercourse and our character depend. In doing so, he had introduced into his analysis a simple observation about the principles of human nature that had been ignored by modern philosophy, that man's natural indigence had somehow gone hand in hand with a love of improvement which he would exercise whenever he felt secure enough to do so. Indeed, as has already been suggested, the business of extending this principle to every aspect of human life had been Smith's singular contribution to the science of man. It had allowed him to suggest that a reasonably stable society will follow a material, moral, political and intellectual path of development that was more natural and more secure than one which was determined by the whims of its sovereigns, and it was he who had developed the stadial model of civilization's progress that was to be one of the lasting legacies of his exploration of the science of man to philosophy, history and the social sciences. In this respect it had been a deeply Epicurean enterprise.

But it had been an Epicurean enterprise shaped by Hume's notably sceptical theory of knowledge, by his provocative claim that the mind was, in the last resort, the Empire of the Imagination, and by that loathing of priestcraft which had identified him in Europe as a philosopher bearing the mark of a true *philosophe*. Smith's scepticism had been more circumspect and his attitude to priestcraft more discrete; he never challenged the general principles of Hume's theory of human nature, but he regarded them as principles to be explored and developed rather than taken at face value. It had been Hume who had made his project for developing a science of man based on a study of the sentiments possible, but it had been left to Smith to consider how the imagination responds to different sorts of event in the natural and moral worlds, and to develop his own radical theory of sympathy to explain how we acquire these senses of justice, morality and taste on which our capacity for sociability, survival and happiness depends. It had been an inquiry which led him to his own peculiarly sceptical conclusions. His ethics had shown that what many think of as the voice of conscience or the deity has its origins in the complicated processes of sympathetic interaction, thus gently reducing it to a form of false consciousness which Christians would inevitably find objectionable. In his jurisprudence and his political economy he had viewed the business of government and politics through the eyes of the sceptical observer who preferred to encourage the governing classes to liberalize their systems of public administration, rather than speculate on utopian solutions to the problem of promoting liberty and prosperity. And although he never shared Hume's notoriety as a public infidel, few Scots were in any doubt where his religious sympathies lay. The Glasgow clergy had sensed that infidelity on his appointment to the professorship of Logic and Metaphysics in 1751; Edmund Burke had been among those who had scoffed at his defence of Hume's notably non-Christian death as a typical manifestation of the clannishness of modern non-believers; James Boswell had irreverently dubbed his old professor as 'an infidel in a bag-wig'. 'Ascanius' – who was probably the Earl of Buchan – writing in the *Bee* in 1791 put the contemporary view well: 'In many respects, Adam Smith was a chaste disciple of Epicurus, as that philosopher is properly understood ... O venerable, amiable, and worthy man, why was you not a Christian?'[2]

Not many thought of Hume and Smith's project as a genuinely 'scientific' contribution to knowledge, one which had established undoubted truths about man and society, politics and history. Thomas Reid, with the sharp intelligence of a Christian philosopher, was fully prepared to admit that Hume had demonstrated that the foundations of a science of man must be based on a study of our beliefs about the world, but thought that much work remained to be done on their metaphysical properties and on the organization of the mind. Hugh Blair and Lord Kames appreciated the importance Smith attached to the sense of taste in shaping the understanding, but were sure that its roots were hard-wired in the constitution of the mind and that its effects could not simply be explained in terms of ingenious speculations about the experience of common life. William Robertson had drawn heavily on Smith's understanding of the progress of civilization in his work on the history of Europe and America but had preferred to think of that process as teleologically driven by a deity whose being, nature and purposes would always remain unclear. The *Theory of Moral Sentiments* was criticized by the intelligent, and in many ways sympathetic, Sir James Mackintosh in the influential dissertation on the progress of ethics he wrote for the *Encyclopaedia Britannica* in 1815, on the grounds that it was based on a theory of sympathy that begged more questions about the nature and powers of that fundamental property of human nature than it answered, and could therefore scarcely be regarded as a secure foundation for a genuine *science* of morals.

Most important of all, as Biancamaria Fontana has shown, by the early nineteenth century, the *Wealth of Nations* itself was coming under fire from the formidably intelligent young men who circled round Francis Jeffrey's *Edinburgh Review*, the most acute critical voice of the political, scientific and literary culture of a post-Enlightenment age. Most of them were Dugald Stewart's pupils, who had been taught to admire the *Wealth of Nations* for its comprehensive, philosophical treatment of political economy, for its erudition and elegance, for the *esprit de système* which informed it, and above all for its unfailingly liberal sentiments. Smith's theory was undoubtedly plausible, but was it true? For the ferociously clever Francis Horner, Smith's thinking lacked rigour and left unanswered too many questions about the nature and scope of the science of political economy and that of government. It was too much a tract for its times, which all too often relied on the persuasive power of rhetoric rather than on hard analysis to sustain its axioms. That said, he was prepared to admit, rather patronizingly, that 'the popular and plausible and loose hypothesis is as good for the vulgar as any other'.[3]

Horner was questioning the ability of a sceptical Hume–Smith conception of science to sustain the sort of analysis demanded by a later generation. He and the younger members of Dugald Stewart's class wanted a philosophy which furnished hard political and economic truths about the principles of economics and good government to advance the cause of constitutional and political reform, rather than one which was merely designed to refresh the political understanding of the intelligent citizens and legislators of a previous age. Indeed the question of how the principles of the *Wealth of Nations* could be corrected, refined and recast for use in new political, economic and intellectual environments was to be the task of successive generations of editors.

It was no accident that one of the pieces of his work that Smith was prepared to save from the flames was his essay on the history of astronomy, which he had begun in the 1740s, had kept beside him for most of his intellectual life, and was apparently still tinkering with at the end. It is a piece which has much to say about Smith's own conception of science.[4] It was an essay about the origins of philosophical thought, the creation of philosophical systems, and the appeal which philosophy has to its public. Philosophy's roots, Smith suggested, lay in the psychological need to explain the unexpected, to soothe the imagination and to restore the mind to a state of cognitive order and tranquillity. It was not an activity to appeal to primitive man or to those who lived in a state of chronic insecurity; under those circumstances philosophy would only generate amazement, fear and superstition. Philosophy would only perform its psychological and social functions when men had the security and leisure to reflect on the world, to attend to 'that train of events which passes around them' and to detect unexplained irregularities in the workings of nature. It was wonder rather than any hope of material gain that provided the spur to philosophy, and it was the pleasure involved in seeking 'the invisible chains which bind together all these disjointed objects' that was its own reward. Thus it was not the task of the historian of philosophy to consider philosophy's contribution to the progress of truth but rather to consider 'how far each of them was fitted to sooth the imagination, and to render the theatre of nature a more coherent, and therefore a more magnificent spectacle, than otherwise it would have appeared to be'.[5] Indeed it was the glory of Newton's philosophy that he had developed a system of philosophy that conquered all opposition 'and has advanced to the acquisition of the most universal empire that was ever established in philosophy. His principles, it must be acknowledged, have a degree of firmness and solidity that we should in vain look for in any other system. The most sceptical cannot avoid feeling this.'[6] It was a system of philosophy that appealed to his contemporaries' sense of truthfulness and, so Smith implied, it would only reign until that sense of truthfulness was undermined. The claim that Smith had made of Newton's philosophy was the same as the claim he made for his own. It was the claim of a philosopher who, for all the scale and scope of his own philosophy, had no illusions about the nature of its authority.

Notes and Sources

ABBREVIATIONS
Smith's Works

All references are to the Glasgow Edition of the works of Adam Smith.

Corr.   *Correspondence*, ed. E.C. Mossner and I.S. Ross (1987)
EPS   *Essays on Philosophical Subjects*, ed. W.P.D. Wightman, J.C. Bryce and I.S. Ross (1980)
LJ   *Lectures on Jurisprudence*, ed. R.L. Meek, D.D. Raphael and P.G. Stein (1978)
LR   *Lectures on Rhetoric and Belles Lettres*, ed. J.C. Bryce (1983)
TMS   *The Theory of Moral Sentiments*, ed. D.D. Raphael and A.L. Macfie (1976)
WN   *An Inquiry into the Nature and Causes of the Wealth of Nations*, ed. R.H. Campbell and A.S. Skinner (1978)

Smith's Biographers

Campbell and Skinner   R.H. Campbell and A.S. Skinner, *Adam Smith* (London, 1982)
Rae   J. Rae, *Life of Adam Smith* (London, 1895)
Ross   I.S. Ross, *The Life of Adam Smith* (Oxford, 1995)
Scott   W. R. Scott, *Adam Smith as Student and Professor* (Glasgow, 1937)
Stewart   D. Stewart, 'Account of the Life and Writings of Adam Smith, LL.D.', ed. I.S. Ross in *Essays on Philosophical Subjects*, ed. W.P.D. Wightman, J.C. Bryce and I.S. Ross (Oxford, 1980), pp. 264–351

Libraries

EUL   Edinburgh University Library
GUL   Glasgow University Library
NLS   National Library of Scotland
SRO   Scottish Record Office

PROLOGUE

1. Hume, *The Letters of David Hume*, vol. ii, p. 314.
2. *Corr.*, p. 337.
3. *Corr.*, pp. 286–7.
4. Stewart, p. 327n.
5. Ibid., p. 303.
6. Ibid., p. 327.
7. *EPS*, p. 245.
8. *Corr.*, pp. 223–4.

Notes on Sources

Smith's first serious biography, Dugald Stewart's 'Account of the Life and Writings of Adam Smith, LL.D.', was written for the Royal Society of Edinburgh and published in 1794 and remains an indispensable source. Stewart knew Smith well in the later years of his life, and understood the intellectual and political milieu in which he lived. His extended essay was frequently reprinted with later editions of Smith's works and presents what has become the canonical portrait of its subject. Rae's *Life of Adam Smith*, written at a time of revived interest in the literary world of eighteenth-century London and Edinburgh, was the first serious attempt to set Smith's life in wider social and political contexts. It is well, though by no means flawlessly, researched, and jauntily written. Scott's *Adam Smith as Student and Professor*, based on extensive use of Glasgow University's archives, is an essential introduction to Smith's early years at Kirkcaldy and Glasgow and to his professorial career. Ross's *Life of Adam Smith* is a deeply researched modern attempt to set Smith's life and works in contemporary contexts and one to which every modern Smith scholar must remain indebted. I certainly am.

Of the shorter lives, Campbell and Skinner's brief *Adam Smith* deserves more attention than it generally receives. D.D. Raphael's *Adam Smith* is the work of the doyen of Smith scholars and an editor of the Glasgow edition of Smith's works. J.Z. Muller's *Adam Smith in His Time and Ours* is lively and opinionated. James Buchan's *Adam Smith and the Pursuit of Perfect Liberty* is informed, intelligent and by far the best short introduction to Smith's life and works.

I. A KIRKCALDY UPBRINGING

1. Stewart, p. 269.

2. *The Bee or Literary Weekly Intelligencer*, iii (11 May 1791), pp. 164–7.

3. *Corr.*, p. 275.

4. Withrington and Grant, eds., *The Statistical Account of Scotland by Sir John Sinclair*, vol. x. *Fife*, pp. 505–65.

5. Dennison and Coleman, *Historic Kirkcaldy*.

6. Durie, *The Scottish Linen Industry in the Eighteenth Century*, pp. 16–17. See also Durie, 'Lairds, Improvement, Banking and Industry in Eighteenth Century Scotland', pp. 21–30.

7. Durie, *The Scottish Linen Industry*, p. 16.

8. Loch, *A Tour through most of the Trading Towns and Villages of Scotland*.

9. Warden, *The Linen Trade Ancient and Modern*, p. 561.

10. Withrington and Grant, *Statistical Account of Scotland*, vol. x. *Fife*, pp. 505–65.

11. [Oswald], *Memorials of the Rt. Hon. James Oswald of Dunnikier*, Preface.

12. Sedgwick, *History of Parliament: The House of Commons 1715–54*, 'Oswald, James'.

13. [Oswald], *Memorials of the Rt. Hon. James Oswald of Dunnikier*, p. 122.

14. Stewart, pp. 300, 333.

15. *WN*, pp. 376–8, 412.

16. *WN*, p. 461.

17. *WN*, p. 49.

18. The story is told in the Kirkcaldy Council Book 1716–42 (KYD/1/1/3, pp. 154, 158, 167, 168–70). I am grateful to the burgh archivist for permission to use these records.

19. Ibid., pp. 174, 217.

20. Ibid., pp. 299–300.

21. Eutropius, *Breviarum Historiae Romanae*, intro.

22. Chambers, *Domestic Annals of Scotland*, vol. iii, pp. 584–5.

23. Moore, 'The Enlightened Curriculum: Liberal Education in Eighteenth Century British Schools', pp. 97–116.

24. Mizuta, ed., *Adam Smith's Library: A Catalogue*, no. 574.

25. Ross, p. 15.

26. Epictetus, *The Discourses of Epictetus*, p. 287.
27. Ibid., p. 306.
28. Ibid., pp. 292, 17.
29. *TMS*, p. 283.
30. *TMS*, pp. 291–2.
31. *Spectator*, no. 6, 7 March 1710/11.

Notes on Sources

On the history of Kirkcaldy see the Rev. T. Fleming's excellent 'Parish of Kirk-caldy' in *The Statistical Account of Scotland . . .*, edited by Withrington and Grant, and Dennison and Coleman's *Historic Kirkcaldy*. In thinking about Smith's education at the parish school. Moore's 'The Enlightened Curriculum: Liberal Education in Eighteenth Century British Schools' has been invaluable. The discussion of the *Spectator* draws on my own work. See my *Hume*, chapter 2 and the references cited there, and my 'Politics and Politeness in the Reigns of Anne and the Early Hanoverians'.

2. GLASGOW, GLASGOW UNIVERSITY AND FRANCIS HUTCHESON'S ENLIGHTENMENT

1. Defoe, *Tour thro the Whole Island of Great Britain*, p. 334.
2. What follows is indebted to the essays in Devine and Jackson, eds., *Glasgow. Volume I: Beginnings to 1830*.
3. Smout, *A History of the Scottish People, 1560–1830*, pp. 258–66.
4. Smout, 'The Glasgow Merchant Community in the Seventeenth Century', pp. 53–71.
5. Devine, *The Tobacco Lords. A Study of the Tobacco Merchants of Glasgow and their Trading Activities*, p. 171; Devine, 'The Scottish Merchant Community 1680–1740'.
6. *WN*, p. 493.
7. Sher, 'Commerce, Religion and Enlightenment in Eighteenth-century Glasgow', in *Glasgow*, p. 318.
8. Gray, ed., *Memoirs of the Life of Sir John Clark of Penicuick . . .*, p. 248.
9. Defoe, *Tour thro the Whole Island of Great Britain*, p. 338.
10. Gibson, *The History of Glasgow, from the Earliest Accounts to the Present Time*, p. 114.
11. Knox, *The Works of John Knox*, pp. 619–21.
12. Emerson, 'Politics and the Glasgow Professors, 1690–1800', pp. 21–39.
13. Robert, Viscount Molesworth, *An Account of Denmark as it was in the*

Year 1692, preface. On Molesworth generally, see Jones, 'The Scottish Professoriate and the Polite Academy 1720–40', pp. 89–117.

14. G. Turnbull–Molesworth, 3 Aug. 1722, *Historical Manuscripts Commission. Report on Manuscripts in Various Collections*, vol. viii (1913).

15. Molesworth, ibid.

16. [H. Blair], 'Hutcheson's Moral Philosophy', *Edinburgh Review,* i, 1755/56, pp. 9–23.

17. Hutcheson, *A System of Moral Philosophy*, vol. i, pp. xxvi, xxxii–iii, xxxv.

18. Leechman, *The Temper, Character and Duty of a Minister of the Gospel*, pp. 5, 12, 17.

19. On Hutcheson's Dublin career see Brown, *Francis Hutcheson in Dublin 1719–1730: The Crucible of his Thought*, and McBride, 'The School of Virtue: Francis Hutcheson, Irish Presbyterianism and the Scottish Enlightenment'.

20. Wodrow, *Analecta or Materials for a History of Remarkable Providences*, vol. iv, p. 190.

21. Ibid., pp. 186–7.

22. Scott, *Francis Hutcheson*, p. 93.

23. Sher, 'Commerce, Religion and the Enlightenment'.

24. Defoe, *Tour thro the Whole Island of Great Britain*, p. 334.

25. Carlyle, *Anecdotes and Characters of the Times*, p. 38.

26. *Corr.*, p. 309.

27. Chamberlayne, *Magnae Britanniae Notitia*, pp. 12–13.

28. Ross, p. 42. For Loudon, see Moore, 'The two systems of Francis Hutcheson: on the origins of the Scottish Enlightenment', pp. 43–4.

29. Hutcheson, *System of Moral Philosophy*, vol. i, pp. iv–v 'Preface Giving some Account of the Life, Writings, and Character of the Author' by W. Leechman.

30. Brougham, *Lives of Men of Letters and Science who flourished in the time of George III*, vol. i, p. 483.

31. Stewart, pp. 270–71.

32. *Corr.*, p. 309.

33. Krieger, *The Politics of Discretion: Pufendorf and the Acceptance of Natural Law*, p. 13.

34. Pufendorf, *The Law of Nature and Nations: Or a General System of the Most Important Principles of Morality, Jurisprudence and Politics*, p. 623.

35. Ibid., p. 625.

36. Ibid., p. 624.

37. Pufendorf, *On the Duty of Man and Citizen According to Natural Law*, p. 35.

38. [Hutcheson], 'To the Author of the *London Journal*', *London Journal*, 21 November 1724.

39. Mandeville, *The Fable of the Bees: or Private Vices, Publick Benefits*, vol. i, pp. 323–4.

40. Ibid., p. 343.

41. Ibid., p. 331.

42. Ibid., p. 37.

43. Hutcheson, *An Inquiry into the Original of our Ideas of Beauty and Virtue*, p. 93.

44. Ibid., p. 186.

45. Ibid., p. 9.

46. Ibid., pp. 114–15.

47. Hutcheson, *System of Moral Philosophy*, vol. i, p. 14.

48. Hutcheson, *Inquiry*, p. 178.

49. Cited in Moore, 'The two systems of Francis Hutcheson', p. 59.

Notes on Sources

For Smith's student life, see particularly Scott and Ross.

Glasgow's history has been neglected, but see the pioneering essays contributing to *Glasgow, Volume 1: Beginnings to 1830*, edited by Devine and Jackson. The tobacco trade has been authoritatively studied by Devine in *The Tobacco Lords: A Study of the Tobacco Merchants of Glasgow and their Trading Activities*. The history of the university badly needs modern treatment but see Scott, J.D. Mackie's dated *The University of Glasgow 1451 to 1951* and R.L. Emerson's 'Politics and the Glasgow Professors 1690–1800', in *The Glasgow Enlightenment*, edited by Hook and Sher.

On Pufendorf, see his *On the Duty of Man and Citizen*, ed. J. Tully, R. Tuck, *Philosophy and Government 1572–1651* and I. Hont, 'The Language of Sociability and Commerce: Samuel Pufendorf and the Theoretical Foundation of the "Four Stages" Theory', in his *Jealousy of Trade: International Competition and the Nation-State in Historical Perspective*. On Mandeville, see his *Fable of the Bees: or Private Vices, Publick Benefits*, edited by F.B. Kaye, and E.J. Hundert's *The Enlightenment's Fable: Bernard Mandeville and the Discovery of Society*.

Hutcheson has been extensively studied, mostly in the misleading belief that he was 'the father of the Scottish Enlightenment'. The standard biography – W.R. Scott's *Francis Hutcheson: His Life, Teaching and Position in the History of Philosophy* – is dated but still useful. See also T.D. Campbell, 'Francis Hutcheson: "Father" of the Scottish Enlightenment', in *The Origins and Nature of the Scottish Enlightenment*, edited by Campbell and Skinner. For his career in Dublin see M. Brown, *Francis Hutcheson in Dublin 1719–1730* and Ian McBride's excellent 'The School of Virtue:

Francis Hutcheson, Irish Presbyterians and the Scottish Enlightenment'. On the elusive relation between his moral and political thought see James Moore, 'The Two Systems of Francis Hutcheson: On the Origins of the Scottish Enlightenment' and K. Haakonssen, 'Natural Law and Moral Realism: The Scottish Synthesis'.

3. PRIVATE STUDY 1740–46: OXFORD AND DAVID HUME

1. Ross, p. 58 and the *St James's Chronicle*, Saturday, 31 July 1790.

2. He was nominated by the Glasgow Senate but David Raynor has suggested to me that his guardian, William Smith, the Duke of Argyll's secretary, may have had a hand in the election. Smith himself was certainly well aware of his guardian's value in such matters; in 1742 he told his mother to alert Smith to the fact that there would shortly be another vacancy for a Snell exhibition (*Corr.*, p. 2).

3. [N. Amhurst], Terrae–Filius, nos. vii and xliii.

4. Quoted in Ward, Georgian Oxford, p. 132.

5. Sutherland and Mitchell, eds., *The History of the University of Oxford. Vol. 5 The Eighteenth Century*, pp. 115–16.

6. WN, pp. 760–61.

7. Jones, *Balliol College: A History*, pp. 162, 165.

8. Davis, *Balliol College*, p. 159.

9. *St James's Chronicle*, Saturday, 31 July 1790.

10. *Corr.*, p. 1.

11. *Corr.*, p. 3.

12. Stewart, p. 271.

13. Ibid., pp. 271–2.

14. *TMS*, pp. 308–9. See also *EPS*, p. 303.

15. *TMS*, p. 139.

16. 'De la Grandeur', in P. Nicole, *Oeuvres Philosophiques et Morales*. Translated by N. Keohane and quoted in *Philosophy and the State in France. The Renaissance to the Enlightenment*, pp. 296–7.

17. *TMS*, p. 123.

18. *LR*, p. 97.

19. *TMS*, p. 33.

20. Marivaux, *Journaux et Oeuvres Diverses*, p. 475.

21. Ibid., pp. 475–6

22. 'C'est la société, c'est toute l'humanité même qui en tient la seule école qui soit convenable, école toujours ouverte, où tout l'homme étudie les autres,

et en est étudié à son tour, où tout l'homme est tour à tour écolier et maître. Cette science reside dans le commerce que nous avons tous, et sans exception, ensemble' (Marivaux, *Journaux et Oeuvres Diverses*, p. 476).

23. '. . . un tissu d'événements qui lui ont donné une certaine connaissance de la vie et du caractère des hommes' (Marivaux, *La Vie de Marianne, ou Les Aventures de Madame la Comtesse de ***, p. 85).

24. *TMS*, p. 143.

25. *Boswell in Extremes 1776–1778*, p. 11.

26. Hume, 'My Own Life', *Essays Moral, Political and Literary*, p. xxxiv.

27. Mossner, *The Life of David Hume*, pp. 144–5.

28. *Monthly Review,* vol. 22, 1797, pp. 57ff. The story was repeated in a slightly different form by McCulloch, *Sketch of the Life and Writings of Adam Smith, LL.D.*, p. 8. The story comes from John Leslie (1766–1832), the future Professor of Mathematics at Edinburgh and an ardent Humean. He was tutor to Smith's nephew and heir, David Douglas, in 1787–8. I am very grateful to David Raynor for the reference and the attribution.

29. Hume, *A Treatise of Human Nature*, p. xvi.

30. Ibid., p. 415.

31. Ibid., p. 363.

32. Ibid., p. 427.

33. Ibid., pp. 316–17.

34. Hume, *Essays Moral, Political and Literary*, pp. 37–8.

35. [Adam Ferguson], 'Of the Principle of Moral Estimation. A Discourse between David Hume, Robert Clerk and Adam Smith', *The Manuscripts of Adam Ferguson*, p. 207.

Notes on Sources

For Smith's Oxford career see Stewart and Ross.

For Oxford see Sutherland and Mitchell's *The History of the University of Oxford. Vol. 5 The Eighteenth Century*, J. Jones, *Balliol College: A History* and H.W.C. Davis, *Balliol College*.

Although the literature on Hume's *Treatise* is vast and multifaceted it pays surprisingly little attention to Hume's ambitions to develop a Science of Man and to its significance for Smith's own philosophical development. However, the following are useful: R. Popkin's classic 'David Hume: His Pyrrhonism and his Critique of Pyrrhonism', in Chappell's *Hume*; D.W. Livingston's *Hume's Philosophy of Common Life*; D.D. Raphael's '"The True Old Humean Philosophy" and its influence on Adam Smith', in *David Hume: Bicentenary Papers*, edited by G.P. Morice; and D. Fate Norton's *David Hume: Common-Sense Moralist, Sceptical Metaphysician*. I have written rather more fully about the historicity of Hume's approach to the study of human nature in my own *Hume*.

4. EDINBURGH'S EARLY ENLIGHTENMENT

1. 'Ad.Smith Ll.D 1723–1790'. EUL MSS, La. II 451/2, ff. 429–34.
2. *Corr.*, pp. 24–5.
3. Mudie, *The Modern Athens,* p. 162.
4. Fletcher, *Political Works,* p. 193.
5. *Corr.*, p. 68. Smith's comment that the merchants had little understanding of trading with the plantations is curious coming from one who mingled with the Glasgow merchant community and listened carefully to their conversation. Glasgow merchants had learned how to evade the Navigation Acts two decades before the Union.
6. *Scots Magazine,* 33, 1771, pp. 340–44.
7. Emerson, 'The Philosophical Society of Edinburgh 1737–1743'.
8. *Select Transactions of the Honourable the Society for Improvement in the Knowledge of Agriculture in Scotland,* p. 1.
9. MacLaurin, *An Account of Sir Isaac Newton's Philosophical Discoveries,* pp. vi–vii.
10. Carlyle, *Anecdotes and Characters,* p. 30.
11. Cameron, *Bank of Scotland,* pp. 45–6.
12. [David Hume], 'A True Account of the Behaviour and Conduct of Archibald Stewart, Esq. Late Lord Provost of Edinburgh', reprinted in J.V. Price, *The Ironic Hume,* pp. 154–74.
13. Sher, *Church and University in the Scottish Enlightenment,* pp. 37–44.
14. MacInnes, *Clanship, Commerce and the House of Stuart 1603–1788,* pp. 204–5, 211–13.
15. W. Crosse, 'Some considerations by way of Essays upon the means of civilizing the Highlands' (1748), NLS MS S201.
16. Pinkerton, ed., *The Minute Book of the Faculty of Advocates. Vol. 2: 1713–1750,* p. 225.
17. SRO GD110/963/7. I am very grateful to David Raynor for this reference.
18. [H. Home], *Essays upon Several Subjects concerning British Antiquities,* Introduction.
19. Lieberman, 'The Legal Needs of a Commercial Society: The Jurisprudence of Lord Kames', and Phillipson, 'The Civic Leadership of Post Union Scotland'.
20. Home, *Elements of Criticism,* Introduction.

21. Allardyce, ed., *Scotland and Scotsmen in the Eighteenth Century: From the MSS of John Ramsay, Esq. of Ochtertyre*, vol. i, pp. 194–5.
22. Quoted in Shapin, 'Property, Patronage and the Politics of Science: The Founding of the Royal Society of Edinburgh', p. 10.
23. Allardyce, *Scotland and Scotsmen*, vol. i, pp. 204–5.
24. *Boswell, Laird of Auchinleck*, p. 385.
25. Tytler, *Memoirs of the Life and Writings of the Honourable Henry Home of Kames*, vol. i, p. 218.
26. *EPS*, pp. 259–61.

Notes on Sources

This chapter develops my own work on Edinburgh's post-Union history, the gist of which is to be found in 'Culture and Society in the Eighteenth Century Province: The Case of Edinburgh and the Scottish Enlightenment', and in 'Politics, Politeness and the Anglicisation of Early Eighteenth-Century Scottish Culture'. On the Union debate see *A Union for Empire: Political Thought and the Union of 1707*, edited by J. Robertson. A very dated introduction to Edinburgh's clubs and societies is to be found in D.D. McElroy's *Scotland's Age of Improvement: A Survey of Eighteenth Century Literary Clubs and Societies*. Edinburgh University lacks an extended modern history but see D.B. Horn, *A Short History of the University of Edinburgh 1556–1889* and Anderson, Lynch and Phillipson's *The University of Edinburgh: An Illustrated History*. The history of the Church and moderate Presbyterianism is the subject of R.B. Sher's seminal *Church and University in the Scottish Enlightenment: The Moderate Literati of Edinburgh*. For the history of the legal profession, see my *The Scottish Whigs and the Reform of the Court of Session 1785–1830*. Colin Kidd's *Subverting Scotland's Past. Scottish Whig Historians and the Creation of an Anglo-British Identity* deals brilliantly with the challenge the Highland problem presented to Scots law. Lord Kames's role as a cultural entrepreneur is still not properly studied but A.F. Tytler, Lord Woodhouselee's *Memoirs of the Life and Writings of the Honourable Henry Home of Kames* and I.S. Ross's *Lord Kames and the Scotland of his Day* are both essential reading.

5. SMITH'S EDINBURGH LECTURES: A CONJECTURAL HISTORY

1. Tytler, *Memoirs of the Life and Writings of the Honourable Henry Home of Kames*, vol. i, pp. 266–7.

2. Ross, p. 86.

3. Tytler, *Memoirs of the Life and Writings of the Honourable Henry Home*, vol. 1, pp. 266–7.

4. Sher, *Church and University in the Scottish Enlightenment*, p. 115.

5. Blair, *Lectures on Rhetoric and Belles Lettres*, vol. 2, p. 22n.

6. *LR*, Intro., p. 12.

7. *LR*, p. 26.

8. *LR*, p. 42.

9. *LR*, p. 8.

10. *LR*, p. 203.

11. *LR*, p. 9.

12. *LR*, pp. 9, 203–4.

13. *LR*, p. 204.

14. *LR*, pp. 223–4.

15. *LR*, p. 5.

16. *LR*, p. 55.

17. *LR*, pp. 56–7. Cf. Mandeville's devastating character sketch in 'A Search into the Nature of Society' in *The Fable of the Bees*, pp. 331–3.

18. *LR*, p. 63.

19. *LR*, pp. 111–12.

20. *LR*, pp. 142–6.

21. *LJ*, pp. 352, 494.

22. [Henry Home], *Essays upon Several Subjects concerning British Antiquities*, pp. 4, 24.

23. Sklar, *Montesquieu*, ch. 1 and Sonenscher, *Before the Deluge*, ch. 2.

24. Montesquieu, *The Spirit of the Laws*, p. 310.

25. Ibid.

26. Cited in Kapossy, 'Virtue, Sociability and the History of Mankind', p. 244.

27. Stewart, p. 275n.

28. Montesquieu, *Spirit of the Laws*, p. 3.

29. Hume, 'Of National Characters', *Essays Moral, Political and Literary*, pp. 197–215.

30. Moore, 'Natural Rights in the Scottish Enlightenment'.

31. Stewart, pp. 321–2. The text of the paper is now lost.

32. *LJ*, p. 5.

33. *LJ*, p. 7.

34. *LJ*, p. 17.

35. *LJ*, pp. 14–16.

36. *LJ*, pp. 208–9. See also p. 338.

37. *LJ*, pp. 221, 218.

38. *LJ*, pp. 208–35.
39. *LJ*, p. 264.
40. *LJ*, p. 252.
41. *LJ*, p. 260.
42. Between 1754 and 1764 the Select Society debated questions relating to the desirability of entails on four occasions, on the value of primogeniture and female succession on five occasions and the question of whether aristocracy or democracy posed a greater threat to liberty on three occasions. *Advocates Manuscripts*, NLS, 23.1.1.
43. *LJ*, p. 6.
44. Hutcheson, *A System of Moral Philosophy*, vol. ii, p. 255.
45. Ibid.
46. Hutcheson, *A Short Introduction to Moral Philosophy*, p. 307.
47. Ibid., p. 308.
48. *LJ*, p. 333.
49. *LJ*, p. 334.
50. *LJ*, p. 338.
51. Locke, *Two Treatises of Government*, pp. 296–7.
52. *LJ*, p. 341.
53. EUL MSS. La II 451/2. The possibility that they met in the winter of 1749–50 cannot be ruled out.
54. Rae, p. 33.
55. EUL MSS. La II. 451/2.

Notes on Sources

Historians have treated this formative period in Smith's intellectual career very gingerly on account of the exiguous and often equivocal data about the circumstances in which Smith gave his lectures and the content of the lectures themselves. This data certainly can be read in a variety of ways and I am very grateful to David Raynor for having devoted so much time and trouble to a sceptical scrutiny of the conjectural account given here. However, our conversations and correspondence have convinced me that my account of the circumstances in which Smith lectured on rhetoric and jurisprudence, of the vexed question of whether he gave one course – on rhetoric, to which he may have added lectures on jurisprudence in 1749–50 – or two distinct courses, one on rhetoric and another on jurisprudence, is as plausible as any other and has the additional advantage of being supported by my account of the intellectual milieu in which the lectures were given. In matters as important as this, biographers must be prepared to conjecture if they are to have any hope of providing a coherent account of their subjects' lives and the development of their thought and if they are to generate fresh thinking on important biographical matters. Anyway, as Henry Home once said to James Boswell, 'with that spring of thought, that kind of sally for which he was ever remarkable, "You'll not go to hell for conjecturing"' (*Boswell: The Applause of the Jury*, p. 36).

On Smith's rhetoric S.J. McKenna's *Adam Smith: The Rhetoric of Propriety* has transformed a neglected and important field. See also W.S. Howell, 'Adam Smith's Lectures on Rhetoric: An Historical Assessment'. I have found Q. Skinner's *Reason and Rhetoric in the Philosophy of Hobbes* particularly suggestive. On Smith's theory of language, see C.J. Berry, 'Adam Smith's Considerations on Language' and M. Dascal, 'Adam Smith's Theory of Language', and, for the wider context, Hans Aarsleff's classic *The Study of Language in England 1780–1860*.

On Smith's jurisprudence and its place in the history of western political thought, Istvan Hont's *Jealousy of Trade: International Competition and the Nation-State in Historical Perspective* is of fundamental importance. I have also learned much from K. Haakonssen's *The Science of a Legislator: The Natural Jurisprudence of David Hume and Adam Smith*. See also D. Lieberman's 'Adam Smith on Justice, Rights, and Law', in *The Cambridge Companion to Adam Smith*.

6. PROFESSOR OF MORAL PHILOSOPHY AT GLASGOW, I. 1751–9

1. *Corr.*, p. 100.
2. *Corr.*, pp. 334–6.
3. *Corr.*, pp. 4–5.
4. Devine, *The Tobacco Lords*, p. 11.
5. *Boswell's Journal of a Tour to the Hebrides*, p. 364.
6. Cited in Peters, 'Glasgow's Tobacco Lords', pp. 364–6.
7. Gibson, *The History of Glasgow*, pp. 114, 120.
8. WN, p. 374.
9. Smout, *A History of the Scottish People*, pp. 379–90.
10. Thomson, *An Account of the Life, Lectures and Writings of William Cullen*, vol. i, p. 46.
11. Walker, ed., *The Correspondence of James Boswell and John Johnston of Grange*, p. 7.
12. *Corr.*, pp. 5–6. Jardine, *Outlines of Philosophical Education*, p. 26.
13. *Corr.*, pp. 5–6.
14. James Wodrow–Samuel Kenrick, 21 January 1752, Wodrow–Kenrick Correspondence. Dr William's Library MSS 24.157 (16).
15. Jardine, *Outlines of Philosophical Education*, p. 24.

16. Ibid., pp. 85ff.

17. 'Book of the Foulis Exhibition 1913', *Proceedings of the Glasgow Bibliographical Society*, vol. ii, 1913, pp. 70–73.

18. Scott, p. 149.

19. Denina, *Essay on the Revolutions of Literature*, reprinted in the *Scots Magazine* (1764).

20. Carlyle, *Anecdotes and Characters of the Times*, p. 38.

21. WN, p. 267 and note 12.

22. *The Defects of an University Education and its Unsuitableness to a Commercial People*, p. 16.

23. [W. Thom], *The Motives which have determined the University of Glasgow to desert the Blackfriars Church and betake themselves to a Chapel* . . .

24. [W. Thom], *The Scheme for Erecting an Academy in Glasgow*, pp. 33–4.

25. There is an authoritative account of Smith's book-collecting and the subsequent history of his library in *Adam Smith's Library: A Catalogue*, ed. Mizuta, pp. xvii–xxiii.

26. Allardyce, ed., *Scotland and Scotsmen in the Eighteenth Century*, vol. i, p. 403n.

27. Richardson, *Discourses on Theological and Literary Subjects*, pp. 507–8.

28. Rae, p. 50.

29. Stewart, pp. 274–5.

30. Allardyce, ed., *Scotland and Scotsmen*, vol. i, pp. 462–3.

31. Stewart, pp. 275–6.

32. *St James's Chronicle*, Saturday, 31 July 1790.

33. Walker, ed., *Correspondence of James Boswell and John Johnston of Grange*, p. 7.

34. Sinclair, *Sketches of Old Times and Distant Places*, p. 9.

35. Allardyce, ed., *Scotland and Scotsmen*, vol. i, p. 463.

36. Rae, p. 61.

37. Ross, p. 214.

38. *Corr.*, p. 25.

39. *Corr.*, p. 12.

40. *Corr.*, pp. 9–10.

Notes on Sources

Scott, Campbell and Skinner, Stewart and Ross are essential sources for this period in Smith's academic career. For the history of the university, see the notes to chapter 2. For Glasgow's clubs and societies, see J. Strang, *Glasgow and its Clubs*. For the remarkable Foulis Press see P. Gaskell's *A Bibliography of the Foulis Press* and J. Maclehose's *The Glasgow University Press*.

7. *THE THEORY OF MORAL SENTIMENTS* AND THE CIVILIZING POWERS OF COMMERCE

1. *WN*, p. 790.
2. Hume, 'Of Commerce', *Essays Moral, Political and Literary*, p. 261.
3. Hume, 'Of Money', *Essays Moral, Political and Literary*, p. 281.
4. Hume, 'Of Interest', *Essays Moral, Political and Literary*, p. 300.
5. Hume, 'Of Refinement in the Arts', *Essays Moral, Political and Literary*, pp. 270–71.
6. Ibid.
7. Smith's two reviews are published in *EPS*, pp. 232–54.
8. Hume's list of the founders of modern philosophy is to be found in the introduction to the *Treatise*, p. xvii. It reads 'Mr. *Locke*, my Lord *Shaftsbury*, Dr. *Mandeville*, Mr. *Hutchinson*, Dr. *Butler*, &.
9. It is perhaps worth noting that an enterprising small-time Edinburgh printer, W. Gray and W. Peter, reprinted the ninth edition of the *Fable of the Bees* in 1755.
10. *EPS*, pp. 250–51.
11. *TMS*, p. 9.
12. *TMS*, p. 9. In Cicero, the agonies of the rack are invoked in order to show that even the worst pain will seem less acute if we feel we are suffering for a noble cause. For Smith, we like to feel that these agonies will be mitigated by sympathy. Cicero, *De Finibus Bonorum et Malorum*, ed. H. Rackham, Loeb Classics (London, 1914), pp. 261–3.
13. *TMS*, p. 16.
14. *TMS*, p. 19.
15. *TMS*, p. 41.
16. *LJ*, p. 497.
17. *Corr.*, p. 43.
18. *TMS*, pp. 51–2.
19. *TMS*, p. 50.
20. *TMS*, p. 82.
21. *TMS*, p. 82.
22. *TMS*, p. 83.
23. *TMS*, pp. 84–5.
24. *TMS*, pp. 113–14.
25. *TMS*, p. 83.
26. *TMS*, p. 342.

Notes on Sources

The literature on the *Theory of Moral Sentiments* is vast. The best short introductions are D.D. Raphael's important introduction to the edition of the *TMS* cited here and K. Haakonssen's introduction to the Cambridge edition of 2002. Raphael's 'The Impartial Spectator' is also essential reading.

The Stoic dimensions of Smith's thinking, over-emphasized in my view, are discussed by Raphael, and by V. Brown, *Adam Smith's Discourse. Canonicity, Commerce and Conscience*, Athol Fitzgibbons, *Adam Smith's System of Liberty, Wealth and Virtue*, and G. Vivenza, *Adam Smith and the Classics: The Classical Heritage in Adam Smith's Thought*. The nature of his engagement with Rousseau is discussed by E.G. West in 'Adam Smith and Rousseau's *Discourse on Inequality*: Inspiration or Provocation?' and brilliantly by M. Ignatieff in *The Needs of Strangers*.

Much attention has been paid to the problem of setting Smith's moral theory in wider contexts. As their titles suggest, T.D. Campbell's *Adam Smith's Science of Morals* and A.S. Skinner's *A System of Social Science* view the *TMS* as part of an attempt to place the study of morality on a scientific basis. J. Dwyer in *The Age of the Passions: An Interpretation of Adam Smith and Scottish Enlightenment Culture* views Smith's theory in the context of the Scots' interest in sensibility and sentiment. D. Marshall in *The Figure of Theater: Shaftesbury, Defoe, Adam Smith, and George Eliot* considers the theatricality built into the language of sentiment. Two important works, C. Griswold's *Adam Smith and the Virtues of Enlightenment* and S. Fleischacker's *A Third Concept of Liberty: Judgment and Freedom in Kant and Adam Smith*, rightly remind us that Smith's moral theory is first and foremost a theory of ethics.

8. PROFESSOR OF MORAL PHILOSOPHY AT GLASGOW, 2. 1759–63

1. *Corr.*, p. 39. This sounds like a reasonable business arrangement, although it is worth noting that the profits to be made out of philosophy were strikingly less favourable than those available to a successful historian. It was the *History of England* that made Hume a rich man. On the returns of authorship see Sher, *The Enlightenment and the Book*, ch. 3. On the publication history of the *Theory of Moral Sentiments* see his 'Early Editions of Adam Smith's Books in Britain and Ireland, 1759–1804'.

2. *Corr.*, p. 35.

3. *Corr.*, p. 40.

4. *Corr.*, pp. 33–6.

5. James Wodrow–Samuel Kenrick, 10 July 1759, Wodrow–Kenrick Correspondence, Dr William's Library MSS 24.157 (33).

6. *Diary of George Ridpath, 1755–1761* (Edinburgh, 1922). Cited in *On Moral Sentiments: Contemporary Responses to Adam Smith*, ed. J. Reeder, pp. 30–32. James Wodrow–Samuel Kenrick, 10 July 1759, Dr William's Library MSS 24.157 (33).

7. David Raynor makes the case for attributing the review to Hume in 'Hume's Abstract of Adam Smith's *Theory of Moral Sentiments*'. Raphael and Sakamoto reinforce it in 'Anonymous Writings of David Hume'.

8. *Annual Register* (1759). Reprinted in *On Moral Sentiments*, ed. Reeder, pp. 50–57.

9. *Corr.*, pp. 46–7.

10. *On Moral Sentiments*, ed. Reeder, pp. 33–50.

11. *Corr.*, p. 43.

12. *Corr.*, p. 49.

13. *On Moral Sentiments*, ed. Reeder, p. 66.

14. *Corr.*, pp. 54–5.

15. Rousseau, *The Discourses and Other Early Political Writings*, p. 148.

16. Stewart, p. 292.

17. *Corr.*, p. 27.

18. *Corr.*, p. 38.

19. What follows based on *Corr.*, pp. 41–73.

20. *Corr.*, p. 30.

21. *Corr.*, p. 29.

22. *Corr.*, p. 29.

23. *Corr.*, pp. 31–2.

24. *Corr.*, p. 70.

25. *Corr.*, p. 84.

26. *Corr.*, p. 98.

27. Namier and Brooke, *The History of Parliment*, 'Fitzmaurice, T.'

28. Stewart, p. 347.

29. Brown, 'Adam Smith's First Russian Followers'.

30. It is suggestive that the only recalcitrant colleague who made him lose his temper was the Professor of Natural History John Anderson, a natural *frondeur* who had a gift for personalizing every issue and who seems to have marked out Smith as a target. Anderson claimed that 'their high words frequently brought them very near to blows', Samuel Kenrick–James Wodrow, 22 February 1785, Wodrow–Kenrick Correspondence, Dr William's Library MSS 24.157 (92).

31. Scott, p. 213.

32. Stewart, p. 300.

33. *LJ*, p. 401.

34. *LJ*, p. 401.
35. *LJ*, p. 404.
36. *LJ*, p. 487. It should be noted that although the first set of lecture notes of 1762–3 provides a fuller and more comprehensively illustrated discussion of Smith's jurisprudence than the notes of the revised later version, which is dated 1766, it is incomplete; one of the volumes of the student's notes is missing. The second set of notes is complete, although it provides a more streamlined, less densely illustrated account of Smith's theory, and is the one that is cited here.
37. *LJ*, p. 487.
38. *LJ*, pp. 488–9.
39. *LJ*, p. 492.
40. *LJ*, pp. 493–4.
41. *LJ*, pp. 347–8.
42. Stewart, p. 300.
43. *LJ*, p. 494. Cf. *LJ*, pp. 355–6.
44. Scott, p. 151.
45. *Corr.*, p. 9.
46. *Corr.*, p. 69.

Notes on Sources

On the bibliographical history of the *Theory of Moral Sentiments* see *A Critical Bibliography of Adam Smith*, edited by K. Tribe; on its reception see the useful anthology *On Moral Sentiments. Contemporary Responses to Adam Smith*, edited by J. Reeder. On the subsequent career of Smith's pupil Thomas Petty Fitzmaurice, see L.B. Namier and J. Brooke, *The History of Parliament: The House of Commons 1754–1790*.

On the development of Smith's political economy see R.L. Meek and A.S. Skinner's classic 'The Development of Adam Smith's Ideas on the Division of Labour', reprinted in Skinner's *A System of Social Science: Papers Relating to Adam Smith*.

On Smith's state of health and the interesting suggestion that the effects of overwork were complicated by hypochondria see M. Barfoot's 'Dr William Cullen and Mr Adam Smith: A Case of Hypochondriasis'.

9. SMITH AND THE DUKE OF BUCCLEUCH IN EUROPE 1764–6

1. *Corr.*, p. 36.
2. Carlyle, *Anecdotes and Characters*, p. 199.

3. The list of books is given in *Corr.*, p. 58.

4. *Corr.*, pp. 95–6.

5. Tytler, *Memories of the Life and Writings of . . . Henry Home of Kames*, vol. i, pp. 272–3n.

6. Stewart, pp. 306–7.

7. Quoted in Bonnyman, 'Agricultural Improvement in the Scottish Enlightenment', p. 61.

8. According to Carlyle, when Townshend proposed giving Hallam a pension of £100 to compensate for losing his pupil, Buccleuch replied, 'No . . . it is my desire that Hallam may have as much as Smith, it being a Great Mortification to him, That he is not to Travel with me' Carlyle, *Anecdotes and Characters*, p. 142n.

9. Carlyle, ibid. Dalrymple's comment was made to Horace Walpole: Ross, pp. 195–6.

10. D. Hume–Comtesse de Boufflers, 15 July 1766, Hume, *Letters of David Hume*, vol. ii, p. 63.

11. Quoted in Ross, 'Educating an Eighteenth-Century Duke', in *The Scottish Tradition: Essays in Honour of R.G. Cant*, p. 185.

12. Ibid., p. 184.

13. Quoted in Taillefer, *Vivre à Toulouse sous l'Ancien Régime*, p. 341.

14. *WN*, p. 726.

15. *TMS*, p. 120.

16. Taillefer, *Vivre à Toulouse*, p. 201; Godechot, *La Revolution Française dans le Midi Toulousain*, ch. 1; Schneider, *The Ceremonial City. Toulouse Observed 1738–1780*, ch. 1.

17. *Corr.*, pp. 101–2; Ross, 'Educating an Eighteenth-Century Duke', pp. 178–97; Bonnyman, 'Agricultural Improvement in the Scottish Enlightenment', ch. 2.

18. *Corr.*, pp. 102–3.

19. Ross, pp. 207–9.

20. Clayden, *Early Life of Samuel Rogers*, p. 95.

21. Faujas Saint Fond, *Travels in England, Scotland, and the Hebrides*, vol. ii, p. 241.

22. Ross, 'Educating an Eighteenth-Century Duke', p. 183.

23. *Corr.*, p. 97.

24. *Corr.*, p. 108.

25. Hume, *Letters of David Hume*, vol. i, p. 524. A change of ministry deprived Hertford of his post but not before securing a pension of £400 for life for Hume. Mossner, *Life of David Hume*, pp. 493–4.

26. Quoted in Ross, *Lord Kames and the Scotland of his Day*, p. 286.

27. Rae, p. 199.

28. Stewart, pp. 302–3.

29. Rae, p. 197.

30. 'Etat des habits linge et effet apartenant a Monsieur Smith', Scott, pp. 261–2.

31. Ross, pp. 213–14.

32. WN, p. 467.

33. Ross, p. 214.

34. The full title of Mirabeau's *Rural Philosophy* is *Philosophie rurale, ou économie générale et politique de l'agriculture, réduite à l'ordre immuable, des lois physiques & morales qui assurent la prospérité des empires.* The full title of Quesnay's book is *Physiocratie, ou constitution naturelle du gouvernement le plus avantageux au genre humain.*

35. The copy of *Physiocratie* that Quesnay presented to Smith is listed in Mizuta, *Adam Smith's Library*, no. 1388.

36. WN, p. 679.

37. *Corr.*, p. 113.

38. WN, p. 678.

39. Stewart, p. 304.

40. Hume, *Letters of David Hume*, vol. ii, p. 205.

41. WN, pp. 663–4.

42. I am indebted to Istvan Hont's discussion of the *économistes'* project in *Jealousy of Trade*, esp. ch. 5.

43. WN, p. 665.

44. WN, p. 673.

45. WN, p. 674.

46. WN, p. 380. Hont, *Jealousy of Trade*, pp. 189–92, 368–72.

47. 'An Extract from Rural Philosophy (1763)', in Meek, ed., *Precursors of Adam Smith*, p. 111.

48. *Corr.*, p. 118.

49. *Corr.*, pp. 114–16.

50. *Corr.*, p. 121.

51. *Corr.*, p. 121. It is not known to whom this letter was addressed. Ross suggests Lady Frances Scott; David Raynor more plausibly suggests Townshend, Campbell Scott's stepfather.

Notes on Sources

Stewart, Ross and Rae deal pretty fully with Smith and Buccleuch's tour. On the physiocrats, see Dugald Stewart's influential discussion of the significance of their thought for Smith in Stewart, pp. 339–48, R.L. Meek's *Precursors of Adam Smith* and T.J. Hochstrasser's, 'Physiocracy and the Politics of

Laissez-faire', in *The Cambridge History of Eighteenth-Century Political Thought*, edited by M. Goldie and R. Wokler. See also two important recent discussions of the historical contexts in which their theory was developed: Hont's *Jealousy of Trade: International Competition and the Nation-State in Historical Perspective* and M. Sonenscher's *Before the Deluge: Public Debt, Inequality, and the Intellectual Origins of the French Revolution.*

10. LONDON, KIRKCALDY AND THE MAKING OF THE *WEALTH OF NATIONS* 1766–76

1. Bonnyman, 'Agricultural Improvement in the Scottish Enlightenment', ch. 1.

2. *Corr.*, pp. 328–34, esp. notes 1–2.

3. Campbell and Skinner, pp. 139–40.

4. *Corr.*, pp. 122–4.

5. *Corr.*, p. 252.

6. *Corr.*, p. 125.

7. Rae, pp. 259–60.

8. *Corr.*, pp. 155–6. On an earlier visit to Kirkcaldy to visit James Oswald, Hume had written of crossing the Firth of Forth, 'Oh that horrid sea-sickness! Are there no chairs from the ferry to your house?' Hume, *Letters of David Hume*, vol. ii, p. 95.

9. Carlyle, *Anecdotes and Characters*, p. 250.

10. Stuart, *Memoire of Frances, Lady Douglas*, pp. 52–3. I am grateful to David Raynor for this reference.

11. Bonnyman, 'Agricultural Improvement in the Scottish Enlightenment', p. 225.

12. *Corr.*, pp. 156, 180.

13. *Corr.*, p. 140.

14. *WN*, p. 678.

15. *WN*, pp. 312, 299.

16. Hamilton, 'The Failure of the Ayr Bank'.

17. *WN*, pp. 316–17.

18. *Corr.*, pp. 162–3.

19. *Corr.*, pp. 163–4.

20. *Corr.*, p. 168.

21. *Boswell: The Ominous Years*, p. 264.

22. *The Bee or Literary Weekly Intelligencer*, iii (11 May 1791).

23. *Corr.*, pp. 173–9; 'get my lug in my lufe' means 'I'll get my ears boxed'.

24. *Corr.*, p. 186.

25. Hume, 'Of Public Credit', *Essays Moral, Political and Literary*, pp. 360–61.
26. *WN*, p. 614. cf. p. 630.
27. 'Smith's Thoughts on the State of the Contest with America, February 1778', *Corr.*, pp. 376–85. It was first published by G.H. Gutteridge in *American Historical Review*, vol. xxxviii, 1933, pp. 714–20.
28. *WN*, p. 617.
29. *WN*, p. 616.

Notes on Sources

Ross, Rae and Campbell and Skinner deal reasonably fully with this period. B.D. Bonnyman's PhD thesis, 'Agricultural Improvement in the Scottish Enlightenment: The Third Duke of Buccleuch, William Keir and the Buccleuch Estates, 1751–1812', raises important questions about Smith's involvement in the reorganization of the Buccleuch estates in Scotland and calls attention to a neglected aspect of Smith's career.

11. THE *WEALTH OF NATIONS* AND SMITH'S 'VERY VIOLENT ATTACK . . . UPON THE WHOLE COMMERCIAL SYSTEM OF GREAT BRITAIN'

1. There were notices and reviews in the *Annual Register*, the *Monthly Review*, the *Critical Review*, the *London Magazine*, the *Scots Magazine*, the *Edinburgh Weekly Magazine* and the *Hibernian Magazine* (Ross, p. 429).
2. Sher, *The Enlightenment and the Book*, pp. 236–7.
3. *Corr.*, pp. 192, 190, 188.
4. Stewart, p. 310. See also Rothschild, *Economic Sentiments: Adam Smith, Condorcet, and the Enlightenment*, pp. 57–61.
5. Stewart, pp. 309–10.
6. *WN*, pp. 26–7, 138, 715.
7. Hume, *Letters of David Hume*, vol. ii, p. 205.
8. *WN*, p. 49.
9. *WN*, pp. 265–7.
10. *WN*, p. 276n.
11. *WN*, p. 283.
12. *WN*, p. 291.
13. *WN*, pp. 341–2.
14. *WN*, pp. 345–6.
15. *WN*, p. 377.

16. *WN*, pp. 378, 380.

17. *WN*, p. 380.

18. *WN*, pp. 49, 429, 449–50.

19. *WN*, pp. 434–5.

20. *WN*, p. 570.

21. *WN*, p. 493.

22. *WN*, p. 572.

23. *WN*, p. 580.

24. *WN*, pp. 604–5.

25. *A Letter from Governor Pownall to Adam Smith, L.L.D. F.R.S., being an Examination of Several Points of Doctrine, laid down in his 'Inquiry in to the Nature and Causes of the Wealth of Nations'* (London 1776). Reprinted in *Corr.*, pp. 337–76; quote from p. 369.

26. *WN*, p. 456.

27. *WN*, p. 471.

28. *WN*, p. 687.

29. *WN*, p. 706.

30. *WN*, p. 715.

31. *WN*, p. 731.

32. *WN*, p. 764.

33. *WN*, p. 796.

34. *WN*, p. 788.

35. *WN*, p. 810.

36. *WN*, pp. 796–7.

37. *WN*, p. 830.

38. *WN*, p. 924.

39. *WN*, p. 911.

40. Hume, 'Of Public Credit', *Essays Moral, Political and Literary*, pp. 360–61.

41. *WN*, pp. 944–7.

Notes on Sources

Much attention has been paid by recent historians of ideas and intellectual historians to the problem of setting the *Wealth of Nations* in its historical context. For the present writer, the first great attempt to do this was Duncan Forbes' historic 'Scientific Whiggism: Adam Smith and John Millar', and R. L. Meek's 'The Scottish Contribution to Marxist Sociology' in his *Economics and Ideology and Other Essays*. Forbes' pioneering essay was written before the notes on Smith's lectures on jurisprudence of 1762–3 had been published and D. Winch's *Adam Smith's Politics: An Essay in Historiographic Revision* was the first substantial attempt to consider their significance for a historical understanding of the *Wealth of Nations*. The range of the discussion was broadened by K. Haakonssen's *The Science of a Legislator: The Natural Jurisprudence of David Hume and Adam Smith* and complicated by *Wealth and Virtue: The Shaping of Political Economy in the Scottish Enlightenment*, edited by I. Hont and M. Ignatieff. More recently, Emma Rothschild's *Economic Sentiments: Adam Smith, Condorcet, and the Enlightenment* and Hont's *Jealousy of Trade* have addressed the problem of setting Smith's political economy in wider European contexts; the present discussion is much indebted to both.

For those who prefer to read the *Wealth of Nations* as a work of philosophy, S. Fleischacker's *On Adam Smith's* Wealth of Nations: *A Philosophical Companion* is to be recommended.

12. HUME'S DEATH

1. *Corr.*, pp. 187–90.
2. *Corr.*, pp. 192–3.
3. *Corr.*, pp. 193–4.
4. Quoted in Ross, pp. 291–2.
5. *Corr.*, pp. 186–7.
6. *Corr.*, pp. 185–6.
7. *Corr.*, pp. 190–91.
8. *Corr.*, pp. 216–17.
9. *Corr.*, p. 206.
10. *Corr.*, pp. 194–5.
11. *Corr.*, p. 208.
12. *Corr.*, pp. 210–12.
13. *Corr.*, p. 203.
14. *Corr.*, p. 216.
15. *Corr.*, p. 206.
16. *Corr.*, pp. 217–21.
17. *Corr.*, pp. 203–4.
18. Cited in Rae, pp. 312–13. See also Aston, 'Horne and Heterodoxy: The Defence of Anglican Beliefs in the Late Enlightenment'.
19. Allardyce, ed., *Scotland and Scotsmen in the Eighteenth Century*, vol. i, pp. 466–7.
20. *Boswell in Extremes, 1776–1778*, pp. 270–71.
21. *Corr.*, p. 251.
22. *Corr.*, pp. 223–4. Edmund Curll was a notorious hack biographer of the previous generation.

23. Cited in Ross, p. 302.
24. Hume, 'Of Tragedy', *Essays Moral, Political and Literary*, p. 220.
25. 'Of the Imitative Arts', *EPS*, p. 176.
26. 'Of the Imitative Arts', *EPS*, pp. 178–9.
27. 'Of the Imitative Arts', *EPS*, p. 178.
28. 'Of the Imitative Arts', *EPS*, p. 187.
29. 'Of the Imitative Arts', *EPS*, p. 209.
30. 'Of the Imitative Arts', *EPS*, p. 192.
31. 'Of the Imitative Arts', *EPS*, p. 194.
32. 'Of the Imitative Arts', *EPS*, p. 204.
33. 'Of the Imitative Arts', *EPS*, p. 205.
34. Ross, p. 380.
35. *Corr.*, p. 227.
36. *Corr.*, pp. 190, 213.
37. *Corr.*, pp. 227–8.
38. *Corr.*, p. 228.
39. *Corr.*, pp. 252–3.

Notes on Sources

Rae and Ross write well about this episode in Smith's life. On the other hand, Smith's work on aesthetics and the imitative arts has been almost completely ignored. For two alternative approaches to these essays see P. Jones, 'The Aesthetics of Adam Smith', in *Adam Smith Reviewed*, edited by Jones and A.S. Skinner, and N. De Marchi's 'Smith on Ingenuity, Pleasure, and the Imitative Arts', in *The Cambridge Companion to Adam Smith*.

13. LAST YEARS IN EDINBURGH 1778–90

1. *Corr.*, pp. 193, 190.
2. Youngson, *The Making of Classical Edinburgh 1750–1840*, pp. 61–5. The bridge collapsed in 1769, less than two years after it had been opened. This, together with its length and the Edinburgh winds, discouraged many old-town residents from settling in a suburb which now seemed perilously far from the centre of public life.
3. I am very grateful to Anthony Lewis for valuable information drawn from Edinburgh City Archives for help on this point.
4. Rae, pp. 326–7.
5. John Brewer has a memorable account of the London Customs House at work in *The Sinews of Power: War, Money and the English State, 1688–1783*, pp. 211–17.

6. Thompson, ed., *The Anecdotes and Egotisms of Henry Mackenzie, 1745–1831*, pp. 91–2.

7. Campbell and Skinner, pp. 200–2.

8. Henry Dundas–Lords of Treasury, 2 November 1782, NLS, Melville MSS/Acc2761.

9. Ross, pp. 332–3.

10. *Corr.*, pp. 249–50.

11. Thompson, *Anecdotes and Egotisms of Henry Mackenzie*, p. 124. There is a reasonably reliable history of the club in McElroy, *Scotland's Age of Improvement*, pp. 168–70.

12. Playfair, 'Biographical Account of James Hutton . . .', *Transactions of the Royal Society of Edinburgh*, (1797) vol. v., pp. 117, 112.

13. Stewart, p. 331.

14. [Kay], *A Series of Original Portraits and Caricature Etchings by the late John Kay*, vol. i, pp. 72–5.

15. [Scott], *The Miscellaneous Prose Works of Sir Walter Scott, Bart.*, p. 840.

16. EUL. MSS. La. II, 451–2, ff. 429–34.

17. *Corr.*, p. 253.

18. Ross, p. 351.

19. *Corr.*, p. 287.

20. 'Henry Mackenzie's Book of Anecdotes', NLS MS 2537. Quoted in Ross, p. 343.

21. Allardyce, ed., *Scotland and Scotsmen in the Eighteenth Century*, vol. i, p. 468.

22. *Corr.*, pp. 275–6.

23. [Walpole], *The Letters of Horace Walpole, Fourth Earl of Orford*, vol. xii, p. 252.

24. *Corr.*, p. 269.

25. *Corr.*, p. 266.

26. *Corr.*, p. 266.

27. *WN*, p. 654.

28. *WN*, p. 744.

29. *WN*, p. 733.

30. *WN*, p. 754.

31. *WN*, p. 752.

32. *WN*, p. 755.

33. Tribe, ed., *A Critical Bibliography of Adam Smith*, pp. 19–20.

34. *Corr.*, pp. 280–81.

35. *Corr.*, p. 281.

36. *Corr.*, pp. 308–9.
37. Quoted in Ross, p. 374.
38. The story first appears in [Kay], *A Series of Original Portraits ... by the late John Kay*, vol. i, pp. 74–5.
39. Cited in Ross, p. 376.
40. *The Bee or Literary Weekly Intelligencer*, iii (11 May 1791), p. 166.
41. *Corr.*, pp. 308–9.
42. *Corr.*, pp. 310–11.
43. *Corr.*, p. 320.
44. *The Bee or Literary Weekly Intelligencer*, iii (11 May 1791), p. 166.
45. [Reid], *The Correspondence of Thomas Reid*, p. 104.
46. *TMS*, p. 216.
47. *TMS*, p. 216.
48. *TMS*, p. 229.
49. *TMS*, pp. 232–3.
50. *TMS*, p. 237.
51. Romilly, *Memoirs*, vol. i, p. 403.
52. Ibid.
53. Stewart's account of Smith's character concludes his biographical memoir. Stewart, pp. 329–32.

Notes on Sources

Rae and Ross are essential reading. D.D. Raphael's introduction to the Glasgow edition of the *Theory of Moral Sentiments* provides the most thorough and thoughtful discussion of Smith's amendments, although its conclusions are somewhat different to those proposed here.

1. *TMS*, p. 3.
2. *The Bee or Literary Weekly Intelligencer*, iii (11 May 1791), p. 167.
3. Fontana, *Rethinking the Politics of Commercial Society: The Edinburgh Review 1802–1832*, p. 47. See also Collini et al., *That Noble Science of Politics. A Study in Nineteenth-century Intellectual History*, esp. ch. 1.
4. 'The Principles which lead and direct Philosophical Enquiries; illustrated by the History of Astronomy', in *EPS*, pp. 31–105.
5. Ibid., p. 46.
6. Ibid., pp. 104–5.

Bibliography of Works Cited

Aarsleff, H., *The Study of Language in England 1780–1860* (Princeton, 1967).

Allardyce, A. (ed.), *Scotland and Scotsmen in the Eighteenth Century: From the MSS of John Ramsay, Esq. of Ochtertyre*, 2 vols. (Edinburgh, 1888).

Anderson, R.D., Lynch, M. and Phillipson, N., *The University of Edinburgh: An Illustrated History* (Edinburgh, 2003).

Aston, N., 'Horne and Heterodoxy: The Defence of Anglican Beliefs in the Late Enlightenment', *English Historical Review* (1993), pp. 895–919.

Barfoot, M., 'Dr William Cullen and Mr Adam Smith: A Case of Hypochondriasis', *Proceedings of the Royal College of Physicians of Edinburgh* (1991), pp. 204–14.

Berry, C.J., 'Adam Smith's Considerations on Language', *Journal of the History of Ideas* (1974), pp. 130–38.

[Blair, H.], 'Hutcheson's Moral Philosophy', *Edinburgh Review* (1755–6).

Blair, H., *Lectures on Rhetoric and Belles Lettres* (London, 1818).

Bond, D.F. (ed.), *The Spectator* (Oxford, 1965).

Bonnyman, B.D., 'Agricultural Improvement in the Scottish Enlightenment: The Third Duke of Buccleuch, William Keir and the Buccleuch Estates, 1751–1812', PhD thesis, University of Edinburgh, 2004.

'Book of the Foulis Exhibition 1913', *Proceedings of the Glasgow Bibliographical Society* (1913).

Boswell's Journal of a Tour to the Hebrides with Samuel Johnson, 1773, ed. F.A. Pottle and C.H. Bennett (New York, 1961).

Boswell: The Ominous Years 1774–1776, ed. C. Ryskamp and F.A. Pottle (London, 1963).

Boswell in Extremes 1776–1778, ed. C.M. Weis and F.A. Pottle (New York, 1970).

Boswell, Laird of Auchinleck 1778–1782, ed. J.W. Reed and F.A. Pottle (New York, 1977).

Boswell: The Applause of the Jury 1782–1785, ed. I. Lustig and F.A. Pottle (London, 1981).

Brewer, J., *The Sinews of Power: War, Money and the English State, 1688–1783* (London, 1989).

Brougham, Viscount, *Lives of Men of Letters and Science who flourished in the time of George III* (London, 1845).

Brown, A.H., 'Adam Smith's First Russian Followers', in *Essays on Adam Smith*, ed. A.S. Skinner and T. Wilson (Oxford, 1975), pp. 247–73.

Brown, M., *Francis Hutcheson in Dublin 1719–1730: The Crucible of his Thought* (Dublin, 2002).

Brown, V., *Adam Smith's Discourse. Canonicity, Commerce and Conscience* (London, 1994).

Buchan, J., *Adam Smith and the Pursuit of Perfect Liberty* (London, 2006).

Cameron, A., *Bank of Scotland* (Edinburgh, 1995).

Campbell, R.H. and Skinner, A.S. *Adam Smith* (London, 1982).

Campbell, R.H. and Skinner, A.S. (eds.), *The Origins and Nature of the Scottish Enlightenment* (Edinburgh, 1982).

Campbell, T.D., *Adam Smith's Science of Morals* (London, 1971).

Campbell, T.D., 'Francis Hutcheson: "Father" of the Scottish Enlightenment', in *The Origins and Nature of the Scottish Enlightenment*, ed. R.H. Campbell and A.S. Skinner (Edinburgh, 1982), pp. 167–85.

Carlyle, A., *Anecdotes and Characters of the Times*, ed. J. Kinsley (London, 1973).

Chamberlayne, J., *Magnae Britanniae Notitia: or the Present State of Great Britain with diverse Remarks upon the Ancient State thereof* (London, 1735).

Chappell, V.C. (ed.), *Hume* (New York, 1966).

Clayden, P.W., *Early Life of Samuel Rogers* (London, 1887).

Collini, S., Winch, D. and Burrow, J., *That Noble Science of Politics. A Study in Nineteenth-century Intellectual History* (Cambridge, 1983).

Dascal, M., 'Adam Smith's Theory of Language', in *The Cambridge Companion to Adam Smith*, ed. K. Haakonssen (Cambridge, 2006), pp. 79–111.

Davis, H.W.C., *Balliol College* (London, 1899).

The Defects of an University Education and its Unsuitableness to a Commercial People: With the Expedience and Necessity of Erecting at Glasgow, an Academy, for the Instruction of Youth. In a letter to J.M. Esq. (London, 1762).

Defoe, D., *Tour thro the Whole Island of Great Britain*, ed. G.D.H. Cole (London, 1962).

De Marchi, N., 'Smith on Ingenuity, Pleasure, and the Imitative Arts', in *The Cambridge Companion to Adam Smith*, ed. K. Haakonssen (Cambridge, 2006), pp. 136–57.

Denina, C.M., *Essay on the Revolutions of Literature* (Glasgow, 1763), reprinted in the *Scots Magazine* (1764), pp. 465–7.

Dennison, E.P. and Coleman, R., *Historic Kirkcaldy. The Archaeological Implications of Development* (Edinburgh, 1995).

Devine, T.M., *The Tobacco Lords. A Study of the Tobacco Merchants of Glasgow and their Trading Activities c. 1740–90* (Edinburgh, 1975).

Devine, T.M., 'The Scottish Merchant Community 1680–1740', in *The Origins and Nature of the Scottish Enlightenment*, ed. R.H. Campbell and A.S. Skinner (Edinburgh, 1982), pp. 26–41.

Devine, T.M. and Jackson, G. (eds.), *Glasgow. Volume I: Beginnings to 1830* (Manchester, 1995).

Durie, A.J., 'Lairds, Improvement, Banking and Industry in Eighteenth Century Scotland: Capital and development in a Backward Economy', *Papers of the Ninth Scottish Historical Conference* (1978), pp. 21–30.

Durie, A.J., *The Scottish Linen Industry in the Eighteenth Century* (Edinburgh, 1979).

Dwyer, J., *The Age of the Passions: An Interpretation of Adam Smith and Scottish Enlightenment Culture* (East Linton, 1998).

Emerson, R.L., 'The Philosophical Society of Edinburgh 1737–1743', *British Journal of the History of Science* (1979), pp. 154–91.

Emerson, R.L., 'Politics and the Glasgow Professors, 1690–1800', in *The Glasgow Enlightenment*, ed. A. Hook and R.B. Sher (Glasgow, 1995), pp. 21–39.

Epictetus, *The Discourses of Epictetus*, ed. C. Gill (London, 1995).

Eutropius, *Breviarum Historiae Romanae*, trans. and ed. H.W. Bird (Liverpool, 1992).

Faujas Saint Fond, B., *Travels in England, Scotland, and the Hebrides* (Glasgow, 1907).

[Ferguson, A.], 'Of the Principle of Moral Estimation. A Discourse between David Hume, Robert Clerk and Adam Smith', *The Manuscripts of Adam Ferguson*, ed. V. Merolle (London, 2006), pp. 207–15.

Fitzgibbons, A., *Adam Smith's System of Liberty, Wealth and Virtue* (Oxford, 1995).

Fleischacker, S., *A Third Concept of Liberty: Judgment and Freedom in Kant and Adam Smith* (Princeton, 1999).

Fleischacker, S., *On Adam Smith's* Wealth of Nations: *A Philosophical Companion* (Princeton, 2004).

Fletcher, A., *Political Works*, ed. John Robertson (Cambridge, 1997).

Fontana, B., *Rethinking the Politics of Commercial Society: The* Edinburgh Review *1802–1832* (Cambridge, 1985).

Forbes, D., 'Scientific Whiggism: Adam Smith and John Millar', *Cambridge Journal* (1954), pp. 643–70.

Gaskell, P., *A Bibliography of the Foulis Press* (London, 1964).

Gibson, J., *The History of Glasgow, from the Earliest Accounts to the Present Time* (Glasgow, 1777).

Godechot, J., *La Revolution Française dans le Midi Toulousain* (Toulouse, 1986).

Gray, J.M. (ed.), *Memoirs of the Life of Sir John Clerk of Penicuick . . .* (Scottish History Society, 1892).

Griswold, C., *Adam Smith and the Virtues of Enlightenment* (Cambridge, 1999).

Haakonssen, K., *The Science of a Legislator: The Natural Jurisprudence of David Hume and Adam Smith* (Cambridge, 1981).

Haakonssen, K., 'Natural Law and Moral Realism: The Scottish Synthesis', in *Studies in the Philosophy of the Scottish Enlightenment*, ed. M.A. Stewart (Oxford, 1990), pp. 61–85.

Haakonssen, K., 'Introduction', in Adam Smith, *The Theory of Moral Sentiments* (Cambridge, 2002).

Haakonssen, K. (ed.), *The Cambridge Companion to Adam Smith* (Cambridge, 2006).

Hamilton, H., 'The Failure of the Ayr Bank', *Economic History Review*, n.s. vol. 8, 3 (1956), pp. 405–17.

Hochstrasser, T.J., 'Physiocracy and the Politics of *Laissez-faire*', in *The Cambridge History of Eighteenth-Century Political Thought*, ed. M. Goldie and R. Wokler (Cambridge, 2006), pp. 419–42.

[Home, H.], *Essays upon Several Subjects concerning British Antiquities . . . composed anno M.DCC.XLV.* (Edinburgh, 1747).

Home, H., *Elements of Criticism* (Edinburgh, 1762).

Hont, I., *Jealousy of Trade: International Competition and the Nation-State in Historical Perspective* (Cambridge, Mass., 2005).

Hont, I. and Ignatieff, M. (eds.), *Wealth and Virtue. The Shaping of Political Economy in the Scottish Enlightenment* (Cambridge, 1983).

Hook, A. and Sher, R.B. (eds.), *Glasgow Enlightenment* (Glasgow, 1995).

Horn, D.B., *A Short History of the University of Edinburgh 1556–1889* (Edinburgh, 1967).

Howell, W.S., 'Adam Smith's Lectures on Rhetoric: An Historical Assessment', in *Essays on Adam Smith*, ed. A.S. Skinner and T. Wilson (Oxford, 1975), pp. 11–43.

[Hume, D.], 'A True Account of the Behaviour and Conduct of Archibald Stewart, Esq. Late Lord Provost of Edinburgh' (1747). Reprinted in J.V. Price, *The Ironic Hume* (Austin, Tex., 1965), pp. 154–74.

Hume, D., *The Letters of David Hume*, ed. J.Y.T. Greig (Oxford, 1969).

Hume, D., *A Treatise of Human Nature*, ed. L.A. Selby-Bigge (Oxford, 1978).

Hume, D., *Essays Moral, Political and Literary*, ed. E.F. Miller (Indianapolis, 1985).

Hundert, E.J., *The Enlightenment's Fable: Bernard Mandeville and the Discovery of Society* (Cambridge, 1994).

Hutcheson, F., *A Short Introduction to Moral Philosophy* (Glasgow, 1753).

Hutcheson, F., *A System of Moral Philosophy*, 2 vols. (London, 1755).

Hutcheson, F., *An Inquiry into the Original of our Ideas of Beauty and Virtue*, ed. W. Leidhold (Indianapolis, 2004).

Ignatieff, M., *The Needs of Strangers* (London, 1984).

Jardine, G., *Outlines of Philosophical Education illustrated by the Method of teaching the Logic . . . in the University of Glasgow* (Glasgow, 1825).

Jones, J., *Balliol College: A History* (Oxford, 1997).

Jones, P., 'The Scottish Professoriate and the Polite Academy 1720–40', in *Wealth and Virtue. The Shaping of Political Economy in the Scottish Enlightenment*, ed. I. Hont and M. Ignatieff (Cambridge, 1983), pp. 89–117.

Jones, P., 'The Aesthetics of Adam Smith', in *Adam Smith Reviewed*, ed. P. Jones and A.S. Skinner (Edinburgh, 1992), pp. 56–78.

Kapossy, B., 'Virtue, Sociability and the History of Mankind in Iselin's Contribution to the Swiss and European Enlightenment', PhD thesis, University of Cambridge, 2003.

[Kay, J.], *A Series of Original Portraits and Caricature Etchings by the late John Kay* (Edinburgh, 1877).

Keohane, N., *Philosophy and the State in France. The Renaissance to the Enlightenment* (Princeton, 1980).

Kidd, C., *Subverting Scotland's Past. Scottish Whig Historians and the Creation of an Anglo-British Identity* (Cambridge, 1993).

Knox, J., *The Works of John Knox*, ed. D. Laing (Edinburgh, 1846–64).

Krieger, L., *The Politics of Discretion: Pufendorf and the Acceptance of Natural Law* (Chicago, 1969).

Leechman, W., *The Temper, Character and Duty of a Minister of the Gospel. A Sermon Preached before the Synod of Glasgow and Ayr at Glasgow. April 7th, 1741*, 3rd edn (Glasgow, 1742).

Lieberman, D., 'The Legal Needs of a Commercial Society: The Jurisprudence of Lord Kames', in *Wealth and Virtue. The Shaping of Political Economy in the Scottish Enlightenment*, ed. I. Hont and M. Ignatieff (Cambridge, 1983), pp. 203–34.

Lieberman, D., 'Adam Smith on Justice, Rights, and Law', in *The Cambridge Companion to Adam Smith*, ed. K. Haakonssen (Cambridge, 2006), pp. 214–45.

Livingston, D.W., *Hume's Philosophy of Common Life* (Chicago, 1984).

Loch, D., *A Tour through most of the Trading Towns and Villages of Scotland* (Edinburgh, 1778).

Locke, J., *Two Treatises of Government*, ed. Peter Laslett (Cambridge, 1988).

McBride, I., 'The School of Virtue: Francis Hutcheson, Irish Presbyterians and the Scottish Enlightenment', in *Political Thought in Ireland since the Seventeenth Century*, ed. D.G. Boyce, R.R. Eccleshall and V. Geoghegan (London, 1993), pp. 73–99.

McCulloch, J.R., *Sketch of the Life and Writings of Adam Smith, LL.D.* (Edinburgh, 1855).

McElroy, D.D., *Scotland's Age of Improvement: A Survey of Eighteenth-Century Literary Clubs and Societies* (Pullman, Wash., 1969).

MacInnes, A., *Clanship, Commerce and the House of Stuart 1603–1788* (East Linton, 1996).

McKenna, S.J., *Adam Smith: The Rhetoric of Propriety* (Albany, NY, 2006).

Mackie, J.D., *The University of Glasgow 1451 to 1951* (Glasgow, 1948).

MacLaurin, C., *An Account of Sir Isaac Newton's Philosophical Discoveries*, ed. Patrick Murdoch (London, 1750).

Maclehose, J., *The Glasgow University Press* (Glasgow, 1931).

Mandeville, B., *The Fable of the Bees: or Private Vices, Publick Benefits*, ed. F.B. Kaye (Indianapolis, 1988).

Marivaux, P., *Journaux et Oeuvres Diverses*, ed. F. Deloffre and M. Gilot (Paris, 1969).

Marivaux, P., *La Vie de Marianne, ou Les Aventures de Madame la Comtesse de ****, ed. M. Gilot (Paris, 1978).

Marshall, D., *The Figure of Theater: Shaftesbury, Defoe, Adam Smith and George Eliot* (New York, 1986).

Mason, R.A. (ed.), *Scotland and England 1286–1815* (Edinburgh, 1987).

Meek, R.L., 'The Scottish Contribution to Marxist Sociology', in R.L. Meek, *Economics and Ideology and Other Essays* (London, 1967), pp. 34–50.

Meek, R.L. (ed.), *Precursors of Adam Smith 1750–1775* (London, 1973).

Mizuta, H. (ed.), *Adam Smith's Library: A Catalogue* (Oxford, 2000).

Montesquieu, C.-L., *The Spirit of the Laws*, ed. A. Cohler, B. Miller and H. Stone (Cambridge, 1989).

Moore, J., 'The two systems of Francis Hutcheson: on the origins of the Scottish Enlightenment', in *Studies in the Philosophy of the Scottish Enlightenment*, ed. M.A. Stewart (Oxford, 1990), pp. 37–59.

Moore, J., 'Natural Rights in the Scottish Enlightenment', in *The Cambridge History of Eighteenth Century Political Thought*, ed. M. Goldie and R. Wokler (Cambridge, 2006), pp. 291–316.

Moore, T.O., 'The Enlightened Curriculum: Liberal Education in Eighteenth Century British Schools', PhD thesis, University of Edinburgh, 1999.

Morice, G.P. (ed.), *David Hume: Bicentenary Papers* (Edinburgh, 1977).

Mossner, E.C., *The Life of David Hume* (Oxford, 1970).

Mudie, R., *The Modern Athens: A Dissection and Demonstration of Men and Things in the Scotch Capital* (London, 1825).

Muller, J.Z., *Adam Smith in His Time and Ours* (Princeton, 1995).

Namier, L.B. and Brooke, J., *The History of Parliament: The House of Commons 1754–1790* (London, 1964).

Norton, D.F., *David Hume: Common-Sense Moralist, Skeptical Metaphysician* (Princeton, 1982).

[Oswald, J.], *Memorials of the Rt. Hon. James Oswald of Dunnikier* (Edinburgh, 1825).

Peters, C.M., 'Glasgow's Tobacco Lords: An Examination of Wealth Creators in the Eighteenth Century', PhD thesis, University of Glasgow, 1990.

Phillipson, N.T., 'Culture and Society in the Eighteenth Century Province: The Case of Edinburgh and the Scottish Enlightenment', in *The University in Society, Vol. 2, Europe, Scotland and the United States from the 16th to the 20th Century*, ed. L. Stone (Princeton, 1974), pp. 407–48.

Phillipson, N.T., 'The Civic Leadership of Post Union Scotland', *Juridical Review* (1976), pp. 97–120.

Phillipson, N.T., 'Politics, Politeness and the Anglicisation of Early Eighteenth-Century Scottish Culture', in *Scotland and England 1286–1815*, ed. R.A. Mason (Edinburgh, 1987), pp. 226–46.

Phillipson, N.T., *Hume* (London, 1989).

Phillipson, N.T., *The Scottish Whigs and the Reform of the Court of Session 1785–1830* (Edinburgh, 1990).

Phillipson, N.T., 'Politics and Politeness in the Reigns of Anne and the Early Hanoverians', in *The Varieties British of Political Thought*, ed. J.G.A. Pocock et al. (Cambridge, 1993), pp. 211–45.

Pinkerton, J.M. (ed.), *Minute Book of the Faculty of Advocates, Vol. 2, 1713–1750* (Edinburgh, 1980).

Popkin, R., 'David Hume: His Pyrrhonism and his Critique of Pyrrhonism', in *Hume*, ed. V.C. Chappell (New York, 1966), pp. 53–98.

Pufendorf, S., *The Law of Nature and Nations: Or a General System of the Most Important Principles of Morality, Jurisprudence and Politics*, trans. B. Kennett, 5th edn (London, 1749).

Pufendorf, S., *On the Duty of Man and Citizen According to Natural Law*, ed. J. Tully (Cambridge, 1991).

Rae, J., *Life of Adam Smith* (London, 1895).

Raphael, D.D., 'The Impartial Spectator', in *Essays on Adam Smith*, ed. A.S. Skinner and T. Wilson (Oxford, 1975), pp. 83–99.

Raphael, D.D., '"The True Old Humean Philosophy" and its Influence on

Adam Smith', in *David Hume: Bicentenary Papers*, ed. G.P. Morice (Edinburgh, 1977), pp. 23–38.

Raphael, D.D., *Adam Smith* (Oxford, 1985).

Raphael, D.D. and Sakamoto, T., 'Anonymous Writings of David Hume', *Journal of the History of Philosophy*, 28 (1990), pp. 271–81.

Raynor, D., 'Hume's Abstract of Adam Smith's *Theory of Moral Sentiments*', *Journal of the History of Philosophy*, 22 (1984), pp. 51–79.

Reeder, J. (ed.), *On Moral Sentiments: Contemporary Responses to Adam Smith* (Bristol, 1997).

[Reid, T.], *The Correspondence of Thomas Reid*, ed. P. Wood (Edinburgh, 2002).

Richardson, W., *Discourses on Theological and Literary Subjects. By the late Rev. Archibald Arthur with an Account of Some Particulars of his Life and Character* (Glasgow, 1803).

Robertson, J. (ed.), *A Union for Empire: Political Thought and the Union of 1707* (Cambridge, 1995).

Romilly, S., *Memoirs* (London, 1840).

Ross, I.S., *Lord Kames and the Scotland of his Day* (Oxford, 1972).

Ross, I.S., 'Educating an Eighteenth-Century Duke', in *The Scottish Tradition: Essays in Honour of R.G. Cant*, ed. G.W.S. Barrow (Edinburgh, 1974), pp. 178–97.

Ross, I.S., *The Life of Adam Smith* (Oxford, 1995).

Rothschild, E., *Economic Sentiments: Adam Smith, Condorcet, and the Enlightenment* (Cambridge, Mass., 2001).

Rousseau, J.-J., *The Discourses and Other Early Political Writings*, ed. V. Gourevitch (Cambridge, 1997).

Schneider, R.A., *The Ceremonial City. Toulouse Observed 1738–1780* (Princeton, 1995).

[Scott, W.], *The Miscellaneous Prose Works of Sir Walter Scott, Bart.* (Edinburgh, 1854).

Scott, W.R., *Francis Hutcheson: His Life, Teaching and Position in the History of Philosophy* (Cambridge, 1900).

Scott, W.R., *Adam Smith as Student and Professor* (Glasgow, 1937).

Sedgwick, R., *History of Parliament: The House of Commons 1715–54* (London, 1970).

Select Transactions of the Honourable the Society for Improvement in the Knowledge of Agriculture in Scotland, ed. R. Maxwell (Edinburgh, 1743).

Shapin, S., 'Property, Patronage and the Politics of Science: The Founding of the Royal Society of Edinburgh', *British Journal for the History of Science* (March 1974), pp. 1–41.

Sher, R.B., *Church and University in the Scottish Enlightenment: The Moderate Literati of Edinburgh* (Edinburgh, 1985).

Sher, R.B., 'Commerce, Religion and the Enlightenment in Eighteenth-Century Glasgow', in *Glasgow, Volume I: Beginnings to 1830*, ed. T.M. Devine and G. Jackson (Manchester, 1995), pp. 312–59.

Sher, R.B., 'Early Editions of Adam Smith's Books in Britain and Ireland, 1759–1804', in *A Critical Bibliography of Adam Smith*, ed. K. Tribe (London, 2002), pp. 13–26.

Sher, R.B., *The Enlightenment and the Book: Scottish Authors and their Publishers in Eighteenth Century Britain, Ireland and America* (Chicago, 2006).

Sinclair, J., *Sketches of Old Times and Distant Places* (London, 1875).

Skinner, A.S., *A System of Social Science: Papers Relating to Adam Smith* (Oxford, 1979).

Skinner, Q., *Reason and Rhetoric in the Philosophy of Hobbes* (Cambridge, 1996).

Sklar, J.N., *Montesquieu* (Oxford, 1987).

Smout, T.C., 'The Glasgow Merchant Community in the Seventeenth Century', *Scottish Historical Review* (1968), pp. 53–70.

Smout, T.C., *A History of the Scottish People, 1560–1830* (London, 1969).

Sonenscher, M., *Before the Deluge: Public Debt, Inequality and the Intellectual Origins of the French Revolution* (Princeton, 2007).

Stewart, D., 'Account of the Life and Writings of Adam Smith, LL.D', ed. I.S. Ross, in *Essays on Philosophical Subjects*, ed. W.P.D. Wightman, J.C. Bryce and I.S. Ross (Oxford, 1980).

Stewart, M.A. (ed.), *Studies in the Philosophy of the Scottish Enlightenment* (Oxford, 1990).

Strang, J., *Glasgow and its Clubs* (Glasgow, 1857).

Stuart, L., *Memoire of Frances, Lady Douglas* (Edinburgh, 1985).

Sutherland, L.S. and Mitchell, L.G. (eds.), *The History of the University of Oxford. Vol. 5 The Eighteenth Century* (Oxford, 1986).

Taillefer, M., *Vivre à Toulouse sous l'Ancien Régime* (Paris, C., 2000).

[Thom, W.], *The Scheme for Erecting an Academy in Glasgow* (Glasgow, 1762).

[Thom, W.], *The Motives which have determined the University of Glasgow to desert the Blackfriars Church and betake themselves to a Chapel …* (Glasgow, 1765).

Thompson, H.W. (ed.), *The Anecdotes and Egotisms of Henry Mackenzie, 1745–1831* (Oxford, 1927).

Thomson, J., *An Account of the Life, Lectures and Writings of William Cullen M.D.* (Edinburgh, 1859).

Tribe, K. (ed.), *A Critical Bibliography of Adam Smith* (London, 2002).

Tuck, R., *Philosophy and Government 1572–1651* (Cambridge, 1993).

Tytler, A.F., Lord Woodhouselee, *Memoirs of the Life and Writings of the Honourable Henry Home of Kames*, 3 vols., 2nd edn (Edinburgh, 1814).

Vivenza, G., *Adam Smith and the Classics: The Classical Heritage in Adam Smith's Thought* (Oxford, 2001).

Walker, R.S. (ed), *Correspondence of James Boswell and John Johnston of Grange* (London, 1966).

[Walpole, H.], *The Letters of Horace Walpole, Fourth Earl of Orford*, ed. Mrs Paget Toynbee (Oxford, 1913–15).

Ward, W.R., *Georgian Oxford* (Oxford, 1958).

Warden, A.J., *The Linen Trade Ancient and Modern* (London, 1864).

West, E.G., 'Adam Smith and Rousseau's *Discourse on Inequality*: Inspiration or Provocation?' *Journal of Economic Issues* 5 (1971), pp. 56–70.

Winch, D., *Adam Smith's Politics: An Essay in Historiographic Revision* (Cambridge, 1978).

Withrington, D.J. and Grant, I.R. (eds.), *Statistical Account of Scotland by Sir John Sinclair*, vol. x. *Fife* (Edinburgh, 1978).

Wodrow, R., *Analecta or Materials for a History of Remarkable Providences* (Edinburgh, 1843).

Youngson, A.J., *The Making of Classical Edinburgh 1750–1840* (Edinburgh, 1966).Acknowledgements

Index

In this index, Adam Smith is abbreviated to AS except in the main entry under his name. His papers and publications appear under their titles; all other publications are given under individual authors. Page numbers in *italics* refer to illustrations in the text.

INDEX